The chapters in this text are logically and clearly organized around levels of understanding that are intuitive and easy to follow. They offer dynamic examples that will keep students engaged. Readers will learn to connect theory and practice, helping them become better researchers and better consumers of research.

—Lynette D. Nickleberry, SUNY Empire State College

This is a must-read text for both new and seasoned researchers. Every topic in the text is comprehensively explained with excellent examples.

—Francis Godwyll, University of West Florida

This text provides clear and concise discussions of qualitative, quantitative, and mixed-methods research for the new scholar-practitioner. The use of questioning and visuals affords students the opportunity to make connections and reflect on their learning.

—Holly Haynes, Truett McConnell University

The edited nature of this book provides a multitude of rich perspectives from well-respected authors. This book is a must-have for introductory research methods students.

—Eric D. Teman, University of Wyoming

This is an excellent read for anyone interested in understanding research; the book provides good clarity and practical examples. . . . It is a pragmatic book that translates research concepts into practice.

—Peter Memiah, University of West Florida

Research Design and Methods

With a Foreword by Michael Quinn Patton

Sara Miller McCune founded SAGE Publishing in 1965 to support the dissemination of usable knowledge and educate a global community. SAGE publishes more than 1000 journals and over 800 new books each year, spanning a wide range of subject areas. Our growing selection of library products includes archives, data, case studies and video. SAGE remains majority owned by our founder and after her lifetime will become owned by a charitable trust that secures the company's continued independence.

Los Angeles | London | New Delhi | Singapore | Washington DC | Melbourne

Research Design and Methods

An Applied Guide for the Scholar-Practitioner

Gary J. Burkholder
Walden University

Kimberley A. Cox
Walden University

Linda M. Crawford
Walden University

John H. Hitchcock
Abt Associates Inc.

With a Foreword by Michael Quinn Patton

Los Angeles | London | New Delhi
Singapore | Washington DC | Melbourne

FOR INFORMATION:

SAGE Publications, Inc.
2455 Teller Road
Thousand Oaks, California 91320
E-mail: order@sagepub.com

SAGE Publications Ltd.
1 Oliver's Yard
55 City Road
London, EC1Y 1SP
United Kingdom

SAGE Publications India Pvt. Ltd.
B 1/I 1 Mohan Cooperative Industrial Area
Mathura Road, New Delhi 110 044
India

SAGE Publications Asia-Pacific Pte. Ltd.
18 Cross Street #10-10/11/12
China Square Central
Singapore 048423

Printed in the United States of America

Library of Congress Cataloging-in-Publication Data

ISBN 978-1-5443-4238-2

Library of Congress Control Number: 2019945278

Acquisitions Editor: Helen Salmon
Editorial Assistant: Megan O'Heffernan
Content Development Editor: Chelsea Neve
Production Editor: Rebecca Lee
Copy Editor: QuADS Prepress Pvt. Ltd.
Typesetter: Hurix Digital
Proofreader: Tricia Currie-Knight
Indexer: Laurie Andriot
Cover Designer: Ginkhan Siam
Marketing Manager: Shari Countryman

19 20 21 22 23 10 9 8 7 6 5 4 3 2 1

CONTENTS

FOREWORD

Michael Quinn Patton

In the agricultural age, success required land. In the industrial age, success required capital. In the information age, success requires knowledge. With the right knowledge, you can acquire land and capital. With the right knowledge, you can become more effective at whatever you choose to do both personally and professionally. However, information alone is not knowledge. The internet is filled with information but yields very little by way of knowledge. Knowledge comes from synthesizing research findings, observations from practice, insights from experts, interpretation based on theory, and ongoing learning.

This book will tell you what you need to do to make a contribution to knowledge worthy of an advanced degree. That's what it means to be awarded an advanced degree, that you have made an original contribution to knowledge. That may sound daunting. It may evoke anxiety and doubt. One source of anxiety you may experience, common among graduate students, is worry about whether the results will turn out the way you hope they turn out. Abandon that notion right now. Your task, indeed your responsibility, is not to produce desired results. Your task, indeed your responsibility, is to find out the answer to your research question. There is no right or wrong answer. There is nothing to prove. The world is the way it is. Your task, indeed your responsibility, is to contribute to our understanding of how the world works. In so doing, you will be engaged in inquiry, learning, discovery, and deeper questioning. Bring to your inquiry an open mind. Be prepared to follow the data wherever it takes you, to see what your research reveals, and to make sense of what you find. Forget about proving something. Focus on discovery.

Your task, indeed you responsibility, is to formulate a researchable question, identify methods that will help you pursue an answer to that question, systematically gather the appropriate data, document what you do every step along the way, organize and interpret your data, and report the findings. Quality is judged by the relevance and significance of your question, the extent to which your proposed research design will help you answer the question, careful and systematic implementation of your design to gather valid and reliable data, and thoughtful analysis. Nowhere in that process are you obligated to prove a certain result. Your obligation is to engage in serious and thoughtful inquiry, to interpret your findings with attention to both the strengths and weaknesses of your methods and data, and to place your findings in the larger context of knowledge within your field. In so doing, you will acknowledge those who have contributed knowledge before you and you will end by proposing inquiry questions for future knowledge generation. This book will tell you how to fulfill each of the steps along the way so that you make a contribution to knowledge and, in recognition of that contribution, attain your advanced degree thereby joining the worldwide community of scholar-practitioners.

DEVELOPING A MIND-SET OF INQUIRY

While the short-term purpose of your research is to fulfill the requirements for an advanced degree, the larger and longer-term purpose is to develop a mind-set of inquiry. Effectiveness as a scholar-practitioner involves ongoing inquiry, continuous learning, and application of research skills to whatever endeavors you undertake. Let me, then, preview for you eight things you are going to have the opportunity to learn that will serve you in good stead the rest of your life. In the spirit of Stephen Covey's best-selling *Seven Habits of Highly Effective People*, these are the *Eight Habits of Highly Effective Scholar-Practitioners.*

1. *Savvy and discriminating research consumption.* Whether you ever conduct original research again, you cannot help but be a consumer of research in this knowledge age. The challenge is becoming a *sophisticated consumer of research.* We are inundated constantly by research findings. A lot of it is junk. A lot of it is opinion disguised as research. A lot of it is biased. A lot of it is fabricated. And, a lot of it provides new insights and knowledge that will make you more effective in whatever you do. The trick is to know how to tell the difference. The scholar-practitioner mind-set is to engage new research findings by asking questions that may require digging deeper: What design produced those findings? What data were gathered and how were the data analyzed? How do these findings fit with other research in the field? Within what theoretical framework was the inquiry conducted? What are the practice implications of the findings, if any? A scholar-practitioner mind-set of inquiry means that you will not accept news headlines about research findings at face value but will look behind those headlines, using your research knowledge and skills, to determine the significance and relevance of the findings to your own work and life.

2. *Asking meaningful and important questions.* One of the first things you will do is work on formulating your research question. In everyday life, we are sloppy about how we frame questions. Learning to ask researchable questions with potentially actionable answers, the hallmark of the scholar-practitioner, is a skill that will serve you well the rest of your life. You will listen more astutely to how people frame their inquiries, the questions they ask, the format of those questions, and whether the questions are posed in ways that could possibly be answered. A sophisticated scholar-practitioner is a sophisticated question asker. It all begins with good questions.

3. *Critical thinking skills.* Scholar-practitioners are critical thinkers. Presumably, to reach the stage of working on an advanced degree, you already have some critical thinking skills. You may even think you're quite a rigorous thinker. Get ready to go deeper, not just to design and complete your research but in all that

you do. The stakes can be quite high. Philosopher Hannah Arendt devoted much of her life to trying to understand how the Holocaust could have occurred. Having experienced totalitarianism while young in Germany during World War II, then having fled as conditions worsened, she came to believe that thinking rigorously in public deliberations and acting democratically were intertwined. Totalitarianism is built on and sustained by deceit and thought control. To resist efforts by the powerful to deceive and control thinking, Arendt (1968) believed that people needed to practice thinking. Toward that end, she developed "eight exercises in political thought." She wrote that "experience in thinking . . . can be won, like all experience in doing something, only through practice, through exercises" (p. 4). From this point of view, I invite you to consider your research inquiry as an opportunity to practice thinking, to do what Arendt hoped her exercises in political thought would do—namely, help us "to gain experience in *how* to think." Her exercises "do not contain prescriptions on what to think or which truths to hold" but, rather, on the act and process of thinking. For example, Arendt thought it important to help people think conceptually,

> to discover the real origins of original concepts in order to distill from them anew their original spirit which has so sadly evaporated from the very keywords of political language—such as freedom and justice, authority and reason, responsibility and virtue, power and glory—leaving behind empty shells. (pp. 14–15)

Your research will involve examining the history of key concepts, how they had been applied in the past, and their relevance for today. This is an exercise in critical thinking, as will be all aspects of your inquiry.

4. *Advanced interviewing skills.* Many of you are likely to use interviewing as one of your inquiry methods. Becoming a skilled interviewer will enhance the validity and trustworthiness of the data you collect through interviewing. But becoming a skilled interviewer will also make you a more effective practitioner in the knowledge age. Every interaction with other human beings offers opportunities to inquire into their worldview, perspective, experiences, opinions, feelings, and behaviors. Knowing how to ask inviting and engaging questions, to listen attentively, to probe astutely, and to follow up on what you hear—these are the elements of effective interviewing and they will serve you well not only in conducting research but also in your relationships with family members, significant others, colleagues, and all you encounter on your life's journey.

I find interviewing people invigorating and stimulating—the opportunity for a short period of time to enter another person's world. I'm personally convinced that to be a good interviewer you must like doing it. This means being interested in what people have to say. You must, yourself, believe that the thoughts and experiences of the people being interviewed are worth knowing. In short, you must have the utmost respect for these persons who are willing to share with you some of their time to help you understand their world. If you include interviewing in your research, this will be an opportunity not only to deepen your skills but also to reflect on how you approach interactions of all kinds with other people. How good are you at asking questions? How good are you at listening? How skilled are you at making it comfortable for people to tell you their stories? How confident are you as an interviewer in our modern interview society, a core aspect of the knowledge age? Scholar-practitioners engage in ongoing learning and development of key inquiry skills such as in-depth interviewing.

5. *Astute observational skills.* Every interview is also an observation. With our heads buried in our devices these days, we miss a lot of what goes on around us. All of science is based on, indeed depends on, astute, focused, deep, and discerning observation. The great thinkers have all been great observers: Aristotle, Copernicus, Newton, Darwin, Einstein, Jung, Goodall, and whoever have been the pioneers in your own specialized scholar-practitioner field. Skilled interviewing involves more than just looking. It involves *seeing*. It involves knowing what to look for. It requires distinguishing signal from noise, astute pattern recognition, and an openness to be witness to whatever is unfolding before you. In our everyday lives, we walk around in a fog, engrossed in our own thoughts, operating on preconceived ideas, immersed in selective perception, operating on biases, and generally oblivious. To move into an observational mind-set means to lift the fog, stop the internal noise and gaze outward into the intriguing panorama of complex reality, open the mind to new possibilities and seeing things in new ways, in short, to become a skilled scholar-practitioner observer. Skill at observation, like interviewing skills, will serve you well not only in conducting research but also in all aspects of your life.

6. *Rigorous meaning-making skills.* All data have to be interpreted. Data do not speak for themselves. Making sense of data is a quintessential inquiry competence and skill. One aspect of analysis and interpretation, as with data collection itself, whether through interviewing or observation, involves distinguishing signal from noise. What is significant? What are the patterns and themes that are worth paying attention to? What do they mean? How do those meanings inform your understanding of the world and, through enhanced understanding, your actions in the world, *your* practice as a scholar-practitioner? One of the pitfalls of analysis is letting your preconceptions, selective perceptions, biases, and preferred ways of seeing things dominate your data interpretation. Rigorous analysis requires rigorous critical thinking. This includes triangulation: looking across different kinds of data (interviews, observations, documents) and diverse interpretive frameworks (previous research findings, alternative theories, competing conceptual frameworks) to figure out what interpretation best fits the data, not your hopes for the data, but the actual data. Rigorous analysis requires a disciplined search for data that don't fit the dominant pattern, for alternative explanations, and a willingness to be the devil's advocate in your own research. As with the other skills I've previewed, becoming better at making sense of data will serve you well not only in your research but also in deciding the value of all kinds of findings and propositions that you will encounter

as you are bombarded with allegations about how the world is from all sides. Astute sense-making, skilled interpretation, and rigorous meaning-making are what will move you from understanding to action in the knowledge age.

7. Integrating theory and practice. Kurt Lewin (1890–1947), pioneer of applied social psychology, famously observed, "There is nothing as practical as a good theory." At the core of being an effective scholar-practitioner is knowing how to integrate theory and practice. The purpose of theory is to explain how the world functions. The purpose of practice is to make a difference in the world. Clearly, knowing how the world functions is essential for knowing how to make a difference in the world. That is what is meant by practical theory. In much of academia, theory and practice are separated. There are courses on theory and other courses on practice. The scholar-practitioner, then, faces the challenge of drawing on theory to inform practice and using lessons from practice to deepen and enrich theory. Let me give you an example using brain research.

Brain research reveals that the human brain is where theory and practice are integrated. The evidence from social and behavioral science is that to make decisions when we are faced with complex choices in new situations, we fall back on a set of rules and standard operating procedures that predetermine what we will do, that effectively short-circuit genuine situational adaptability. The evidence is that we are running most of the time on preprogrammed tapes. That has always been the function of social norms, rules of thumb, and scientific paradigms. Faced with a new situation, we turn to old and comfortable patterns (sometimes consciously, sometimes unconsciously). This may help explain why so many researchers find that the approaches in which they are trained, and with which they are most comfortable, *just happen* to be particularly appropriate in each new inquiry they engage in—time after time after time.

Several interdisciplinary fields of inquiry have provided insights into how we manage decision-making in the face of complexity. Decision sciences have been identifying decision heuristics that cut through the messy, confusing, and overwhelming chaos of the real world so that we can avoid analysis paralysis and take action. We rely on routine "heuristics"—rules of thumb, standard operating procedures, practiced behaviors, and selective perception that can be distorting the has-been.

- The *confidence heuristic:* The *amount* of information we obtain increases our confidence in our judgments, regardless of the accuracy or redundancy of the information.

- The *representativeness heuristic:* This guides our sense-making in new situations by focusing our attention on those aspects of the situation that are most familiar and similar to our previous experiences. We make a new problem or situation *representative* of things we already know, selectively ignoring information and evidence that is unfamiliar or that doesn't fit our preconceptions developed through past experiences.

- The *availability heuristic:* This operates to make sense of new situations by bringing readily to mind things that happened to us recently or information that we come across frequently.

What intersecting and overlapping fields of research on decision-making and brain functioning reveal is that we can't systematically consider every possible variable in a situation. Findings from cognitive science, decision science, and contingency theory triangulate to reveal that what makes thought and action possible is viewing the real world through some kind of framework for making sense of situations, a framework that tells us what factors deserve priority in our sense-making. This readily and inevitably happens unconsciously. It's how our brains work. The issue is whether and how we can become more consciously and intentionally deliberative about how we engage in sense-making and situation recognition. We can do this through ongoing and in-depth reflective practice to become *reflective theory-based practitioners.* We can do this by systematically evaluating our decision-making patterns, engaging in ongoing learning, and deconstructing our design tendencies and methodological decision-making.

Let me reiterate the overall point here. We are already integrating theory and practice in our brains because to practice (or act) at all we make sense of what to do by interpreting the situations we face through some set of theoretical screens and constructs that operate through decision heuristics, cognitive algorithms, paradigm parameters, and mental shortcuts. The issue, then, isn't whether we integrate theory and practice in our brains. The issue is whether we become more intentional and deliberative about how we do so. Toward that end, your inquiry journey will provide an opportunity to exercise greater intentionality and deliberativeness in integrating theory and practice in your own decision-making processes, including especially decisions you make about your research question, design, analysis, and reporting. What you learn about your own patterns and tendencies will have influence far beyond the research you do for your advanced degree.

8. *Systematic evaluative thinking.* The eighth and final thing you are going to have the opportunity to learn that will serve you in good stead the rest of your life is systematic evaluative thinking. This book includes guidance on doing program evaluation. But whether you undertake a formal program evaluation for your research, you will still, inevitably, be engaged in evaluative thinking. This means that you will have to become explicit about criteria you will use to judge quality, validity, relevance, credibility, and utility of research findings and about the processes that generated those findings. Not only does this apply to your own research, which will be evaluated by you, your research committee, and others who read your findings, but systematic evaluative thinking is also critical to your review of the research of others. As you engage in a literature review, you will be employing systematic evaluative thinking to determine which published research is particularly relevant and meaningful for your own inquiry. As you review methodological possibilities and analysis options, you will be engaged in systematic evaluative thinking. This will

require you to get better at generating evaluative criteria and applying those criteria to make judgments about what is significant, meaningful, and important. Pay attention to the criteria you use and the implications of applying those criteria. Like critical thinking, and integrating theory and practice, systematic evaluative thinking is something you can get better at with practice, but only if you pay attention, reflect on your thinking patterns, and learn both about what you are studying and, perhaps even more important, about yourself.

The Eight Habits of Highly Effective Scholar-Practitioners

As I noted at the beginning of this forward, while the short-term purpose of your research is to fulfill the requirements for an advanced degree, the larger and longer-term purpose is to develop a *mind-set of inquiry.* Effectiveness as a scholar-practitioner involves ongoing inquiry, continuous learning, and application of research skills to whatever endeavors you undertake. This foreword has previewed for you eight things you are going to have the opportunity to learn that will be essential in completing your research but, no less important, will serve you in good stead the rest of your life as you become an *effective scholar-practitioner.*

1. Savvy and discriminating research consumption

2. Asking meaningful and important questions

3. Critical thinking skills

4. Advanced interviewing skills

5. Astute observational skills

6. Rigorous meaning-making skills

7. Integrating theory and practice

8. Systematic evaluative thinking

In closing, I'd like to share with you a cautionary tale to inform your inquiry journey.

ON BEING PRESENT FOR THE WHOLE JOURNEY

Master Halcolm was renowned as a wise sage. Students came to him for advice and counsel. When a group of students about to begin research projects came to see Halcolm, he asked them, "What did you learn in your readings this week?"

"We learned that a journey of 1000 miles begins with the first step," replied the students.

"Ah, Yes, the importance of beginnings," smiled Halcolm.

"Yet I am puzzled," said a student. "Yesterday I read that there are 1000 beginnings for every ending."

"Ah, yes, the importance of seeing anything through to the end," confirmed Halcolm.

"Which is more important, to begin or end?" asked a student.

"Two great self-deceptions are asserted by the world's self-congratulators: that the hardest and most important step is the first and that the greatest and most resplendent step is the last. While every journey must have a first and last step, my experience is that what ultimately determines the nature and enduring value of the journey are the steps in between. Each step has its own value and importance. Be present for the whole journey, learners that you are. *Be present for the whole journey.*" (Patton, 2015, pp. 734–735; used with permission)

READINESS

Readiness, in my experience, is primarily a state of mind, being open to new learning and prepared to do the work necessary to apply what you learn. This book has all the resources you need to complete your research and make a contribution to knowledge. Ready. Set. **GO!**

References

Arendt, H. (1968). *Between past and future: Eight exercises in political thought.* New York, NY: Viking Press.

Patton, M. Q. (2015). *Qualitative research and evaluation methods* (4th ed.). Thousand Oaks, CA: SAGE.

PREFACE

One of the hallmarks of graduate education is research. We have been preparing to do research since our earliest years of schooling. Over time, our understanding of the meaning of *research* changes and differs depending on context. For example, students in junior high school conduct research by going to the internet (and perhaps to the library) for information to write a paper about a famous person; in the process, they learn that research is associated with collecting and synthesizing information. In high school, students study the laboratory sciences. At the baccalaureate and master's degree levels, students may write research papers for courses that involve collecting information from an expanded set of resources that integrates and summarizes knowledge in a particular area. There may also be the goal of applying that knowledge to solutions of practical problems. At the doctoral level, students are typically expected to produce original research that adds new knowledge to their discipline of study or use research to solve an applied problem in a novel way.

Research at all levels tends to come with some amount of anxiety. For example, in our earliest undergraduate education courses, we may ask ourselves, "Do I have enough sources to support a five-page paper?" When students come into their doctoral programs, many are told that they have to write the equivalent of a book and that the research process takes several years. To complicate matters, the requirement for research design and statistics courses may raise issues of math and other kinds of analytic performance anxiety. There are also many students who would like to have a doctoral degree but never intend on becoming professional researchers or academics. They may wonder if their programs will require less statistics and other kinds of analysis and research design training, since they plan on continuing to work in their chosen fields of study.

Working professionals who increasingly seek doctoral degrees reflect an increasingly pragmatic focus on education worldwide. In the new knowledge economy of the 21st century, employability has surfaced as a key goal of higher education. No longer focused solely on creating new academics, universities are creating doctoral programs designed for people intending to work outside of academia, those who we will call *scholar-practitioners*. In our experience with distance education, people who otherwise would not be attracted to a doctoral program now have flexible options to achieve a degree that can carry professional prestige, higher salaries, and opportunities for career expansion.

Tenkasi and Hay (2008) defined the scholar-practitioner as one who "ha[s] one foot in each of the worlds of academia and practice and are pointedly interested in advancing the causes of both theory and practice" (p. 49). Hay (2004) provided an example from management in that scholar-practitioners "promise to be boundary-spanners who move between the worlds of academic and business in order to generate two outcomes—new theoretical knowledge and organizational results" (p. 375). Kram, Wasserman, and Yip (2012) used the definition from Tenkasi and Hay (2008), among others, to define the scholar-practitioner as "one who actively engages in developing new knowledge and applying it in practice" (p. 334). Most definitions of scholar-practitioner carry implicit messages about the role of research: (a) scholar-practitioners are likely not positioning themselves as academics, although scholarship is a key part of their identity, and (b) research is important to the scholar-practitioner who seeks to understand and apply theory to solve practical problems arising in the professions. Scholar-practitioners can now be found across multiple disciplines, including health, psychology, business and management, and education. Counted among the ranks are nurse practitioners, school superintendents, counselor-educators, management consultants, and others.

Thus, the scholar-practitioner has a responsibility to gain broad understanding of the philosophical foundations guiding research and the profession, apply the scientific method, gather appropriate evidence situated in the knowledge within the discipline, and solve important problems in practice. One term used frequently in the health care professions is *evidence-based practice*, the goal of which is to combine clinical expertise, theory, and results of research when making key practice decisions and achieving results in patients, businesses, schools, and the many other settings in which scholar-practitioners operate. This is not to say that scholar-practitioners are not interested in theory; one of the primary goals of any researcher is to understand the philosophical underpinnings and the role of theory in the discipline and to use evidence and application that can advance theory. Here, we recognize that many scholar-practitioners have as their goal the application of scientific discovery and theory to problems in practice. It is for these scholar-practitioners that this book is primarily written.

THE PURPOSE OF THE BOOK

In some ways, doing research is like learning a foreign language: It takes dedicated practice to learn the vocabulary; to acquire listening, reading, writing, and speaking skills; and to become proficient in the grammar. It also takes a lot of patience. Our purpose in writing this book is to provide a straightforward and easy-to-understand text for those conducting research in the social, behavioral, health, management, and education sciences (for ease, when we refer to *social sciences* going forward, we will consider that inclusive of these discipline areas) that will help them learn this new language of research. It is written with a specific orientation to the scholar-practitioner who is new at research at the advanced undergraduate or graduate degree levels. We wrote this book understanding that there is a paucity of texts that present the basic concepts of research for scholar-practitioners and establish a foundation on which to build deeper understanding of issues related to research methods relevant to their particular disciplines and interests.

Our intent is not to present detailed analysis of the various epistemologies and traditions of research methods associated with different choices of approaches to inquiry, design, and analysis. Rather, our goal is to provide an overview of the main topics associated with research that will help you establish a foundational understanding of research principles. This, in turn, will allow you to successfully craft a research prospectus or proposal. Each chapter contains an overview with sufficient detail for a basic mastery of the material. Because we recognize the key contributors in specific areas of focus in research, each chapter ends with key resources we consider critical for adequate mastery in that particular aspect of research and inquiry. Consider this book as a way of establishing a foundation for research that serves as an entry into the much richer world of research and all of its interpretations. Joining us in this journey will allow you to seek the most appropriate expression of research in your own work and to develop your own unique voice as a scholar-practitioner.

ORGANIZATION OF THE BOOK

The book is divided into six parts. Parts 1 to 4 address the foundational concepts of research philosophy and theory, design, methods, analysis, and data collection. This is the essential information that every scholar-practitioner needs to have in order to become conversant in research and its methods and a critical consumer of research findings, as well as to begin the process of writing a research proposal. This information also forms the foundation on which you can build your own understanding of theory and research in your discipline and use that new understanding to engage in the research that is most meaningful to answer your research questions of interest.

Part 5 contains detailed exploration of a number of research designs and methodologies, based on our combined experience of more than 80 years of working with scholar-practitioners, that doctoral students in scholar-practitioner programs tend to choose. These are the designs and methodologies that tend to be grounded in practice and naturally address the real-world problems that scholar-practitioners want and need to solve. The information provided will be most useful for students trying to decide whether a particular design most appropriately addresses their research questions. These chapters cannot substitute for a more in-depth analysis of the approach, and for this reason, the additional resources provided will help you achieve the requisite depth of understanding needed to craft a complete proposal and conduct research.

Finally, Part 6 provides information on writing and disseminating research. The chapters on synthesizing and critiquing literature and on writing the proposal help you to turn what you have learned in the first part of the book into a logical, concise, and coherent research proposal. The final chapter helps you to turn the results of your work into a product that can be appreciated by others, including academic and nonacademic audiences.

Below is a brief overview of each chapter.

Part 1: Foundations in Research Design

- *Chapter 1, Introduction to Research*, provides key research vocabulary and the foundations of research. The goal of this chapter is to provide you with the essential building blocks of the language of research on which you can build fluency. In addition, the key steps of the research process are outlined. These steps necessarily link to subsequent chapters in Part 1.

- *Chapter 2, Philosophical Foundations and the Role of Theory in Research*, introduces the role of philosophy and theory and how it shapes research conducted by social scientists. The focus of this chapter is on understanding science as a means of generating knowledge; explanations of ontology and epistemology and why this has bearing on knowledge and the choice of research paradigm and design; positivist, postpositivist, and constructivist/interpretive orientations to understanding truth; and the nature of causality in the social sciences. Also included is an introduction to the role of theory in scientific research.

- *Chapter 3, Conceptual and Theoretical Frameworks in Research*, provides clarity to the role of conceptual and theoretical frameworks in guiding research. Literature-based definitions of conceptual and theoretical frameworks used by other researchers in the literature are explored, and we provide a definition that we use consistently throughout the book. Included is practical guidance on how you can develop a conceptual or theoretical framework that guides development of the research proposal.

Part 2: Research Design and Analysis

- *Chapter 4, Quantitative Research Designs*, provides definitions of design-related terms including *variable, operational definition*, and *levels of measurement*. The remainder of the chapter is focused on providing an overview of common quantitative research designs as well as their strengths and limitations. Included in the chapter is information on sampling and sampling strategies.

- *Chapter 5, Quantitative Analysis*, provides some introductory information regarding analysis and presentation of quantitative data. By use of example, the author provides introduction to important concepts such as the use and presentation of descriptive statistics, effect size to determine required sample size, and issues related to screening and cleaning data.

- *Chapter 6, Qualitative Research Designs*, provides an overview of the purposes of qualitative research and the role of the researcher in qualitative research. There is a brief overview of five qualitative designs most frequently chosen by scholar-practitioner researchers: (1) case study, (2) ethnography, (3) phenomenology, (4) narrative, and (5) grounded theory. The author provides guidance on sample size for various designs and how to achieve trustworthiness, the equivalent to reliability and validity in quantitative studies.

- *Chapter 7, Qualitative Analysis*, introduces issues related to the analysis of qualitative data. The author describes various approaches to coding, such as deductive and inductive techniques, developing a codebook, and teamwork coding. He provides practical examples that demonstrates the use of coding and thematic formation that serves as the foundation of analysis in most qualitative approaches.

- *Chapter 8, Mixed Methods Designs and Approaches*, introduces mixed methods research, which tends to be most misunderstood design and approach. The chapter provides a clear understanding of what it takes to do a mixed methods study correctly and the reasons researchers might choose this particular strategy. Included is a description of the philosophical underpinnings, mixed methods designs, and strategies for integrating quantitative and qualitative methods.

- *Chapter 9: Mixed Methods Analysis* describes issues associated with analysis of quantitative and qualitative data. The authors introduce the concept of data integration and common levels of integration, provide a practical example of the application of data integration, and outline some of the key challenges when conducting mixed methods data analysis.

Part 3: Data Collection

- *Chapter 10, Interviewing Essentials for New Researchers*, provides introductory information around the key issues that arise when conducting interviews. Included in the chapter are distinctions among structured, semistructured, and unstructured interviews as well as the differences between individual and focus group interviews. Included also is a description of the influence of power and culture dynamics in interviews.

- *Chapter 11, Survey Research*, provides an excellent overview of the key considerations for those who create their own instruments. The chapter begins with a definition of survey research and a brief historical overview of the evolution of the methodology. A number of examples of survey research are included that represent multiple disciplines in the social sciences. Also included is an overview of the process of creating a survey instrument.

Part 4: Research Quality and Ethics

- *Chapter 12, Quality Considerations*, describes issues related to quality in qualitative, quantitative, and mixed methods research. The chapter provides an overview of the importance of quality of data sources and methods, data collection, and analysis. Topics include reliability and validity in experimental research designs, specifically focusing on definitions of internal and external validity as well as statistical conclusion and construct validity, and trustworthiness, the equivalent to validity and reliability in quantitative research.

- *Chapter 13, Ethical Considerations*, provides an overview of ethical issues of most relevance to novice researchers. Included in the chapter is a description of the historical evolution of ethical codes, followed by the role of professional associations in research ethics. Other topics include assessing risks and benefits to participation, function and composition of institutional review boards (IRBs), informed consent, and methods for protecting privacy of data. Three topics are addressed that have contemporary importance, including the use of deception in experimental research, conducting research with vulnerable populations, and the ethical implications associated with internet research.

Part 5: Selected Research Designs and Approaches

- *Chapter 14, Phenomenology*, provides a comprehensive overview of an approach that is both a method and a methodology with a rich philosophical tradition. The chapter describes the origins and philosophical underpinnings of phenomenology. Several examples of the use of phenomenology across a variety of disciplines and the research questions that are most appropriate for phenomenology are given. The chapter includes description of issues related to sample size and the role of the researcher in phenomenological research.

- *Chapter 15, Grounded Theory*, provides an overview of the concepts associated with grounded theory approach and analysis. The chapter introduces some of the origins and philosophical underpinnings of grounded theory. Examples of how grounded theory has been used within several disciplines are provided in addition to information on appropriate sample size data collection and analysis. Constant comparative analysis, a feature unique to grounded theory, is described.

- *Chapter 16, Case Study Research*, begins with a definition of case study and a description of the origins and philosophical underpinnings of the approach. Several discipline-specific applications of case study methodology are provided apart from a description of the appropriate research questions addressed by case studies. The chapter includes information on some of the methodology considerations, including sample size, data collection, and data analysis.

- *Chapter 17, Program Evaluation*, describes the foundational role of stakeholders in program evaluation and the logic model of evaluation. The explanation includes key differences between process and formative evaluation and between outcome and summative evaluation. Included are a number of examples of program evaluation across the disciplines as well as methodological aspects of program evaluation such as sample size, data collection and analysis, and issues of quality.

- *Chapter 18, Action Research*, describes what action research is (and is not), the historical origins, and its philosophical underpinnings. Action research is compared with traditional experimental research to highlight the highly practical nature of action research. Included is an explanation of various aspects of the methodology, including data collection and analysis, and sample size determination.

Part 6: Writing and Disseminating Research

- *Chapter 19, Critiquing and Synthesizing the Literature*, provides practical strategies for reviewing literature and writing the literature review section of the research. The chapter highlights the difference between critique and synthesis and includes important considerations and common mistakes in both. The chapter also includes examples of good and poor critique and synthesis.

- *Chapter 20, Writing the Research Proposal*, brings together the information from the previous chapters into a practical guide to understanding and writing the key sections of a research proposal. These sections include the problem statement, purpose statement, research questions, and theoretical and conceptual frameworks that constitute the rationale for the study. Included are tools that can be used to help ensure alignment (or consistency) across the key sections of your research proposal.

- *Chapter 21: Disseminating Research*, introduces the various ways to share the results of research that fit with the researcher's personal and professional goals. The author draws on his extensive experience in dissemination and provides practical advice for those who want to publish in academic journals as well as for those who want to disseminate in other venues, such as places of employment and conferences.

This book is designed for you; it is meant to be a foundational yet flexible resource to help you gain the confidence to conduct scholarly research, whether your goal is purely academic or completed through a scholar-practitioner lens. It is not possible to provide the depth of understanding needed to become an expert in each of the topics described in this book. Use the Key Resources provided at the end of each chapter as a guide for further and deeper exploration. Bring any questions you have to colleagues, your professors, or your dissertation/thesis committee; each of these people can help you achieve the depth of understanding of basic research principles that you will need to complete a successful research study.

Research is a scientific enterprise, but it is also a social enterprise; scientists learn from one another and slowly accumulate a knowledge base in a discipline. Kuhn (1962) wrote that "normal science," the puzzle-solving activity we have just examined, "is a highly cumulative enterprise, eminently successful in its aim, the steady extension of the scope and precision of scientific knowledge" (p. 52). But Hacking (1983) also acknowledged that "there can be heaping up of knowledge without there being any unity of science to which they all add up" (p. 55). Each discipline has a rich store of knowledge, some organized through theories and some not. The important work you do as a researcher steadily extends the scope of knowledge. Social science researchers bring fresh perspectives to their disciplines; engaging that perspective in research helps bring more clarity (or further questions) to specific topics of importance in your field. We hope that this book empowers you to probe with depth and more confidence research topics of most interest to you and to the discipline and that this depth of understanding helps you to craft a research study that addresses the most important questions in your disciplines and professions.

References

Hacking, I. (1983). *Representing and intervening: Introductory topics in the philosophy of natural science.* Cambridge, UK: Cambridge University Press.

Hay, G. W. (2004). Executive PHDs as a solution to the perceived relevance gap between theory and practice: A framework of theory–practice linkages for the study of the executive doctoral scholar-practitioner. *International Journal of Organisational Behavior, 7*(2), 375–393.

Kram, K. E., Wasserman, I. C, & Yip, J. (2012). Metaphors of identity and professional practice: Learning from the scholar-practitioner. *Journal of Applied Behavioral Science, 48*(3), 304–341. doi:10.1177/0021886312439097

Kuhn, T. (1962). *The structure of scientific revolutions*. Chicago, IL: University of Chicago Press.

Tenkasi, R. V., & Hay, G. W. (2008). Following the second legacy of Aristotle: The scholar-practitioner as an epistemic technician. In A. B. Shani, S. A. Mohrman, W. A. Pasmore, B. N. Stymne, & N. Adler (Eds.), *Handbook of collaborative management research* (pp. 49–72). Thousand Oaks, CA: SAGE.

Companion Website

For accompanying student and instructor resources, visit the book's companion website at **https://study.sagepub.com/burkholder1e**.

Instructor resources include:

- Chapter-specific slide presentations highlighting key points from the text, ideal for use in lectures and review.
- Lecture notes which summarize and outline each chapter, providing structure for class lectures.

Student resources include:

- SAGE Research Methods Case Studies, carefully selected to draw connections to real-world examples of research concepts and methods covered in the text.

ACKNOWLEDGMENTS

We are indebted to many people for their support and intellectual contributions during the creation of this book. First, a great thank you to our families and friends for the support and encouragement during the many hours of writing and editing. We extend our deepest appreciation to the chapter contributors. We sought colleagues across institutions who not only had deep expertise in research but also had significant experience working with scholar-practitioners, for whom this book is written. Our colleagues worked with us to refine the vision for the book so that it would be maximally useful for those who are just learning about research and who will continue to advance practice. Many chapter contributors also sought expertise from other colleagues who provided valuable feedback on content and tone. On behalf of the chapter contributors, we thank these colleagues for their insights. Several anonymous reviewers provided feedback that helped us ensure that the book was positioned in the correct way for the scholar-practitioner audience. We used their insights to ensure that our book was inclusive of multiple perspectives, perspectives that are indeed important for early researchers.

We extend our deepest thanks and appreciation to Helen Salmon at SAGE Publishing, who served as our managing editor. She has been enthusiastic about this project from the very beginning. Helen guided us through the process of putting this book together and helped us achieve the best combination of authors and content to ensure its relevance to the scholar-practitioner. Megan O'Heffernan provided valuable assistance in the day-to-day activities associated with the book. We also thank our colleagues at Laureate Education who collaborated with us on an earlier version of the book. Our gratitude also goes to colleagues with whom we have had many hours of dialogue on teaching, the value of research, and service on doctoral dissertation committees. We have grown tremendously as researchers through these dialogues.

Finally, we thank all the students whom we have taught and mentored over the years. When we started out in our academic careers, we did not imagine that our life's work would be about preparing both academic researchers and scholar-practitioners. Through their honest struggles and successes as emerging researchers, our students have taught us much about what they need to understand the research process. We conceptualized this book to meet their specific needs. It is our way of saying *thank you* to all of our students for what they have taught us about teaching research.

The authors and SAGE would like to thank the following reviewers for their feedback:

Rukhsana Ahmed, *University of Ottawa*

Naseem Badiey, *California State University Monterey Bay*

Brandon M. Butler, *Old Dominion University*

Ajay Das, *SUNY Empire State College*

Francis Godwyll, *University of West Florida*

Gavin R. Goldstein, Esq., *Berkeley College*

Holly A. Haynes, *Truett McConnell University*

Dena Kneiss, *University of West Georgia*

Carmen L. McCrink, *Barry University*

Peter Memiah, *University of West Florida*

Lynette Nickelberry, *SUNY Empire State College*

Charol Shakeshaft, *Virginia Commonwealth University*

Eric D. Teman, *University of Wyoming*

ABOUT THE EDITORS

Gary J. Burkholder is a senior research scholar and a senior contributing faculty at Walden University. He graduated from the University of Rhode Island with a PhD in experimental psychology and with MA and BA degrees in psychology; he also earned a bachelor of science degree in engineering from the University of Washington. He has been on the faculty at Walden University, a distance education institution focused primarily on graduate, scholar-practitioner students, since 2001. He has served in several senior academic and business administration roles at Walden University and other institutions, including program director, director of online studies, assistant dean, dean, college vice president, and vice president for academic affairs. In his faculty role, he has mentored more than 90 doctoral dissertation students in the social and behavioral sciences and the health sciences, and he is a past recipient of Walden University's Bernard L. Turner award for excellence in mentoring dissertation students. His research focus spans qualitative, quantitative, and mixed methods, including multivariable statistical analysis and instrument development. He has conducted research in topics that intersect psychology and public health, including those involving exercise and diet behavior change and adherence and predictors of substance use, sex risk, and HIV risk among youth and adults. More recently, his research interests have involved retention and persistence in tertiary education as well as online pedagogy. He has served as author of approximately 70 peer-reviewed publications and collaborated in more than 70 conference presentations; several publications and presentations have involved his doctoral students. He is active in the American Public Health Association, serves as a peer reviewer with the Higher Learning Commission regional accreditation body, and serves as a reviewer for several professional journals in education, psychology, and public health.

Kimberley A. Cox earned her PhD in social psychology from Claremont Graduate University and her master's degree in psychology from Pepperdine University. She received her undergraduate education at the University of California, Irvine, where she earned a bachelor's degree in psychology and a bachelor's degree in criminology, law, and society. For the past 10 years, she has been a faculty member at Walden University, where her work is dedicated to teaching and mentoring future scholar-practitioners.

During this time, she has mentored 45 doctoral students to dissertation completion. She is a past recipient of Walden University's Bernard L. Turner award for excellence in mentoring dissertation students and the Presidential Research Fellowship in Distance Education. She currently teaches doctoral-level courses in research design and methods and applied social psychology. She also serves as a subject matter expert in the design of online courses. Most recently, her academic interests include the application of social psychology principles and theories to social problems and environmental issues with a focus on topics that intersect social psychology, health, and the environment. Prior to her teaching career in higher education, she held various academic and applied research positions, including as a research associate in the Department of Psychiatry and Human Behavior in the College of Medicine at the University of California, Irvine, as a research associate at the Rand Corporation, and as a doctoral research fellow at the NASA Ames Research Center.

Linda M. Crawford, professor emerita at Walden University, received her doctoral degree from the University of Minnesota with emphases in curriculum and educational administration. In her most recent position as director of academic quality and accreditation for Laureate Education, she conducted quality assurance reviews, both domestic and international, at institutional, program, certificate, course, and service levels, including reviews for schools in Saudi Arabia, Ecuador, and Switzerland. She also advised institutions extensively on the faculty perspective related to academic initiatives, including development of new faculty orientation programs, faculty governance, and faculty models. Prior to her work in quality assurance, she held both teaching and administrative positions at all levels of education, including P–12, undergraduate, and graduate education. While serving as an assistant superintendent for a large metropolitan-area school district, she provided direction for research, evaluation, and assessment; P–12 curriculum and instruction; special education; instructional media and technology; state and federal programs, including desegregation, family service cooperatives, and all federal Title programs; policy development and maintenance; and community education. She also initiated online learning within the P–12 environment with a focus on serving homebound students or students otherwise missing school attendance and on providing low enrollment courses across districts. Involved in online education for two decades, she developed and taught courses for multiple universities in the areas of research, measurement and evaluation, curriculum theory and design, instructional practice, and educational law. She has published and presented locally, regionally, and nationally on topics of research, curriculum, educational philosophy, administration, and mentoring doctoral students. Her current research centers on mentoring graduate students and building a sense of community among students in the online environment. She is a two-time recipient of the Walden University Bernard L. Turner Award for excellence in mentoring dissertation students and has also received the Walden University Richard W. Riley College of Education and Leadership Extraordinary Faculty Award.

John H. Hitchcock is a principal associate in the Social and Economic Policy division of Abt Associates. In the past, he held tenured faculty appointments at Ohio University and Indiana University. At each university, he also served as a director of a research center. He earned a PhD in educational psychology; a certificate of advanced study in applied research, focusing on program evaluation; and a master's degree in educational psychology and statistics, all from the University at Albany, State University of New York. He earned a bachelor's degree in psychology from the University of Evansville. He focuses on developing mixed methods research applications, evaluating interventions designed for children with special learning needs, and research syntheses. To date, he has served as a co–principal investigator on four randomized controlled trials, helped the U.S. Department of Education develop standards for evaluating the causal validity of single-case research designs, coauthored more than 45 scholarly works (peer-reviewed journal articles, books, national technical reports, and book chapters), and presented research at conferences more than 125 times. As part of these efforts, he coauthored grant applications that have led to more than US$10 million in funding from federal, state, philanthropic, and international agencies. He has served as an associate editor for *School Psychology Review* and is currently coeditor in chief of the *International Journal of Multiple Research Approaches*. As an international researcher, he served on the executive board of the Mixed Methods International Research Association and has provided consultation to education leaders in Turkey, Saudi Arabia, Kosovo, and Jamaica.

ABOUT THE CONTRIBUTORS

Patricia M. Burbank is a professor at the University of Rhode Island, College of Nursing, and a fellow in the American Academy of Nursing. She is also a faculty member in the Rhode Island Geriatric Education Center. Her master's degree in gerontological nursing and her doctoral degree in nursing science are both from Boston University. Her major teaching responsibilities have been graduate courses in philosophy of science, theoretical foundations of nursing research, and quantitative methods as well as gerontological advanced practice nursing courses. She has been a key member of an interdisciplinary research team examining exercise and nutrition behavior change among older adults using the transtheoretical model of behavior change. This research resulted in several publications, including her book (edited with D. Riebe) *Promoting Exercise and Behavior Change Among Older Adults* (also translated into Japanese). Her other research projects have included studying the outcomes of a fall-prevention program, statewide needs assessment survey of LGBT older adults, examining attitudes toward older adults, and instrument development of the Perspectives on Caring for Older Adults scale. She has also worked in theory development, coauthoring the critical interactionist theory, which combines symbolic interactionism and critical theory. Her book *Vulnerable Older Adults: Issues and Strategies* was a winner of the *Choice* magazine award and the *American Journal of Nursing* Book of the Year award. Most recently, she has teamed with biosensor engineering professor K. Mankodiya in developing smart textiles to monitor gait parameters and help motivate older adults to be more physically active. Research to test these textiles is currently under way. Her current interests also include the benefits of a whole food, plant-based diet and fostering innovation in nursing practice and education.

Paula Dawidowicz has conducted research since 1979 when, in the Air Force, she conducted systems and personnel analyses. Since having earned her PhD in 2001, she has conducted at least three studies a year, culminating in numerous scholarly presentations and articles. She has developed expertise in virtually all qualitative designs and has written and presented on the use of those designs in multiple venues. On graduation, she worked at The Florida Center for Reading Research, where she served as a research associate for two years conducting evaluations of different reading programs, parents' participation in the reading programs, and other aspects of

Florida reading activities. She left there to join Walden University, her alma mater, as a faculty member. Since joining Walden University, she has served as a full-time PhD faculty, as a PhD education content-area specialization coordinator, and as the PhD education research coordinator for more than 12 years in charge of all aspects of the dissertation development process. She conducted her dissertation using what she calls a grounded ethnohistoriographic design, a hybridization of three different qualitative methods designs, examining cultural and educational changes in one state's educational environment as a result of religious diversification. She followed that with a second grounded ethnohistoriographic study focused on a school district and its special education program population. She has a broad area of interests because she looks at systemic connections. She has a PhD in education, postdoc courses in psychology, an MS in health services administration, and a BA in international affairs. She is interested in systems that include the sociological, psychological, and cultural aspects of education and how education can help address cultural issues. Her specific content focuses include logic, critical thinking, argumentation, and systemic thinking. Her current methodological foci are qualitative methods and mixed methods.

Laura Knight Lynn is currently the executive director of the Center for Research Quality at Walden University. In this capacity, she oversees research quality assurance, research process approvals, and research resources and opportunities for students and faculty at the university. She has also served as doctoral faculty supporting many PhD and professional doctorate students as chair and committee member in Walden University's Richard W. Riley College of Education and Leadership. Her previous roles include research and residency coordinator in the Richard W. Riley College of Leadership, executive director of Prism Community Institute, and research scientist at Rehabilitation Foundation, Inc. As an experienced program evaluator for nonprofit programs and as a community-based researcher, she has developed projects and presented and published on health care outcomes research, youth media programs, juvenile justice, after-school programs, English Language Learner programs, and community support programs. Inspired by her work with students and faculty at Walden University, she has also designed research and presented and published on doctoral student research self-efficacy and doctoral student progress and evaluation. Much of her community research and evaluation work fits with mixed method designs that include interviews, document analysis, observations, surveys, and standard questionnaires. Her current area of focus is international doctoral students studying online. She currently has an active research team at Walden University looking at both the impact of African national dissertation research and support opportunities and learning preference for African national doctoral students studying online. She received her PhD in research methodology and human development from Loyola University. She is skilled in both qualitative and quantitative methodologies. She has taught several courses in research design and provided trainings in interviewing techniques for researchers.

Craig A. Mertler is currently an associate professor and director of the EdD program in Leadership & Innovation at Arizona State University. He began his career as a high school biology teacher. He has been an educator for 33 years, 23 of those in higher education and 10 as an administrator (department chair, doctoral program director, and education dean) at Bowling Green State University, the University of West Georgia, and Lynn University. He teaches courses focused on the application of action research to promote educator empowerment, school improvement, and job-embedded professional development and also teaches research methods, statistical analyses, and educational assessment methods. He has served as the research methodology expert on more than 100 doctoral dissertations and master's theses. He is the author of 24 books (including three books on *action research*, and others on *classroom assessment*, and *data-driven instructional decision-making*), 9 invited book chapters, and 22 refereed journal articles. Since 2005, much of Craig's work has centered on the notion of integrating action research into schools. He has conducted numerous in-service training sessions on the action research process in school districts and institutions of higher education in numerous states around the country.

Paul Mihas is the assistant director of qualitative research at the Odum Institute for Research in Social Science at the University of North Carolina at Chapel Hill. Since 2001, he has also served as a qualitative analysis consultant with ResearchTalk Inc. and as a mentor at ResearchTalk's qualitative data analysis camps. He is on faculty at the annual Qualitative Research Summer Intensive in Chapel Hill and at the Inter-University Consortium for Political and Social Research Summer Program in Methods of Social Research. He teaches qualitative methods through the Global School in Empirical Research Methods at the University of St. Gallen, BI Norwegian Business School, and the University of Ljubljana, Slovenia. He is a contributor to the SAGE Research Methods Datasets, an online collection of methods articles on qualitative and quantitative data analysis. His forthcoming publications include a chapter on approaches to qualitative analysis in the *Oxford Research Encyclopedia of Education*. He is the former managing editor of *Social Forces*, a journal of sociology published at the University of North Carolina Press. His academic interests include narrative analysis, strategies for memo writing, and cancer survivorship and identity.

Louis Milanesi received his PhD in social ecology from the University of California, Irvine, in 1991. He is an advocate for pragmatic utilitarian program evaluation practices and has more than 35 years of experience in the field. Most of his work has been in the higher education sector related to academic program planning, development, launch, review, and refinement. He has served six universities and colleges both public and private and within two-year, four-year, and postbaccalaureate master's and doctoral programs. His broad personal experience across both faculty and senior administrative roles facilitates his collaboration with the diverse stakeholders that must coordinate their efforts to deliver effective academic experiences addressing the specific needs of equally diverse segments of students. During his career, he has applied data to empirically demonstrate the need for new programs and curriculum, monitor the effectiveness of existing programs, and, when necessary, guide revisions to curriculum, policies, or extracurricular support mechanisms. He has also served as an award-winning subject matter expert in developing technologies to support institution-wide assessment infrastructure and resources. He also enjoys supporting evaluation practice among small public sector and nonprofit organizations in his expanding spare time. While these organizations contribute much to society daily, particularly at the local level, their constrained resources often limit their ability to effectively capture data and leverage data to their advantage. Consequently, he has partnered with local agencies to help them in learning how best to collect and use data to clearly document their needs, achievements, and value.

Sarah E. P. Munce received her PhD in health services research in the outcomes and evaluation stream at the Institute of Health Policy, Management & Evaluation (IHPME) at the University of Toronto (U of T) in 2014. She also took a number of courses to qualify for a knowledge translation specialization designation. She completed her postdoctoral fellowship at Toronto Rehabilitation Institute–University Health Network (TRI-UHN) in 2018. Her postdoctoral research was recognized by several national and international granting agencies, including a Heart and Stroke Foundation of Canada Fellowship and a Canadian Institutes of Health Research Fellowship. Currently, she is a scientist in the LIFEspan (Living Independently Fully Engaged) Service at TRI-UHN. She is also an assistant professor (status only) in the Department of Occupational Science & Occupational Therapy, Rehabilitation Sciences Institute, and IHPME at the U of T. She does extensive work with the Mixed Methods International Research Association (MMIRA) as the elected membership chair. In addition to her work with MMIRA, she provides a number of lectures on mixed methods research at the U of T, especially in the area of integration. She has published more than 50 peer-reviewed articles. Her program of research involves the development, implementation, and evaluation of transitional care interventions (e.g., self-management, peer support) for individuals with neurological conditions and their caregivers.

Bonnie K. Nastasi is a professor in the Department of Psychology, School of Science and Engineering, at Tulane University. She received her PhD in school psychology from Kent State University in 1986. She codirects a trauma specialization in the school psychology PhD program at Tulane. Her research focuses on the use of mixed methods designs to develop and evaluate culturally appropriate assessment and intervention approaches for promoting mental health and reducing health risks such as sexually transmitted infections (STIs) and HIV, both within the United States and internationally. She has worked in Sri Lanka since 1995 on development of school-based programs to promote psychological well-being and directed a multicountry study of psychological well-being of children and adolescents with research partners in 12 countries from 2008 to 2013. She was one of the principal investigators of an interdisciplinary public health research program to prevent STIs among married men and women living in the slums of Mumbai, India, from 2002 to 2013. She is active in promotion of child rights and social justice within the profession of school psychology and has directed the development of a curriculum for training school psychologists internationally on child rights, a joint effort of International School Psychology Association (ISPA), International Institute of Child Rights & Development, APA's Division 16, and Tulane University's School Psychology program. She is past president of Division 16 and past cochair of APA's Committee for International Relations in Psychology. Currently, she is APA council representative for Division 16 and is president of ISPA.

Anthony J. Onwuegbuzie is a professor and senior research associate in the Faculty of Education at the University of Cambridge. In addition, he is a distinguished visiting professor at the University of Johannesburg, an honorary professor at the University of South Africa, and an honorary visiting scholar in the College of Nursing and Health Sciences at Flinders University. A former secondary school teacher, he teaches doctoral-level courses in qualitative research, quantitative research, and mixed methods research. His research areas primarily involve social and behavioral science topics, including disadvantaged and underserved populations such as minorities, children living in war zones, students with special needs, and juvenile delinquents.

Additionally, he writes extensively on qualitative, quantitative, and mixed methodological topics applicable to multiple disciplines within the field of the social and behavioral sciences. With an *h-index* of 89, he has secured the publication of more than 500 works, including more than 350 journal articles, 50 book chapters, and 5 books, with 5 more books in the pipeline. Furthermore, he has received more than 20 outstanding paper awards. Additionally, he has delivered more than 1,000 presentations and 200 workshops worldwide that include more than 50 keynote addresses across six continents. He is former editor of *Educational Researcher.* Currently, he is editor in chief of the *International Journal of Multiple Research Approaches* and editor of *Research in the Schools.* He is past president of the Mixed Methods International Research Association. Recently, he was a recipient of the 2018 National Research Foundation top honors awards in the science and research field—receiving an "A" rating (cf. http://www.nrf.ac.za/media-room/news/leading-south-african-researchers-recognised-2018-nrf-awards). This rating, which is based on peer evaluation and according to international best practice, recognizes him as a top researcher in South Africa. His overall professional goal is to be a role model for early career researchers and students worldwide—especially those who characterize underrepresented populations (e.g., minorities).

Annie Pezalla is a researcher and faculty member at Hamline University in St. Paul, Minnesota. Her research focuses on at-risk behaviors among children, adolescents, and young adults and on methodological reflexivity in qualitative research, with particular focus on how the *researcher embodies the instrument* of data collection and analysis in social science research, and how self-awareness of that role can promote greater transparency, better scholarship, and deeper relationships with those we research. She has taught extensively in developmental psychology, both for undergraduates and graduate-level students, and she has written, designed, and taught courses in both qualitative and quantitative methods. She also has years of experience teaching academic writing. She has cowritten a book, *Essential Guide to Critical Reading and Writing*, which offers tangible ways for students to apply critical thinking in coursework, navigate academic reading, and produce writing at an appropriate academic level. She has conducted seminars and in-depth residency trainings to graduate-level students on how to craft well-aligned research proposals and then how to carry out the steps of data collection, analysis, and dissemination. She loves to work with those who call themselves *scholar-practitioners*: who are steeped in the research literature of their academic disciplines while also invested in the pragmatic work of their families, schools, or greater communities. She received her PhD in human development and family studies from The Pennsylvania State University.

Justus J. Randolph is an associate professor at the Georgia Baptist College of Nursing at Mercer University in Atlanta, Georgia. He teaches doctoral-level research methods and statistics courses, serves on doctoral committees, and is a methodological and statistical consultant. He is also a member of the Center for Applied Research and Evaluation, which provides methodological and statistical support to university stakeholders, and an associate editor for the *American Journal of Evaluation*. In the past, he has worked for organizations such as the Faculty of Education at the University of Lapland, the Department of Computer Science and Statistics at the University of Eastern Finland, the Department of Elementary Education at Finlandia University, and the Richard W. Riley College of Education and Leadership at Walden University. His international work history was a result of being awarded a Fulbright grant to Finland in 2003. Justus has a PhD in education research and program evaluation and a certification in educational leadership from Utah State University, an MEd in international education from Framingham State University, and a bachelor's degree in English, art history, and philosophy from Weber State University. His primary research areas include scale development, statistics, program evaluation, and meta-analysis, especially as they relate to education and health care outcomes. He has served on more than 40 successful doctoral committees and is the author of two books—*Multidisciplinary Methods in Educational Technology Research and Development* and *Computer Science Education at the Crossroads: A Methodological Review of Computer Science Education Research*—and more than 40 peer-reviewed journal publications.

Kurt Schoch is a higher education and learning professional with more than 35 years' experience in corporate training, organizational development, and higher education. He has been a faculty member and program administrator in the Walden University Richard W. Riley College of Education and Leadership, taught adult education courses for Indiana University, is an adjunct faculty member in the School of Business at the University of Indianapolis, and serves as a leadership coach in the Lacy School of Business MBA program at Butler University. He is currently owner, coach, and consultant for Performance Improvement Consulting, a coaching and consulting business based in Zionsville, Indiana, where he works with clients in business, nonprofit organizations, and higher education to clarify vision, strategize actions, and overcome challenges to making visions come to life. He is a certified professional coach, a certified Everything DiSC® Trainer, a Core Values Index™ certified practitioner, and master practitioner for the Energy Leadership Index

Assessment™. His research interests include the impact of the Baldrige Performance Excellence Criteria on health care and other organizations, introducing a coach approach into faculty–student interactions, using the CIPP model of program evaluation in corporate and nonprofit settings, and continuously learning more about case study research. He has a BA in sociology from Southern Methodist University, an MDiv from Christian Theological Seminary, and an EdD in adult education from Indiana University. He also enjoys biking, kayaking, and spending time with his five grandchildren.

 **Molly S. Stewart** is an assistant research scientist at the Center for Evaluation, Policy, and Research at Indiana University. Her research interests include public policy design and implementation, markets and choice in education, and school law and finance issues. She has published and presented on parent involvement in choice policies, theoretical assumptions underlying choice policies, federal K–12 education policy implementation, leadership preparation in higher education settings, and equity issues in public education policies. Her current research projects and partnerships focus on the U.S. market for private K–12 tutoring, transparency in state education policies and finance, data-based decision-making in K–12 education, and the role of social emotional factors in the schooling experiences of students. She is currently serving as the project manager for the formative evaluation and implementation support activities under the Indiana Student Information to Empower Consortium of Indiana school districts. In addition to evaluation and research activities, she also teaches courses in research methods and public program evaluation for the Indiana University School of Public and Environmental Affairs. She received her doctoral degree from the University of Wisconsin–Madison in 2013.

FOUNDATIONS IN RESEARCH DESIGN

PART I

INTRODUCTION TO RESEARCH

Gary J. Burkholder

INTRODUCTION AND OVERVIEW

In the 19th century, research became an integral part of the university ethos. In the United States specifically, the role of the university assumed a pragmatic function as "American reformers further transformed higher education by stressing the relationship between the university and society through the concept of service and direct links with industry and agriculture" (Altbach, 2011, p. 17). In the United States, this more pragmatic approach was reflected in the requirement that education be more directly connected with the needs of society, such as by ensuring that graduates are well situated to join the workforce. Even today, there is an apparent worldwide shift in focus to employment and employability training, which has opened new paths to professional doctorate degrees oriented toward scholar-practitioners who value the application of theory and research to practical problems.

Science plays a significant role in generating new knowledge that can be used by scholar-practitioners to address practical problems. Aristotle was one of the first who formalized an approach to knowledge generation involving a process of inquiry and analysis; general principles can be formulated from what is observed (induction) and, from these general principles, hypotheses for testing can be derived (deduction). The results of tests of hypotheses can then be used to inform validity of theory. The cycle of induction and deduction is what is responsible for the creation of new knowledge (Gauch, 2003). In the 18th and 19th centuries, rationalism, defined as the belief that knowledge can be created through internal reflection and logic, was superseded by empiricism, the belief that what is known is that which is discoverable by the senses and ultimately measurable. It is empiricism that dominates contemporary scientific research.

The scientific method has led to the discoveries that have revolutionized technology and the ways we use it, our understanding of the nature of the universe, and the eradication of diseases. These discoveries are based on what can be directly seen in the microscope and the telescope and what can be measured and strictly controlled. Those discoveries came from the natural sciences, such as chemistry and biology, colloquially referenced as the *hard sciences*. In the social or *soft sciences*, applying typical scientific standards is more challenging. For example, people behave in expected and unexpected ways that may change in different contexts and times. Thus, it is difficult to isolate one factor that is suspected to cause a certain kind of behavior and measure its impact. This variation in behavior creates a challenge for explanation and prediction. Scientists try to isolate behavior and devise research studies to understand the effects of that behavior; the results are then interpreted and reviewed by the wider community of scientists and the public. Despite measures to isolate variables and validate survey instruments and assessments, thus bringing a measure of objectivity to the process of discovery, interpreting human behavior is ultimately subjective. Such interpretation raises questions about what we can truly know and understand about behavior. Therefore, it is not surprising that people have varying levels of confidence in the social scientific enterprise as well as its evidence-based explanations.

Funk and Rainie (2015) compared the beliefs of scientists from the American Association for the Advancement of Science with those from a random sample of the American public and found some encouraging results: Unsurprisingly, 79% of the adults reported that science has made life easier for most people, and 71% felt that investments in science have paid off in the long run. However, other findings provide a more nuanced examination of attitudes toward science. For example, 88% of scientists believed that it is safe to eat genetically modified foods, whereas only 37% of the adults surveyed believed they are safe. The same, but smaller, differences were found with evolution: Overall, 98% of scientists versus 65% of adults believed that humans have evolved over time. With vaccines, 86% of scientists versus 68% of adults believed that vaccination of children should be required. With climate change, 87% of scientists versus 50% of the public believed it was due to human activity. Compare this with the finding that the public believes that only 57% of scientists agree that climate change has been caused by humans. The differences reflected here are startling and suggest a public misperception about the scientific enterprise. Additionally, Pew Center researchers found that perceptions of science and its contribution to society have decreased among scientists and the American public, both down by about 11 points (Funk & Rainie, 2015).

It is crucial for new social science researchers to be well grounded in the science that underlies their specific disciplines as well as to understand the strengths and limitations of scientific research. Due to the changing social and political contexts in which social scientists operate, it is important to understand the foundations and language of research as well as its methods. With this understanding, you can be prepared to engage in ethically and socially responsible research and enter confidently and knowledgably into the dialogues that characterize scholarship in the disciplines and in debates engaged in by the larger public.

The purpose of this first chapter is to provide an overview of essential terminology of research for scholar-practitioners. The chapter begins with an introduction to research approaches (qualitative, quantitative, and mixed methods) as well as distinctions among research approach, design, and methodology. Each of these will be carefully defined to ensure that there is no confusion during the reading of this book. Finally, the chapter ends with an overview of a description of the key phases of research, the components of which are described in various chapters throughout the book.

INTRODUCTION TO FOUNDATIONAL PRINCIPLES OF RESEARCH

Science is a social endeavor in which scientists and practitioners representing multiple disciplines conduct research that supports and refutes theories (Bourdieu, 1991; Kuhn, 2012). The range of scientific disciplines represent varying perspectives on reality and differences in interpretation of which problems are important. Thus, it is not surprising to learn that each discipline has language and practices specific to its own unique perspectives. Methods that guide research in education, for example, may be different from those that guide research in public health; experimental designs may be a more important standard in some disciplines than others. Thus, not all scientists necessarily adopt the same terminology or ways of conducting research.

Scientific Method

When people think of the scientific method, it usually brings back memories of the high school or college chemistry lab. The researcher measures some chemical, introduces it to the test tube, carefully controls all environmental variables, performs the experiment, and interprets the results. In the social sciences, the research settings are often not laboratories, but rather real-world settings involving individuals and groups. Several researchers have challenged the conventional definition of scientific method (e.g., Bauer, 1992; Windschitl, Thompson, & Braaten, 2008) precisely because specific methods, methodologies, and designs have evolved within the scientific disciplines. Each discipline trains and orients researchers to how questions are asked, theory is approached, and data are collected and analyzed that may be specific to that discipline (Bauer, 1992). For example, Windschitl et al. (2008) proposed an alternative to the traditional scientific method, *model-based inquiry*, in which scientific inquiry is expanded to incorporate the social sciences methods that include testing questions using discipline-specific ways of collecting and analyzing data and expanding the role of science to be evolutionary rather than assuming that any theory or model is the end goal.

So what is it that makes the scientific method (or model-based inquiry) "scientific"? Whenever we describe the scientific process in social science research, the following are the principles we have in mind.

- *The scientific method requires systematic observation.* Scientists depend on careful, objective, and reliable observation to ensure data are as free from error as possible. This is true whether the data are numeric data, as might be collected in a survey, or textual data, as might be collected in interviews.

- *The scientific method involves theory development and subsequent testing of emerging theories.* The goal of science is to generate theory that can then be tested from hypotheses derived from the theory (deduction) or to examine repeated occurrences of events from which a testable theory can be derived (induction). Abduction is a process of finding the simplest explanation for a set of observations and is part of the theory development process (Haig, 2005).

- *The scientific method, as applied to the social sciences, seeks to understand, explain, and predict behavior. This implies understanding cause-and-effect relationships.* The goal of science is to describe what can be seen, use the description to generate theory to explain behavior, and analyze data to test the extent to which the theory consistently explains behavior across time and place.

- *The scientific method seeks objectivity, to the extent possible constrained by its methods.* "Objectivity" in this sense means that observation and analysis are not influenced by the values, biases, and perspectives of the researcher. In survey research, where people provide numerical responses to questions, the researcher is relatively distant from the analysis. In interview research, by comparison, the researcher or research team serves as both the instrument for data collection as well as the means of analysis. The researcher as instrument introduces subjectivity that is recognized and appreciated as an important source of variation that adds richness to interpretation of textual data.

Paradigm

A paradigm is an organizing principle for new ideas and new frameworks for describing phenomena. Houghton, Hunter, and Meskell (2012) defined paradigm (citing Guba & Lincoln, 1994) as "a set of basic beliefs or a frame of reference that explains how individuals perceive the nature of the world and their places in it" (p. 34). Paradigms evolve and not all scientists adhere to the same one. A classic example of a paradigm shift is the change from a simple mechanical view of the structure of matter to a view framed by Einstein's theory of general relativity. The choice of the term *paradigm* in the social sciences has been rather muddled. It seems to be used by various authors both to refer to the philosophical orientations, such as positivism and constructivism (e.g., see Guba & Lincoln, 1994; Houghton et al., 2012), and to describe qualitative, quantitative, and mixed methods research strategies (e.g., see Denzin, 2009; Johnson & Onwuegbuzie, 2004). Reynolds (2007) indicated that many scientific theories are paradigms as well. Part of the reason for the variety in definitions may be because of the close connection between theory and the philosophy underlying the theory.

The term *paradigm* will be used in this book to refer to the constellation of assumptions and orientations, the "presuppositions regarding reality and how it may be understood" (Mittwede, 2012, p. 23) that guide researchers to adopt particular approaches to inquiry and their methods. This includes the ontological and epistemological assumptions underlying reality. This is closely aligned with *philosophical orientations*, terminology commonly used to reference the philosophical assumptions underlying the researcher's worldview and his or her research processes. These philosophical orientations, or paradigms, that guide social science research will be explored further in Chapter 2.

Approaches to Inquiry

We refer to qualitative, quantitative, and mixed methods as *approaches*, similar to how Creswell (2013) employs the term. The quantitative approach, described more fully in Chapters 4 and 5, is primarily deductive. Hypotheses are generated, data are collected, and hypotheses are tested to see if the data provide support for theory. Its hallmarks are the control, to the extent possible and desired, of variables and the collection of numeric data from respondents directly or through observations. Quantitative approaches are frequently used to test theory.

Qualitative approaches to inquiry are primarily for deep explanation of a phenomenon and are often used to develop or validate theory. They are generally inductive, and the data from which the qualitative researcher works are principally textual, or narrative. While qualitative approaches have historically been associated with fields such as anthropology, education, and sociology, they have gained popularity in other sciences, including psychology and public health, since the 1960s and 1970s. The rising recognition of communities and populations marginalized or ignored in research, such as those with race/ethnicity other than white; lesbian, gay, bisexual, and transgender communities; and women, brought a new imperative for an interpretive and explanatory approach to research to understand the experiences of members of these groups and how those experiences map to existing social science theories (e.g., see Smith, 1999, regarding research on indigenous peoples; Kitzinger, 1987, for one view of the marginalization of minority groups from traditional social science research; Lather, 1994, for views on feminism in research; and Stanfield & Rutledge, 1993, for issues of race and ethnicity in research). The qualitative approach to inquiry is explained in more detail in Chapters 6 and 7.

Mixed methods research, the third major approach to inquiry, combines both qualitative and quantitative approaches in a holistic way. Mixed methods as an approach emerged in the 1970s and 1980s. Mixed methods as an approach to inquiry has been examined from philosophical, theoretical, and pragmatic perspectives (Teddlie & Tashakkori, 2008). It is rigorous in terms of justifying and integrating philosophies and theories representing both quantitative and qualitative approaches. Mixed methods studies are described more fully in Chapters 8 and 9.

Design

We refer to research *design* as how the research is structured to answer the research questions. For example, in qualitative research, there are several designs from which to choose, including phenomenology, ethnography, and grounded theory, among others. In quantitative studies, researchers can choose from experimental designs, such as randomized controlled trials; quasi-experimental designs, in which random assignment to groups does not happen; or observational studies. There are also nonexperimental designs that include correlational studies that examine the natural relationships among

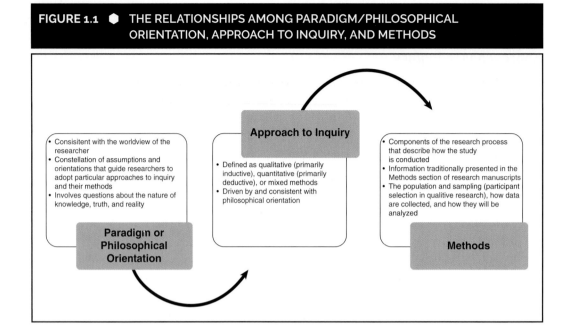

FIGURE 1.1   ◆   THE RELATIONSHIPS AMONG PARADIGM/PHILOSOPHICAL ORIENTATION, APPROACH TO INQUIRY, AND METHODS

variables with no researcher manipulation. The design also includes the fundamental research question(s) guiding the study and the hypotheses where appropriate. Note that the design informs many, if not all, parts of the study methods, such as participant recruitment, instrumentation selection, data collection, and analysis.

Methods

We reserve the term *methods* to describe the various components involved in executing a study. These include the design as previously described, population and sampling, how data are collected, and how they will be analyzed. Together, these details convey to members of the broader scientific community, scientists within the specific discipline, and practitioners who read the studies how the research was (or will be) executed. Together, these components of the research proposal define the methods for the study.

Figure 1.1 provides a graphical representation of the relationship between paradigm/philosophical orientation, approach, and methods and how each is related to and derives from one another. An understanding of these relationships is needed to develop a proposal to conduct a study using a specific design and set of methods.

STAGES OF THE RESEARCH PROPOSAL WRITING PROCESS

A primary purpose of this book is to provide essential information needed to craft a scientific research proposal that will lead to high-quality study. This section provides a basic framework including the steps to guide you in completing the research proposal; more detailed information regarding each step is included throughout the book. We recommend that you use this framework as a cognitive map to guide you in mastering the components required for each of the stages of research presented in subsequent chapters.

1. *Determine an area of interest:* The first step in the research process is to identify an area that you want to research. This first idea can emerge from several sources. It can result from scholarly research, or it may be a problem in the setting in which you work that needs to be addressed. It can also be an idea that you have had that you would like to explore further. Ideas for great research originate for many reasons, and what is important is that any research idea is pursued systematically to determine if it is research worthy.

2. *Reflect on your worldview and orientation to research:* It is important as a scholar-practitioner to be able to articulate your view of the world. Is your interest in prediction, or is it more about explanation and interpretation of experience? Are you more comfortable with distance and objectivity, or do you prefer to have direct contact with your participants and share in the discovery of meaning of their experiences? Do you believe that there is one "Truth," or is "truth" a relative concept that has meaning only in the context of individual or collective experience? This reflection is important for you to articulate because how you read the literature and how you design your study will be driven in part by your views of truth and reality. The importance of worldview and the ways in which philosophical perspectives influence research are described in Chapter 2.

3. *Conduct a thorough literature search:* A systematic literature search is critical to your strategy for identifying a researchable question. Depending on the nature of the research, this can include peer-reviewed research manuscripts, doctoral dissertations, books, and non-peer-reviewed publications such as magazines and newspapers. It might also include nontext data, such as video footage. Data come in numerous forms. More information about literature searches is provided in Chapter 19.

4. *Conduct and write the literature review:* The literature review involves thorough review of books, manuscripts, and other documents, as well as audiovisual artifacts, that you collect. A careful literature review allows you to present the key theoretical and conceptual frameworks guiding your area of research, accumulated knowledge, and the limits of that knowledge. More about the literature review is provided in Chapter 19.

5. *Determine the research problem:* Once the literature has been reviewed, the research problem needs to be identified. This essentially is a statement about what still needs to be answered in your area of scholarship. This is a critical step. Without a clearly articulated problem statement, the research will likely fail to make a contribution to new knowledge in the field. Chapter 20 provides more information on the research problem.

6. *Determine the purpose of the study:* Once you have identified the problem and determined that you have a legitimate research study that adds new knowledge, the purpose of the study needs to be articulated. The purpose of the study provides your readers with a concise statement of the goal of the study. Chapter 20 provides more information on the purpose statement.

7. *Determine the research question:* This is an important step because the research question helps define the scope of the study, guides the development of the problem statement, and influences choice of appropriate research design. Chapter 20 provides more information on the research questions.

8. *Develop the conceptual and/or theoretical framework:* Concepts and theories have a reflexive role in your research: Understanding of the concepts and theories in the discipline related to the topic of interest emerges from the literature review. The conceptual and/or theoretical framework provides a logical structure to the research study that connects research questions, methodology, and design in a way that is internally consistent. Conceptual and theoretical frameworks are described in detail in Chapter 3.

9. *Determine the appropriate research approach:* Based on the research question and the framework, you will need to decide which approach is most relevant for the study. Review of the literature will be a primary source of information guiding the approach and subsequent design. The research approach and design must be consistent with the problem, purpose, and research questions. Chapters 4 through 9 provide more detailed information on research approaches and the designs and analyses consistent with them.

10. *Articulate the methods:* The methods include from whom you will collect the data, how the data will be collected, what instrumentation will be used to collect the data, and how the data will be analyzed. Chapters 4 through 9 provide information on methods associated with qualitative, quantitative, and mixed methods approaches. Chapter 20 provides more information on presenting the methods in a research proposal.

11. *Align paradigm, approach, and methods:* Internal alignment and consistency are critical for a logical proposal. Any changes to any part of the overall proposal can result in inconsistencies among the various sections. Chapter 20 includes more information regarding this alignment.

12. *Gain approval for the study:* All research must undergo a process of approval at the sponsoring institution. Universities, hospitals, and other institutions that sponsor research and receive federal funds have an institutional review board that serves to review and approve research consistent with federal requirements. The responsibility for the institutional review board is to ensure the ethical conduct of research. More about ethics in research will be presented in Chapter 13.

CONCLUSION

Even though research terms are used differently within and across disciplines, what is important is that you understand how terms are being used in this book so as to minimize confusion and maximize clarity of principles. In the end, you decide on the way you will use terms; any use of terminology should be clearly presented in the research proposal and be consistently used. You are the scientist, the scholar-practitioner, and your task is to design and conduct original basic or applied research. The paradigm, approach to inquiry, design, and methods must be internally consistent and logical as well as ethically sound. Any decision you make will require collecting the necessary evidence. As long as you support your claims with solid evidence, it will be difficult for others to question those claims.

References

Altbach, P. G. (2011). Patterns of higher education development. In P. G. Altbach, P. J. Bumport, & R. O. Berdahl (Eds.), *American higher education in the twenty-first century: Social, political, and economic challenges* (pp. 13–36). Baltimore, MD: Johns Hopkins University Press.

Bauer, H. (1992). *Science literacy and the myth of the scientific method.* Urbana: University of Illinois Press.

Bourdieu, P. (1991). The peculiar history of scientific reason. *Sociological Forum, 6*(1), 3–26. doi:10.1007/BF01112725

Creswell, J. W. (2013). *Research design: Qualitative, quantitative, and mixed methods approaches* (4th ed.). Thousand Oaks, CA: SAGE.

Denzin, N. K. (2009). The elephant in the living room: Or extending the conversation about the politics of evidence. *Qualitative Research, 9,* 139–160. doi:10.1177/1468794108098034

Funk, C., & Rainie, L. (2015). Americans, politics and science issues. *Science & Society.* Retrieved from http://www.pewinternet.org/2015/07/01/americans-politics-and-science-issues/

Gauch, H. G. (2003). *Scientific method in practice.* Cambridge, UK: Cambridge University Press.

Guba, E. G., & Lincoln, Y. S. (1994). Competing paradigms in qualitative research. In N. K. Denzin & Y. S. Lincoln (Eds.), *Handbook of qualitative research* (pp. 163–194). Thousand Oaks, CA: SAGE.

Haig, B. D. (2005). An abductive theory of scientific method. *Psychological Methods, 10*(4), 371–388. doi:10.1037/1082-989X.10.4.371

Houghton, C., Hunter, A., & Meskell, P. (2012). Linking aims, paradigm and method in nursing research. *Nurse Researcher, 20*(2), 34–39. doi:10.7748/nr2012.11.20.2.34.c9439

Johnson, R. B., & Onwuegbuzie, A. J. (2004). Mixed methods research: A research paradigm whose time has come. *Educational Researcher, 33*(7), 14–26. doi:10.3102/0013189X033007014

Kitzinger, C. (1987). *The social construction of lesbianism*. Thousand Oaks, CA: SAGE.

Kuhn, T. (2012). *The structure of scientific revolutions* (50th anniversary ed.). Urbana, IL: University of Chicago Press.

Lather, P. (1994). Critical inquiry in qualitative research: Feminist and poststructural perspectives. In B. F. Crabtree, W. L. Miller, R. B. Addison, V. J. Gilchrist, & A. J. Kuzel (Eds.), *Exploring collaborative research in primary care* (pp. 103–114). Thousand Oaks, CA: SAGE.

Mittwede, S. K. (2012). Research paradigms and their use and importance in theological inquiry and education. *Journal of Education & Christian Belief, 16,* 23–40. doi:10.1177/205699711201600104

Reynolds, R. D. (2007). *A primer in theory construction*. Boston, MA: Allyn & Bacon Classics.

Smith, L. T. (1999). *Decolonizing methodologies: Research and indigenous peoples*. London, UK: Zed Books.

Stanfield, J. H., II, & Rutledge, M. (1993). *Race and ethnicity in research methods*. Newbury Park, CA: SAGE.

Teddlie, C., & Tashakkori, A. (2008). *Foundations of mixed methods research: Integrating quantitative and qualitative approaches in the social and behavioral sciences*. Thousand Oaks, CA: SAGE.

Windschitl, M., Thompson, J., & Braaten, M. (2008). Beyond the scientific method: Model-based inquiry as a new paradigm of preference for school science investigations. *Science Education, 92,* 941–967. doi:10.1002/sce.20259

PHILOSOPHICAL FOUNDATIONS AND THE ROLE OF THEORY IN RESEARCH

Gary J. Burkholder and Patricia M. Burbank

INTRODUCTION

Science comprises a body of knowledge originating from systematic observation. The term *traditional science* is sometimes used to describe the scientific method that first evolved to explain physical phenomena and has been broadly applied by social scientists through primarily quantitative approaches to explain human behavior. The traditional science method typically involves the generation or utilization of theory to explain phenomena in the natural world. Theories are then tested using careful methods of observation, data collection, and analysis.

History shows that there is an important role for the merging of *philosophy*, the understanding of the fundamental nature of reality and the processes involved in trying to find the answers to questions regarding its nature (Buckingham & Burnham, 2015), and *science*. A *philosophy of science* addresses fundamental questions about the nature of truth and the underlying assumptions of theories used to describe natural phenomena. In particular, philosophers of *social* science are interested in a number of implications of this intersection of science and philosophy because what happens when chemicals in a laboratory interact appears to be fundamentally different from how humans interact. The differences and similarities between the physical and social sciences have been an ongoing debate among philosophers of science.

One school in the philosophy of science believes that the social and natural sciences are essentially the same and that their methods should closely correspond. They believe that social phenomena can be reduced to physical entities, which can be directly observed and are governed by physical laws. This reflects a reductionist view of science held by philosophers such as Karl Popper, Thomas Nagel, and Richard Dawkins. Others, such as Max Weber and Jurgen Habermas, held the view that the social and natural sciences are inherently different and that explanations of social phenomena are based on interpretivist perspectives grounded in experience and meaning.

This range of views affects different decisions regarding how to answer social science research questions. For example, if you believe that social sciences are similar to natural sciences, then traditional science methods using primarily quantitative approaches are appropriate. On the other hand, if you believe that social sciences are inherently different from natural sciences and that knowledge about human beings can advance only through the discovery of meaning, then the traditional science methods will not work to uncover these meanings. Some refer to *nontraditional* science approaches that include interpretive and hermeneutic methods to explain and understand phenomena. Both approaches are valuable in generating a full range of knowledge in the social sciences, yet the differences raise a number of important questions, including those involving (a) what we can know in the natural sciences versus what we can know in the social sciences; (b) whether there can be laws that govern human behavior, much like the laws that govern physical phenomena; and (c) the nature of causality. It is these questions that this chapter will begin to address.

The purpose of this chapter is to provide a brief introduction to the terminology and concepts associated with the philosophy of science that are most directly applicable to your research. From a purely practical standpoint, it might seem that philosophy does not have anything to do with conducting research. For example, you could imagine conducting a study, collecting and analyzing data, and reporting on those data without considering the philosophical or theoretical aspects of the underlying science. However, as will become clearer in this chapter, your choices of theory, research approaches, and research designs come with sets of assumptions about the nature of truth. More practically for you as a researcher, there needs to be a logical connection between philosophy, theory, approaches, and designs, or what we frequently refer to as *alignment* in this text. Miller and Burbank (1994) wrote,

> Philosophy, theory, and method are interrelated and fit together like pieces in a puzzle. . . . One's philosophical perspectives affect the way one chooses a theoretical perspective. Similarly, the underlying assumptions on which theories are based may limit the research methods. (p. 704)

Our focus in this chapter is the congruence between philosophy, theory, and method; why this congruence is important; and strategies to achieve it.

We begin with a review of two concepts in philosophy, ontology and epistemology. Next, we review the major philosophical perspectives, referred to in Chapter 1 as *paradigms*, found in social and health science research. *Philosophical orientations* refers to the constellation of assumptions about reality that guide the adoption of particular approaches to inquiry and methods. We will review philosophical perspectives including logical positivism, sometimes just called positivism; postpositivism; and constructivism. Next, we present the essentials of theory development to orient you to the role of theory in research. We conclude the chapter with key sources as well as reflection questions that should guide your thinking regarding the underlying assumptions and the role of theory in research.

ONTOLOGY AND EPISTEMOLOGY

Ontology

Ontology addresses the nature of reality and being (Ponterotto, 2005) and the underlying question of whether there is an objective, verifiable reality outside of the researcher, a position associated with *realism*, or whether reality is the result of individual interpretation or social construction, a position associated with *relativism*. Although there are many varieties of realism, realists believe that we perceive objects outside of ourselves whose existence and nature are independent of our perception of them. Realists believe that there is one truth, even though we may never be able to know it. Truth, in this sense, corresponds directly to facts that are observable and knowable (Kukla, 2000).

Antirealism includes many different philosophical positions, such as pragmatism, idealism, rationalism, and relativism. Relativism will be considered here because it is an ontological position closely aligned with several nontraditional, interpretive methods, such as hermeneutic phenomenology. Relativism was described by Clark (1992) as knowledge that is always a representation of reality from a person's particular perspective. Thus, there can be no objective point from which to evaluate the truth of our view outside of our own perspective of the social world. Knowledge is determined by contextual circumstances, including historical, subjective, cultural, or institutional (Kim, 1999).

Epistemology and Ways of Knowing the World

Knowledge. Knowledge is defined as belief that is justified based on facts assumed to be true by an observer. There are multiple ways by which knowledge can be generated. The first is through perception: We know things because we have experienced them with our senses. Experiential knowledge associated with sensory understanding is called *empirical knowledge*. We can also use either inductive or deductive logical and reasoned analysis. For example, professors and employers alike value critical thinking skills, but one does not need to be a scientist to invoke critical reasoning to solve problems. Many of us use the *memory* of situations to arrive at conclusions (knowledge) about what is happening at any given point in time. *Introspection*, reflection on the experience of our own mind, is yet another way of gaining knowledge, which may or may not involve inductive or deductive reasoning and logical thought. In *testimonial* knowledge, we rely on what a trusted other says is credible. Another way of knowing is through *intuition*. For example, people sometimes use hunches to come to understand their world, thereby reaching conclusions about the world that may be based partly or not at all in fact.

Epistemology concerns knowledge. It is the study of knowledge and guides us to ask questions about what we can know and how we can know it, and the reliability of such knowledge (Johnson & Duberley, 2000); it also includes questions that explore the limits of knowledge. From the perspective of science, epistemology concerns what can be known using a scientific approach to understanding the natural world. For example, what can science and the scientific method reveal? Epistemological discussions also include whether the researcher can be a truly objective observer of reality or whether knowledge is really generated through dynamic interpretation of phenomena (Houghton, Hunter, & Meskell, 2012), a reflection of the connection between the "investigator and the investigated" (Mittwede, 2012, p. 26). Some have believed that the relationship between observer and observed could be regarded as completely objective, with the researcher viewing the object of research or the participant in an unbiased, value-free way. Thus, epistemology is concerned with the nature of scientific knowledge and the limits to which science can add new knowledge.

We agree with Hanson (1958), who argued that observation is theory laden and unbiased observation is not possible because researchers are human beings with biases that cannot be completely overcome. This position is often called *modified objectivity*. Other researchers who use nontraditional or interpretive science approaches believe that the best and sometimes only way to generate knowledge about human beings is through a subjective relationship between the researcher and the participants, who cocreate knowledge. Thus, lack of objectivity is fundamental to the process of knowledge generation.

Facts. Scientists discover and confirm facts. "The sun shines" is a fact because it is directly observable and can be verified by multiple bystanders. However, facts are not necessarily stationary; tomorrow, the fact may be that the sun is not shining because you cannot see the sun and it is raining (although it is a fact that the sun still exists behind the clouds!). Facts also result from immutable laws of nature. For example, sodium and chloride can be combined in predetermined proportions to make salt; we accept this as fact because this experiment when repeated multiple times and in multiple contexts achieves the same result.

Facts can change based on new knowledge and new understanding. For many years, scientists believed that gastric ulcers were caused by stress and excess stomach acid. Although Warren and Marshall's (1983) work identified a bacterium as the cause of gastric ulcers, the medical community did not accept these findings for many years. Continued scientific research and discovery ultimately provided undisputable facts that led to a shared understanding of a bacterial cause for ulcers. The two scientists were awarded the Nobel Prize in 2005 for their important work. Their work demonstrates that fact evolves through debate and verification.

Summary

Ontology concerns the nature of reality and the perception of what is *truth*. Epistemology in the philosophy of science refers to scientific knowledge and what constitutes scientific knowledge, how knowledge is generated from the practice of the scientific method, and the nature of the relationship between the researcher and what is being researched. When we are using the scientific method, we base what we know (or what we have come to know) on facts that are observable and verifiable by others. We systematically observe a phenomenon, assemble the facts, and use critical reasoning to arrive at understanding (knowledge) of the phenomenon. For researchers, ontological and epistemological considerations are crucial for understanding the nature of truth and reality as well as how knowledge is generated. How you understand ontology and epistemology orients you toward certain approaches to research; this will become clearer in the discussion of paradigms/philosophical orientations.

PHILOSOPHICAL ORIENTATIONS/PARADIGMS

Your specific philosophical orientation plays a role in predisposing you to research questions that involve particular kinds of research methods. A paradigm is the collection of facts, assumptions, and practices that guide a particular orientation to knowledge generation. The paradigms we review here are positivist, postpositivist, and relativist (we will primarily focus on constructivism, a relativist position). Lincoln, Lynham, and Guba (2011) also included critical theory as one of the philosophical orientations parallel to the other three. Although it is important, our view is that it is usually not considered a philosophy of science orientation but rather a critical realist philosophical perspective. We will return to critical perspectives briefly later in the chapter.

Positivism/Logical Positivism

Positivism emerged primarily from the successes of knowledge generation in the natural sciences. Positivism has its roots in the scientific revolution that occurred during the 15th through 17th centuries and the Enlightenment period, which extended from the late 17th into the early 19th centuries. During the period of the scientific revolution, the natural sciences were flourishing. Nicolaus Copernicus (1473–1543) had used systematic observation to show that the earth revolved around the sun and not the other way around, although this discovery was not accepted as truth at the time. Isaac Newton (1642–1726) invented calculus, which was used to discover the laws governing the physical world. The advances in knowledge, principally due to the successes in the natural sciences, influenced philosophers during the Enlightenment. During this time period, philosophers viewed knowledge as originating from thinking (rationalism; e.g., Rene Descartes and Baruch Spinoza) and observation (empiricism; e.g., John Locke and David Hume) (Johnson & Duberley, 2000). Locke (1632–1704), whom many consider the father of modern empiricism, explained that data collected via the senses are internalized, reflected on, and form the basis of ideas that grow in increasing complexity with the addition of new sense data. In essence, he created a logical argument for the role of experience in the production of knowledge. Scientists examine data as perceived by the senses and inductively generate laws based on those data.

Auguste Comte (1798–1857) was the first philosopher to use the term *positive* to distinguish scientific knowledge from fictitious knowledge, associated with religious teachings, and abstract knowledge, associated with metaphysics

(Johnson & Duberley, 2000). For Comte, positive knowledge is generated from facts derived from sense perceptions; anything not directly attributable to the senses was relegated to the metaphysical realm and thus not considered valid (Mittwede, 2012). Comte believed that just as empirical laws govern the natural world, universal laws would be discovered that govern social behavior. What emerged from the Enlightenment was a view of science that seeks universal laws through objective observation, description, explanation, prediction, and control of natural phenomena.

This view of science was extended to the emerging social sciences in the 19th century. For example, the science of psychology, born in the German university system, continued the split between psychology and religion that had begun with the advent of biology and evolutionary theory. The early German psychologists focused on directly measurable and observable aspects of behavior. The scientific method, which had proven to be highly successful in the natural sciences, was replicated to explain human behavior and cognition. John Stuart Mill (1806–1873) formalized a set of procedures that would become the basis of the scientific method; the scientific experiment was promoted as the optimal means for controlling variables and identifying causal mechanisms. Positivism, based in the methods of the natural sciences, thus became the foundation for knowledge generation in the emerging social sciences.

Logical positivism emerged from a group of philosophers, including Rudolf Carnap and others, who created a positivist philosophy of science by formalizing the language of theories. Logical positivism has also been referred to as the *received view* to recognize the extended influence of positivism on scientific research. Johnson and Duberley (2000) described the four epistemological commitments of logical positivism as follows:

1. Observations of the world through our senses provide the sole foundation for knowledge. Following Comte, those observations could be made in a neutral, value-free manner.

2. What is not observable or is unconscious cannot be included in the realm of scientific knowledge. Anything that is tested empirically must be able to be verified.

3. Methods used in the natural sciences provide the gold standard for scientific knowledge generation.

4. The goal of science is prediction and control.

Each of these commitments has clear roots in positivism; what distinguishes positivism from logical positivism is that in the latter, all data must be observable and verifiable and scientific explanations are based in logic. This distinction provided a clear demarcation between what can be considered scientific and what belongs in the metaphysical realm. The approach of the logical positivists is reductionist, much in the same way that physical laws reduce explanations to the mechanisms that occur at the atomic level.

Postpositivism

As knowledge in the disciplines of physics and the other physical and mathematical sciences rapidly progressed and greatly enhanced our understanding of the world, philosophers such as Karl Popper (1902–1994) and Carl Hempel (1905–1997) realized that there was no way to prove empirical claims to be universally true. Popper was one of the key opponents of the view that verification of theory is the defining feature of science. Rather, in his postpositivist critical rationalist philosophy, he believed that researchers are inherently human and thus fallible. For Popper, *falsifiability*, the ability of a theory to be shown to be false, was a much more important defining feature of science. He also realized that metaphysical knowledge, defined as knowledge that cannot be seen, sometimes spurs scientific discovery. Such knowledge, for example, can come through hunches that lead to hypotheses that can be tested. Thus, he found the complete rejection of metaphysical knowledge by the logical positivists to be overstated. Two other postpositivist philosophers of science, Polanyi (1958) and Hanson (1958), effectively disputed the idea of value-free observations, arguing that all observations are biased in some way by the observer and his or her values and past experience.

Relativism and Constructivism

The relativist perspective has its roots in the philosophy of Immanuel Kant (1724–1804), who posited that reality, or the external world, is shaped by our experiences, which define unique and individual worldviews. We cannot experience reality directly; instead, we experience phenomena, which are then interpreted by our senses. A relativist perspective holds that there is no external, verifiable reality outside of the observer and, because of this, there can be no value-free, objective observations on the part of the researcher. There can also be no shared truth between researcher and participant. Relativism departs significantly from positivism in that it does not assume the existence of any single *true* reality. Constructivism (see Schwandt, 1998, for a more detailed discussion of the constructivist position), a relativist position, posits that meaning and knowledge are constructed through the interactions of individuals and it is through these interactions that shared meanings and *truths* are cocreated (Ponterotto, 2005). What is truth in one context may not be truth in a different context, and all realities are equally valid. Meaning is typically hidden and requires reflection through shared experiences to be discovered.

Guba (1990) identified three points where the constructivist position is at odds with the positivist and postpositivist views. First, facts only make sense in the context of a given theory or value proposition, which means that there can be no single reality. Second, theories can never be fully tested; there will always be competing theories, and no one theory will ever be found that explains the facts completely. Third, objectivity is not possible because the observer's interpretation of what is observed will always be shaped by the value and theoretical systems of the observer. Guba wrote, "The key to openness and the continuing search for ever more informed and sophisticated constructions. Realities are multiple, and they exist in people's minds" (p. 26). Thus, relativist approaches question the plausibility of a single, objective reality or truth (Gershenson, 2013), and their richness lies in the multiple interpretations of the experiences in which humans engage.

In an even more extreme type of constructivism, physical reality is seen as *caused* by consciousness (Harman, 1991). There are some researchers who challenge the *matter-over-mind* position; these researchers tend to represent those interested in Eastern spiritual traditions. One example is the power of meditative states and how meditation is seen as a causal mechanism for changes in physical states (self-healing). Some authors in the popular press who espouse the practice of intentionality apply this philosophical perspective of relativism. They propose that one may control events in the physical world with thoughts, affirmations, and/or intentions (Day, 2010; Hay, 1984; Hicks & Hicks, 2006; McTaggart, 2003).

All these three paradigms—positivism/logical positivism, postpositivism, and relativism (specifically constructivism for our discussion)—are important and can be described in terms of their essential ontological and epistemological positions. The positions not only represent an evolution of scientific understanding but also reflect the various positions scientists take when thinking about the nature of reality. Understanding paradigmatic, ontological, and epistemological positions provides a path for clearly communicating your assumptions concerning your views of the fundamental nature of reality and the nature of knowledge generation.

These paradigms are also closely related to the research approaches to inquiry (qualitative, quantitative, and mixed methods). For example, most quantitative research tends to be more aligned with positivism and postpositivism, whereas qualitative research tends to be aligned more with constructivist paradigms. These are not hard-and-fast distinctions, however. For example, a qualitative researcher may code data with the intent to reduce the data to units that can be analyzed quantitatively; this approach would be more aligned with a positivist epistemology and ontology.

There are many fine tables that provide a clear presentation of these positions (e.g., see Guba, 1990; Lincoln et al., 2011, p. 98). Figure 2.1 is an adaptation and simplification of information provided by Lincoln et al. (2011, p. 98). We show here only two paradigms representing extreme positions; note that your particular philosophical orientation may lie somewhere between the two.

There are three things to consider related to ontology and epistemology that require you to answer some important questions that reflect the way you see the world and influence your natural approach to research. The first consideration is your own ontological orientation. For example, do you believe that there is a reality outside of yourself that is independent of your perception of it, or do you believe that there are multiple truths that depend on individual interpretations of a phenomenon? The second consideration is your own epistemological orientation. For example, does the generation of knowledge happen through a neutral, objective relationship between the researcher and the object of research? Is objectivity a goal, though not truly achievable, or is knowledge discovered or created through the relationship between the researcher and the participants who are researched? The third consideration is

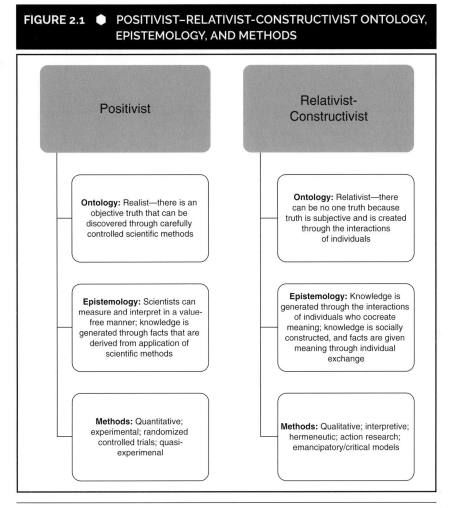

FIGURE 2.1 ● POSITIVIST–RELATIVIST-CONSTRUCTIVIST ONTOLOGY, EPISTEMOLOGY, AND METHODS

Positivist

Ontology: Realist—there is an objective truth that can be discovered through carefully controlled scientific methods

Epistemology: Scientists can measure and interpret in a value-free manner; knowledge is generated through facts that are derived from application of scientific methods

Methods: Quantitative; experimental; randomized controlled trials; quasi-experimenal

Relativist-Constructivist

Ontology: Relativist—there can be no one truth because truth is subjective and is created through the interactions of individuals

Epistemology: Knowledge is generated through the interactions of individuals who cocreate meaning; knowledge is socially constructed, and facts are given meaning through individual exchange

Methods: Qualitative; interpretive; hermeneutic; action research; emancipatory/critical models

Source: Adapted from Lincoln et al. (2011, p. 98).

related to your goals for the research. Are you interested in a distant relationship between yourself and the research participant, or is your goal knowledge generation through interaction with the participants in the research? Each of us has a natural orientation to one or more of these positions, and it is important that you uncover your unique orientation.

Once these questions have been addressed, the next step is to explore the literature on these different perspectives in more detail. There are many good resources, including Crotty (1998) and Mackenzie and Knipe (2006); however, it also requires review of current research in the discipline. Which perspectives have been presented in the research in your area of interest? Is there room for other perspectives that challenge current thinking and potentially add new knowledge in the context of that challenge? What theoretical perspectives influence ontology and epistemology in your discipline? The pursuit and exploration of answers to these questions serve to enrich the quality of your research.

Critical Perspectives

Although we opted not to include critical perspectives as one of the philosophical paradigms, this approach is important and deserves some attention. Critical perspectives derive from Marxist and neo-Marxist theories that examine the ways in which "relationships of domination and exploitation are embedded in the dominant ideas of society" (Burbank & Martins, 2010, p. 30). At the heart of critical theory is acknowledgment of the nature of oppression and how subordinates' acceptance of their social status continues to reinforce their oppression (Kincheloe, McLaren, & Steinberg, 2011).

In their essence, critical theory and critical perspectives seek to understand the nature of oppression and seek the emancipation of oppressed peoples. Emancipation occurs through the process of research with coresearchers (typical of a participatory action framework; see Hacker, 2013), critical evaluation of the contexts in which the research is situated, and the use of research results to make change. Critical theorists are constructivists, on the one hand, but they may also believe that there is a truth that cannot be seen because of its being clouded in power relations. Thus, the relationship between the researcher and what is researched is constantly in flux. Various methods can be used to answer research questions; thus, critical perspectives can be viewed also as being pragmatic. Critical theorists have established lines of scholarship in several important areas, including feminist theory (Gannon & Davies, 2007; Lather, 1994), queer theory (Plummer, 2011), research on indigenous peoples (Smith, 1999), and the intersections of race, gender, and sexuality (Bowleg, 2012), among many others.

Figure 2.2 provides a guide to help you understand some of the key differences in goal, philosophy, and approach to inquiry of research among the positivist, constructivist, and critical-realist positions. The goals of research as predictive, interpretive, and emancipatory are consistent with the writings of Habermas (1971).

FIGURE 2.2 ● **DIFFERENCES IN RESEARCH GOAL, PHILOSOPHY, AND APPROACH AMONG THE POSITIVIST/POSTPOSITIVIST, CONSTRUCTIVIST, AND CRITICAL-REALIST POSITIONS**

Research Philosophy, Goal, and Approach

Philosophy: Positivist/postpositivist	**Philosophy:** Constructivist	**Philosophy:** Critical realist
Goal: Prediction	**Goal:** Understanding	**Goal:** Emancipation
Approach: Primarily quantitative	**Approach:** Primarily qualitative, including interpretive methods	**Approach:** Qualitative or quantitative; focus on critical perspectives

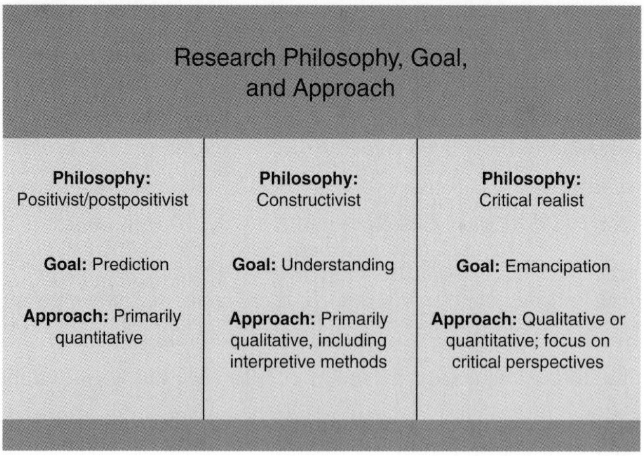

Next, we turn our attention to the role of theory in research. We begin the discussion with a broad understanding of what theories are and how they are constructed. Following the discussion of theories, there are definitions of the key components of theories: concepts, constructs, and hypotheses. Next, we include a brief overview of the role of causality in social science research and its connection to theory. Finally, we close with a presentation of the concept of a continuum of inquiry that brings together the discussion of philosophical perspectives/paradigms and theory in a practical way.

THE ROLE OF THEORY IN RESEARCH

What Is Theory?

Reynolds (2007) described four roles for scientific knowledge: "(1) a method of organizing and categorizing 'things', a typology; (2) predictions of future events; (3) explanations of past events; and (4) a sense of understanding about what causes events" (p. 2). Reynolds conveyed that each of these four roles must contribute significantly to how theory serves as an organizing principle of knowledge and the expected relationships between categories of objects.

The term *theory* is, unfortunately, used differently in different contexts. Part of the reason for this misuse is that, from a philosophy of science standpoint, the definition of theory has evolved over time, and even philosophers of science do not necessarily agree on the definition. There is also a misunderstanding that theory is not important in quantitative or qualitative research. To complicate matters, the word *theory* is used carelessly by new scientists as well as by the general public; the terms *theory* and *hypothesis* are frequently and inappropriately interchanged. For example, a student might state the "theory" that people in the workplace would work harder if they were offered more vacation time. But this is not a theory; rather, it is a speculation (hypothesis) that needs to be tested empirically via the scientific approach. We define theory as *a set of concepts and relational statements that organize scientific knowledge in a focused way*. In addition, we will focus on what Reynolds (2007) called the *causal process form* of theories, which focuses on the potential causal nature of the relational statements constituting theory. In the following sections, we describe each of these components of the definition in more detail.

Theories typically have four purposes: describing, explaining, predicting, and controlling or changing phenomena. These four purposes are hierarchical, with each subsequent purpose including the previous one. At the descriptive level, theories simply *describe* concepts regarding phenomena and the relationships between those concepts. Description serves to increase our understanding of a particular phenomenon. The way we describe a phenomenon orients the reader to particular kinds of explanations (Geertz, 1973). Theories that *explain* answer the question regarding why a phenomenon occurs. They typically refer to occurrences in the past, whereas theories focused on *prediction* build on explanation by focusing on future events. If a theory works well to explain something that happened in the past, it should be able to predict what will happen if the same situation occurs in the future. Last, theories can be applied to *change or control situations*—for example, theories that focus on health behavior change. Some theoreticians, however, do not like the word *control* and have chosen other terms to reflect prediction and control. For example, Kim (1993) uses *prescribe* in place of *control*.

Theories may be used in research in two ways. First, theories are used as a guide for the research process, including selecting research questions and interpreting findings. Second, the research may be a test of the theory itself, measuring the concepts and testing the relationships between the concepts to determine the adequacy of the theory. It is important to recognize that theory has an important place in both quantitative and qualitative research; in fact, most granting agencies will not allow one to submit proposals for atheoretical qualitative research.

Concepts

Concepts are representations of things that exist in reality; they can be specific or vague, abstract or concrete. For example, *dog* would be a very specific, concrete concept; it is a representation that is widely agreed on. *Weight* is an abstract concept that is independent of time and location (Reynolds, 2007). If one were to change it to read *weight of the chair*, this would become a concrete concept. A *construct* is a type of concept that is theoretical in nature and agreed on in terms of what it generally conveys, but it cannot be directly observed. The social sciences contain many examples of constructs, including intelligence quotient, attitudes, and values. Using operational definitions, scientists measure these constructs even though they cannot see them.

Theoretical and Operational Definitions. Concepts have theoretical and operational definitions, which are descriptions in words of the meaning of a concept. Operational definitions may be different for the same concept used in different theories. One example is intelligence. Traditional measures of intelligence, developed by researchers such as David Wechsler, focus on quantitative and verbal reasoning that tends to be highly related to academic achievement. Other researchers have proposed different theoretical definitions of intelligence. For example, David Gardner advanced the theory of multiple intelligences, and Peter Salovey developed a theory around emotional intelligence. Although all scientists may not agree on how a concept is theoretically or operationally defined, you must be very clear in stating how *you* define the concept in your immediate study.

For concepts such as temperature, the operational definition is very clear: It includes use of a thermometer that has been appropriately calibrated and tested. There is little choice or deliberation on the matter of how you might define and measure temperature. For other kinds of concepts and constructs used in the social sciences, operational definitions typically require some kind of assessment that can be either self-reported or administered by a tester. In our example of intelligence, the operational definition is the particular scale that is used to assess it. For example, the Stanford–Binet Intelligence Scales are one instrument used to assess traditional intelligence, and the Mayer–Salovey–Caruso Emotional Intelligence Test is used to assess emotional intelligence. Different theorists have different theoretical definitions of intelligence and thus operationalize it differently using different scales.

Operational definitions are important as well in qualitative research. A qualitative education researcher may be interested in measuring motivation; the raise of a hand in class may be one operational definition of motivation. What is important is that each concept that is the focus of your research study must have a theoretical definition that is accompanied by its appropriate operational definitions. Theoretical and operational definitions communicate clearly to other researchers the choices that guide your study.

Relational Statements. Relational statements describe the relationship between two or more concepts. Theories consist of a number of relational statements that indicate how concepts are hypothesized to relate to one another. Reynolds (2007) identified two kinds of relational statements. Associational statements describe the concepts or constructs that occur (or do not occur) together. A simple example of an associational statement is the correlation statement. For example, "Lower fat diets are associated with lower risk for cardiovascular disease" is an associative statement that represents a positive correlation between dietary fat and risk for disease. The second kind of relational statement is the causal statement. The correlational statement can be converted to a causal statement: "If men and women in the United States have lower levels of fat in their diet, this will cause lower risk for cardiovascular disease." In a causal statement, there is a clear independent variable (dietary fat) that is manipulated to cause a change in the dependent variable (risk for cardiovascular disease). It is important not to confuse correlation and causation; we will return to this point later in the discussion.

Hypothesis. A hypothesis is a special kind of relational statement that provides a conjecture of the relationship between two or more variables that can be directly tested empirically. Hypotheses are best guesses about the relationships between the concepts of a theory. A review of the literature supports the potential relationship between the concepts, but there is no (or limited) empirical evidence for the relationship. The researcher's goal is to test the hypothesis and provide evidence that supports or refutes it. In the ideal case, hypotheses that are derived from existing theory serve as further tests of that theory. It is very important to note that the results of a test of a hypothesis do not *prove* or *disprove* the larger theory. Rather, they provide evidence that either supports, and thus strengthens, the theory or does not support the theory (see Kuhn, 2012, for an excellent discussion on the role of confirmation and disconfirmation of theory).

Reynolds (2007) provided a way to think about the relationship between relational statements and empirical support by stating, "Those with no support are considered hypotheses, those with some support are considered empirical generalizations, and those with 'overwhelming' support are considered laws" (p. 88). In the social sciences, there are probably very few *laws* because the variability of human behavior requires extensive testing of hypotheses over multiple contexts and time periods.

Theoretical Model

Sometimes, researchers use the terms *theory, theoretical model*, and *theoretical framework* synonymously. Theoretical models are visual representations that demonstrate how a subset of concepts constituting a theory are hypothesized to relate to one another. A model can (but may not) include all the concepts of the underlying theory. An example is the health belief model (Rosenstock, 1974), which has been extensively researched and is still used as a theoretical framework today. In public health research, the health belief model has been used to explain people's health-seeking behavior. It links concepts together, such as external environmental cues and perceived health risk. This model is a representation of concepts that have their roots in field theory, originally conceptualized by Kurt Lewin (1890–1947).

Evaluating Theories

McEwen (2011) reviewed the nursing literature and identified the internal and external criteria most often used by researchers to evaluate theories; although the review was focused on nursing literature, the criteria have broad generalizability across disciplines. The four key internal criteria are clarity, consistency, logical adequacy, and simplicity. Theories should be *clear* in terms of definitions of major concepts, with the relationships among those concepts clearly specified. Theories should be internally *consistent* in terms of their major suppositions, logical connections among concepts, and philosophical underpinnings. *Logical adequacy* refers to the propositions in the theory being plausible and creating a coherent structure for the theory. Many argue for *simplicity*, or parsimony, in that the simplest theories that maximally explain the phenomenon should be chosen over more complex theories. However, Dudley-Brown (1997) also suggested that theories might be necessarily complex depending on the phenomenon of interest.

Major external criteria include scope or generality, testability and empirical adequacy, fruitfulness, and usefulness or significance. Theories should have *scope or generality* appropriate to their level of development. Whereas broad scope would be expected of more advanced middle- and higher range theories, which are characterized by more fully developed relationships among concepts that have been empirically tested, narrow scope may characterize newer theories. A theory that is *testable* has qualities that enable it to be tested empirically to determine if it can be supported or not. A theory is *empirically adequate* if the results of the studies conducted to test the theory support it. *Fruitful* theories are those that provide a rich set of concepts that generate multiple relational statements as well as hypotheses for testing. Fruitful theories can thus promote generation of new theories that yield different hypotheses to test. *Useful* theories are those that can be used to address the phenomena of interest or problems within and/or across disciplines. Useful theories enjoy increasingly broad consensus and acceptability.

Reynolds (2007) takes a slightly different position and advocates that theories should not necessarily be compared. He offers four reasons for this. First, because science is not focused on searching for a unitary truth, multiple theories are useful to capture more accurate descriptions of phenomena. Second, theories can never be totally rejected by a single study, and in reality, multiple studies are required over time and across contexts to eventually support or refute a theory. Third, theories may describe processes that affect variables in particular contexts, and these processes may be described differently in different theories. It makes more sense, in his view, to test the extent of influence each process has rather than trying to make a decision about which one is best or correct. Competing theories in this case make sense. Fourth, theories generally cannot be directly compared. Competing theories likely arise because the ones that are in existence fail to account for certain relational statements; thus, comparing them directly would be challenging.

Regardless of the stance you choose, you should understand the theories that guide a specific phenomenon through careful examination in terms of their concepts and relational statements. It may be that your study is able to test relational statements as hypotheses that would be consistent with two different theories. In this case, the goal would not be to compare and contrast but rather to understand the assumptions and limitations of each of the competing theories.

Choosing a Theory to Guide Research

Many studies are published without any reference to a theory guiding the research. The results seem just as valuable and important whether or not there is a theory, so an important question arises as to why theory is important. Even though a research study may not explicitly state a theory, the author of the study always has a particular view of the world. The author also has a particular set of beliefs about the concepts and/or variables and the relationships between them that constitute theory. It is very important to make these theoretical connections explicit in your own research. The connections, when discussed in relation to the existing research in the discipline, provide greater depth of understanding to bridge the relationships between the variables. Acknowledging the theoretical and philosophical connections helps other scientists interpret the results of the study as well as the limitations of those results. The careful use of theory also helps build the case for it.

When you begin to explore an area and conduct a literature review, the theories that others have used typically become apparent. Selecting a theory can seem like a daunting task. As you read more about the theories relevant to your topic area in the discipline, you will be drawn more to some theories than to others. The theories to which you are drawn are most likely those that fit best with your worldview. Before selecting one particular theory to guide your research, examine the underlying assumptions of the theory to ensure that they fit with your philosophical perspectives. One question that is useful to ask yourself in examining assumptions is "What do I have to believe about the world and about human beings in order for me to accept or use this theory?" For example, if you are choosing a theory of human behavior and you hold a basic belief that human beings are unique and active creators of their own actions, then your assumptions are not congruent with those of the theory of behaviorism. Behaviorism posits behavior as a response to external stimuli. Thus, behaviorism would not be an obvious choice for the underlying theoretical and philosophical perspective for your research. However, if you take the position that human behavior is the result of responses to environmental stimuli, as posited by B. F. Skinner, for example, the choice of behaviorism as a theoretical perspective would yield congruence of theory and fundamental assumptions.

Cause and Effect

Correlation, as described earlier, does not necessarily support causation. In correlational relationships, one can have a positive relationship, a negative relationship, or no relationship. If the correlation is positive, the best you can conclude, in the absence of any other evidence, is that when the value of one variable is high (or low), so is the value of the other. You cannot determine which variable is responsible, and it may be that the cause is actually another variable that was not tested. One example of what is commonly described as the *third-variable problem* is the correlation between bars and churches. In general, when the number of bars in a community is high, so is the number of churches (it would seem rather silly that opening bars would somehow cause more churches to open). In this example, one indeed does not cause the other; rather, the increase in each is directly influenced by population growth. Bullock, Harlow, and Mulaik (1994) provided several criteria required to establish causation. First, the two variables must be associated (correlated). Second, the variables must be isolated so that other, extraneous variables are removed as possible causes for the covariation (correlation). Finally, the variable hypothesized to be the causal variable must precede the other in time.

In the laboratory, factors hypothesized to be the cause can be imposed by the research design. For example, we know that when we heat a gas, the heat causes it to expand in a very predictable way. Expansion does not cause the temperature to rise; rather, the expansion is due to increasing the temperature. Determining causal relationships in social behavior is much more challenging. The influences on behavior are so great and varied that controlling for all the possible effects is virtually impossible, even in a laboratory setting. Thus, measuring behavior is imprecise. There are also limits to the control of variables based on ethical principles. For example, a researcher cannot create an experimental group of nonsmokers and ask them to begin smoking in order to examine the causal effects of smoking on depression. People also tend to behave differently when they know that they are being observed, so it is not typically possible to know if the precise, hypothesized cause of the behavior is being measured.

Each of these challenges limits the degree to which we can assert causation in almost every situation involving human behavior. However, research helps scientists make progress in the search for causal relationships. First, longitudinal studies, those that assess people's behavior at multiple time points, can allow researchers the opportunity to determine sequencing in time, a critical requirement for causality. Second, replicating studies across multiple contexts and times can help solidify evidence that a particular relationship is durable and specific variables are causal. One example of how evidence over time leads to causal assumptions is the extensive evidence of the correlational relationship between smoking and lung cancer. The cumulative evidence of the association between tobacco use and lung cancer, controlling for the potential effects of other variables, has been overwhelming. Thus, correlation studies test for the extent to which variables change in a coordinated fashion, typically in naturalistic settings, without determining why the variables behave as they do. Cause-and-effect studies focus on determining which variable is responsible for the change.

CONCLUSION

The ways in which worldview and paradigms, theory, approaches to inquiry, and methods interact are complicated. Houghton et al. (2012) provide a good discussion of the connections between aims, paradigms, and methods in research, which may be helpful to you in your own research. We provided context about research philosophy and theory that can give you a rich set of ideas on the types of studies available to you. It is always good to spend time reflecting on your orientation to the world. For example, are you more positivist in terms of ontology (i.e., you believe that there is one true reality) or constructivist/interpretivist (i.e., you believe that there are multiple local realities based on unique circumstances of time and place)? Understanding the answer to this question can help orient you to those approaches to inquiry that make the most sense and are consistent with your own views of the world.

Figure 2.3 provides a visual to demonstrate that the research process is not necessarily as linear as one might think. Your worldview influences the theories on which

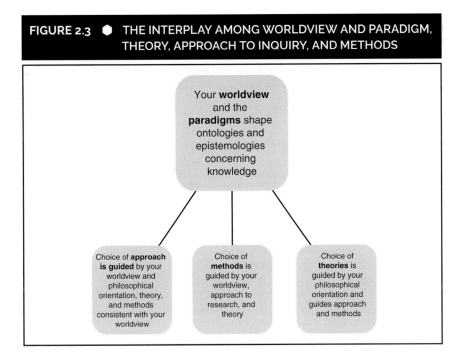

FIGURE 2.3 ● THE INTERPLAY AMONG WORLDVIEW AND PARADIGM, THEORY, APPROACH TO INQUIRY, AND METHODS

you focus and the research approaches with which you are most comfortable; however, it is also true that the process of research can change your view of the world. In addition, researchers should not be constrained by any one method. Multiple methods can be brought together to answer your research question. Understanding the critical roles that paradigm, theory, approach to inquiry, and methods play in the research process can guide you to create a research project that is as traditional or as critical/emancipatory as your goals dictate.

Questions for Reflection

1. Write down your ontological and epistemological views on the nature of truth, knowledge, and reality. Based on your reflections, decide whether your worldview aligns most closely with a positivist, postpositivist, constructivist, or critical-realist position.

2. Based on your articulation of your worldview, describe what this means for how you view science. How will this affect the kind of research approach you choose?

3. Describe, from an ontological perspective, your own ontology, that is, your view of "reality." In other words, do you consider yourself a realist or a relativist? Given your view, what types of research designs might you consider that are consistent with this position?

4. Consider an area in your discipline that you would like to research. What do you see as the ultimate goal of your research? For example, are you seeking more traditional outcomes, such as those that can be achieved through experimental studies, or is the goal more emancipatory and participatory in that the outcomes are influenced by coresearchers and other stakeholders?

5. Discuss what might happen if your philosophy of science, choice of theory, and method are not congruent.

Key Sources

Crotty, M. (1998). *The foundations of social research: Meaning and perspective in the research process*. Thousand Oaks, CA: SAGE.

Green, K., & LeBihan, J. (1996). *Critical theory and practice: A coursebook*. London, UK: Routledge.

Hayden, J. A. (2013). *Introduction to health behavior theory*. Burlington, MA: Jones & Bartlett Learning.

Johnson, P., & Duberley, J. (2000). *Understanding management research: An introduction to epistemology*. Thousand Oaks, CA: SAGE.

Kuhn, T. (2012). *The structure of scientific revolutions* (50th anniversary ed.). Urbana, IL: University of Chicago Press.

Malhotra-Bentz, V., & Shapiro, J. J. (1998). *Mindful inquiry in social research*. Thousand Oaks, CA: SAGE.

Reynolds, P. D. (2007). *A primer in theory construction*. Boston, MA: Pearson.

References

Bowleg, L. (2012). The problem with the phrase "women and minorities": Intersectionality, an important theoretical framework for public health. *American Journal of Public Health, 102*(7), 1267–1273. doi:10.2105/AJPH.2012.300750

Buckingham, W., & Burnham, D. (2015). *The philosophy book: Big ideas simply explained*. London, UK: Penguin Group.

Bullock, H. E., Harlow, L. L., & Mulaik, S. (1994). Causation issues in structural modeling research. *Structural Equation Modeling Journal, 1*, 253–267. doi:10.1080/10705519409539977

Burbank, P. M., & Martins, D. C. (2010). Symbolic interactionism and critical perspective: Divergent or synergistic? *Nursing Philosophy, 11*, 25–41. doi:10.1111/j.1466-769X.2009.00421.x.

Clark, T. W. (1992). Relativism and the limits of rationality. *The Humanist, 52*, 25–42.

Crotty, M. (1998). *The foundations of social research: Meaning and perspective in the research process*. Thousand Oaks, CA: SAGE.

Day, L. (2010). *How to rule the world from your couch*. New York, NY: Atria Books.

Dudley-Brown, S. L. (1997). The evaluation of nursing theory: A method for our madness. *International Journal of Nursing Studies, 34*, 76–83. doi:10.1016/S0020-7489(96)00024-7

Gannon, S., & Davies, B. (2007). Postmodern, poststructural, and critical theories. In S. N. Hesse-Biber (Ed.), *Handbook of feminist research: Theory and praxis* (pp. 71–106). Thousand Oaks, CA: SAGE.

Geertz, C. (1973). *The interpretation of cultures: Selected essays*. New York, NY: Basic Books.

Gershenson, C. (2013). The implications of interactions for science and philosophy. *Foundations of Science, 18*, 781–790. doi:10.1007/s10699-012-9305-8

Guba, E. (1990). *The paradigm dialog*. Newbury Park, CA: SAGE.

Habermas, J. (1971). *Knowledge and human interests* (J. J. Shapiro, Trans.). Boston, MA: Beacon Press. (Original work published 1968)

Hacker, K. (2013). *Community-based participatory research*. Thousand Oaks, CA: SAGE.

Hanson, N. R. (1958). *Patterns of discovery*. Cambridge, UK: Cambridge University Press.

Harman, W. (1991). *A re-examination of the metaphysical foundations of modern science*. Petaluma, CA: Institute of Noetic Sciences.

Hay, L. (1984). *You can heal your life*. Carlsbad, CA: Hay House.

Hicks, E., & Hicks, J. (2006). *The law of attraction: The basics of the teachings of Abraham*. Carlsbad, CA: Hay House.

Houghton, C., Hunter, A., & Meskell, P. (2012). Linking aims, paradigm and method in nursing research. *Nurse Researcher, 20*(2), 34–39. doi:10.7748/nr2012.11.20.2.34.c9439

Johnson, P., & Duberley, J. (2000). *Understanding management research: An introduction to epistemology*. Thousand Oaks, CA: SAGE.

Kim, H. S. (1993). Putting theories into practice: Problems and prospects. *Journal of Advanced Nursing, 18,* 1632–1639.

Kim, H. S. (1999). Critical reflective inquiry for knowledge development in nursing practice. *Journal of Advanced Nursing, 29*(5), 1205–1212. doi:10.1046/j.1365-2648.1999.01005.x

Kincheloe, J. L., McLaren, P., & Steinberg, S. R. (2011). Critical pedagogy and qualitative research: Moving to the bricolage. In Y. S. Lincoln, S. A. Lynham, & E. G. Guba (Eds.), *Handbook of qualitative research* (pp. 162–177). Thousand Oaks, CA: SAGE.

Kuhn, T. (2012). *The structure of scientific revolutions* (50th anniversary ed.). Urbana, IL: University of Chicago Press.

Kukla, A. (2000). *Social constructivism and the philosophy of science.* London, UK: Routledge.

Lather, P. (1994). Critical inquiry in qualitative research: Feminist and poststructural perspectives. In B. F. Crabtree, W. L. Miller, R. B. Addison, V. J. Gilchrist, & A. J. Kuzel (Eds.), *Exploring collaborative research in primary care* (pp. 103–114). Thousand Oaks, CA: SAGE.

Lincoln, Y. S., Lynham, S. A., & Guba, E. G. (2011). Competing paradigms in qualitative research. In N. K. Denzin & Y. S. Lincoln (Eds.), *Handbook of qualitative research* (pp. 96–127). Thousand Oaks, CA: SAGE.

Mackenzie, N., & Knipe, S. (2006). Research dilemmas: Paradigms, methods, and methodology. *Issues in Educational Research, 16,* 1–11.

McEwen, M. (2011). Theory analysis and evaluation. In M. McEwen & E. M. Wills (Eds.), *Theoretical basis for nursing* (3rd ed., pp. 89–106). Philadelphia, PA: Wolters Kluwer/Lippincott Williams & Wilkins.

McTaggart, L. (2003). *The field: The quest for the secret force of the universe.* London, UK: Element.

Miller, J. R., & Burbank, P. M. (1994). Congruence among philosophy, theory and method in nursing research. In Workgroup of European Nurse Researchers (Ed.), *The contribution of nursing research: Past–present–future: Vol. 2. Proceedings at the 7th Biennial Conference* (pp. 704–709). Oslo, Norway: Falch Hurtigtrykk.

Mittwede, S. K. (2012). Research paradigms and their use and importance in theological inquiry and education. *Journal of Education and Christian Belief, 16*(1), 23–40. doi:10.1177/205699711201600104

Plummer, K. (2011). Critical humanism and queer theory: Living with the tensions. In N. K. Denzin & Y. S. Lincoln (Eds.), *The SAGE handbook of qualitative research* (pp. 195–212). Thousand Oaks, CA: SAGE.

Polanyi, M. (1958). *Personal knowledge: Towards a post-critical philosophy.* Chicago, IL: University of Chicago Press.

Ponterotto, J. G. (2005). Qualitative research in counseling psychology: A primer on research paradigms and philosophy of science. *Journal of Counseling and Clinical Psychology, 52*(2), 126–136. doi:10.1037/0022-0167.52.2.126

Reynolds, P. D. (2007). *A primer in theory construction.* Boston, MA: Pearson.

Rosenstock, I. M. (1974). Historical origins of the health belief model. *Health Education Monographs, 2*(4), 328–335. doi:10.1177/109019817400200403

Schwandt, T. A. (1998). Constructivist, interpretivist approaches to human inquiry. In N. K. Denzin & Y. S. Lincoln (Eds.), *The landscape of qualitative research: Theories and issues* (pp. 221–259). Thousand Oaks, CA: SAGE.

Smith, L. T. (1999). *Decolonizing methodologies: Research and indigenous peoples.* London, UK: Zed Books.

Warren, J. R., & Marshall, B. (1983). Unidentified curved bacilli on gastric epithelium in active chronic gastritis. *Lancet, 1,* 1273–1275. doi:10.1016/S0140-6736(83)92719-8

CONCEPTUAL AND THEORETICAL FRAMEWORKS IN RESEARCH

Linda M. Crawford

At the outset of planning your research, you set the study into a framework that justifies the study and explains its structure or design. This framework is like a foundation for a house. It provides the essential support for the study components and also clarifies the context of the study for the reader, much like a house blueprint. By constructing this framework, you not only justify and explain the study to others but also check your own understanding of the need for the study, how the study is conceived, what knowledge it will add regarding the topic, and how the elements of the study design align with the problem identified for the study.

This chapter builds on the philosophical foundations presented in Chapter 2 by addressing the framework for a research study. One of the difficulties for new researchers in developing a framework for a study is that conceptual and theoretical frameworks are defined and described differently by different authors, and the definition of what is considered a study framework may vary by institution. This chapter explores those various definitions to provide a spectrum of understanding of conceptual and theoretical frameworks. This chapter also provides the purpose of the conceptual framework, sources from which these frameworks are derived, and how conceptual frameworks are presented. Given the discrepancy in definitions of conceptual and theoretical frameworks, the term *conceptual framework* will serve as the overriding term for the chapter and will be differentiated from the term *theoretical framework*. Finally, some guidance in how to approach the conceptual and theoretical frameworks for your study is provided.

LITERATURE-BASED DEFINITIONS OF CONCEPTUAL FRAMEWORKS

Before exploring the various understandings of conceptual frameworks in depth, it is helpful to compare multiple definitions of the term. Some authors view conceptual and theoretical frameworks as synonymous. Interestingly, some research design authors do not provide description or definition of either conceptual or theoretical frameworks, even if they discuss theory; for example, see this omission in Leedy and Ormrod (2016). Please note that this omission from texts does not justify excluding a conceptual framework from a study. A conceptual framework provides the orientation to the study and assists both the researcher and the reader in seeing how the study contributes to the body of knowledge on the topic, how elements of the study align, and how the study design and methodology meet rigorous research standards. In summary, a conceptual framework is incredibly important.

Table 3.1 displays various authors' definitions of conceptual framework. A conceptual framework may be defined broadly as theory or literature review, or it may be defined more narrowly as the factors and variables addressed in a study (Maxwell, 2017; Miles, Huberman, & Saldaña, 2014). Essentially, all definitions of conceptual framework provide a context for the study, but the scope of that context varies among authors.

Ravitch and Riggan

Ravitch and Riggan (2017) presented the most comprehensive understanding of conceptual framework. Indeed, they devoted an entire book to the topic. Their main point was that a conceptual framework is an argument for the study and that argument has two parts. First, the argument establishes the importance of and intended audience for the study. Second, the argument demonstrates alignment among research questions, data collection, and data analysis, as well as the use of rigorous procedures to conduct the study. They posited that the conceptual framework both

TABLE 3.1 ● DEFINITIONS OF CONCEPTUAL FRAMEWORKS	
Author(s)	**Definition**
Ravitch and Riggan (2017)	"An argument about why the topic one wishes to study matters, and why the means proposed to study it are appropriate and rigorous." (p. 5)
Miles et al. (2014)	"[An explanation], either graphically or in narrative form, [of] the main things to be studied—the key factors, variables, or constructs—and the presumed relationships among them." (p. 20)
Maxwell (2013)	"The actual ideas and beliefs that you hold about the phenomena studied, whether these are written down or not; this may also be called the 'theoretical framework' or 'idea context' for the study." (p. 39)
Marshall and Rossman (2016)	"The first major section of the proposal—the conceptual framework—demands a solid rationale. In examining a specific setting or set of individuals, the writer should show how she is studying instances of a larger phenomenon. By linking the specific research questions to larger theoretical constructs, to existing puzzles or contested positions in a field, or to important policy issues, the writer shows that the particulars of this study serve to illuminate larger issues and therefore hold potential significance for that field." (p. 6)

informs and describes the development of research questions, design selection, data collection, data analysis, and presentation of findings.

Miles, Huberman, and Saldaña

A major contribution to the idea of conceptual framework presented by Miles et al. (2014) is the graphical representation of the conceptual framework, which will be explored later in this chapter. They promoted spending significant time in developing and representing the conceptual framework. That process encourages a closer assessment of how a study's variables are related, how study participants are characterized, and how data collection instruments are selected.

Maxwell

Maxwell (2013) discussed conceptual frameworks in relation to qualitative research design. For Maxwell, the conceptual and theoretical frameworks are synonymous. Maxwell presented the terms as synonymous because he viewed the conceptual framework as presenting a theory of the phenomenon under investigation (p. 39). A major point of Maxwell's contribution is that the researcher must build, or construct, the conceptual framework from personal experience, prior research, and published theory into a coherent representation of the study.

Marshall and Rossman

Marshall and Rossman (2016) described conceptual framework as providing a rationale for the study. The idea of rationale is close to Ravitch and Riggan's (2017) view of conceptual framework as an argument for the study. Marshall and Rossman also emphasized the importance of grounding a conceptual framework in the literature published on the topic under study.

All definitions demonstrate the importance of the relationship of the conceptual framework to the roots of the study purpose and the alignment of study parts. They also indicate ways that a conceptual framework makes the construction of a study clearer, cleaner, and more straightforward. However, another consideration is how researchers define the term *theoretical framework*, particularly in relation to the conceptual framework.

LITERATURE-BASED DEFINITIONS OF THEORETICAL FRAMEWORKS

The definitions of conceptual framework are confounded by the fact that some authors do not differentiate between conceptual and theoretical frameworks. Maxwell (2013), Robson and McCartan (2016), and Merriam and Tisdell (2016) consider the terms synonymous. Anfara and Mertz (2015) do not explicitly relate conceptual and theoretical frameworks, but they imply a synonymous relationship between them. Some authors (Marshall & Rossman, 2016; Miles et al., 2014) offer no discussion of the relationship between conceptual and theoretical frameworks.

Merriam and Tisdell (2016) defined theoretical framework as "the underlying structure, the scaffolding or frame of your study" (p. 85), which seems close to some of the definitions of conceptual framework provided earlier. Anfara and Mertz (2015) defined theoretical frameworks as "any empirical or quasi-empirical theory of social and/or psychological processes, at a variety of levels . . . that can be applied to the understandings of phenomena" (p. 15).

A clear definition of theoretical frameworks and the relationship between theoretical and conceptual frameworks comes from Ravitch and Riggan (2017). They defined theoretical frameworks as follows:

> In the case of theoretical frameworks, the "parts" referred to in this definition are *theories*, and the thing that is being supported is the relationships embedded in the conceptual framework. More specifically, we argue that the parts are *formal* theories; [*sic*] those that emerge from and have been explored using empirical work. (pp. 11–12)

Ravitch and Riggan (2017) required that the theoretical framework be based on published, identifiable theories. Private conceptualizations or theoretical constructions do not qualify. In addition, they held that the theoretical framework resides within the conceptual framework and is not synonymous with it. *In other words, the conceptual framework presents the overall structure of the study, and the theoretical framework within it explains the relationships that are explored within the study.*

RECOMMENDED DEFINITIONS OF CONCEPTUAL AND THEORETICAL FRAMEWORKS

I recommend that conceptual and theoretical frameworks not be considered synonymous, and I align the definitions used in this text with the guidance provided by Ravitch and Riggan (2017). I adopt Ravitch and Riggan's definition of conceptual framework as "an argument about why the topic one wishes to study matters, and why the means proposed to study it are appropriate and rigorous" (p. 5). For example, a conceptual framework for a study on learning styles would present the reason(s) why studying the particular aspect of learning styles is important, with that reason rooted in the literature; for whom studying the particular aspect of learning styles might make a difference; and how the planned design and methods of the study are appropriate and rigorous.

Furthermore, I differentiate between conceptual and theoretical frameworks, conceiving theoretical framework as an explanation of how the study relates to the generation or testing of theory. Building on Ravitch and Riggan (2017), I define *theoretical framework* as an element of a conceptual framework that situates the relationships explored in the study into the context of developing or testing formal theories.

Consistent with Ravitch and Riggan (2017), the theoretical framework should do the following:

1. Identify the theory cluster. A theory cluster combines theories into categories, such as theories of learning style, organizational communication, and language acquisition.

2. Identify specific theories relevant to that cluster, including the originator or source and the major propositions and hypotheses of each theory.

3. Identify the theory selected for the study. This includes specifying the specific theory within the cluster that will be used, the propositions of the theory that relate to the specific study, and the review of prior studies using that theory as a focus.

4. State how the study will contribute to the body of knowledge related to the theory.

Following the earlier learning style study example, the theory cluster would be learning style theory. There are several different learning style theories, such as Kolb's experiential learning theory model (Kolb, 1984, 2015) and the Dunn and Dunn learning style model (Dunn, Dunn, & Price, 1984). Of course, there are more learning style theorists, but these two are presented for the purpose of this example. Within a theoretical framework, if you were doing this study, you would present the major theories that are relevant to the study.

Notice that a theory often has the originator's name associated with it, such as Einstein's theory of relativity, Gardner's theory of multiple intelligences, and Freud's psychosexual theory of human development. Notice, too, that the publication dates for theories are often old. Theories require significant testing over time to be verified. Theories supported by research survive the test of time. Theories not supported by research lose usefulness and eventually fall away, are revised, or are replaced by new theories.

Having identified the theory cluster and the specific theories within the cluster that are related to the study problem, the theories must be explicated. In other words, their major propositions or hypotheses need to be presented. For example, Kolb's (2015) theory holds that individuals show a preference for one of four learning styles—accommodating, converging, diverging, and assimilating—and each style has a certain set of characteristics. These styles and characteristics would need to be summarized along with any other major propositions or hypotheses of the theory. As another example, Dunn and Dunn's theory (Dunn et al., 1984) offers five stimulus areas—environmental, emotional, sociological, physiological, and psychological—and each of these five areas are associated with certain elements. These areas and elements, along with any other major propositions or hypotheses, would need to be summarized. These two learning theories are very different from each other. The next task for the researcher is to select the theory most relevant to the study.

For the example of a learning style theory study, consider that the researcher is investigating whether student standardized test scores vary according to the time of day students are tested in relation to their preferred learning style. Since the researcher has explicated both Kolb's and Dunn and Dunn's theories, the researcher has shown that the Dunn and Dunn theory has explicit propositions with regard to time of day as a factor in learning, whereas the Kolb theory does not. Therefore, the researcher selects the Dunn and Dunn theory for inclusion in the theoretical framework, giving that rationale. A review of research on the physiological element of time of day in Dunn and Dunn's theory situates the proposed study within the professional conversation that is related to that theory. Finally, the researcher describes how the proposed study will contribute to using the theory for explanation and prediction.

EXAMPLE OF HOW A THEORETICAL FRAMEWORK RELATES TO A STUDY

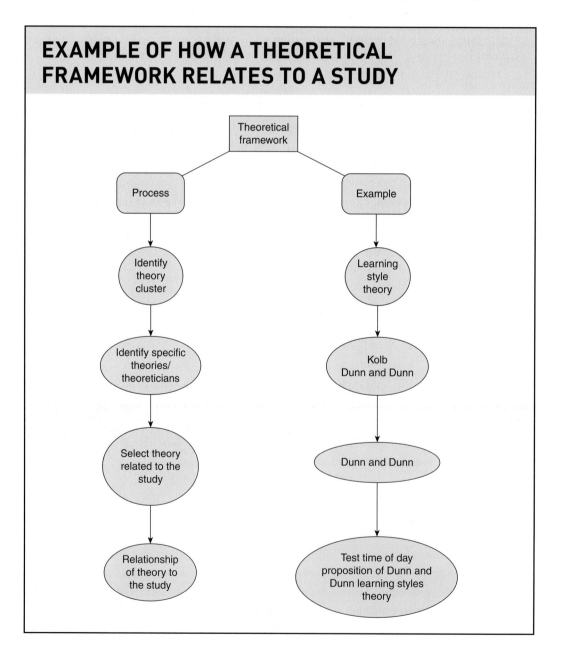

PURPOSE OF CONCEPTUAL FRAMEWORKS

To construct an informative conceptual framework, the researcher must under-stand the purpose of a conceptual framework. Different authors present the purpose of conceptual frameworks in different ways (Table 3.2). Some authors focus on the conceptual framework as argumentation for the study (Marshall & Rossman, 2016; Ravitch & Riggan, 2017). Other authors see the conceptual framework as explana-tory (Anfara & Mertz, 2015; Miles et al., 2014). Merriam and Tisdell (2016) viewed the conceptual framework, which they termed theoretical framework, as generating elements of the research design and methods, whereas Robson and McCartan (2016) emphasized variable relationships and research design. Maxwell (2013) combined pur-poses of the conceptual framework into clarification, explanation, and justification.

TABLE 3.2 ● PURPOSE OF CONCEPTUAL FRAMEWORKS

Author(s)	Purpose
Ravitch and Riggan (2017)	Argue for why the topic matters and why the proposed design and methodology are appropriate and rigorous (p. 5)
Miles et al. (2014)	Explain relationships among key factors/variables/constructs of the study (who and what will be studied) (p. 20)
Maxwell (2013)	Clarify, explain, and justify methods (pp. 39–40)
Robson and McCartan (2016)	Specify variable relationships and research design (p. 68)
Marshall and Rossman (2016)	Argue for study in terms of meaning and contribution to improving the human condition (p. 67)
Merriam and Tisdell (2016)	Generate study problem, research questions, data collection, data analysis, and interpretation of findings (p. 86)
Anfara and Mertz (2015)	Explain variable relationships (p. 15)

Figure 3.1 displays the various purposes of conceptual frameworks: (a) argumenta-tion, (b) explanation, and (c) generation. Argumentation focuses on the importance of studying the topic, the appropriateness of the design, and the rigor of the meth-ods. Explanation stresses the relationships among who and what will be studied. Generation gives rise to the problem, research questions, and methods of a study.

FIGURE 3.1 ● PURPOSES OF CONCEPTUAL FRAMEWORKS

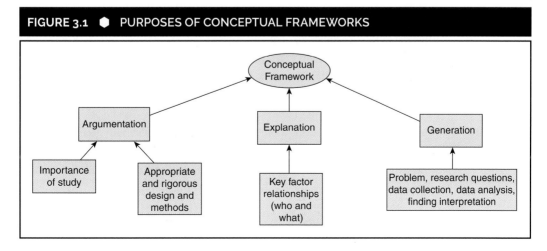

I recommend that you incorporate the three purposes—argumentation, explanation, and generation—when constructing your conceptual framework. By doing so, you will build a comprehensive model that will aid in justifying your study, clarifying the relationships explored in the study, and aligning design elements. As you build the conceptual framework toward these purposes, you must root the framework in verifiable sources.

SOURCES OF CONCEPTUAL FRAMEWORKS

A source for a conceptual framework is the principal element forming the basis for the development of the framework (Ravitch & Riggan, 2017). You may think of it as the impetus for the conceptual framework. There are three sources for a conceptual framework: (1) experience, (2) literature, and (3) theory.

Experience

Ravitch and Riggan (2017), Maxwell (2013), Robson and McCartan (2016), Marshall and Rossman (2016), and Booth, Colomb, Williams, Bizup, and Fitz-gerald (2016) all allowed for personal interests, experiences, intuitions, and hunches as stimuli for a conceptual framework, although none of them believed that personal experience alone is sufficient. For example, your personal experience observing leadership styles in an organization may stimulate in you a desire to conduct a study on a certain aspect of leadership, but a literature review might reveal that that aspect has already been deeply studied or that there is scant support in the profession for investigating that aspect. Personal issues may point you in the direction of a study topic, but the topic must have meaning for others in the field. In other words, there must be evidence that others in the field share your concern and that addressing the concern will advance knowledge. Such evidence rests in literature and a theoretical base to support a conceptual framework for a study.

Literature

An essential source for your conceptual framework is the published research literature related to your topic. Ravitch and Riggan (2017), Maxwell (2013), Robson and McCartan (2016), Merriam and Tisdell (2016), and Marshall and Rossman (2016) advocated for rooting the conceptual framework in the literature associated with the topic of study. Of singular importance is that your study is based on a need documented from the literature. For example, following the idea in the prior paragraph, your personal experience may point to a desire to study a certain aspect of leadership. Of importance, though, is that you find out from the literature the extent to which that aspect has already been studied, what is still not understood about it, and whether or not the discipline needs to remedy the lack of knowledge (Booth et al.,

2016). The literature review provides the evidence for the argumentation contained in a conceptual framework.

Theoretical Framework

An additional source for your conceptual framework is theory (Anfara & Mertz, 2015; Marshall & Rossman, 2016; Maxwell, 2013; Ravitch & Riggan, 2017; Robson & McCartan, 2016), and this source is expressed in the theoretical framework. The study may be focused on generating new theory or on testing theory that has already been constructed (Creswell & Poth, 2018). For example, your study may focus on describing how leaders distribute power in an organization. In other words, the focus is on developing an explanation, or theory, of how power distribution functions in a certain kind of organization. Or your study may focus on testing some theory of power distribution that has already been developed to determine if it accurately explains how power is distributed within a certain group. Whether generating or testing theory, the conceptual framework contains the theoretical framework, or theoretical context, for the study.

Summary of Sources of Conceptual Frameworks

As shown in Figure 3.2, there are three sources, or stimuli, for creating a conceptual framework: (1) experience, (2) literature, and (3) theory. Although personal experience may instigate a research idea, personal experience is not sufficient to support a conceptual framework for a research study. The conceptual framework must be rooted in the professional literature. The literature provides the rationale for the study by exposing what is not yet known or understood about a phenomenon. The third source for a conceptual framework is theory, integrated as the theoretical framework. Is there already a theory that needs to be tested? Is there no existing viable theory of the phenomenon and does one need to be developed? Thus, experience may prompt a conceptual framework, the literature must provide the argumentation for pursuing the research idea, and the study must be situated in relation to generating or testing theory.

FIGURE 3.2 ● SOURCES OF CONCEPTUAL FRAMEWORKS

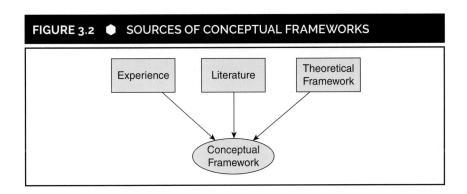

PRESENTATION OF CONCEPTUAL FRAMEWORKS

There are two ways to present a conceptual framework—graphically and narratively. If you are crafting a research study for a thesis or dissertation, your institution will probably expect that, at a minimum, you describe the conceptual framework narratively, with optional figures to support clarity of presentation. This section will examine means of exhibiting a conceptual framework.

Graphic Presentation

Some authors favor a diagrammatic portrayal of a conceptual framework using a concept map, with or without an accompanying narrative (Marshall & Rossman, 2016; Maxwell, 2013; Merriam & Tisdell, 2016; Miles et al., 2014; Robson & McCartan, 2016). A concept map is a pictorial portrayal of relationships. It shows how one idea or concept connects to other ideas or concepts.

Miles et al. (2014) provided several fine examples of graphic presentations and concept maps describing conceptual frameworks. As an additional example, Figure 3.3 shows a graphical conceptual framework for a mixed methods study that examined the influence of specific dimensions of supervisor support (mentoring, coaching, task support, and social support) on transfer motivation and training transfer to determine whether transfer motivation mediates the relationships between dimensions of supervisor support and training transfer (Schindler, 2012).

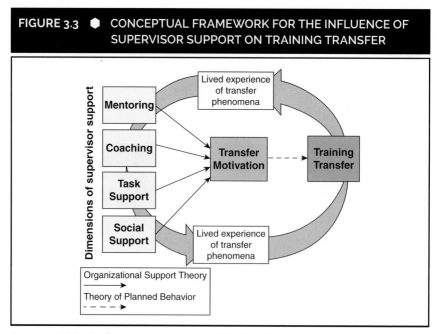

FIGURE 3.3 ● CONCEPTUAL FRAMEWORK FOR THE INFLUENCE OF SUPERVISOR SUPPORT ON TRAINING TRANSFER

Source: L. A. Schindler (personal communication, July 15, 2015).

Figure 3.3 reflects the purpose of the mixed methods study, which was to understand the influence of specific dimensions of support (mentoring, coaching, task support, and social support) on transfer motivation and training transfer. In the quantitative portion of this study, the author examined the relationships between dimensions of supervisor support and training transfer and the degree to which transfer motivation mediates those relationships. In the qualitative portion of the study, the author explored participants' lived experiences of transfer phenomena (i.e., supervisor support, transfer motivation, and training transfer). Both organizational support theory and the theory of planned behavior provided support for this study (Schindler, 2012).

Miles et al. (2014) noted that forcing the graphic onto one page rather than multiple text pages allows you to see and adjust all the parts of the study as a unit as well as to see inconsistencies and contradictions. Going through this process lends cohesiveness to the study design. You should expect development of the graphic to be an iterative process with several versions until it finally accurately represents the study. During this iterative process, how you are writing about the study in text and how you are graphically representing the study become mutually informative and mutually formative. Miles et al. further suggested that you should challenge yourself to avoid overly global graphics with ubiquitous two-way arrows that do not clearly demonstrate the flow of the study.

Like Miles et al. (2014), Robson and McCartan (2016) advocated presenting the conceptual framework in graphic format. Robson and McCartan provided six specifications for developing that graphic:

1. Contain the graphic on one page.

2. Include multiple inputs, such as prior research, including pilot studies; relevant theories; hunches with regard to the phenomenon or variable relationships; and thoughts of other professionals in the field.

3. Attain internal consistency within the graphical map.

4. Expect to produce multiple iterations of the framework graphic.

5. Include an item, rather than exclude it, if unsure.

6. Simplify the graphic as you learn from experience.

If you attend to each of the six specifications listed, you will develop a solid graphical presentation of your conceptual framework.

Narrative Presentation

Ravitch and Riggan (2017) were less supportive of a graphical presentation. Although they saw that graphical and narrative presentations of the conceptual framework can work well, they preferred a text-based presentation of conceptual framework when there is a question about presentation. Ravitch and Riggan provided strong examples of narratively presented conceptual frameworks in relation to design, data collection, data analysis, and presentation of findings.

Recommendation

I advocate narrative presentation of the conceptual framework accompanied by a graphic. The effort to create a one-page graphical model of a study will assist you in coherently conceptualizing the study, determining appropriate alignment of research design elements, and communicating the essential elements to others. Another benefit of a graphical conceptual framework is that it lifts you from the burden of words, in which some researchers can become mired, and allows you to see the study and interrelationships as a picture. In that way, a graphic provides you with an organizing tool that conveys meaning to readers more simply than written text. I maintain, though, that you must also present the conceptual framework in clearly written text. Narrative presentation of the conceptual framework clarifies key aspects of the study foundation and conveys an understanding of the overall study in the context of knowledge in the discipline.

SUMMARY

In this chapter, I explored definitions of conceptual and theoretical frameworks. I advocated that conceptual and theoretical frameworks should not be considered synonymous but should be understood as different concepts, congruent with the assertions of Ravitch and Riggan (2017). As shown in Figure 3.4, three

FIGURE 3.4 ● PURPOSES AND SOURCES OF CONCEPTUAL FRAMEWORKS

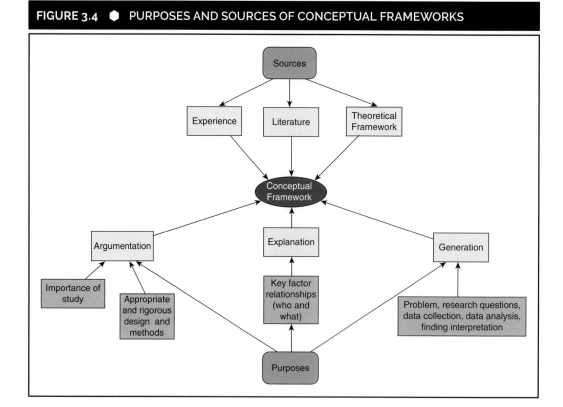

purposes identified for conceptual frameworks—argumentation, explanation, and generation—are rooted in the three sources of experience, literature, and theory. As part of the conceptual framework, the theoretical framework shows how the study relates to generating or testing theory and explains the relationships that are explored within the study. Finally, I recommended graphical presentation of a conceptual framework accompanied by narrative explication.

Questions for Reflection

1. How do you distinguish between conceptual and theoretical frameworks?

2. Why is personal experience a valid but insufficient stimulus for a study's conceptual framework?

3. How might the presentation of a conceptual framework in both narrative and graphical formats help both the conceptualization and communication of a study?

Key Sources

Anfara, V. A., & Mertz, N. T. (2015). *Theoretical frameworks in qualitative research* (2nd ed.). Thousand Oaks, CA: SAGE.

Miles, M. B., Huberman, A. M., & Saldaña, J. (2014). *Qualitative data analysis: A methods sourcebook* (3rd ed.). Thousand Oaks, CA: SAGE.

Ravitch, S. M., & Riggan, M. (2017). *Reason & rigor: How conceptual frameworks guide research* (2nd ed.). Thousand Oaks, CA: SAGE.

References

Anfara, V. A., & Mertz, N. T. (Eds.). (2015). *Theoretical frameworks in qualitative research* (2nd ed.). Thousand Oaks, CA: SAGE.

Booth, W. C., Colomb, G. G., Williams, J. M., Bizup, J., & Fitzgerald, W. T. (2016). *The craft of research* (4th ed.). Chicago, IL: University of Chicago Press.

Creswell, J. W., & Poth, C. N. (2018). *Qualitative inquiry & research design: Choosing among five approaches* (4th ed.). Thousand Oaks, CA: SAGE.

Dunn, R., Dunn, K., & Price, G. E. (1984). *Learning style inventory.* Lawrence, KS: Price Systems.

Kolb, D. A. (1984). *Experiential learning: Experience as the source of learning and development.* Englewood Cliffs, NJ: Prentice Hall.

Kolb, D. A. (2015). *Experiential learning: Experience as the source of learning and development* (2nd ed.). Upper Saddle River, NJ: Pearson Education.

Leedy, P. D., & Ormrod, J. E. (2016). *Practical research: Planning and design* (11th ed.). Boston, MA: Pearson.

Marshall, C., & Rossman, G. B. (2016). *Designing qualitative research* (6th ed.). Thousand Oaks, CA: SAGE.

Maxwell, J. (2013). *Qualitative research design: An interactive approach* (3rd ed.). Thousand Oaks, CA: SAGE.

Maxwell, J. (2017). Foreword. In S. M. Ravitch & M. Riggan (Eds.), *Reason & rigor: How conceptual frameworks guide research* (2nd ed., pp. xi–xiii). Thousand Oaks, CA: SAGE.

Merriam, S. B., & Tisdell, E. J. (2016). *Qualitative research: A guide to design and implementation* (4th ed.). San Francisco, CA: Jossey-Bass.

Miles, M. B., Huberman, A. M., & Saldaña, J. (2014). *Qualitative data analysis: A methods sourcebook* (3rd ed.). Thousand Oaks, CA: SAGE.

Ravitch, S. M., & Riggan, M. (2017). *Reason & rigor: How conceptual frameworks guide research* (2nd ed.). Thousand Oaks, CA: SAGE.

Robson, C., & McCartan, K. (2016). *Real world research* (4th ed.). Chichester, UK: Wiley.

Schindler, L. A. (2012). *A mixed methods examination of the influence of dimensions of support on training transfer* (Doctoral dissertation). Available from ProQuest Dissertations and Theses database. (Order No. 3547454). Retrieved from http://search.proquest.com/docview/1268753273? accountid=14

RESEARCH DESIGN AND ANALYSIS

PART II

QUANTITATIVE RESEARCH DESIGNS

Kimberley A. Cox

A research design describes a detailed plan for answering a research question. In quantitative research, where the researcher seeks to understand and describe a phenomenon, behavior, or issue using numerical data and statistical analysis, this includes elements such as the specific structural features of the study, measurement of variables, and strategy for sampling. Together, these elements link the research question to the data.

The goals of this chapter are to (a) introduce you to some of the specialized vocabulary that is used in quantitative research and (b) provide an overview of quantitative designs to guide you toward selecting an appropriate and credible design for your research projects. I begin this chapter with a brief discussion of frequently encountered terms and concepts in quantitative research. I follow with an overview of common types of randomized experimental, quasi-experimental, and nonexperimental designs. Last, I describe some of the common sampling strategies in quantitative research.

VARIABLES

The design of a study often begins with curiosity about an abstract idea or phenomenon that cannot be directly measured, such as motivation or autonomy. That is, interest may begin with a *concept*, an "abstraction, a representation of an object, or one of that object's properties" (Frankfort-Nachmias & Nachmias, 2008, p. 24) that does not exist in a physical sense (Loseke, 2013). A *construct* typically refers to a type of concept that theoretically holds an agreed-on meaning but cannot be directly observed. Concepts are common in many disciplines because of their usefulness as "heuristics devices" of communication (Frankfort-Nachmias & Nachmias, 2008, p. 24). Due to their subjective nature, concepts may hold different meanings from person to person. Therefore, it is necessary to translate concepts into variables.

A *variable* is a measurable attribute or characteristic that varies in value. Whereas a concept may hold many different meanings, a variable is a concept translated into a measurable attribute that holds different values. For example, a concept such as autonomy could mean one's sense of control in defining and carrying out work in the context of a job setting (Heidemeier & Wiese, 2014), or it could mean one's experience of psychological freedom or interpersonal distance from persons in positions of authority, such as parents, in the context of adolescent development (Van Petegem, Vansteenkiste, Soenens, Beyers, & Aelterman, 2015). The process of translating a concept, such as autonomy, into a variable that can be empirically tested is called *operationalization*, and the result of this translation is an operational definition (Loseke, 2013).

Operationalization

Your task in the process of operationalization is to determine the procedures for measuring your concepts of interest. The result is an *operational definition*, which is a definition that describes a variable based on the specific procedures for measuring or manipulating it, and in doing so, it "bridge[s] the conceptual-theoretical and empirical-observational levels" (Frankfort-Nachmias & Nachmias, 2008, p. 28). For any particular variable, there are potentially countless possible operational definitions.

For example, returning to the concept of autonomy, Van Petegem et al. (2015) conducted a longitudinal study to examine whether adolescents' oppositional defiance toward their parents led to greater autonomy. The researchers operationally defined autonomy on the dimensions of distance and volition as measured by adolescents' self-reported scores on the Emotional Independence subscale of the Psychological Separation Inventory (Hoffman, 1984, as cited in Van Petegem et al., 2015) and the Choicefulness subscale of the Self-Determination Scale (Sheldon, Ryan, & Reis, 1996, as cited in Van Petegem et al., 2015), respectively. Heidemeier and Wiese (2014) also conducted a longitudinal study on autonomy, but they examined the concept through a different line of research inquiry—whether women's achievement goals and autonomy would affect their readjustment to work on returning to the workplace after maternity leave. Heidemeier and Wiese operationally defined autonomy as the women's self-reported scores on a Freedom scale that was part of a larger battery of assessments.

The above examples illustrate that translating a concept into a variable can result in various definitions, but through the process of operationalization, the researchers provided definitions for their readers that clearly described the variable based on the specific procedures used for measuring it. Just as these researchers operationally defined the same concept in different ways, you will make a series of decisions to arrive at operational definitions that are aligned with your particular research question. A good starting point in the process is to determine a variable's level (or scale) of measurement.

Levels of Measurement

The choice of a variable's level of measurement typically coincides with writing an operational definition. Your choice is important because a variable's level of measurement will inform the type of statistical analysis that you can perform to analyze the data, which, in turn, influences your interpretation of the findings. Measurement involves the assignment of values, such as labels or numbers, to represent the attributes of a variable. These values are assigned to one of four levels or scales of measurement: (1) nominal, (2) ordinal, (3) interval, or (4) ratio. Some variables can have values on any one of these scales depending on the procedure used for its measurement. For example, educational attainment could be represented by category and measured as high school diploma, bachelor's degree, master's degree, and doctoral degree. Educational attainment could also be represented by a number and measured as the number of years of education completed.

Nominal Scale. The values of a nominal scale reflect a name, label, or category represented with words. This level of measurement enables you to classify things, individuals, or responses into groups that share a common attribute. The values reflect differences in quality (type), not quantity (amount) and, therefore, have no corresponding mathematical properties. An example of a nominal variable is marital status. Although researchers can assign numbers to represent the values of the categories they create, such as 1 = *Single* and 2 = *Married*, these numbers are arbitrary and have no intrinsic meaning.

Ordinal Scale. The values of an ordinal scale share the properties of the nominal scale in that they classify things, individuals, or responses into groups that share a common attribute, but these values imply a meaningful order or rank on some dimension. This level of measurement, therefore, communicates the position of values relative to one another, such as lower or higher or less than or more than. The distance between values, however, may not be equal. Therefore, it may not be possible to make meaningful mathematical comparisons between any two values on an ordinal scale. A common example of an ordinal variable is socioeconomic status (SES), which can be classified most generally as low, middle, and high. The difference between low SES and middle SES may not be the same as the difference between middle SES and high SES.

Interval Scale. The values of an interval scale share the properties of nominal and ordinal scales, but the distance between any two values is equal. This level of measurement, therefore, communicates the rank of values with equal differences in the distance between each value. For example, temperature on the Fahrenheit or Celsius scales represents an interval scale. A difference in temperature of 72 °F and 75 °F is the same as a difference in temperature of 89 °F and 92 °F such that the 3-degree difference represents the same amount of energy regardless of where it is located on the scale. An interval scale, however, does not have a true or fixed zero point that reflects the absence of the attribute being measured. There is no absence of temperature, for example, at 0 °F.

In some disciplines, there is debate about treating the scores obtained from rating scales, such as a Likert scale that presents adjective options along a continuum (e.g., strongly disagree, disagree, uncertain, agree, and strongly agree), as interval data rather than as ordinal data (Norman, 2010). This practice is debatable because the differences between the adjective options may be perceived differently depending on the perception of the responder. Although further discussion on this debate is beyond the scope of this chapter, in practice, many researchers treat Likert scale data as interval-level data although the scale yields ordinal-level data.

Ratio Scale. The values of a ratio scale share the properties of nominal, ordinal, and interval scales, but this scale has a fixed zero point. This level of measurement, therefore, communicates the rank of values with equal differences represented by the distance between each value, and there is a true zero point that reflects the absence of the attribute being measured. Thus, researchers measure values on a ratio scale starting at zero. Length and weight, for example, are data that are measured on a ratio scale because they have a fixed zero point representing absence of the attribute.

Types of Variables

Independent Variable. The independent variable is the presumed factor that causes a change in the situation or phenomenon under study. In experimental designs, it is the variable that is varied or is manipulated across groups or conditions. For example, if you were interested in studying the impact of a recycling campaign on recycling behavior, the type of recycling campaign, such as its presence or absence, would serve as the independent variable. By instituting the recycling campaign (independent variable), you anticipate change in recycling behavior because of its presence.

Some researchers only use the term *independent variable* for experimental designs that involve the manipulation or control of the potential causal factor. When a research design is nonexperimental, such as in correlational research, the term *predictor variable* is commonly used instead. Researchers also tend to refer to variables that reflect intrinsic characteristics of the study population that cannot be manipulated or controlled, such as gender or age, as *subject variables* or *attribute variables* rather than as independent variables.

Dependent Variable. The dependent variable is the presumed effect or outcome. In experimental designs, it is the variable that is measured to determine if the independent variable had an effect. That is, the outcome of the dependent variable depends on the independent variable. Returning to the recycling campaign example, the dependent variable would be recycling behavior. In nonexperimental research designs, the term *criterion variable* is commonly used rather than the term *dependent variable.*

In a study on residential curbside recycling behavior, Schultz (1999) conducted an experiment to investigate whether feedback interventions designed to activate personal norms and social norms—that is, beliefs about one's behavior and beliefs about other people's behavior, respectively—lead to an increase in recycling among residential households. The independent variable was the feedback intervention with five types: (1) recycling plea, (2) plea plus information, (3) plea plus neighborhood feedback, (4) plea plus individual household feedback, and (5) a control condition. Schultz collected data over a 17-week period on households' (a) frequency of participation in curbside recycling, (b) average amount of material recycled per week, and (c) proportion of nonrecyclable materials placed in recycling bins. Each of these three recycling behaviors represented the dependent variables.

Mediator. A mediator is a variable that mediates the effect of the independent variable on the dependent variable because it stands between or links them in the sequence of their relationship (Baron & Kenny, 1986). Researchers might include a mediator in their study as a potential explanation for why an independent variable, through the mediating variable, has an effect on a dependent variable. For example, González, Swanson, Lynch, and Williams (2016) conducted a study to investigate various psychosocial factors (e.g., need satisfaction at work) as mediator variables that could explain the underlying link between SES and physical and mental health as illustrated in Figure 4.1.

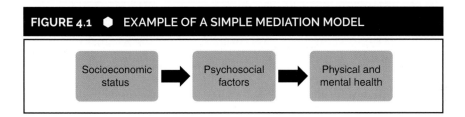

FIGURE 4.1 ● EXAMPLE OF A SIMPLE MEDIATION MODEL

Moderator. A moderator is a variable that influences the strength and/or direction of the relationship between an independent variable and a dependent variable. For example, in their study about the relationship between the search for and presence of meaning in life and work stress, Allan, Douglass, Duffy, and McCarty (2016) examined three facets of meaningful work as potential moderators of this relationship. The researchers hypothesized that meaningful work might moderate (i.e., change) the relationship between meaning in life and perceptions of work stress as illustrated in Figure 4.2.

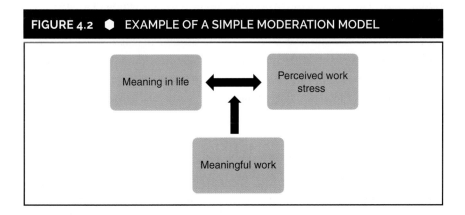

FIGURE 4.2 ● EXAMPLE OF A SIMPLE MODERATION MODEL

Confound. A confound generally refers to two categories of variables that could potentially have an undesired influence on the results of a study. One category called *extraneous variables* refers to factors other than the independent variable that were not measured, but could potentially confound or affect the relationship between the dependent variable and the independent variable. Researchers can use design techniques, such as random assignment, to minimize their influence.

Another category refers to factors that can occur during a study that could also potentially affect the dependent variable, such as boredom or motivation on the part of participants. For example, during the course of a study involving a lengthy recycling campaign, participants might lose motivation over time, or their awareness of being observed might be responsible for any changes in their recycling behavior rather than the campaign's actual components.

TYPES OF QUANTITATIVE RESEARCH DESIGNS

All research designs have strengths and weaknesses. Your selection of a research design rests largely on weighing these strengths and weaknesses given your study's research question, problem, and purpose. Although only a selection of common examples from three main types of designs are presented in this chapter, their basic components can serve as a guide for designing more sophisticated studies to meet the needs of a variety of research projects. The design notation used below is based on Campbell and Stanley's (1966) seminal work. This notation reflects a shared language that researchers commonly use to communicate about quantitative research designs by way of a diagram, where the letter X refers to the independent variable or treatment, and the letter O refers to the dependent variable or observation. When a design calls for more than one independent variable (e.g., multiple interventions) and/or more than one dependent variable (e.g., multiple measures), a subscript numeral is often used, such as X_1 and X_2 or O_1 and O_2, respectively. The letter R is used to denote random assignment. Each group is displayed on a separate line in the diagram. Although the examples presented below depict two groups, the designs can include more. Last, the placement of the notations conveys a temporal sequence that should be read from left to right reflecting the steps in the study procedures.

Randomized Experimental Designs

The goal in designing an experiment is to determine whether there is a causal link between the independent variable and dependent variable. The design of an experiment identifies the operational definitions of these variables and the randomization procedure, which refers to the method used to randomly assign participants to groups or conditions. An experiment that is designed well with alignment to the research question and hypotheses provides a strong foundation for making inferences about causation.

Many experimental designs call for a comparison between one or more groups or conditions. The experimental group or condition is exposed to a treatment of the independent variable, where a treatment could mean things such as a task, event, or intervention, and the control group or condition is not. The important difference, then, between the groups or conditions is the independent variable; both groups are equivalent and encounter the same conditions with the exception of exposure to the independent variable.

A significant feature of randomized experimental designs is *control*. Control refers to the procedures that researchers use, such as sampling and random assignment, to minimize threats to the internal validity of a study. Controlling for differences between groups before introducing the independent variable minimizes differences in participants within each of the groups or conditions and minimizes any potential confounds that could affect the observed outcome. The strength of randomized experimental designs is this feature of control that maximizes internal validity—that is, the extent to which the treatment (independent variable) is responsible for the outcome (dependent variable).

One method to achieve control is to design the experiment such that any factors or procedures are held as constant as possible across groups with the exception of manipulation of the independent variable. For example, all participants might complete a test or activity under the same conditions, such as location, time of day, and so on. Although such steps minimize differences, participants are inherently not all the same. Therefore, a second method called *random assignment* is used to achieve control.

Random assignment is a distinguishing feature of randomized experimental designs. It refers to a procedure for assigning participants to groups or conditions such that each participant has the same chance of being assigned to any given group or condition. Shadish, Cook, and Campbell (2002) presented seven methods of randomization, such as simple random assignment, batch randomization, and random assignment from matches or strata. Randomization affords the assurance of equivalent groups at the beginning of the study except for the treatment (independent variable). This equivalence enables causal inferences with more confidence: If the groups differ on the dependent measure after the treatment, it can be said with confidence that the difference was caused by the independent variable, not by the characteristics of the participants. Randomization is not without its controversies in scientific circles, however. One such controversy is the debate around the potential ethical implications of random assignment. The main arguments in favor and opposition of random assignment are covered in more detail in Shadish et al. (2002).

To broadly summarize, experiments are characterized by (a) their control, which is executed through the planning of experimental procedures and random assignment of participants, and (b) a comparison between groups or conditions based on manipulation of an independent variable. In the following section, I describe common randomized experimental designs.

Posttest-Only Control Group Design. In a posttest-only control group design, participants are randomly assigned to the experimental and control groups before presentation of the independent variable (X). Participants in the experimental group are exposed to a treatment, and the control group is not. The two groups are measured on the dependent variable (O) after (or during) exposure to the independent variable. This design can be illustrated as follows:

$$R \quad X \quad O$$
$$R \quad \quad O$$

The lack of a pretest in this design eliminates any potential carryover or practice effects that are possible when multiple measures of the dependent variable are used. There are also some situations where a pretest may not be possible or practical. Therefore, this type of design is most appropriate when the availability or use of a pretest is prohibitive or known to interact with the independent variable. Although random assignment allows for the assumption that the groups are equivalent, there is not complete assurance that this is the case. Without a pretest, your ability to determine whether any differences observed between the groups on the dependent variable are due to the independent variable (or potentially a confounding variable) is limited. In addition, the potential for loss of participants due to attrition is a possible concern because without a pretest, there is no way to compare participants who dropped out of the study with those who remained in the study (Shadish et al., 2002). Therefore, when possible, the addition of a pretest is recommended.

Pretest–Posttest Control Group Design. In a pretest–posttest control group design, participants are randomly assigned to the experimental and control groups. Each group is measured on the dependent variable (O_1) followed by presentation of the independent variable (X). Participants in the experimental group are exposed to a treatment, and the control group is not. Both groups are then measured again on the dependent variable (O_2). This design can be illustrated as follows:

$$R \quad O_1 \quad X \quad O_2$$
$$R \quad O_1 \qquad O_2$$

With the addition of the pretest, this design can address whether any differences exist between the groups before introduction of the independent variable. If the results reveal that the groups differ on the posttest measure (O_2), but not the pretest measure (O_1), you have confidence to report that the independent variable is responsible for the observed outcome. This design is well suited to manage attrition, but potential threats to internal validity still exist, such as testing and instrumentation. Testing refers to the potential for a pretest to affect participants' performance on the posttest. Instrumentation refers to the possibility of procedural changes in the use of an instrument between administration of the pretest and posttest.

There are numerous variations to the pretest–posttest control group design that can be tailored to the needs of a particular research context. For example, this design can be extended to compare more than one treatment (e.g., two different types of instructional delivery) with two experimental groups each receiving a level of the independent variable and a control group. This design can be illustrated as follows:

$$R \quad O_1 \quad X_A \quad O_2$$
$$R \quad O_1 \quad X_B \quad O_2$$
$$R \quad O_1 \qquad O_2$$

It is also possible to include a second control group if your goal is to determine if a pretest measure affects participants' scores on the posttest measure. This design, called the *Solomon four-group design*, can be illustrated as follows:

$$R \quad O_1 \quad X \quad O_2$$
$$R \quad O_1 \quad \quad O_2$$
$$R \quad \quad X \quad O_2$$
$$R \quad \quad \quad O_2$$

Factorial Designs. The designs presented so far allow you to vary one independent variable (X) at a time. Factorial designs, by comparison, permit you to vary several independent variables within a single experiment. For example, in the simplest of factorial designs, called a 2 × 2 factorial design, there are two independent variables, referred to as factors, each with at least two levels. Participants are randomly assigned to one of four possible combinations of experimental treatment (X_{A1B1}, X_{A1B2}, etc.). The four groups are measured on the dependent variable (O) after (or during) exposure to the independent variable. This design can be illustrated as follows:

$$R \quad X_{A1B1} \quad O$$
$$R \quad X_{A1B2} \quad O$$
$$R \quad X_{A2B1} \quad O$$
$$R \quad X_{A2B2} \quad O$$

The main advantages of factorial designs are that they allow you to test several hypotheses or predictions of the relationship between variables or the study's outcome at the same time because they accommodate combinations of treatments and they permit the testing of interactions among factors. This type of design allows for an examination that is wider in scope to determine, for example, if a combination of treatments is more effective than a single treatment. Factorial designs are typically more suitable for settings that afford a great deal of control over the various combinations, such as in laboratory research (Shadish et al., 2002).

Quasi-Experimental Designs

Not all research questions can be answered with a randomized experimental design because of the nature of the problem under study, ethical issues, and/or practical constraints. Research often involves the study of naturally occurring groups or groups for which membership is self-selected or intact prior to an investigation. As such, it may not be possible or ethical to change an individual's group assignment or randomly assign group members into experimental and control groups. In these situations, a quasi-experimental design may be an appropriate choice. Although quasi-experimental designs share some commonalities with experimental designs, such as the comparison of groups on a dependent variable, the key difference is the lack of random assignment of participants to groups.

The lack of random assignment in quasi-experimental designs means that the groups may not initially be equal or similar. This presents the challenge of ruling out other alternative explanations that could be responsible for any observed outcome. For example, groups for which individuals self-select their membership may differ for any number of reasons other than the treatment or manipulation of the independent variable. A quasi-experimental design, then, would not afford you with the same confidence in making causal inferences that you would have from a randomized experimental design.

In this section, I present two main types of quasi-experimental designs identified by Cook and Campbell (1979) to illustrate their general elements: nonequivalent groups design and time-series design. These designs involve collecting data from at least two nonequivalent groups and collecting multiple observations over time, respectively. There are, however, numerous types of quasi-experimental designs that can accommodate various research projects. I recommend the seminal works by Campbell and Stanley (1966) and Cook and Campbell (1979) for their extensive coverage of quasi-experimental designs.

Nonequivalent Groups Designs. In nonequivalent groups designs, participants are not assigned to groups at random. The term *nonequivalent* is used because without randomization, there may be characteristics of the participants that are responsible for any observed difference between the groups other than the independent variable. When only a posttest is used, the *posttest-only design with nonequivalent groups* (Cook & Campbell, 1979) involves two or more groups, including an experimental group that is exposed to the treatment (X), where a treatment could mean things such as a task, event, or intervention, and a control group that is not. The two groups are measured on the dependent variable (O) after (or during) exposure to the independent variable. This design can be illustrated as follows:

$$X \quad O$$
$$O$$

This design has limited use without a pretest and randomization. With the addition of a pretest, the *pretest–posttest design with nonequivalent groups* (Cook & Campbell, 1979) holds greater credibility. Here, both groups are measured on the dependent variable (O_1) followed by presentation of the independent variable (X). Participants in the experimental group are exposed to a treatment, and the control group is not. Both groups are then measured again on the dependent variable (O_2). This design can be illustrated as follows:

$$O_1 \quad X \quad O_2$$
$$O_1 \qquad O_2$$

Time-Series Designs. In time-series designs, participants in the experimental and control groups are measured on multiple observations of the same dependent variable (O_1, O_2, etc. for any number of observations) before and after exposure to some treatment (X). Time-series designs enable you to identify trends in change of the dependent variable that may be attributed to the impact of the treatment. There are several variations of the simplest of time-series designs, called the *simple interrupted time-series design with a nonequivalent control group* (Cook & Campbell, 1979), which can be illustrated as follows in this example involving eight observations:

$$O_1 \quad O_2 \quad O_3 \quad O_4 \quad X \quad O_5 \quad O_6 \quad O_7 \quad O_8$$
$$O_1 \quad O_2 \quad O_3 \quad O_4 \qquad O_5 \quad O_6 \quad O_7 \quad O_8$$

Nonexperimental Designs

Correlational Design. When your goal is to understand the nature of the relationship or association between naturally occurring variables that cannot be manipulated, a correlational design may be an appropriate choice. A key difference from experimental designs is that the values of variables in a correlational design are measured, but they are not manipulated. Therefore, a correlational design cannot provide information about the direction of the causal relationship between variables; this unknown is called the *bidirectionality problem* (Does A cause B, or does B cause A?). A correlational design also cannot provide information on whether a confound is the plausible explanation of the relationship between A and B; this unknown is called the *third variable problem* because it is not clear whether a third variable C might explain the relationship between A and B. The lack of manipulation of variables, the bidirectionality problem, and the third variable problem means that a correlational design limits your ability to make causal inferences (Hatfield, Faunce, & Job, 2006).

A correlational design is not to be confused with the statistical test called correlational analysis or the correlational coefficient statistic. A researcher's lack of confidence in inferring causation from data obtained from a correlational design is due to the nature of this type of design, not the statistical test used to analyze the data (Hatfield et al., 2006). Researchers can perform correlational analysis on data collected from randomized experimental designs, such as the pretest–posttest control group design, and make causal inferences based on the results of this analysis because the data were collected with the rigor characteristic of experimental design.

Despite the potential problems of bidirectionality and third variables, correlation research can enable researchers to make predictions. If there is a correlation between two variables, then knowing the scores of one of the variables can be used to predict the scores of the other variable. Researchers compute these predictions using statistical tests. When there is one predictor variable, simple linear regression is the statistical test used to investigate the linear relation between the two variables. When there is more than one predictor variable, multiple regression is the statistical test used. The findings from correlational research often lead to investigating potential causal relations under the controls of experimental research designs.

SAMPLING

The process of selecting participants for a research study is called *sampling*. The goal in sampling is to select a sample from the population that is most representative of that population to maximize generalizability and minimize sampling error. Sampling error refers to the variability or difference between characteristics of the population and sample. A *population* refers to an entire set or collection, and a *sample* refers to a subset of the population. Strategies to select a sample can be broadly categorized as *probability sampling* or *nonprobability sampling*. Your choice of sampling strategy will determine the extent to which you can make generalizations from the findings about the sample to the target population.

Probability Sampling

In probability sampling (also called random sampling), the selection of participants is determined by chance, with each member of a population having an equal chance of being selected. As a result, you can state the probability for which each member of the population will be included in the sample. Probability sampling is advantageous because the sample is more likely to be representative of the population, which would allow you to make inferences about the population based on findings from the sample. There are three common types of probability sampling: (1) simple random sampling, (2) systematic random sampling, and (3) stratified random sampling.

Simple Random Sampling. Simple random sampling involves drawing a sample so that every member of a population has an equal chance of being selected. This type of sampling implies that you can obtain a numbered list of the population from which to draw the sample. You could flip a coin or use a table of random numbers to select members when the sample size is small. For larger sample sizes, random number generators, such as those available in some software programs, are more efficient.

Systematic Random Sampling. Systematic random sampling begins with randomly selecting a member from the population, and then, sampling proceeds with selecting every *n*th member. To begin, the population size is divided by the desired sample size to obtain *n*, and then participants are selected from every *n*th member.

Stratified Random Sampling. Stratified random sampling requires prior knowledge of a characteristic from the population that may be related to the dependent variable. This characteristic is used to form sampling strata (subgroups). Members of the population are first categorized based on their value on this characteristic. Then, a percentage of members from these strata is randomly selected based on the ratio known in the population. Nationwide surveys often use stratified random sampling where the population is stratified, for example, by geographic region. The goal of this sampling strategy is to obtain a sample that represents the population on the stratified characteristic. It is the appropriate strategy to use when it is important that the ratio of subgroups in the sample reflect the population from which they are drawn.

Nonprobability Sampling

In nonprobability sampling (also called nonrandom sampling), the probability of selection is not known. That is, each member of a population does not have an equal chance of being selected. Researchers frequently use nonprobability sampling for a variety of reasons that may preclude the feasibility of probability sampling, such as time or difficulty. In such circumstances, nonprobability sampling strategies are more feasible. There are three common types of nonprobability sampling: (1) convenience sampling, (2) purposive sampling, and (3) quota sampling.

Convenience Sampling. Convenience sampling refers to selecting a sample based on availability. For example, much psychological research has been conducted with convenience samples of undergraduate college students because of their availability. Researchers are limited, however, in their ability to speak to the representativeness of a sample to a population when it is selected through convenience sampling.

Purposive Sampling. Purposive sampling refers to selecting a sample based on a particular purpose that meets the needs of the study. This sampling method is often used when there is interest in a specific characteristic that only certain people possess, such as a specific life experience or skill. For example, Chueh and Chang (2013) used purposive sampling to select a sample of male veterans residing in a nursing home for a study that sought to investigate the effects of a therapeutic intervention on veterans' depressive symptoms. As with convenience sampling, a weakness of purposive sampling lies in the sample's potential lack of representativeness to a population.

Quota Sampling. Quota sampling is similar to stratified random sampling except that the probability of selection is unknown. In this sampling strategy, a quota or proportion for each stratum (subgroup) is determined that will proportionally represent a particular characteristic of interest in the population from which a sample is selected.

CONCLUSION

The elements of a research design in quantitative research describe the detailed plan for answering a research question and link the research question to the data. Your research question, problem, and purpose will guide you toward selecting the research design that is most appropriate for your particular study. Your selection of the appropriate design is important because the design communicates to others the plan for your study and influences your ability to draw valid conclusions.

Questions for Reflection

1. Why is operationalization an important step in the research process?

2. What considerations should you take into account when determining the appropriate research design for a quantitative study?

3. In what way does your choice of sampling strategy influence your interpretation of findings?

Key Sources

Campbell, D. T. (1957). Factors relevant to the validity of experiments in field settings. *Psychological Bulletin, 54*(4), 297–312. doi:10.1037/h0040950

Campbell, D. T., & Stanley, J. C. (1966). *Experimental and quasi-experimental designs for research.* Chicago, IL: Rand McNally.

Carifio, J., & Perla, R. J. (2007). Ten common misunderstandings, misconceptions, persistent myths, and urban legends about Likert scales and Likert response formats and their antidotes. *Journal of Social Science, 3,* 106–116. doi:10.3844/jssp.2007.106.116

Cook, T. D., & Campbell, D. T. (1979). *Quasi-experimentation: Design and analysis issues for field settings.* Skokie, IL: Rand McNally.

Crano, W. D., Brewer, M. D., & Lac, A. (2015). *Principles and methods of social research* (3rd ed.). New York, NY: Routledge.

Shadish, W. R., Cook, T. D., & Campbell, D. T. (2002). *Experimental and quasi-experimental designs for generalized causal inference.* Boston, MA: Houghton Mifflin.

References

Allan, B. A., Douglass, R. P., Duffy, R. D., & McCarty, R. J. (2016). Meaningful work as a moderator of the relation between work stress and meaning in life. *Journal of Career Assessment, 24*(3), 429–440. doi:10.1177/1069072715599357

Baron, R. M., & Kenny, D. A. (1986). The moderator–mediator variable distinction in social psychological research: Conceptual, strategic, and statistical considerations. *Journal of Personality and Social Psychology, 51*(6), 1173–1182. doi:10.1037/0022-3514.51.6.1173

Campbell, D. T., & Stanley, J. C. (1966). *Experimental and quasi-experimental designs for research.* Chicago, IL: Rand McNally.

Chueh, K., & Chang, T. (2013). Effectiveness of group reminiscence therapy for depressive symptoms in male veterans: 6-month follow-up. *International Journal of Geriatric Psychiatry, 29,* 377–383. doi:10.1002/gps.4013

Cook, T. D., & Campbell, D. T. (1979). *Quasi-experimentation: Design and analysis issues for field settings.* Skokie, IL: Rand McNally.

Frankfort-Nachmias, C., & Nachmias, D. (2008). *Research methods in the social sciences* (7th ed.). New York, NY: Worth.

González, M. J., Swanson, D. P., Lynch, M., & Williams, G. C. (2016). Testing satisfaction of basic psychological needs as a mediator of the relationship between socioeconomic status and physical and mental health. *Journal of Health Psychology, 21*(6), 972–982. doi: 10.1177/1359105314543962

Hatfield, J., Faunce, G. J., & Job, R. F. S. (2006). Avoiding confusion surrounding the phrase "correlation does not imply causation." *Teaching of Psychology, 33*(1), 49–51. doi:10.1207/s15328023top3301_9

Heidemeier, H., & Wiese, B. S. (2014). Achievement goals and autonomy: How person–context interactions predict effective functioning and well-being during a career transition. *Journal of Occupational Health Psychology, 19*(1), 18–31. doi:10.1037/a0034929

Loseke, D. R. (2013). *Methodological thinking: Basic principles of social research design.* Thousand Oaks, CA: SAGE.

Norman, G. (2010). Likert scales, levels of measurement and the "laws" of statistics. *Advances in Health Science Education, 15*(5), 625–632. doi:10.1007/s10459-010-9222-y

Schultz, P. W. (1999). Changing behavior with normative feedback interventions: A field experiment on curbside recycling. *Basic & Applied Social Psychology, 21*(1), 25–36. doi:10.1207/15324839951036533

Shadish, W. R., Cook, T. D., & Campbell, D. T. (2002). *Experimental and quasi-experimental designs for generalized causal inference.* Boston, MA: Houghton Mifflin.

Van Petegem, S., Vansteenkiste, M., Soenens, B., Beyers, W., & Aelterman, N. (2015). Examining the longitudinal association between oppositional defiance and autonomy in adolescence. *Developmental Psychology, 51*(1), 67–74. doi:10.1037/a0038374

QUANTITATIVE ANALYSIS

Justus J. Randolph

The ability to understand and analyze data is a critical competency in the information age. Quantitative analysis allows for reducing the complexity of our data-rich world into more easily understandable parts. It helps "classify, extrapolate, and predict, allowing us to build powerful models of reality" (Orlin, 2018, p. 198). Finally, it helps you become better-informed citizens, make better personal choices, and inform academic and professional decisions as scholar-practitioners. However, quantitative data analysis is intimidating for many. Misconceptions that originate in analysis can have serious consequences, including the perpetuation of discriminatory practices, belief in pseudoscience, and "poor decisions as to what products and services to purchase, which politicians to believe, and how to interpret information as to one's health, wealth, and abilities" (Huck, 2016, p. xxviii).

While no single chapter can completely help remedy quantitative intimidation or statistical misconceptions, it is my goal to lessen them by providing some prerequisite knowledge in quantitative analysis for further study. It is outside the scope of this chapter to provide instruction on how to conduct the hundreds of different statistical procedures available to date. Therefore, I provide an overview of key terms in quantitative analysis and then present a simple method for choosing a statistical analysis technique given a research question, how to choose an appropriate number of participants, and how to conduct a basic data analysis once data are collected. After reading this chapter, you should be familiar enough with the fundamentals of quantitative data analysis to plan and propose procedures for your own quantitative study.

KEY TERMS IN QUANTITATIVE ANALYSIS

The study of quantitative analysis can be difficult because groups of researchers use different terms to mean the same concept and the same terms to mean different concepts. So I begin this chapter with a set of definitions and explanations that hopefully will clarify some of the terminology. Specifically, I discuss three sets of terms that confused me when I began to study quantitative research: (1) descriptive and inferential statistics, (2) variable types, and (3) variable roles.

Descriptive and Inferential Statistics

The goal of descriptive statistics is to summarize a set of data. Four ways to summarize data are by their (1) frequency (i.e., how many cases are in each category), (2) central tendency (i.e., which responses are the most common or the best measure of the center), (3) variation (i.e., how the responses spread out around the center), and (4) position (i.e., how one score relates to the set of scores, e.g., percentile rank).

The goal of an inferential analysis is to draw a conclusion (inference) about a large group, or *population*, based on data from a subset of that large group, known as a *sample*. There are many different inferential analyses that you will study in courses dedicated to statistics. It is best practice to conduct an exploratory analysis with descriptive statistics prior to conducting an inferential analysis. Such exploratory analysis will help you decide if the inferential results are appropriate, accurate, and meaningful.

Variable Types

Variables are classified by the measurement levels of nominal, ordinal, interval, and ratio. *Categorical* refers to variables measured at the nominal level, variables that have no inherent order (e.g., U.S. states—Minnesota, Massachusetts, Utah, etc.), to follow the naming conventions found in many statistical programs and textbooks. *Dichotomous* variables are categorical variables having only two categories (e.g., yes or no). *Ordinal* refers to variables that have an inherent order but not an equal distance between units (e.g., choices on a scale that assess the level of satisfaction with a product). Furthermore, I define *continuous* variables as those measured at either the interval (characterized by levels having the same distance between them, e.g., degrees on the Fahrenheit scale) or the ratio (those having the same characteristic as interval variables with the caveat that there is an absolute zero, e.g., height in meters) level. Thus, by *variable type*, I mean whether a variable is categorical, ordinal, or continuous. Being able to identify variables by their type is an essential first step in deciding which statistical analysis technique to use later.

Variable Roles

There are two major classifications of quantitative research: experimental and correlational. Experimental research seeks to determine cause and effect. Note that in some texts, *experimentation* exclusively refers to manipulation of a treatment, such as randomization of people to study conditions (e.g., treatment vs. control). Here, I use a broader definition to mean any research that entails causal inference. The variable that is anticipated to be the cause is called the *independent* variable, and the variable that is anticipated to be the effect is called the *dependent* variable. Experimental researchers often also use *control variables* (or *covariates*) to account for other factors besides the independent variable that may influence the dependent variable. So, in experimental research, the variable roles can be referred to as *independent*, *dependent*, or *control*. Here is an example of a purpose statement for an experimental study: *The purpose of this study is to compare customer satisfaction rates* (dependent variable) *between customers who talk immediately to a live customer service representative and those who are initially routed through an automated tree* (independent variable), *controlling for the number of prior calls to the service* (control variable).

In contrast, correlational research does not establish cause and effect but rather reveals the associations between existing variables. Correlational researchers strive to predict an outcome from a set of one or more predictors; they use the terms *predictor* and *outcome* to specify variable roles. Here is an example purpose statement for a correlational study: *The purpose of this study is to determine the relationship between hours of sleep* (predictor) *and grade point average* (outcome) *for senior high school students.*

CHOOSING AN APPROPRIATE STATISTICAL ANALYSIS

The first step is extracting information about each variable from the research question. The second step is matching that variable information with the appropriate statistical analysis. Once you know what type of statistical analysis you will use, you can use additional resources to find out more about that type of analysis and under what circumstances your data and the planned analysis will be a good match.

Extracting Variable Information From the Research Question

From experience, I can usually quickly tell whether a research project is on track from the research question alone. A good quantitative research question should have enough information so that one can infer the type of research that will be conducted (e.g., experimental or correlational) and the variable types and roles. It is also common to include information on the participants and the settings in a research question. Chapter 20 provides more detailed information on how to write a good research question.

This example research question for a posttest-only with control group design will be used throughout the chapter:

> *To what degree is there a difference in the mathematics posttest scores between students in a rural high school who receive a traditional teaching method and those who receive an experimental teaching method?*

From this research question, you can infer much about the study itself. From the term *experimental*, you know that this is an experimental or quasi-experimental study. There is only one posttest variable, a control group, and no pretest. This is what Shadish, Cook, and Campbell (2002) call a *posttest-only with control group* design. The term *difference* indicates that this a study testing the null hypothesis of no differences between the experimental and control groups (see Chapter 20 for a discussion of null hypothesis testing).

You can infer certain information about variable role and type from the research question. In terms of variable roles, type of teaching method is the independent variable, and posttest score is the dependent variable. In terms of variable types, the independent variable is a categorical variable with two categories (experimental and control). Since the categorical variable has only two categories, it is a dichotomous variable. The dependent variable (scores on a mathematics test) is a continuous variable. There are no control variables.

The characteristics of the variables described in the example research question provide the information needed to choose an inferential statistical analysis. Table 5.1 is a tool you can use to map information about the variables in your research question. Based on your research question, if you cannot complete any relevant cell in such a table, then your research question might need revision. With an adequately detailed quantitative research question, you can complete the table and then determine the correct analysis using the method explained in the following section. Table 5.1 has been completed for our example research question.

TABLE 5.1 ● MATRIX FOR EXTRACTING VARIABLE CHARACTERISTICS

Variable Role	Variable Description	Variable Type	If Categorical, No. of Categories
For experimental studies			
Independent variable(s)	Teaching method	Categorical	Two
Dependent variable(s)	Posttest score	Continuous	
Control variable(s)			
For correlational studies			
Predictor variable(s)			
Outcome variable(s)			

Identifying the Type of Statistical Analysis From the Variable Properties

Once you have extracted the properties of the variables from your research question, you can use a table such as Table 5.2 to choose the appropriate inferential analysis. In the example research question, there is one dichotomous independent and one continuous dependent variable, so Table 5.2 shows us that an independent samples t test is the appropriate analysis. You can learn more about the analyses shown in Table 5.2, as well as other inferential analyses and their underlying assumptions, in statistical texts such as Field (2018), Mertler and Vannatta (2016), Pallant (2013), Micceri (1989), and Wilcox (2012). The point here is to understand how to choose the initial inferential analysis from a research question.

Once you have a solid research question and know which statistical analysis to apply to the data, your next step is to choose an appropriate number of study participants.

TABLE 5.2 ● CHOOSING A STATISTICAL ANALYSIS FROM THE PROPERTIES OF THE VARIABLES IN THE RESEARCH QUESTION		
Independent/Predictor Variable	**Dependent/Outcome Variable**	**Inferential Statistical Analysis**
One dichotomous variable	One continuous variable	Independent samples *t* test
Two continuous variables (when comparing the means between two variables)		Dependent samples *t* test
One categorical variable with three or more categories	One continuous variable	Analysis of variance
Two continuous variables (when examining the degree of association between two variables)		Bivariate correlation/simple regression
Two or more variables of any type	One continuous variable	Multiple linear regression/ analysis of covariance
Two categorical variables		Chi-square analysis
Two or more variables of any type	One dichotomous variable	Binary logistic regression
Two or more variables of any type	Two or more variables of any type	Multivariate analysis of variance/multivariate analysis of covariance
Three or more continuous variables		Repeated measures

Note: The analyses listed above are parametric analyses that have a strict set of assumptions that need to be met. If those assumptions are not met, there are many robust, nonparametric alternate analyses that one can use (Wilcox, 2012).

CHOOSING THE NUMBER OF PARTICIPANTS

In this section, I introduce some terms you will encounter in relation to sample size. Following this is a simple method from Field (2018) for finding the minimum number of participants needed for a basic statistical analysis.

Terms Related to Sample Size

Power. In the statistical sense, the term *power* is the probability of *correctly* concluding that a result *was not* due to chance (i.e., a true, positive conclusion). The greater the power, the lower the probability of making a Type II error—that is, incorrectly concluding that a result was due to chance (i.e., a false, negative conclusion). How high should a study's power be? More power is always better, but a common convention is that a study should be powered at least to .80. In other words, the probability of a making a Type II error should be 20% or less. Greater power requires greater sample sizes.

Alpha. In contrast, alpha (α) is the probability of *incorrectly* concluding that a result *was not* due to chance, which is called a Type I error (i.e., a false, positive conclusion). A common convention is that a study should adhere to an overall alpha value of .05, meaning that the probability of a making a Type I error should be 5% or less. Lower alpha values require larger sample sizes.

Effect Size. Effect size quantifies the magnitude, or strength, of a result as small, medium, or large between groups or between variables. If you are wondering whether you should plan for a small, medium, or large effect size, the best approach is to review the effect sizes from previous research on your topic. The smaller the effect size, the larger the sample needs to be in order to detect it. See Middlemiss Maher, Markey, and Ebert-May (2013) for a down-to-earth discussion of effect sizes and Deng (2005) for information on effect size and sample size conventions often used in dissertation research.

Power, alpha, and effect size are not the only important parameters for determining an appropriate sample size, however. The next section provides a description of an easy method for estimating an appropriate sample size for a basic study when taking into account the number of predictors being examined.

Field's Method for Determining Sample Size

Field (2018) provides a simple method for determining sample size when there is one continuous dependent/outcome variable. Other often-cited resources such as Cohen (2008), Dattalo (2008), and Faul, Erdfelder, Lang, and Buchner (2007) provide further information on how to conduct sample size analyses for complex research designs. Field's method requires you to know two things: (a) how many independent/predictor variables there are in the study and (b) the expected strength of the effect size you want to be able to detect (i.e., small, medium, or large). The more independent/predictor variables you use and the smaller the effect size you want to be able to detect, the greater is the sample size you will need.

TABLE 5.3 ● RECOMMENDED SAMPLE SIZES FOR SMALL, MEDIUM, AND LARGE EFFECTS GIVEN THE NUMBER OF INDEPENDENT/PREDICTOR VARIABLES

Total No. of Independent/ Predictor Variables	No. of Participants		
	Small Effect Size	Medium Effect Size	Large Effect Size
1	387	55	25
2	476	68	31
3	539	77	36
4	590	85	40
5	635	92	43
6	667	98	46

Source: Adapted from Figure 9.9 of Field (2018).

Note: The assumptions for using this table are as follows: (a) there is one continuous outcome variable, (b) power is .80, (c) Type 1 error probability is .05, and (d) there is one tested predictor.

You can use Table 5.3 to find the minimum number of participants needed to ensure that there is sufficient power to detect a small, medium, or large effect size. Conventions for small, medium, and large standardized mean difference effect sizes in the social sciences are .20, .50, and .80, respectively (Cohen, 2008). For the example research question, there is one independent variable, so 387, 55, or 25 participants would be needed to detect a small, medium, or large effect, respectively. For more sophisticated sample size analyses, there are a variety of computer programs for determining sample size to choose from (see Dattalo, 2009).

So far, you have acquired information on analyzing the variable properties from a given research question, identifying the appropriate inferential analysis, and determining the number of participants based on the desired effect size. Next, the procedures involved in analyzing data once they have been collected are described. That process begins with preparing the data for analysis.

PREPARING DATA FOR ANALYSIS

Once data are collected, there is preparation work required before statistical analysis can begin. This includes setting up a data file and cleaning the data to find any mistakes. There are several user-friendly books on data management and preparing data for analysis that can give you some time-saving suggestions, such as Field (2018), Mertler and Vannatta (2016), and Pallant (2013).

Creating a Data File

A spreadsheet is created in such a way that variables are arranged in columns and the data for each case are arranged in rows. The first row of the spreadsheet usually contains short variable labels. Figure 5.1 is an example of what a spreadsheet for our example research question might look like (using SPSS software)—with 10 cases, 5 of which received the control teaching method (hereafter the *control*

FIGURE 5.1 ● TEN-CASE EXAMPLE DATA SET

✎ case.id	👥 group	✎ possttest
1.00	Control Group	82.05
2.00	Control Group	64.47
3.00	Control Group	87.40
4.00	Control Group	62.95
5.00	Control Group	76.09
6.00	Experimental Group	95.21
7.00	Experimental Group	96.55
8.00	Experimental Group	92.13
9.00	Experimental Group	86.39
10.00	Experimental Group	71.21

group) and 5 that received the experimental teaching method (hereafter *the experimental group*).

From left to right in Figure 5.1, the variable names are displayed in the first row. They are *case.id*, *group*, and *posttest*. The case.id variable provides a unique identifier for each case, which is very helpful if you ever need to sort your data. The group variable indicates whether the participant was in the experimental group or the control group. The posttest variable contains the mathematics posttest score for each case. For example, we see that Case 1 was a participant in the control group and had a score of 82.05.

Cleaning Data

When manually inputting data into a spreadsheet, there are likely to be data entry mistakes. For example, it is very easy to add extra digits when typing (e.g., a 9 becomes a 90); this affects the validity of your statistical conclusions. So, prior to analysis, clean the data by carefully checking for data entry mistakes. Double entry, in which two people independently enter data, is often used to counter this problem. Sometimes, examining descriptive statistics and visualizing your data is the only way to identify small errors in a large data set.

You need to evaluate the extent of missing data. It is important to examine whether the missing data are random or systematic. If data are missing at random, you would expect about a similar number of data points to be missing from particular groups of participants (e.g., older and younger people might tend to skip survey items in the same way). If the data are missing systematically, you will notice that the missing data would be disproportionally greater in one group than in another (e.g., older people might tend to skip responses to specific questions more than younger people). Graham (2009) and Meyers, Gamst, and Guarino (2016) provide strategies for dealing with missing data, such as simply excluding cases with missing data, replacing missing data with a mean, or using advanced techniques such as multiple imputation of missing data.

CALCULATING DESCRIPTIVE STATISTICS

Descriptive statistics reduce the complexity of your data set by summarizing them into two sets of statistics: (1) central tendency (i.e., a measure of the center) and (2) variation (i.e., a measure of how your data are spread around the center). They provide an important snapshot of the sample and can also provide some preliminary information on the generalizability of the sample. Here are some measures of central tendency for the mathematics posttest variable in the example study:

Mean = 81.44.

Median = 84.22.

Mode: There is no mode; none of the cases have the same posttest score.

The standard deviation is the most common measure of central tendency; the range is also frequently used. Here are the measures of variation for the mathematics posttest variable in our example study:

Standard deviation = 12.27.

Minimum = 62.95.

Maximum = 96.55.

VISUALIZING THE DATA

Displaying data visually in figures, such as bar graphs, histograms, line graphs, plots, and pie charts, is an essential step in any statistical analysis. My best single piece of advice is to use figures to tell most of the story and let the sophisticated statistics be the footnotes for those who are interested in the details. As Wilkinson and the Taskforce on Statistical Inference (1999) noted, "Graphics broadcast, statistics narrowcast" (p. 597). For example, Figure 5.2 is a dot plot from the example data. Each dot is a participant's posttest score. From this figure alone, you can start to see that the posttest scores in the experimental group differed from the posttest scores in the control group. Nicol (2010), Nicol and Pexman (2010), McCandless (2010, 2012), Rosling (2006), Tufte (1990, 1997, 2001, 2006), and Tukey (1977) provide advice and examples on how to create compelling evidence and explanations through data visualization. There are many good programs to choose from for data visualization and analysis, such as IBM SPSS (which was used for this chapter), SAS, Stata, and JMP. R. Silver (2015) provides a review of statistical software.

FIGURE 5.2 ● DOT PLOT OF POSTTEST SCORES FOR PARTICIPANTS IN THE CONTROL GROUP AND EXPERIMENTAL GROUP

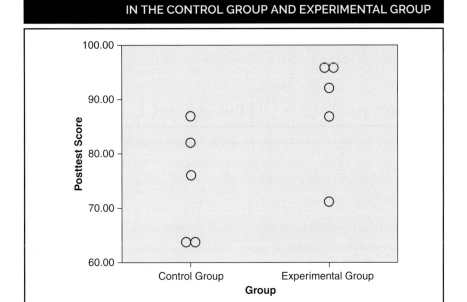

Variable	Group	Group Statistics			
		N	Mean	Standard Deviation	Standard Error of the Mean
Posttest score	Control	5	74.59	10.72	4.80
	Experimental	5	88.30	10.32	4.62

TABLE 5.4 ● DESCRIPTIVE STATISTICS FOR THE CONTROL AND EXPERIMENTAL GROUPS

CONDUCTING THE INFERENTIAL ANALYSIS

Once you have conducted a descriptive analysis and visualized your data, it is typical to perform an inferential analysis. The variable mapping in Table 5.1 indicated that we should use an independent samples *t* test. The output from an independent samples *t* test typically includes the descriptive statistics for each group (Table 5.4) and the results of the *t* test (Table 5.5). As shown in Table 5.4, the mean and standard deviation for the control group were 74.59 and 10.72, respectively; the mean and standard deviation for the experimental group were 88.30 and 10.32, respectively. Table 5.5 shows that the mean difference between the two groups was 13.71—indicating that the mean of the experimental group was 13.71 points higher than the mean of the control group. Also provided is a 95% confidence interval for the mean difference, which spans from –1.64 to 29.06. Remember that the purpose of inferential statistics is to make an inference from a sample to a population. The practical interpretation of the confidence interval is that it is a plausible range of values for the mean difference in the population from which our sample was drawn (Cumming & Finch, 2005). In other words, while the mean difference for our sample was 13.71, the mean difference in the population is likely to be between –1.64 and 29.06. When the confidence interval contains zero, it corresponds to a difference that is not statistically significant. However, a result's statistical significance may be unrelated to its practical significance—that is, its usefulness in the real world (Kirk, 1996).

DRAWING AND STATING CONCLUSIONS

The results of statistical analysis help answer the research question. First, review the research question: *To what degree is there a difference in the mathematics posttest scores between students in a rural high school who receive a traditional teaching method and students who receive an experimental teaching method?*

Looking at Table 5.5, the results show that the posttest mean difference was 13.71 points in favor of the experimental group. The 95% confidence interval tells us that, given chance, the plausible range of the mean difference in the population is from –1.64 to 29.06, which is quite large. The .073 in the "Significance" column (i.e., the *p* value) indicates that there was a 7.3% probability of getting a mean difference of 13.71 or less, just by chance. In other words, there was no statistically significant

TABLE 5.5 ● RESULTS OF AN INDEPENDENT SAMPLES *T* TEST FOR THE EXAMPLE DATA

					95% Confidence Interval of the Difference	
t	df (Degrees of Freedom)	Significance (Two Tailed)	Mean Difference	Standard Error of the Difference	Lower	Upper
2.06	8	.073	13.71	6.66	–1.64	29.06

t Test for Equality of Means

difference between the groups. There are many discipline-specific guidelines for drawing and stating conclusions from a quantitative analysis (e.g., American Psychological Association, 2010; Applebaum et al., 2018; Cooper, 2010; Nicol, 2010; Nicol & Pexman, 2010). Generally, you communicate them in a table, as in Table 5.5, and by stating the conclusion in a sentence, such as the following:

Participants who received the experimental teaching method scored on average 13.71 points higher on the posttest than participants who received the traditional teaching method, 95 CI [–1.64, 29.06]. The difference was not statistically significant, t(8) = 2.06, p = .07.

CONCLUSION

Figure 5.3 summarizes the steps in quantitative analysis. Starting with the research question, determine which statistical analysis is appropriate. From there, compute

FIGURE 5.3 ● SUMMARY OF THE QUANTITATIVE DATA ANALYSIS PROCESS

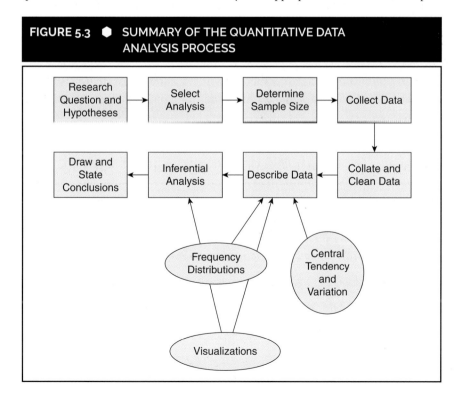

the required sample size, which will inform the scope of your data collection process. After (or as) you collect data, clean the data to prepare for descriptive analysis that includes measures of central tendency and variability along with charts as appropriate for visualization. Once you have sufficiently described and visualized the data, the next step is inferential analysis. Finally, you use the data to answer your research question by drawing and stating conclusions.

Do not worry if some of the discussion above is confusing. The point here is to provide an example of the process of analyzing data using a software program and drawing conclusions from the results. The details of data analysis will become much clearer as you take statistics classes and conduct your own study.

Reflection Questions

Think about a study you might conduct based on your research interests.

1. Based on the research question guiding your study, what are the key variables in your study, and what are their characteristics? Create a table similar to Table 5.1 using your variables.

2. Based on the characteristics of the variables, what statistical analysis is most appropriate? Refer to Table 5.2.

3. Based on the number of independent/predictor variables, what number of participants would be appropriate to identify a small, a medium, and a large effect? Refer to Table 5.3.

4. What steps would you likely go through to carry out the analysis?

5. How would you draw and state conclusions for your study?

Key Resources

These resources are sorted from the least to the most advanced.

Salkind, N. J. (2016). *Statistics for people who (think they) hate statistics* (6th ed.). Thousand Oaks, CA: SAGE.

Field, A. (2018). *Discovering statistics using SPSS* (5th ed.). Thousand Oaks, CA: SAGE.

Pallant, J. (2013). *SPSS survival manual* (5th ed.). New York, NY: McGraw-Hill.

Tabachnik, B. G., & Fidell, L. S. (2007). *Using multivariate statistics*. Boston, MA: Pearson.

Mertler, C. A., & Vannatta, R. A. (2016). *Advanced and multivariate statistical methods* (5th ed.). Glendale, CA: Pryczak.

McCormick, K., & Salcedo, J. (2017). *SPSS statistics for data analysis and visualization*. Indianapolis, IN: Wiley.

References

American Psychological Association. (2010). *Publication manual of the American Psychological Association* (6th ed.). Washington, DC: Author.

Applebaum, M., Cooper, H., Kline, R. B., Mayon-Wilson, E., Nezu, A. M., & Rao, S. M. (2018). Journal article reporting standards for quantitative research in psychology: The APA Publication and Communications Board Task Force Report. *American Psychologist, 73*, 3–25. doi:10.1037/ampoooo191

Cohen, J. (2008). *Statistical power analysis for the behavioral* sciences (2nd ed.). New York, NY: Taylor & Francis.

Cooper, H. (2010). *Reporting research in psychology: How to meet journal article reporting standards* (6th ed.). Washington, DC: American Psychological Association.

Cumming, G., & Finch, S. (2005). Inference by eye: Confidence intervals and how to read pictures of data. *American Psychologist, 60*(2), 170–180. doi:10.1037/0003-066X.60.2.170

Dattalo, P. (2008). *Determining sample size: Balancing power, precision, and practicality.* New York, NY: Oxford University Press.

Dattalo, P. (2009). A review of software for sample size determination. *Evaluation & the Health Professions, 32*(3), 229–248. doi:10.1177/0163278709338556

Deng, H. (2005). Does it matter if non-powerful significance tests are used in dissertation research? *Practical Assessment Research & Evaluation, 10*(16). Retrieved from https://pareonline.net/getvn.asp?v=10&n=16

Faul, F., Erdfelder, E., Lang, A.-G., & Buchner, A. (2007). GPower 3: A flexible statistical power analysis program for the social, behavioral, and biomedical sciences. *Behavior Research Methods, 39*(2), 175–191. doi:10.3758/BF03193146

Field, A. (2018). *Discovering statistics using SPSS* (5th ed.). Thousand Oaks, CA: SAGE.

Graham, J. W. (2009). Missing data analysis: Making it work in the real world. *Annual Review of Psychology, 60*, 549–576. doi:10.1146/annurev.psych.58.110405.085530

Huck, S. W. (2016). *Statistical misconceptions* (Classic ed.). New York, NY: Routledge.

Kirk, R. E. (1996). Practical significance: A concept whose time has come. *Psychological and Educational Measurement, 56*(5), 746–759. doi:10.1177/0013164496056005002

McCandless, D. (2010, July). *David McCandless: The beauty of data visualization* [Video file]. Retrieved from https://www.ted.com/talks/david_mccandless_the_beauty_of_data_visualization

McCandless, D. (2012). *The visual miscellaneum: A colorful guide to the world's most consequential data.* New York, NY: HarperCollins.

Mertler, C. A., & Vannatta, R. A. (2016). *Advanced and multivariate statistical methods* (5th ed.). Glendale, CA: Pryczak.

Meyers, L. S., Gamst, G. C., & Guarino, A. J. (2016). *Applied multivariate research: Design and interpretation* (3rd ed.). Thousands Oaks, CA: SAGE.

Micceri, T. (1989). The unicorn, the normal curve, and other improbable creatures. *Psychological Bulletin, 105*(1), 156–166. doi:10.1037/0033-2909.105.1.156

Middlemiss Maher, J., Markey, J. C., & Ebert-May, D. (2013). The other half of the story: Effect size analysis in quantitative research. *CBE-Life Sciences Education, 12,* 345–351. doi:10.1187/cbe.13-04-0082

Nicol, A. A. M. (2010). *Presenting your findings: A practical guide to creating tables* (6th ed.). Washington, DC: American Psychological Association.

Nicol, A. A. M., & Pexman, P. M. (2010). *Displaying your findings: A practical guide for creating figures, posters, and presentations* (6th ed.). Washington, DC: American Psychological Association.

Orlin, B. (2018). *Math with bad drawings: Illuminating the ideas that shape our reality*. New York, NY: Black Dog & Levanthal.

Pallant, J. (2013). *SPSS survival manual* (5th ed.). New York, NY: McGraw-Hill.

Rosling, H. (2006, February). *Hans Rosling: The best stats you've ever seen* [Video file]. Retrieved from https://www.ted.com/talks/hans_rosling_shows_the_best_stats_you_ve_ever_seen

Shadish, W. R., Cook, T. D., & Campbell, D. T. (2002). *Experimental and quasi-experimental designs for generalized causal inference*. Boston, MA: Houghton Mifflin.

Silver, C. N. (2015). Software for statistical analyses. In N. Balakrishnan, T. Colton, B. Everitt, W. Piegorsch, F. Ruggeri, & J. L. Teugels (Eds.), *Wiley StatsRef: Statistics reference online*. New York, NY: Wiley. doi:10.1002/9781118445112.stat06182.pub2

Tufte, E. R. (1990). *Envisioning information*. Cheshire, CT: Graphics Press.

Tufte, E. R. (1997). *Visual explanations: Images and quantities, evidence and narrative*. Cheshire, CT: Graphics Press.

Tufte, E. R. (2001). *The visual display of quantitative information* (2nd ed.). Cheshire, CT: Graphics Press.

Tufte, E. R. (2006). *Beautiful evidence*. Cheshire, CT: Graphics Press.

Tukey, J. W. (1977). *Exploratory data analysis*. New York, NY: Pearson.

Wilcox, R. (2012). *Introduction to robust estimation and hypothesis testing* (3rd ed.). Boston, MA: Elsevier.

Wilkinson, L., & Taskforce on Statistical Inference. (1999). Statistical methods in psychology journals: Guidelines and explanations. *American Psychologist, 54*(8), 594–604. doi:10.1037/0003-066X.54.8.594

QUALITATIVE
RESEARCH DESIGNS

Linda M. Crawford

This chapter introduces qualitative research. Qualitative research often focuses on generating theory, and it is more commonly used at the initial stages of understanding a phenomenon. As an overview, this chapter presents definitions and purposes of qualitative research, descriptions of predominant qualitative research designs along with how to select a qualitative design, and discussion of key concepts for qualitative research, including sampling logic, trustworthiness, and the researcher's role. The information in this chapter will provide you with baseline understanding of qualitative research. Our hope is that you use this information as a foundation for reading, studying, and practicing qualitative research.

DEFINITION AND PURPOSE
OF QUALITATIVE RESEARCH

Experts provide varying definitions of qualitative research. Several of the most prominent definitions follow. Denzin and Lincoln (2018) defined *qualitative research* in terms of a *situated activity*.

> *Qualitative research* is a situated activity that locates the observer in the world. Qualitative research consists of a set of interpretive, material practices that make the world visible. These practices transform the world. They turn the world into a series of representations, including field notes, interviews, conversations, photographs, recordings, and memos to the self. At this level, qualitative research involves an interpretive, naturalistic approach to the world. This means that qualitative researchers study things in their natural settings, attempting to make sense of, or interpret, phenomena in terms of the meanings people bring to them. (p. 10)

Creswell (2013) extended Denzin and Lincoln's (2018) definition by placing more emphasis on the process of qualitative research.

> Qualitative research begins with assumptions and the use of interpretive/theoretical frameworks that inform the study of research problems addressing the meaning individuals or groups ascribe to a social or human problem. To study this problem, qualitative researchers use an emerging qualitative approach to inquiry, the collection of data in a natural setting

sensitive to the people and places under study, and data analysis that is both inductive and deductive and establishes patterns or themes. The final written report or presentation includes the voices of participants, the reflexivity of the researcher, a complex description and interpretation of the problem, and its contribution to the literature or a call for change. (p. 44)

Merriam and Tisdell (2016) offered a simplified definition of *qualitative research:* "Basically, qualitative researchers are interested in *understanding meaning people have constructed,* that is, how people make sense of their world and the experiences they have in the world" (p. 15).

In contrast to Merriam and Tisdell (2016), Schwandt (2015) offered a complex definition of *qualitative inquiry.*

> *Qualitative* is a not-so-descriptive adjective attached to the varieties of social inquiry that have their intellectual roots in *hermeneutics, phenomenological sociology,* and the *Verstehen* tradition. Many scholars use the phrase *qualitative inquiry* as a blanket designation for all forms of social inquiry that rely primarily on qualitative data (i.e., data in the form of words). . . . To call a research activity qualitative inquiry may broadly mean that it aims at understanding the *meaning* of *human action.* . . . Because the adjective is used in so many different ways, it does not clearly signal a particular meaning or denote a specific set of characteristics for qualitative research. . . . Broadly speaking, qualitative methods are procedures including unstructured, open-ended interviews and participant observation that generate qualitative data . . . . One, however, could easily generate qualitative data via an open-ended interview, transform those data into numbers, and analyze them by means of nonparametric statistics. Hence, what precisely comprises a so-called qualitative method is not all that clear. (pp. 256–257)

In essence, Schwandt (2015) spotlighted vagueness and breadth in the definition of qualitative research, Merriam and Tisdell (2016) centered on understanding the world, Creswell (2013) focused on the process of conducting qualitative research, and Denzin and Lincoln (2018) emphasized the possibility that qualitative research can transform the world. What sense, then, can the student make of qualitative research, and why do it?

There are some commonalities that can be derived from the various definitions of qualitative research:

1. Occurs in natural rather than controlled settings

2. Collects data as words, pictures, or other kinds of aural, visual, or textual artifacts

3. Incorporates participants' voice into the presentation of findings

4. Describes some phenomenon as experienced by individuals or groups

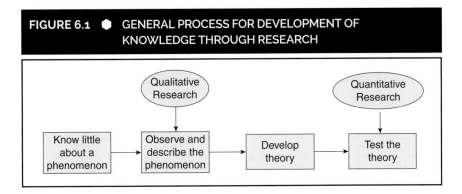

FIGURE 6.1 ● GENERAL PROCESS FOR DEVELOPMENT OF KNOWLEDGE THROUGH RESEARCH

The last point above leads us to the purpose of qualitative research. The primary purpose of qualitative research is to describe phenomena that occur in the world. By describing what is occurring, we develop complex understandings that can be used to build theories, or explanations, for how phenomena work in the world. The theories that are developed using qualitative research can then be tested using quantitative research. Figure 6.1 displays this general process.

Qualitative research tends to be exploratory, with the function of gaining understanding of complex phenomena through observation and description. Synthesizing the characteristics of qualitative research and its purpose, I define *qualitative research* as follows:

> *Qualitative research is an exploratory investigation of a complex social phenomenon conducted in a natural setting through observation, description, and thematic analysis of participants' behaviors and perspectives for the purpose of explaining and/or understanding the phenomenon.*

Qualitative research, similar to quantitative research, is structured according to a selected research design. I now review qualitative research designs and how to select an appropriate design for a qualitative study.

QUALITATIVE RESEARCH DESIGN AND DESIGN SELECTION

A research study has an overall structure. That structure carries certain conventions that have been accepted over time by researchers to establish rigor. Qualitative researchers use various terms to designate the structure of qualitative research, such as *genre* (Marshall & Rossman, 2016), *approach* (Creswell, 2013; Creswell & Creswell, 2018), *strategy* (Robson & McCartan, 2016), and *tradition* (Creswell, 1998). In this chapter, the term *design* will be used to indicate the overall structure of a qualitative research study.

Qualitative Research Designs and Purposes

All qualitative research is descriptive, but different qualitative designs accomplish description in different ways (Glesne, 2016). There are five main categories commonly presented in qualitative research texts: (1) case study, (2) ethnography, (3) phenomenology, (4) narrative, and (5) grounded theory (Creswell & Poth, 2018; Marshall & Rossman, 2016; Robson & McCartan, 2016). These five designs do not encompass all possible qualitative designs, but they cover the kinds of research scholar-practitioners are likely to perform. Therefore, this discussion focuses on these five designs in terms of purpose, unit of analysis, and predominant data collection tools. You are already familiar with the terms *purpose* and *data collection*. A new term, *unit of analysis*, refers to the entity around which analysis is organized (Trochim, 2006b). Understanding the unit of analysis for each qualitative research design is one key to selecting the appropriate design for your study.

Case Study.   The purpose of a qualitative case study is to describe the interactions of a bounded unit in relation to some phenomenon (Merriam & Tisdell, 2016). There are different schools of thought on what should be emphasized in a case study. Some argue that the process is the most distinct feature of a case study (Yin, 2018); others argue that the bounded unit is the identifying feature of a case study (Merriam & Tisdell, 2016). I agree with Merriam and Tisdell that the bounded unit must be identified to qualify something as a "case."

A bounded unit is

> a single entity, a unit around which there are boundaries. You can "fence in" what you are going to study. The case then, could be a single person . . . , a program, a group, an institution, a community or a specific policy. (Merriam & Tisdell, 2016, p. 38)

For example, if a study intends to describe how information gathered from patients during hospital admission was processed and used by the hospital for patient care, the study would have a bounded unit—hospital. There could be one case (i.e., one hospital) or several cases (i.e., several hospitals). If, on the other hand, a study intends to describe how patients experience the admission process, regardless of hospital or regardless of how the hospital uses the admission information, then there is no bounded unit; the focus is on individual experience. In the first instance, the unit of analysis is the hospital, allowing for a case study; in the second instance, the unit of analysis is the individual patient, likely a phenomenological study.

Case studies are differentiated from some of the other qualitative designs by the data collected. Case studies seek to paint a comprehensive picture of a bounded unit around some phenomenon, such as a picture of how one higher education institution responds to allegations of sexual harassment. To do that, multiple data sources are explored, including sources such as interviews, observations, meeting agendas and minutes, policies, reports, and artifacts. A case study, then, is much like a jigsaw puzzle. It requires putting together various pieces to form a composite picture of what is occurring in the bounded unit. Case study is quite close to ethnography, but there are also distinctions between case study and ethnography (Merriam & Tisdell, 2016).

Ethnography. Although both case study and ethnography investigate a bounded unit, ethnography differs from case study in that it requires long-term immersion in a cultural group to collect data. Ethnographic research is rooted in anthropology and sociology and has the purpose of interpreting the functioning of a cultural group in relation to some phenomenon. Although case study entails considering any bounded unit as eligible for study, ethnography insists on a culture-sharing group that has been intact long enough to have discernable patterns of ideas, beliefs, values, behaviors, and rituals (Creswell & Poth, 2018). What constitutes a cultural group is not entirely clear, however. Schwandt (2015) reported that more than 300 definitions have been published for the term *culture.* Schwandt suggested that *culture,* for ethnographic research, may be defined "in terms of meaning, symbolism, language, and the discourse drawing respectively on phenomenology, cultural anthropology, structuralism, semiotics, *cultural studies,* and critical theory" (p. 55). Merriam and Tisdell (2016) were more specific in defining *culture* as "the beliefs, values, and attitudes that structure the behavior patterns of a specific group of people" (p. 29).

Responding to Merriam and Tisdell (2016), then, a cultural group, the unit of analysis for an ethnographic study, would have a common and discernible set of beliefs, values, and attitudes. For example, an ethnographer might study the communication patterns in a rural community, the power structure within teenage gangs, or gender roles within a certain religious denomination. Because cultural groups are bounded units, similar to case study, you may be wondering how case study and ethnography differ. The distinction lies predominantly in the manner of data collection.

A defining characteristic of ethnography, different from case study, is that the researcher lives within and participates in the culture for a period of time, sometimes for several years, rather than just observing it from collected information, as in a case study (Suryani, 2008). The ethnographic researcher becomes immersed in the culture. Data sources are not so different from case study data sources (interviews, observations, meeting agendas and minutes, policies, reports, and other artifacts), but ethnographies have the added component of intense fieldwork diaries that serve as records of observations made on-site. Ethnography requires fieldwork. For example, an ethnographic study of communication patterns in a rural community would require involvement in the community for a period of time, noting, for example, who goes to the coffee shop and who does not go to the coffee shop and what are the topics of conversation in the coffee shop. The researcher would likely also participate in the conversations. Ethnographies and case studies, however, do not explore individual experiences regarding a phenomenon. That is accomplished using phenomenological studies.

Phenomenology. Phenomenological studies seek to understand the experiences of a set of individuals who share a common experience. The purpose, then, of a phenomenological study is to describe the lived experiences of individuals in relation to an identified phenomenon (Creswell & Poth, 2018).

The unit of analysis for phenomenology is some set of individuals that shares a common characteristic related to the phenomenon of study. For example, for a study of principals' experience of the applicability of their training programs to the real-life work of educational leadership, the researcher would interview a number of principals from multiple locations, rather than in a bounded unit (case study) or cultural group (ethnography). Based on the interviews, the researcher would derive themes that incorporate the essence of shared experiences of the group. In other words, the researcher would collect individual experiences and then discern across those individual experiences a shared, lived experience (Marshall & Rossman, 2016).

The primary data collection tool for phenomenology is in-depth individual interviews, although strategies such as observations and document analyses have also been used (Creswell & Poth, 2018; Moustakas, 1994). The individual interviews are analyzed and brought together into a description of shared experiences. If the desired focus is on individual rather than shared experience, narrative analysis is the optimal choice.

Narrative. The purpose of narrative research is to tell stories, "first person accounts of experience told in story form having a beginning, middle, and end. Other terms for these stories of experience are biography, life history, oral history, autoethnography, and autobiography" (Merriam & Tisdell, 2016, p. 34). Narrative research does not seek to derive a shared meaning from individual experiences, as does phenomenology, but seeks to understand the meaning of individual experiences in relation to a phenomenon. Marshall and Rossman (2016) noted that narrative research has been criticized as overly focused on the individual rather than on the collective experience of a phenomenon, but narrative research has indeed resulted in significant contribution to knowledge.

A fine example of the contributory nature of narrative research is that done by Paige (2007). Paige collected life stories from 13 formative technology users to discern the places of self-directed informal learning and formal career development processes in career-directed learning. Using the individual life stories as the unit of analysis, Paige likened self-directed learning to entrepreneurial learning and found that such learning benefits from strategic guidance and self-reflection. He concluded that there is a necessity for instructors, or trainers, to model their own learning process as a potential learning strategy for their students. This modeling, he found, would lead to students' recognizing their own learning strategies and creating their own learning stories. With that developed skill, students would gain more control over their own learning and harness their informal learning experiences for new learning. Based on the results of the narrative study, Paige recommended that corporate trainers incorporate self-directed learning, particularly story-based self-reflection, into formal career development programs. The findings from his award-winning dissertation have been disseminated in a book chapter (Paige, 2008), two articles (Paige, 2009a,

2010a), and three invitational conference presentations (Paige, 2009b, 2010b, 2013). In addition, his work has been cited by others in the field multiple times demonstrating that narrative research can contribute to new knowledge.

The unit of analysis for narrative research is the individual. The researcher collects stories from individuals, primarily from interviews, which tell the story of the individual in relation to the phenomenon under study. Both phenomenological and narrative researchers collect information from individuals. One difference between phenomenological and narrative research is that phenomenological research requires the participation of multiple individuals, and, even though narrative researchers usually collect stories from multiple individuals, narrative research could involve the story of only one person. A second difference between phenomenological and narrative research is that phenomenological researchers look for themes among the individual stories, whereas narrative researchers analyze each story as a distinct unit. In narrative research, other artifacts can add information to the telling of the story, such as documents (including journals, emails, and letters); photographs; and video and audio records (Marshall & Rossman, 2016). The additional artifacts serve to enhance and support the story told in interviews.

Grounded Theory. As noted earlier, the primary purpose of all qualitative research is to describe phenomena that occur in the world, leading to complex understandings that can build toward theories. Although all qualitative research designs contribute to that purpose, the grounded theory design is specifically focused on theory development (Corbin & Strauss, 2015; Merriam & Tisdell, 2016; Saveyne & Robinson, 1997).

Even though there is consensus that the purpose of grounded theory studies is to develop theory, there is less agreement about the unit of analysis within this design. For example, some authors have argued that a set of participants with a shared experience is the unit of analysis (Creswell & Poth, 2018), whereas others have proposed that the social situation of interest is the more appropriate unit of analysis (Clarke, Friese, & Washburn, 2018). Robson and McCartan (2016) stated that for grounded theory studies, "no particular type of 'field' is called for. Such studies have been carried out in a very wide variety of settings" (p. 162). The unit of analysis, then, is not a defining characteristic for grounded theory studies. The purpose of generating theory can be accomplished with a variety of participant sets.

Whatever the participant set, the major data collection strategy for grounded theory studies is interview, although other forms of data collection, such as observations and documents, may be used (Creswell & Poth, 2018; Robson & McCartan, 2016). Interviews in grounded theory research are often iterative, meaning that the questions can change as interviews progress and new areas of exploration are encountered. An initial interview might query participants on their experience related to the process or activity under study, with emphasis on the sequence of events related to the phenomenon. Follow-up interviews might query participants on specifics of the phenomenon itself, causes for the phenomenon, how the participant interacted with the phenomenon, and what happened as a result (Creswell & Poth, 2018).

TABLE 6.1 ◆ SUMMARY OF QUALITATIVE RESEARCH DESIGN SPECIFICATIONS			
Qualitative Design	**Major Purpose**	**Unit of Analysis**	**Primary Data Collection**
Case study	Describe behavior of a bounded unit in relation to a phenomenon	Bounded unit	Multiple sources
Ethnography	Describe behavior of a cultural group in relation to a phenomenon	Cultural group	Immersion in culture for an extended time period; multiple sources
Phenomenology	Describe themes and patterns of lived experiences across individuals in relation to a phenomenon	Individuals sharing a common experience	Interviews
Narrative	Describe individual stories in relation to a phenomenon	Individuals	Interviews
Grounded theory	Develop theory	Unspecified	Interviews

Summary of Qualitative Research Designs and Design Selection

If a qualitative study is deemed appropriate for a research study, the next task is to select a particular qualitative design. Table 6.1 provides a summary of five qualitative designs and their major purpose, unit of analysis, and primary data collection strategy.

By considering the study problem, purpose, and research question(s) in the context of Table 6.1, you can explore, and ultimately select, the qualitative design that best matches your study. Typically, you will need to consider several designs before deciding on the one that will provide the best overall structure for your intended study. Once a design is chosen, you must consider how to choose study participants, which is a matter of sampling logic.

SAMPLING LOGIC

After selecting the research design, your next step is to identify the sources that will provide information (data) to answer your research question(s). In quantitative research, this step requires identifying the population of interest and drawing a sample from that population sufficient in size and statistical power to represent, and generalize to, that population. Quantitative studies generally use *probability sampling* to represent a population. Qualitative studies, though, are not concerned with representing a population but, instead, are focused on relevance to the research question(s). Qualitative studies use nonprobability sampling, also called *purposive sampling*, to identify those who can provide data for the study (Schwandt, 2015). Schwandt indicated that there are two critical issues in qualitative sampling logic, or purposive sampling: (1) establishing criteria for choosing study participants and (2) describing a strategy for determining that selected participants meet the established criteria.

Participant Selection

To select participants for a qualitative study, you need to provide eligibility criteria. You need to look closely at the research question and then identify the characteristics needed of study participants to answer that research question. For example, if your research question was "How do female executives in Fortune 500 companies experience work–family balance?" your participant criteria would be the following:

1. Female gender

2. Executive position, and *executive position* would need definition

3. Employed in a Fortune 500 company, and *Fortune 500 company* would need definition

4. Family association, and *family association* would need definition

Defining terms is very important. For example, does *family* include only women who have a spouse and/or children, or does it include single women with no children but obligations to parents or other relatives? In this example, only women who meet the definitions of *executive* in a Fortune 500 company and who have a family would be eligible for the study. Notice that the research question does not ask about work–life balance, but about work–family balance, evidencing the need for clarity and specificity in the research question.

With participant criteria clearly delineated, you then need to describe how you find appropriate participants. Miles, Huberman, and Saldaña (2014) summarized purposive sampling strategies, such as snowballing (asking the current participant for a referral to a next participant), convenience (using those who are readily available), and opportunistic (capitalizing on unexpected leads). Which sampling strategy to use depends largely on feasibility. Feasibility requires that there is a sufficient number of people meeting your participant criteria available to you and that you truly can access them. If, for example, you know of only a few people who meet participant criteria, but those few may know others, then snowballing may be appropriate. If, for example, the study requires access to financial records of a company, and those records are not publicly available, you must determine if it is feasible to obtain those records with permission of the company.

The mention of *records* in the last paragraph is important, as in qualitative research, documents may serve as data sources. For example, case study procedures might include examining meeting agendas and minutes, policy statements, calendars, and other records. If you decide to collect such data sources, you will need to explain your rationale for doing so and your criteria for including those sources. The same requirements apply for including these data sources as for including human participants in your research.

At this introductory stage, it is not necessary to understand all the purposive sampling strategies. It is important to understand that qualitative sampling is based on relevance, rather than representativeness, and that, as a researcher, you must describe the criteria for inclusion of data sources in the study and how those data sources are selected, with consideration for their availability and accessibility. That does leave the question, though, of how many participants, documents, or other sources should be included in a qualitative study. That question is addressed through understanding the concept of *saturation*.

Saturation

Important questions in qualitative research include the amount of data you should collect, from how many people, and from how many documents or observations. *Saturation* is the relevant concept here. Two criteria have to be achieved in order to reach saturation: (1) Continued analysis yields no new information and (2) there are no unexplained phenomena (Marshall & Rossman, 2016; Saumure & Given, 2008). It is easy to think that you have achieved saturation when no new information is being derived from the data, but remember that the second condition has to be fulfilled as well. For the second condition to be fulfilled, the data gathered must be sufficient to answer the research question(s).

This vagueness makes it difficult to decide on the specific number of people from whom data will be collected. You cannot always predict the number of people to be interviewed or documents to be reviewed to reach saturation. You should, though, provide an estimate of the number of people, documents, observations, or hours of recorded transcripts that are expected, with the option of continuing on if saturation is not attained or stopping earlier if saturation is already attained (Merriam & Tisdell, 2016; Patton, 2015). The estimate can be informed by reading other studies that have used a similar design and/or addressed the same or similar topics. You should also provide a description of how saturation will be recognized, which is a matter of design trustworthiness.

TRUSTWORTHINESS IN QUALITATIVE STUDIES

As described in Chapter 12, quantitative researchers rely on the concepts of reliability, internal and external validity, and replicability to legitimate their studies. The counterparts for qualitative researchers are dependability, credibility, transferability, and confirmability (Guba & Lincoln, 1989; Lincoln & Guba, 1985). In this section, I first define the four terms presented in the previous sentence; after that, I describe strategies related to evidencing trustworthiness of a qualitative study

Definitions

Dependability. Dependability in qualitative research is akin to reliability in quantitative research. *Reliability* means that the instruments used to collect data produce consistent results across data collection occurrences. For example, a metal tape measure will likely be more reliable than a cloth tape measure because a metal tape measure will not stretch as will a cloth one. Reliability can be estimated statistically. In qualitative studies, the concept of statistical reliability does not apply.

Instead, qualitative studies must meet a standard of dependability. *Dependability* means that there is evidence of consistency in data collection, analysis, and reporting. It also means that any adjustments or shifts in methodology, which can occur in qualitative studies, are documented and explained in a fashion that is publicly accessible. Inquiry audits and triangulation are the most common methods of establishing dependability (Guba & Lincoln, 1989; Merriam & Tisdell, 2016).

Credibility. Internal validity in quantitative research confirms that the data collected matches the research question. In other words, if the research question is about motivation, the data collected must be about motivation. Credibility is the parallel concept for qualitative studies. *Credibility* means that the findings of the study are believable given the data presented (Merriam & Tisdell, 2016). Credibility is established using strategies such as prolonged engagement, persistent observation, peer debriefing, negative case analysis, progressive subjectivity, member checking, triangulation, and reflexivity (Guba & Lincoln, 1989; Merriam & Tisdell, 2016). If you were conducting a qualitative study, you would not need to use all the strategies related to credibility; rather, you would select the strategy or strategies most appropriate for your study.

Transferability. Transferability relates to the quantitative concept of external validity. External validity provides a measure of the extent to which the findings of the study, based on a sample, are generalizable to the population of interest for the study. Even though the purpose of qualitative research is not to generalize from a sample to a population, a qualitative study must have some meaning beyond the immediate instance of the study. Determining the applicability of the findings of a qualitative study to other situations is predominantly a responsibility of the person in the other situation. The researcher's responsibility with regard to transferability is to provide sufficient description of the setting and the assumptions of the study so that a reader can make informed application of the findings of the study (Trochim, 2006a). Transferability is supported by using thick descriptions and maximum variation (Merriam & Tisdell, 2016).

Confirmability. Quantitative research aims at objectivity, extracting the researcher from the study as much as possible so that the findings of the study are disassociated from any researcher bias. Qualitative research admits researcher subjectivity, but its methods must be based on verifiable procedures, analyses, and conclusions. In other words, confirmability requires that other informed researchers would arrive at essentially the same conclusions when examining the same qualitative data (Guba & Lincoln, 1989). Guba and Lincoln (1989) proposed a confirmability audit as the primary means of establishing confirmability.

Strategies to Evidence Trustworthiness

As identified earlier with each definition, there are multiple strategies available to establish trustworthiness of a study. Table 6.2 summarizes the strategies associated with each of the four aspects of trustworthiness defined earlier.

TABLE 6.2 ◆ SUMMARY OF TRUSTWORTHINESS CRITERIA AND RELATED EVIDENTIARY STRATEGIES	
Trustworthiness Criterion	**Strategies**
Dependability	• Inquiry audit • Triangulation
Credibility	• Prolonged engagement • Persistent observation • Peer debriefing • Negative case analysis • Progressive subjectivity • Member checking • Triangulation • Reflexivity
Transferability	• Reflexivity • Thick description • Maximum variation
Confirmability	• Confirmability audit

In the next section, I will briefly describe each of the strategies listed in Table 6.2.

Audit Trails. I consider inquiry and confirmability audits together under the idea of audit trails. "An audit trail in a qualitative study describes in detail how data were collected, how categories were derived, and how decisions were made throughout the inquiry" (Merriam & Tisdell, 2016, p. 252). Audit trails are derived from field notes as well as from memos or reflection journals about decisions made during the research process. "Essentially, it [the audit trail] is a detailed account of how the study was conducted and how the data were analyzed" (Merriam & Tisdell, 2016, p. 253). These reflective documents become available to other analysts to assess the dependability and confirmability of the study.

Triangulation. Triangulation is the use of more than one source to verify the basis of a claim. Although researchers sometimes limit the concept of triangulation to multiple data sources, triangulation can also be established using "multiple investigators, multiple theoretical perspectives, or multiple methods. The central point of the procedure is to examine a conclusion (assertion, claim, etc.) from more than one vantage point" (Schwandt, 2015, p. 307). Triangulation might imply *three*, but it should be interpreted as *multiple*, which is more than one but not necessarily three.

Prolonged Engagement. Ethnographic studies, in particular, rely on prolonged engagement. Prolonged engagement requires presence and involvement at the study site for an extended period of time, often several years. There are three purposes for prolonged engagement: (1) to build rapport and trust, (2) to derive enough information to mitigate misunderstandings, and (3) to understand more deeply the context and culture of the study environment (Guba & Lincoln, 1989).

Persistent Observation. Persistent observation accompanies prolonged engagement. It means that the observations recorded are sufficient to provide depth of understanding through collection of details (Guba & Lincoln, 1989). This definition is vague because what is sufficient is a matter of judgment, but consider persistent observation in alignment with the concept of saturation described earlier.

Peer Debriefing. Peer debriefing involves engagement with a qualified colleague, someone who is not involved in the study, in ongoing discussions of study progress, in data analyses, and in tentative findings. The role of the peer is to pose questions that assist you in clarifying conclusions and excising researcher bias. A key to peer debriefing is rapport between you and the peer as well the peer's own experience as a qualitative researcher, as both will inform the kinds of questions the peer poses (Guba & Lincoln, 1989).

Negative Case Analysis. For qualitative studies, you need to record data collection instances that are divergent from the majority of derived themes and patterns, known as negative cases, noting the strength of such negative cases. If the presence of such divergent cases is weak, then the derived patterns and themes receive more confidence (Guba & Lincoln, 1989). You should, however, be vigilant that a divergent, or negative, case may point in a direction that requires further study.

Progressive Subjectivity. Although subjectivity is inevitable in qualitative research, it is not appropriate to let this subjectivity run unchecked. You must acknowledge your subjectivity by revealing, monitoring, and controlling its influence on data collection and interpretation, a process known as progressive subjectivity. This progressive subjectivity is recorded in three steps: (1) prior to data collection, you would record your conceptualization and expectations; (2) during the study, you would regularly note developing conceptualizations and expectations; and (3) a peer reviewer would examine your notations and challenge your interpretations, as needed (Guba & Lincoln, 1989).

Reflexivity. Progressive subjectivity is closely associated with reflexivity. Reflexivity obliges you to document in field notes, memos, or journals your self-critical analyses of biases, your role in and responses to the research process, and any adjustments made to the study based on ongoing analysis (Schwandt, 2015).

Member Checking. Qualitative researchers sometimes interpret member checking only as having study participants review and confirm their interview transcripts, but member checking is more than transcript review. Member checking, also called respondent validation, "is systematically soliciting feedback about your data and conclusions from the people you are studying" (Maxwell, 2013, p. 126). Notice that member checking involves not only having participants examine data, such as transcripts, but also having participants provide feedback on findings as they emerge. As Merriam and Tisdell (2016) wrote, "The process involved in member checks is to take your preliminary analysis back to some of the participants and ask whether your interpretation 'rings true'" (p. 246).

Thick Description. *Thick description* means that the research report contains "a description of the setting and participants of the study, as well as a detailed description of the findings with adequate evidence presented in the form of quotes from participant interviews, field, notes, and documents" (Merriam & Tisdell, 2016, p. 257). There are, then, three elements to thick description: (1) description of the setting, (2) description of the participants, and (3) adequate evidence to support the findings. You must use your own judgment to determine what is adequate, and not too little or too much, evidence to support findings. Peer debriefing can support that judgment.

Maximum Variation. Merriam and Tisdell (2016) discussed maximum variation as a means of strengthening transferability. Maximum variation is a sampling strategy that intentionally diversifies study participants to create greater applicability of the study to a variety of situations. This strategy may not be useful if the study is focused on understanding a particular set of participants.

Thus far in this chapter, I have defined qualitative research and its purposes, examined qualitative study designs, and considered how to establish the trustworthiness of a qualitative study. In the next section, I discuss the role of the researcher.

ROLE OF THE RESEARCHER

If you are undertaking a qualitative study, then you as the researcher serve as the primary data collection instrument. You serve as this instrument through your direct observations, your participation in interviews, and your analysis of documents. This role as primary instrument of data collection brings you into an intimate relationship with your setting, your participants, and your data analysis, yielding a duality to your presence in a study as both a participant and an observer in varying degrees ranging from complete participant to complete observer (Creswell & Poth, 2018).

Complete Participant

If you are a complete participant in a qualitative research study, you will behave as a full member of the unit of analysis. For example, if you were a complete participant in a study of neighborhood watch groups, you would become a member of the watch group, live in the neighborhood, and engage in neighborhood activities as any other community member would. Benefits of the complete participant role include very deep understanding of how the participants experience the study's phenomenon of focus and the development of trusting relationships with participants. Challenges with complete participation include potential loss of perspective and difficulty recording observations accurately while fully engaged in activities.

Participant-Observer

Another variation of the researcher role is the participant-observer role. In the participant-observer role, you share actively with the study participants but also step back from the activities so as to be an observer. For example, in a study of how members of a volunteer community group negotiate task distribution, you might join the group and participate in some activities, but you would also step out to observe other activities and conduct interviews. Benefits and challenges of the participant-observer role are similar to those for the complete participant role, but may be mitigated somewhat by the balancing of both roles, with weight toward the participant role.

Observer-Participant

With the observer-participant role, the balance shifts to the observer side. As observer, you would not engage in activities with your participants. As participant, you would be present in the setting, and the study participants would be aware of your direct observation. For example, for a case study of how school board members manage conflict, you might attend board meetings, interview board members, and examine related documents, but you would not participate in board deliberations, make presentations to the board, or otherwise interact with the board. Benefits of the observer-participant role include facility of recording data contemporaneously with observations and the opportunity to collect data within settings and from groups to which the researcher does not have access of full membership. Deficits of the observer-participant role include loss of information that comes from full engagement and potential influence of observer presence on participant behavior.

Complete Observer

The researcher in the complete observer role is not present in the setting or with the participants. The study participants do not see or hear you, and you either collect data remotely, through technology, or from archival documents. For example, in a study of the visible and audible reactions of patients to a painful medical procedure, you might collect videotapes, with permission of course, and later analyze the body, facial, and verbal language exhibited. Benefits of the complete observer role include the opportunity to collect data when researcher presence would be intrusive or the setting is at a distance. Another benefit is the absence of influence of the researcher's presence on participant behavior. Deficits of the complete observer role include loss of information from engaging directly with study participants and inability to use some data collection strategies, such as interviews and focus groups.

Each of the four research roles requires particular skills to be used effectively, such as how to observe a situation without influencing it and how to be fully engaged in an activity and yet collect data regarding it. Whichever role you assume depends on the circumstances of the study. You must disclose your selected role with a clear and well-articulated rationale. If the role changes during the course of the study, you must document that change and the rationale for the change.

CONCLUSION

If you are pursuing a qualitative research design, I advise you to read the relevant sources in this chapter's Key Sources section and also read multiple studies that have used the design you are considering. Qualitative research is not easy. A substantial amount of practice is needed to collect and analyze qualitative data.

Questions for Reflection

1. How does understanding the purpose of each qualitative design help in design selection for a particular study?

2. What is the difference between representativeness and relevance in sampling?

3. What are ways to evidence the trustworthiness of a qualitative study?

4. How might various researcher roles affect the conduct of a study?

Key Sources

Case Study

Stake, R. E. (1995). *The art of case study research.* Thousand Oaks, CA: SAGE.

Yin, R. K. (2018). *Case study research: Design and methods* (6th ed.). Thousand Oaks, CA: SAGE.

Ethnography

Agar, M. H. (1996). *The professional stranger: An informal introduction to ethnography* (2nd ed.). San Diego, CA: Academic Press.

Geertz, C. (1973). *The interpretation of cultures.* New York, NY: Basic Books.

Madison, D. S. (2012). *Critical ethnography: Method, ethics, and performance* (2nd ed.). Thousand Oaks, CA: SAGE.

Wolcott, H. F. (2008). *Ethnography: A way of seeing* (2nd ed.). Plymouth, UK: AltaMira Press.

Phenomenology

Moustakas, C. E. (1994). *Phenomenological research methods.* Thousand Oaks, CA: SAGE.

Van Manen, M. (2016). *Researching lived experience: Human science for an action sensitive pedagogy* (2nd ed.). New York, NY: Routledge.

Narrative

Clandinin, D. J., & Connelly, F. M. (2000). *Narrative inquiry: Experience and story in qualitative research.* San Francisco, CA: Jossey-Bass.

Czarniawska, B. (2004). *Narratives in social science research.* Thousand Oaks, CA: SAGE.

Grounded Theory

Corbin, J., & Strauss, A. (2015). *Basics of qualitative research: Techniques and procedures for developing grounded theory* (4th ed.). Thousand Oaks, CA: SAGE.

Glaser, B. G., & Strauss, A. L. (1999). *The discovery of grounded theory: Strategies for qualitative research.* New Brunswick, NJ: Aldine Transaction.

References

Clarke, A. E., Friese, C., & Washburn, R. S. (2018). *Situational analysis: Grounded theory after the interpretive turn* (2nd ed.). Thousand Oaks, CA: SAGE.

Corbin, J., & Strauss, A. (2015). *Basics of qualitative research: Techniques and procedures for developing grounded theory* (4th ed.). Thousand Oaks, CA: SAGE.

Creswell, J. W. (1998). *Qualitative inquiry and research design: Choosing among five traditions.* Thousand Oaks, CA: SAGE.

Creswell, J. W. (2013). *Qualitative inquiry & research design: Choosing among five approaches* (3rd ed.). Thousand Oaks, CA: SAGE.

Creswell, J. W., & Creswell, J. D. (2018). *Research design: Qualitative, quantitative, and mixed methods approaches* (5th ed.). Thousand Oaks, CA: SAGE.

Creswell, J. W., & Poth, C. N. (2018). *Qualitative inquiry & research design: Choosing among five approaches* (4th ed.). Thousand Oaks, CA: SAGE.

Denzin, N. K., & Lincoln, Y. S. (2018). Introduction: The discipline and practice of qualitative research. In N. K. Denzin & Y. S. Lincoln (Eds.), *The SAGE handbook of qualitative research* (5th ed., pp. 1–26). Thousand Oaks, CA: SAGE.

Glesne, C. (2016). *Becoming qualitative researchers: An introduction* (5th ed.). Boston, MA: Pearson.

Guba, E. G., & Lincoln, Y. S. (1989). *Fourth generation evaluation.* Newbury Park, CA: SAGE.

Lincoln, Y. S., & Guba, E. G. (1985). *Naturalistic inquiry.* Beverly Hills, CA: SAGE.

Marshall, C., & Rossman, G. B. (2016). *Designing qualitative research* (6th ed.). Thousand Oaks, CA: SAGE.

Maxwell, J. A. (2013). *Qualitative research design: An interactive approach* (3rd ed.). Thousand Oaks, CA: SAGE.

Merriam, S. B., & Tisdell, E. J. (2016). *Qualitative research: A guide to design and implementation* (4th ed.). San Francisco, CA: Jossey-Bass.

Miles, M. B., Huberman, A. M., & Saldaña, J. (2014). *Qualitative data analysis: A methods sourcebook* (3rd ed.). Thousand Oaks, CA: SAGE.

Moustakas, C. E. (1994). *Phenomenological research methods.* Thousand Oaks, CA: SAGE.

Paige, R. D. (2007). *The relationship between self-directed informal learning and the career development process of technology users* (Doctoral dissertation). Available from ProQuest

Dissertations and Theses database (Order No. 3244821). Retrieved from http://search.proquest .com/docview/304762834? accountid=14872

Paige, R. D. (2008). The relationship between self-directed informal learning and the career development process. In H. Nilsen & E. Perzycka (Eds.), *The teacher for the knowledge society* (pp. 71–95). Høgskolen i Nesna, Norway: Organ for FoU-publikasjoner.

Paige, R. D. (2009a, Fall). Self-directed learning and the mind-set of successful entrepreneurial learning. *ATEA Journal, 37*(1), 16–21.

Paige, R. D. (2009b, May). *Self-directed learning and the mind-set of successful entrepreneurial learning.* Paper presented at NISOD International Conference on Teaching and Leadership Excellence, Austin, TX.

Paige, R. D. (2010a). Beyond student-centered instruction: A model for teaching learning-to-learn strategies. *International Journal of Interdisciplinary Social Sciences, 5*(5), 299–308.

Paige, R. D. (2010b, August). *Beyond student-centered instruction: A model for teaching learning-to-learn strategies.* Paper presented at the Fifth International Social Sciences Conference, Cambridge, UK.

Paige, R. D. (2013, October). *The entrepreneurial learner: How people learn-to-learn and learn to apply what they have learned.* Paper presented at the Instructional Technology Conference, Middle Tennessee State University, Murfreesboro, TN.

Patton, M. Q. (2015). *Qualitative research & evaluation methods* (4th ed.). Thousand Oaks, CA: SAGE.

Robson, C., & McCartan, K. (2016). *Real world research* (4th ed.). Chichester, UK: Wiley.

Saumure, K., & Given, L. M. (2008). Data saturation. In L. M. Given (Ed.), *The SAGE encyclopedia of qualitative research methods* (Vol. 2, pp. 195–196). Thousand Oaks, CA: SAGE.

Saveyne, W., & Robinson, R. (1997). Qualitative research issues and methods: An introduction for educational technologists. In D. Jonassen (Ed.), *Handbook of research for educational communications and technology* (pp. 1171–1195). New York, NY: Macmillan.

Schwandt, T. A. (2015). *The SAGE dictionary of qualitative inquiry* (4th ed.). Thousand Oaks, CA: SAGE.

Suryani, A. (2008). Comparing case study and ethnography as qualitative research approaches. *Jurnal Ilmu Komunikasi, 5*(1), 117–127.

Trochim, W. M. K. (2006a). Qualitative validity. In W. M. K. Trochim (Ed.), *Research methods knowledge base* (October 2006 ed.). Retrieved from http://www.socialresearchmethods.net/ kb/unitanal.php

Trochim, W. M. K. (2006b). Unit of analysis. In W. M. K. Trochim (Ed.), *Research methods knowledge base* (October 2006 ed.). Retrieved from http://www.socialresearchmethods.net/kb/unitanal.php

Yin, R. K. (2018). *Case study research: Design and methods* (6th ed.). Thousand Oaks, CA: SAGE.

QUALITATIVE ANALYSIS

Paul Mihas

INTRODUCTION

This chapter provides an introduction to qualitative data analysis, which refers to an array of tools of inquiry, including coding, memo writing, and diagrams. I focus on textual data and describe various approaches to coding, such as deductive and inductive techniques, developing a codebook, and teamwork coding. I also discuss objectives of analysis, such as the rich description of data—condensing copious amounts of textual or visual data into presentable findings—and identifying patterns across data—that is, discerning conceptual similarities called "themes." In theoretical studies, researchers synthesize the interconnected themes into a cohesive understanding of phenomena. Finally, I describe how researchers might use codes to analyze the relationship between demographic characteristics and codes and present products of analysis, including matrices and diagrams.

CODING

Focusing the Researcher Gaze

This chapter focuses largely on coding and how researchers can employ it to construct themes and generate evocative findings. Coding is the process of applying topical names to pieces of data and using these topics to recognize and name larger conceptual patterns across data (see Table 7.1). It is a way of seeing—of focusing on topics that reveal meaning—based on one's research questions. For example, a researcher specifically studying friendship might create codes such as *best friend*, *childhood friend*, *co-worker friend*, and *managing friendships*, but a study on another topic, such as surviving cancer, might simply use a code for *friendship* without developing more specific codes around this matter. The topic of the study and research questions provide direction in regard to which codes, broad or specific, will best serve you as you dwell on the language of the data. A descriptive study on a new transit policy would have different codes from a more theoretical study on social identity formation.

Researchers in the design phase not only determine the possible theoretical or conceptual framework that will guide their coding but also consider other tools for analysis such as memo writing and

TABLE 7.1 ● TYPES OF CODES, DEFINITIONS, AND UTILITY

Type of Codes	Definition	Utility
A priori (deductive codes)	Predetermined topics familiar to the researcher from a literature review or from fieldwork knowledge or from knowledge of the population	Common in studies with a conceptual or theoretical framework Useful in assessing how data fit (or do not fit) the topics from a framework
Inductive ("emerging" codes)	"New" topics that researchers discern as they review data Topics that "surface" beyond the initial codes	Useful in data-driven, participant-centered studies Provide insight into how participants frame their lifeworld
In vivo codes	Use evocative language of participants to construct a code	Useful in data-driven studies aiming to privilege participant voices, rather than formal, academic language
Descriptive codes	Address the fundamental *who*, *what*, *where*, and *when* of the data	Essential in providing a rich portrayal of phenomena or events
Interpretive codes	Capture an abstract or conceptual topic aimed at addressing the *how* or *why* of the data	Useful in developing abstract themes or building theory
Emotion coding	Address explicit or implicit emotional states	Useful in reporting on how emotions are activated in particular contexts
Values coding (Saldaña, 2013)	Capture how individuals prioritize particular beliefs, events, or conditions	Provides insight into motivation and behavior Useful in assessing the implicit value structure inscribed in a narrative
Versus coding (Saldaña, 2013)	Constructed to capture the tension between two opposing topics, such as reality versus fantasy	Useful when looking for relationships between topics Useful when assessing how participants construct "absolutes"

Note: These code types are not all mutually exclusive, nor is this list exhaustive.

quotation diagrams, called *episode profiles*, that capture logical relationships among illuminating quotations from a transcript (Fryer et al., 2015; Maietta, 2006).

First-Cycle Coding: Deductive and Inductive Coding

After collecting and transcribing data, researchers use what has been called *first-cycle coding* (Saldaña, 2013). First-cycle coding refers to both deductive and inductive coding in early data engagement (Miles, Huberman, & Saldaña, 2014). Deductive codes are predetermined (a priori) codes based on a literature review or theoretical framework; they are topics to which the researcher is sensitized perhaps even before data collection. Hence, if a conceptual framework constructed from a literature review drives the inquiry, the researcher would typically adopt codes from this framework. This initial phase reveals the analytical reach of these deductive codes.

In contrast, inductive coding engages topics that are unanticipated in data as the researcher pays close attention to both the text and the subtext. That is, data can be analyzed informationally or discursively—or both. You can focus on the content of the data, such as actions, actors, and consequences, or on elements of how the narrative data are structured, framed, or conveyed, such as emphases, repetitions, and negations. Rather than relying on codes that are within easy reach—those from a conceptual framework—inductive coding focuses on surfacing topics that researchers discern as especially relevant, such as metaphorical language revealing a keen perspective or a different angle on familiar constructs.

Numerous variations of first-cycle coding have been categorized, including emotion, values, versus, motif, and causation coding (Saldaña, 2013). Table 7.1 provides definitions and uses for several types of first-cycle coding. In grounded theory, this is referred to as *open coding*, the initial, inductive phase of analysis (Charmaz, 2014). Deciding on a particular coding strategy will depend on whether you are studying processes, events, settings, or society and culture more broadly and, relatedly, whether the unit of analysis is the individual, dyad, event, setting, or organization.

Descriptive Coding

Codes also span a spectrum from descriptive to interpretive. Descriptive codes are codes that capture the *who, what, where*, and *when* of the data (Maietta, Hamilton, Swartout, & Petruzzelli, 2018). These codes, lower on the conceptual ladder than abstract codes, allow you to keep track of actors, actions, settings, and behaviors. In other words, who is doing what to whom? In the following journal entry, for example, a student living in North Carolina writes about living through a hurricane in 1999. Descriptive codes might include *media, speculation, parents, decision making*, and *tracking the storm*. A benefit of coding for a surface-level code such as *parents* allows the researcher to later gather all data referencing parents to assess what the data reveal about the role of parents in young adults' experiences of a natural disaster.

EXAMPLE: APPLYING CODES

The news said this morning that the hurricane is headed for us. But, as of 8:00 a.m., classes were still on the go. The rain has set in and the winds picked up a little more since yesterday.	**media**
Everybody is talking about the storm and whether or not it's actually gonna hit. During my 10:00 class, I received word that classes were canceled as of 2:00 today and tomorrow. After my 12:00 class I headed back to my apartment and called my mama to tell her the good news:	**speculation**
	parents
NO CLASS. She insists that I come home because of the possibility of Floyd being as bad as forecasters say. Being that my mama worries so consistently about me, I packed up my things and began home. (East Carolina University, 1999)	**tracking the storm**
	decision making

In Vivo Coding: Participant Words as Codes

When using an inductive lens, researchers can construct codes based on the verbatim language of participants. Consider the following example from the hurricane study: "Finding eggs, bread, and milk were like finding gold." Researchers might use *finding gold* as a code for any narrative suggesting items that have a sudden increase in value. The participant's language captures the sense of discovering a commonplace item that now has high worth. These *in vivo* codes are used when the participant's language vividly captures lived experience, what it is like to inhabit their lives.

Interpretive Coding

Interpretive coding requires moving up the conceptual ladder to identify and name higher level topics. Beyond coding for surface-level topics such as setting and actors, these codes require the researcher to identify topics that are more abstract and evocative in nature. They address the *how* and *why* questions. In the hurricane paragraph, the survivor mentions the "news," the official "word" from campus, and her mother's imperatives. An interpretive code, *voices of authority*, captures the declarations and requests that she references. Its abstract nature indicates a higher level inference and helps explain, not just describe, what is happening in the data.

Beyond coding for content, you might also code for narrative or discursive strategies in data. There are numerous strategies for doing so (Burman & Parker, 1993; Potter & Wetherell, 1987). For example, discursive coding might pay attention to textual strategies such as primacy (what comes first in a narrative), negation (negative language), distortion (e.g., exaggerations), emphasis (text treated with more regard), isolation (expressions that stand out from the rest of a transcript), repetition (repeated phrases), incompletion (unfinished thoughts), and uniqueness (unusual expressions) (Alexander, 1988). This approach fits studies aimed at not only identifying what participants say but also how they release information and how they make claims using specific narrative techniques.

Size of Textual Segments

Apart from which topics to select as codes, researchers must also address the size of the textual unit to which a code is applied. Coding a paragraph suggests attention to context; coding a smaller fragment suggests attention to nuance. Simultaneous coding (Saldaña, 2013) refers to coding the same textual unit multiple ways—that is, to codes that overlap. Simultaneous coding also means you are paying attention to the multiple aspects of the text—that is, seeing several topics at once: setting, action, actor, emotion(s), value(s), and so on.

Code Relationships: Identifying Primary and Secondary Codes

Moving forward with codes from first-cycle coding requires making judicious decisions regarding which codes best fit the data—which ones have risen to distinction—and which ones can be deleted, renamed, or merged with existing codes. Another objective is creating a hierarchical or otherwise relational coding structure; for this reason, we might organize topics into primary codes (or *categories* as they are called in grounded theory) and secondary codes, or subcodes.

For example, in a study on experiencing chemotherapy, one might have identified the following codes in first-cycle coding: *renewed intimacy with partner, edginess, veins burning, sleeping more, "hiding the tears," making home more comfortable, "eating different food," "chemo brain," new routines, remembering healthier times,* and *seeking fresh entertainment.* It is important to now move from all codes occupying the same level of importance to a more defined structure that requires considering the broad and the specific. For example, a primary code (or category) called *physical changes* could encompass *veins burning, sleeping more, "eating different food," edginess, "hiding the tears,"* and *"chemo brain."* Similarly, the primary code *emerging self* could encompass *remembering healthier times, renewed intimacy with partner, new routines, making home more comfortable,* and *seeking fresh entertainment.* The objective is to consider logical relationships among primary codes and subcodes.

In grounded theory, a similar process, axial coding, invites the researcher to determine the interconnections among the categories created from the first round of coding. Once the initial set of categories is determined, the researcher proceeds through an iterative process of connecting the categories to subcategories (Corbin & Strauss, 2015). For example, in the chemotherapy study, we might recognize the conceptual link between *emerging self* and *physical changes* and create a new category that relates to both topics—the *embodied self.*

Developing a Codebook

As researchers develop codes, they formalize them in a codebook that includes a list of codes, subcodes, and their definitions. In grounded theory, a definition might include the code's properties and dimensions (Corbin & Strauss, 2015). For example, the code *cancer survivor* might have a property called *visibility* (as a survivor) and a dimension from high to low. A survivor who is open about his or her status would demonstrate

CODE STRUCTURE: PRIMARY CODES AND SUBCODES

Physical changes

- Edginess
- "Hiding the tears"
- "Chemo brain"
- Sleeping more
- Veins burning
- "Eating different food"

Emerging self

- Renewed intimacy with partner
- Remembering healthier times
- New routines
- Seeking fresh entertainment
- Making home more comfortable

high visibility as a survivor, whereas someone who is reluctant to discuss his or her cancer journey would demonstrate low visibility. In more general approaches to operationalizing codes—appropriate in descriptive and pragmatic studies—a definition might simply include guidance on how the code should be applied, information on the origin of the code, an example from the data, and reflection on how the code is intended to contribute to the study (Fryer et al., 2015; Maietta, 2006).

In defining a code, you might go a step further and decide that the definition contains topics that can be elevated to subcodes. For more information on developing code definitions, see Miles et al. (2014). Figure 7.1 illustrates how one might revisit the codebook throughout the coding process. See SAGE (2019) for an example of a codebook.

FIGURE 7.1   ●   STEPS FOR CODING AND ANALYSIS

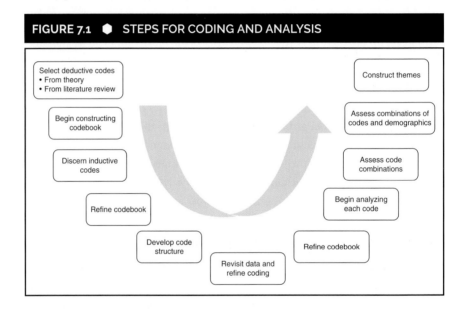

EXAMPLE DEFINITION

The following example illustrates a code definition, *Instrumental Relationships with Doctors*, from a study on rural health.

Instrumental Relationships with Doctors refers to unavoidable encounters between physicians and patients, but ones that lack genuine rapport and two-way communication. That is, interviewees recognize doctors' value and expertise but only within a one-way communication channel-one where information flows from doctor to patient. This is largely an instrumental relationship where a doctor is playing a role rather than engendering a productive, ongoing bond. Patients seem to give control to physicians as soon as they are "handed over" to them, rather than developing a personal relationship that develops their full agency.

Example: "I taught Sunday school this past Sunday. The doctor don't like for me to do it. I got out of it. I taught the adult Sunday school class—we're Methodists at Plateau for about fifteen or twenty years, I reckon, and the doctor made me give it up."

Why this code is important to the study: This inductive code adds nuance to the relationship between patient and physician and explains why some doctors are not referred to by name.

Teamwork and Intercoder Agreement

Teamwork in qualitative studies might involve multiple coders reviewing a subset of data to develop initial topics and then meeting to refine these topics into an initial codebook. With an established codebook, team members can divide the data and each can code his or her respective subset of transcripts. Alternatively, they might code the same subset and convene again to assess intercoder agreement (Burla et al., 2008; Lombard, Snyder-Duch, & Bracken, 2002; Neuendorf, 2002).

Intercoder agreement refers to the extent to which two or more coders have applied the same codes to the same text segments given an established coding scheme. It can be considered a psychometric exercise or a heuristic tool to examine consensus between and among coders. As a psychometric exercise, it provides a kappa statistic or percentage, evidence for the coding schema reliably fitting the data by more than one researcher. The kappa statistic is used to measure the extent to which coders achieve agreement beyond any agreement expected to occur by chance alone. Though qualitative researchers have not agreed on an absolute threshold for an acceptable kappa, a criterion of .80 or higher is considered excellent by a number of researchers (Banerjee, Capozzoli, McSweeney, & Sinha, 1999; Krippendorff, 1980; Popping, 1988). As a heuristic tool, intercoder agreement might be used to primarily provide a conversation regarding consensus. That is, having two coders code the same data can bring to the surface codes that have not been adequately defined or codes that might need to be divided into subcodes.

Conceptual Relationships Among Codes

Asking Questions Using Codes. Analysis requires thinking with data as well as thinking with codes. This means reviewing quotations to synthesize the texture and nuance of what participants convey as well as considering codes and their conceptual relationship with other codes in a higher level synthesis. In describing quotations coded to a topic, the researcher might present the condensed meaning across quotations as well as illustrate the range of sentiments and rationales. For example, in a study of oral history data and experiences with health and illness, a report on the code *sense of surrender* illustrates three participants' accounts of submitting to illness and death:

> Wasn't anything they could do about it. He died in about three days.

> I didn't realize [he] was dying, but he got worse off all night. We didn't know it.

> I think it was a heart attack, although they never did fully know. He wasn't in real good health and just passed away in the night. (Southern Oral History Program Collection #4007, 1980–2006)

The full report of quotations provides a wider range of voices and experiences, providing evidence for the code and examples of its relevance across data. Participants do not question but simply surrender to what happens, evidencing a kind of fatalism, whether it is sudden death or the removal of a limb. In analysis, our task is not simply to present representative voices but to illustrate the range of voices. Even a sentiment or situation that shows up only once can inform a study and contribute to an array that can be further explored in a follow-up, perhaps quantitative, study.

Assessing Code Co-Occurrences. Beyond mining the meaning of a single code, researchers can assess code combinations to construct a multiple-concept code. That is, they can use codes to ask analytic questions of how codes share meaning or how one code might reveal unknowns about other codes. When analyzed together, codes may make more sense than when they are simply summarized separately. For example, the following paragraph from the hurricane study has been coded as both *time* and *assessing physical environment.*

> Rivers have rise[n] an unbelievable tremendous amount since yesterday. Apparently Floyd dumped an enormous amount of rain on eastern NC and showed no mercy. Houses and roads are flooded from the rain yesterday and now rivers are rising. A group of friends and I had made plans to head to Salem, VA, for the weekend. What should have been a four-hour trip turned out to be seven hours due to closed roads. Around 11:30 p.m. we crashed into our motel rooms and awaited the morning. (East Carolina University, 1999)

The participants are coping not only with an altered physical setting but also with altered time. Co-occurring codes that are applied to the same excerpts can be recon-ceptualized as a multiple-concept code, *elongated time.* This code captures how what is happening to the physical environment also seems to affect the experience of time itself.

Co-occurrences can also happen at the level of the transcript rather than at the level of the quotation. For example, a code about *limited transportation* may illustrate how a rural participant is limited to a small geographic area, whereas the code *lack of proactivity*, applied elsewhere in the transcript, shows how the participant may avoid medical assistance.

> I sold my old car and I could ride a bus right to work and back.

> I always shied away from doctors, and I wouldn't go to them. But I knew there was something wrong with me and they made an appointment. (Southern Oral History Program Collection #4007, 1980–2006)

Together, these quotations and the associated codes suggest a higher level topic that we might call *proximal reliance*, capturing one's tendency to rely on nearby support but avoiding more distant (and intimidating) medical assistance. Bridging or combining codes in this way suggests a more complex topic—a multiple concept that tells a story within or across transcripts, condensing numerous textual accounts into a higher level topic (Maietta et al., 2018).

Using Codes to Construct Themes. Though individual transcripts might have identifiable threads, the term *theme* is best reserved for patterns distinguishable across many or all documents. In addition to the cross-cutting nature of themes, they are also topics that meaningfully integrate other codes. For example, in the hurricane study, researchers identified codes for *luck* and *guilt*. Reviewing the codes side by side—that is, in reviewing the respective sets of quotations—we see that these codes reveal more together than they do separately. Claims of being lucky, in light of revelations regarding guilt, give each code more conceptual depth. Researchers can conceptualize this connection by constructing a multiple-concept code, such as the *luck–guilt tradeoff* (Mihas, 2014). Combining codes to construct a more meaningful topic is not only a comparative task, it also gives rise to a larger claim, finding, or metastory. Rather than merely summarizing *luck* and *guilt* as separate sections in a paper, asking how they conceptually *vibrate* with each other takes analysis to more suggestive territory. Constructing themes goes beyond summary to integration.

Analyzing Demographics, Themes, and Codes. Themes can also be discerned by combining codes and demographic variables. Demographic variables might be deductive attributes such as gender, age, and ethnicity, but they can also be inductive attributes based on what the researchers discern in the data. In the hurricane study, the code *partying* can be transformed into the variable *partiers*. This attribute categorizes participants who attended hurricane parties and did not anticipate the extent of the ultimate damage. How you might use these demographics in analysis brings the focus back to the codes. You might, for example, find that certain codes are evident in the older adults' transcripts and that other codes are evident in the younger individuals' data. Themes can then be constructed based on these distinctions (e.g., *indestructible youth*). Another example is a study of chronic muscle pain, where analysis of narratives regarding pain management indicated differences based on gender. Women adopted a *quest narrative*, while men espoused a *restitution narrative*. That is, women sought a solution for their physical pain that transcended medicine, whereas men sought closure within the context of medicine. Hence, *quest narrative* and *restitution narrative* become themes linked to gender, elevating the differences between men and women to a conceptual plane (Ahlsen, Bondevik, Mengshoel, & Solbrække, 2014).

Using Codes to Build Theory. Theories in qualitative research often address a process or phenomenon, its contexts, and its consequences. That is, we use theory to not only describe a process but also explain what keeps it in place, what destabilizes it, and what outcomes it generates (Corbin & Strauss, 2015). Hence, we might say that theories go beyond themes in providing a more fully articulated explanation for behavior or action. Codes help us build theory by allowing us to keep track of the elements of this unfolding process—conditions that foster it and variations in how it is experienced. For example, in a study on the rural experience of health care, we identify a central code, *instrumental relationship with doctors* and then use other codes to elaborate on how this relationship is played out. Hence, we tell the story of how individuals participate in a process—actions, interactions, and reactions. Examining codes with theory development in mind produces hypotheses about how the phenomenon and the participants interact (Leedy & Ormrod, 2013; Merriam, 2009). (For an example, see Charmaz 1999.)

PRODUCTS OF ANALYSIS: CONDENSING FINDINGS INTO MATRICES AND DIAGRAMS

Matrices

A common product of analysis is a narrative report and illustrative quotations of reflecting themes that have risen to prominence, but products of analysis can include matrices, charts, and diagrams. Rather than focusing on frequencies, which can be misleading in qualitative inquiry, researchers can use matrices to show relationships between codes—how combinations of codes lead to a distinctive narrative. A matrix is a form of synthesis, a place to get a "good view" of the data (Miles et al., 2014). It allows us to step back and see primary codes in relation to other codes.

EXAMPLE

This matrix condenses information from a study on experiencing a hurricane. The matrix is based on axes of agency and types of environment—imposed and constructed. "Imposed environment" refers to the established conditions of the storm; "constructed environment" refers to being creative in finding refuge or changing one's built environment for survival.

Types of Environment and Agency

	Imposed Environment	Constructed Environment
Survivor as **Disempowered**	• Storm overpowering the participant • Participant frustrated with FEMA • Storm personified as villain	• Experiencing instrumental intimacy ("misery loves company") • Participants connected yet feeling hopeless
Survivor as **Empowered**	• Participant joining forces with neighbors • Solidarity and increased prosocial behavior	• Survivor proactive in managing the stages of the strom • Participants strategizing shelter with strangers and neighbors

FIGURE 7.2 ● DIAGRAM OF THE CONNECTION AMONG THREE CODES WITH ILLUSTRATIVE QUOTES

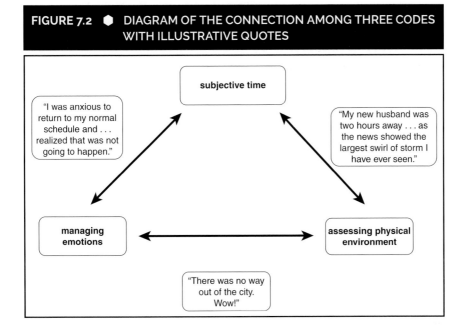

Diagrams

Another research product is a diagram. The example in Figure 7.2 shows the connections among three codes—*subjective time*, *managing emotions*, and *assessing physical environment*—in the hurricane study. The diagram captures the constellation of primary codes in the data and how they are linked to one another. Diagrams are a product of analytic synthesis, a visual technique designed to make a claim by positioning codes and linking them. The connections show the reader what has been learned during the research journey, something that could not have been produced without "empirical intimacy"—dwelling in data and taking systematic inventory of data and indispensable topics (Truzzi, 1974). Illustrative quotations are used to provide further evidence of the connections.

CONCLUSION

In this chapter, I provided an overview of techniques used in qualitative analysis. After collecting data, you begin engaging data from a particular point of departure—perhaps from a conceptual framework or from an exploratory perspective. You apply codes to data and define these codes, thus identifying patterns across data. You also show what stands out from the pattern—the paradoxes and contradictions. Analysis allows the assessment of co-occurrences of codes—topics that repeatedly show up together in the same excerpts or transcripts. Codes that share "space" might also share meaning. They reveal unknowns about the other and allow us to move up the conceptual ladder. Qualitative analysis requires examining codes both within and across data, as well as constructing products such as diagrams and matrices to synthesize findings.

Questions for Reflection

1. Consider the following paragraph from the hurricane data mentioned in this chapter:

   And then there was darkness. Never before had I lived without electricity. Without this necessity it left me feeling very alone. I noticed people cooking outside and I met many of my neighbors that I never really had gotten to know. During the first day without power I had decided that I would drive back to PA because the electricity was not supposed to come back on for a few days. That idea failed miserably, though. All roads out of Greenville were flooded. This left me feeling completely helpless and even more alone.

   Try coding this paragraph using some of the coding approaches discussed in this chapter—inductive coding, in vivo coding, and interpretive coding.

2. Begin writing a definition of one of the codes you used in the previous exercise. How will you determine how this code will be applied in other data?

3. Notice how your codes above suggest tangible, surface-level topics or abstract topics higher on the conceptual ladder. Are there other differences among your codes, such as codes capturing actions versus codes capturing feelings, that you notice?

Key Sources

Charmaz, K. (2014). *Constructing grounded theory* (2nd ed.). Thousand Oaks, CA: SAGE.

Corbin, J., & Strauss, A. (2015). *Basics of qualitative research: Techniques and procedures for developing grounded theory*. Thousand Oaks, CA: SAGE.

Creswell, J., & Poth, C. (2018). *Qualitative inquiry and research design: Choosing among five approaches*. Thousand Oaks, CA: SAGE.

Daiute, C. (2014). *Narrative inquiry: A dynamic approach*. Thousand Oaks, CA: SAGE.

Miles, M., Huberman, A. M., & Saldaña, J. (2014). *Qualitative data analysis: A methods sourcebook* (3rd ed.). Thousand Oaks, CA: SAGE.

Saldaña, J. (2016). *The coding manual for qualitative researchers*. Thousand Oaks, CA: SAGE.

References

Ahlsen, B., Bondevik, H., Mengshoel, A. M., & Solbrække, K. N. (2014). (Un)doing gender in a rehabilitation context: A narrative analysis of gender and self in stories of chronic muscle pain. *Disability and Rehabilitation, 36*(5), 359–366.

Alexander, I. (1988). Personality, psychological assessment, and psychobiography. *Journal of Personality, 56*, 265–294.

Banerjee, M., Capozzoli, M., McSweeney, L., & Sinha, D. (1999). Beyond kappa: A review of interrater agreement measures. *Canadian Journal of Statistics, 27*(1), 3–23.

Burla, L., Knierim, B., Barth, J., Liewald, K., Duetz, M., & Abel, T. (2008). From text to codings: Intercoder reliability assessment in qualitative content analysis. *Nursing Research, 57*(2), 113–117.

Burman, E., & Parker, I. (1993). *Discourse analytic research: Repertoires and readings of texts in action.* New York, NY: Routledge.

Charmaz, K. (1999). Stories of suffering: Subjective tales and research narratives. *Qualitative Health Research, 9*(3), 362–382.

Charmaz, K. (2014). *Constructing grounded theory* (2nd ed.). Thousand Oaks, CA: SAGE.

Corbin, J., & Strauss, A. (2015). *Basics of qualitative research: Techniques and procedures for developing grounded theory.* Thousand Oaks, CA: SAGE.

East Carolina University. (1999). *Listening to history: Telling our stories about the flooding of 1999* (History 5135, Manuscripts and Rare Book Collection). Greenville, NC: Author.

Fryer, C., Passmore, S., Maietta, R., Petruzzelli, J., Casper, E., Brown, N., . . . Quinn, S. (2015). The symbolic value and limitations of racial concordance in minority research engagement. *Qualitative Health Research, 26*(6), 830–841.

Krippendorff, K. (1980). *Content analysis: An introduction to its methodology.* Thousand Oaks, CA: SAGE.

Leedy, P. D., & Ormrod, J. E. (2013). *Practical research: Planning and design.* Boston, MA: Pearson.

Lombard, M., Snyder-Duch, J., & Bracken, C. C. (2002). Content analysis in mass communication assessment and reporting of intercoder reliability. *Human Communication Research, 28*(4), 587–604.

Maietta, R. (2006). State of the art: Integrating software with qualitative analysis. In L. Curry, R. Shield, & T. Wetle (Eds.), *Improving aging and public health research: Qualitative and mixed methods* (pp. 117–139). Washington, DC: American Public Health Association and the Gerontological Society of America.

Maietta, R., Hamilton, A., Swartout, K., & Petruzzelli, J. (2018). *ResearchTalk's Qualitative Data Analysis Camp* (Short course conducted by ResearchTalk, Inc.). Carrboro, NC: ResearchTalk.

Merriam, S. B. (2009). *Qualitative research: A guide to design and implementation.* San Francisco, CA: Jossey-Bass.

Mihas, P. (2014, May). *Load-bearing codes: Coding the connections.* Paper presented at the International Congress of Qualitative Inquiry, Urbana, IL.

Miles, M., Huberman, A. M., & Saldaña, J. (2014). *Qualitative data analysis: A methods sourcebook* (3rd ed.). Thousand Oaks, CA: SAGE.

Neuendorf, K. (2002). *The content analysis guidebook.* Thousand Oaks, CA: SAGE.

Popping, R. (1988). On agreement indices for nominal data. In W. E. Saris & I. N. Gallhofer (Eds.), *Sociometric research: Vol. 1. Data collection and scaling* (pp. 90–105). New York, NY: St. Martin's Press.

Potter, J., & Wetherell, M. (1987). *Discourse and social psychology: Beyond attitudes and behavior.* Newbury Park, CA: SAGE.

SAGE. (2019). *Learn to build a codebook for a generic qualitative study.* Retrieved from http://methods.sagepub.com/Datasets

Saldaña, J. (2016). *The coding manual for qualitative researchers.* Thousand Oaks, CA: SAGE.

Southern Oral History Program Collection #4007. (1980–2006). *Southern historical collection.* Chapel Hill, NC: University of North Carolina at Chapel Hill, Wilson Library.

Truzzi, M. (1974). *Verstehen: Subjective understanding in the social sciences.* Reading, MA: Addison-Wesley.

MIXED METHODS DESIGNS AND APPROACHES

Bonnie K. Nastasi

A major premise of this chapter is that research methods can be portrayed on a continuum from quantitative to qualitative, with mixed methods somewhere in the center. Chapters 4 and 6 address quantitative and qualitative methodologies. This chapter draws on that background to focus on the important issues relevant to the mixing of methods. Framing the discussion is the assumption that mixed methods research (MMR) can facilitate the exploration of complex research questions such as those related to translating research to practice and policy, thereby extending the potential contributions of qualitative or quantitative methods studies alone.

An important first step in decision making about research methods is consideration of the purpose of research. Newman, Ridenour, Newman, and DeMarco (2003) provided a typology of nine research purposes with specific connections to methods. The purposes that call for quantitative methods include prediction, extending knowledge, measuring change, and testing new ideas. Those that call for qualitative methods include understanding complex phenomena, generating new ideas, examining the past, and having personal, social, or organizational impact. Newman and colleagues proposed that a ninth purpose, informing constituencies, relies on both qualitative and quantitative methods. Furthermore, they proposed that several purposes could be extended through mixed methods: (a) extending knowledge base, (b) understanding complex phenomena, (c) generating or testing new ideas, and (d) having personal, social, or organizational impact.

Given this differentiation of method by purpose, how do we distinguish quantitative, qualitative, and mixed methods? In general,[1] quantitative methods are based in the hypothetical–deductive and postpositivist traditions of science and rely on statistics to represent the occurrence of phenomena and to test predictions (hypotheses) based on deductions from existing research and theory. Qualitative methods are based on the constructivist and interpretive traditions and rely on verbal and visual representations (e.g., through narrative, observations, artifacts). In contrast to the deductive approach in quantitative research, qualitative research is an inductive form of inquiry. Finally, quantitative research embodies an etic perspective based on existing theory and research as interpreted by the researcher, and qualitative research is characterized by an emic perspective designed to capture

---

[1] This qualifier applies to most distinctions between quantitative, qualitative, and mixed methods research; there are exceptions for most rules. As an example, it is possible for a quantitative researcher to describe phenomena without using tests or deductive processes.

the perspective of those being studied and/or identify theory grounded in real-life experience. MMR, characterized by the mixing of quantitative and qualitative, is intended to capitalize on the strengths of each of these traditions in order to extend our understanding of phenomena and to inform science, practice, and policy through the integration of emic and etic perspectives.

The purpose of this chapter is to introduce MMR, address key philosophical and design issues, and answer questions about MMR and why researchers choose to mix qualitative and quantitative methods. The chapter begins with an explanation of MMR and why researchers choose a mixed methods approach. Following this is a discussion of philosophical underpinnings of MMR. Next is a discussion of types of MMR designs, followed by a discussion of the process of integrating quantitative and qualitative findings.

WHAT IS MIXED METHODS RESEARCH?

MMR, stated simply, is the integration of quantitative and qualitative data collection and analysis to answer specific research questions; it can be viewed as the center of the quantitative–qualitative continuum. However, MMR is much more complex than merely the collection of both qualitative and quantitative data in a single study. In the past two decades, methodologists have engaged in discussion and debate about what constitutes MMR, the types of MMR, when and how to apply mixed methods, and the interplay between the researcher's philosophy and choice of methods, among other issues. The result of these discussions is reflected in publication of two editions of the *Handbook of Mixed Methods Research* (Tashakkori & Teddlie, 2003, 2010), the *Journal of Mixed Methods Research*, and a plethora of books and articles. The writings in the field not only address philosophical and design issues but also provide examples of applications of MMR. For methodologists, the consideration of the questions surrounding MMR can be overwhelming and impede its use. At the same time, lack of understanding of the complexity and expected rigor can lead to poorly designed studies. Planned and conducted in a systematic way, MMR can enhance our understanding of phenomena in ways that extend beyond the use of qualitative or quantitative designs alone.

WHY DO RESEARCHERS USE MIXED METHODS?

The decision to use MMR depends on your purpose. Newman et al. (2003) and others (e.g., Tashakkori & Teddlie, 2003) have argued that purpose drives the choice of design and methods. Greene, Caracelli, and Graham (1989) identified purposes for using MMR in evaluation research: (a) triangulation (seeking convergence), (b) complementarity (seeking clarification or elaboration), (c) development (informing later stages of research program), (d) initiation (seeking new perspectives), and (e) expansion (extending breadth and depth). More complex schemes for classifying purpose have been suggested as well, for example, Bryman's (2006) 16-type scheme for classifying research purpose (for detail, see Bryman's article). As a general rule, research purpose and questions determine the choice of design and methods. For those of you choosing MMR, your decision must stem from research questions that cannot be answered by quantitative or qualitative methods alone.

The value of qualitative and quantitative methods in MMR. Hausman et al. (2013) describe the use of MMR in the development of contextually relevant measures of outcomes in violence prevention programs. Through a participatory process of involving stakeholders in the community, the researchers developed community-defined constructs relevant to established measures. The qualitative data, gathered through focus groups, led to the development of community-defined indicators of the effectiveness of violence prevention programs. These indicators were then matched to items from existing, previously validated measures to inform the development of new culturally relevant measures; this was followed by quantitative data collection (administration of new measures) and factor analysis to establish instrument validity. The process resulted in development of new culturally relevant constructs not reflected in preexisting measures. For additional examples of the use of MMR in instrument development, see Hitchcock and Nastasi (2011), Hitchcock, Nastasi, et al. (2005), Hitchcock, Sarkar, et al. (2006), and Nastasi, Hitchcock, Burkholder, et al. (2007).

Morgan (2007) extends the considerations around research purpose and draws distinctions among qualitative, quantitative, and MMR based on the connections between theory and data, researcher and research process, and data and inference, which all follow from the research purpose.

1. *Theory–data connection.* In most qualitative research, data analysis can be described as an *inductive* process; that is, the meaning of data is derived from the viewpoint of the participants. For example, children might describe what they view as psychological well-being. In quantitative research, data analysis is *deductive*, such that the meaning of data depends on existing theory and research. For example, hypotheses are derived by existing empirically supported theory. In MMR, the collection of both qualitative and quantitative data lends itself to an *abductive* approach, in which researchers can integrate meanings of constructs, such as psychological well-being, based on an integration of the inductive and deductive reasoning. Thus, MMR researchers modify existing definitions based on perspectives of research participants as reflected in data.

2. *Researcher–research relationship.* In qualitative research, the researcher generally assumes a *subjective* stance regarding the research process. For

example, the researcher's perspective influences research questions and data collection and analysis. In quantitative research, the researcher assumes an *objective* stance, thus attempting to engage in the research process without personal bias; instead, existing theory might guide the development of research questions, data collection, analysis, and so on. MMR researchers assume an *intersubjective* perspective by attempting to integrate an objective stance drawn from existing theory with a subjective stance drawn from personal worldview.

3. *Data–inference relationship.* In qualitative research, the interpretation of data is assumed to be specific to the *context* in which the research occurred—for example, a specific elementary school. In quantitative research, the data are interpreted with an assumption of *generality*; that is, the findings can be applied to elementary schools in general. In MMR, findings are assumed to be *transferable* to other similar settings—for example, to elementary schools with similar contextual features (demographics, location).

These descriptions of MMR characterize the method as a complex yet powerful approach to research. If your research interests are aligned with an MMR approach, you need to integrate the inductive approach with one that is also deductive. You need to seek an intersubjective connection between yourself as the researcher and your topic of interest. Last, you need to characterize your data inference connection as one that is transferable between context-specific settings and one that is general. All these considerations must be addressed. For further details, see Morgan (2007) and Nastasi, Hitchcock, and Brown (2010).

In addition to considerations about research purpose, your philosophical and theoretical perspectives are critical. Indeed, MMR has been identified as a third paradigm to distinguish it from quantitative (first) and qualitative (second) research. I explore these issues in the next section.

PHILOSOPHICAL UNDERPINNINGS OF MMR: WHAT IS THE THIRD PARADIGM?

Underlying methodological decisions are

> philosophical assumptions that researchers bring to their inquiries . . . [assumptions about] what knowledge warrants our attention, how knowledge is learned, the nature of reality and values, and also the historical and political perspectives that individuals bring to research. (Creswell & Tashakkori, 2007, p. 305)

Johnson and Onwuegbuzie (2004) defined a *research paradigm* as "a set of beliefs, values, and assumptions that a community of researchers has in common regarding the nature and conduct of research . . . a research culture" (p. 24).[2] Applying the concept of research culture, they describe MMR as the *third paradigm* with philosophical foundations that distinguish it from the first (quantitative) and second (qualitative) paradigms. The philosophical foundations of quantitative research are positivist or, more recently, postpositivist, with a focus on objectivity, context-free generalizability, and causality. The foundations of qualitative research are constructivist or interpretive, with a focus on subjectivity, context specificity, and multiple constructions of reality. The most common depiction of the third (alternative) paradigm for MMR is *pragmatism* (see Johnson & Onwuegbuzie, 2004; Maxcy, 2003; Morgan, 2007; Nastasi et al., 2010; Tashakkori & Teddlie, 1998, 2003). Morgan (2007) described pragmatism as grounded in *practical* questions that include purpose (Is MMR the best way to answer the research questions?), context (What is appropriate given the setting?), and consequences or implications (Will the research lead to change at social or policy level?).

Greene (2007) and Denscombe (2008) adopt the *dialectical* perspective, founded on the intersubjective nature of MMR. Greene's *dialectical* perspective emphasizes the potential divergence or conflict of views between the researcher and the researched and the integration of these. For example, in participatory research, one might focus on integrating the etic perspective of the researcher and the emic perspective of the participants (Nastasi, Hitchcock, Sarkar, et al., 2007). The dialectical perspective is also inherent in Descombe's *communities of practice* model, involving partnership of researchers and practitioners (e.g., teachers). Critical to the dialectical perspective is the value of MMR that results from the potential conflict between subjective and objective views inherent in qualitative and quantitative data, respectively. Applied to Descombe's communities of practice, the tension between researchers and practitioners can facilitate a process that leads to thinking informed by both stakeholder groups. The differences in perspectives can challenge the etic view of researchers— that is, their worldview informed by theory and research. These differences can also make explicit the practitioners' emic views, worldviews informed by their experiences and understanding of the context. Integration of etic and emic views can help ensure the application of research to practice and alter the perspectives of both researchers and practitioners.

Furthermore, Mertens (2003, 2007) proposed the *transformative (–emancipatory)* perspective that incorporates the pragmatist and the dialectical perspectives. Mertens (2007) described the transformative approach as "a cyclical model of mixed methods research . . . as a way of involving the community in research decisions and the collection of data that can be used for social justice purposes" (p. 224). The purpose of research from the transformative (–emancipatory) perspective is to understand

---

[2] Johnson and Onwuegbuzie (2004) and Denscombe (2008) describe the MMR as a paradigm that depicts a *research community*, consistent with the thinking of Kuhn (1962). As discussed in Denscombe, the four characteristics of paradigm (according to Kuhn) are as follows: (1) specific set of problems that are important to advancing science, (2) shared practices or research techniques, (3) shared identity among researchers, and (4) community of researchers.

Contributions of the dialectical perspective: Emic + Etic = Derived Etic. Harkness et al. (2006) used a mixed methods design—specifically, qualitative semistructured interviews and quantitative structured questionnaires—to develop a cross-cultural child temperament measure that was relevant to the cultures in seven countries. Using data from parent descriptors of their children (emic) and existing child development theories and measures (etic), the researchers developed instruments that reflected convergence of emic and etic perspectives (derived etic) that could be applied to cross-cultural research. Important to their work was the identification of descriptors that reflected convergence from parents' interview data across the seven countries, thus achieving consensus on what might be described as universal descriptors of child temperament. This method contrasts with the application of an etic perspective (e.g., measures of temperament developed and validated in the United States) in cross-cultural research.

social, cultural, and political realities from perspectives of stakeholders and to create change through researcher–participant partnerships. The pragmatic view is reflected in the intended consequences, to empower participants to bring about social change or action through the participatory research process. The dialectical perspective is evident in efforts to integrate emic and etic perspectives through the participatory process. Thus, the transformative (–emancipatory) framework focuses on the consequences of research (the pragmatic) and involves research participants as collaborators (the dialectical).

Mertens (2007, p. 223) described the educational reform work of Thomas (2004, cited in Mertens, 2007) as an example of transformative evaluation research that integrates scientific methods with political activism, "an evolving entity that is developed through a co-constructive process involving the evaluators, school staff members, parents, and students." This perspective is inherent also in participatory approaches focused on social change and capacity building in domestic and global contexts, such as those of Eade (1997), Nastasi, Hitchcock, Sarkar, et al. (2007), and Nelson and Prilleltensky (2005).

The use of MMR to address research questions from pragmatic, dialectical, and transformative perspectives speaks to MMR's potential to address more complex questions through the mix of qualitative and quantitative research. An example of this potential can be seen in the work of researchers who study the implementation of evidence-based interventions (EBIs) to answer questions about how to translate EBIs to practical settings. Recall from Chapter 4 the value of experimental research, for example, randomized controlled trials (RCTs), for testing the efficacy of an intervention. Such testing occurs under highly controlled conditions that might not match the conditions in real-world contexts. Even RCTs conducted in natural settings to test intervention effectiveness require some level of control to promote internal validity. This level of control is not always possible as practitioners attempt to implement EBIs. To address these challenges, implementation scientists have begun to use MMR to better understand the necessary conditions for effective interventions.

To do this, researchers use quantitative designs, such as RCTs, to test effectiveness of the intervention and use qualitative methods, such as observation and interviews, to document the conditions under which the intervention was conducted (Fixsen, Naoom, Blase, Friedman, & Wallace, 2005).

Implementation scientists also use MMR to study the process of implementation and adaptation of EBIs (Lee, Altschul, & Mowbray, 2008). For example, researchers might use qualitative research (interviews, observations) to understand the current context and population, make relevant modifications to an EBI to better fit the target culture and context, and then test the effectiveness of the modified intervention using quantitative methods. Furthermore, mixed methods can be used to explore the translation of research and policy to practice (Beidas et al., 2013). Such research holds promise for the application of MMR to address real-world challenges and to facilitate social and political change.

Using MMR to facilitate translation of research to practice. Goldstein, Kemp, Leff, and Lochman (2013) described and illustrated the use of mixed methods in participatory action research to facilitate the adaptation of EBIs to different contexts and populations. The process involves selecting an EBI, collecting qualitative data through focus group interviews with the target population, making revisions and piloting the revised program using an experimental (quantitative) design, collecting additional qualitative data from program implementers, making further revisions, and testing the intervention using RCTs with the target population. As described by Goldstein and colleagues, the process is an iterative application of a sequential process—qualitative (Qual) → quantitative (Quan) → Qual → Quan—in which data from each step informs the next. You might also consider the use of both qualitative and quantitative during each step of the process, thus Qual + Quan → Qual + Quan, and so on.

TYPES OF MMR

Mixed methodologists have proposed multiple schemes for categorizing mixed methods designs, ranging from basic to complex (Creswell, 2009; Nastasi et al., 2010; Onwuegbuzie & Collins, 2007; Teddlie & Tashakkori, 2006; Teddlie & Yu, 2007). Nastasi et al. (2010) proposed five typologies to depict the array of the MMR designs. In this chapter, I focus primarily on basic designs, with brief attention to more complex designs.

For the purposes of our discussion, a *research strand* refers to the completion of a three-phase/stage cycle of research: (1) conceptualization, (2) experiential, and (3) inferential (see Teddlie & Tashakkori, 2009). *Conceptualization* refers to establishing theoretical and empirical foundations, identifying research purpose, and formulating research questions. *Experiential* refers to data collection and analysis. *Inferential* refers to interpretation and application/dissemination of findings. In the next section, I expand these three phases to encompass a 10-step research process.

There are three basic design typologies: Type I, based on the number of research strands; Type II, the manner in which data are mixed; and Type III, the stage of the research process in which mixing occurs. *Type I* refers to whether research is monostrand or multistrand (see Tashakkori & Teddlie, 2003; Teddlie & Tashakkori, 2009). *Monostrand* refers to a study involving a single cycle (strand) from conceptualization to inference; this is typical of a single research study in which one generates research questions, collects and analyzes data (in this case, using mixed methods), and disseminates the findings. *Multistrand* refers to use of multiple cycles as one might use in a program of research that includes a series of studies. That is, the researcher engages in several conceptualization–experiential–inferential cycles, which are linked by long-term research goals, typically with the findings of one study influencing the purpose and questions of the next study.

Type II addresses the mixing of qualitative and quantitative methods, specifically *types* of data (qualitative and quantitative); *dominance*, the priority or relative importance of qualitative and quantitative (e.g., are qualitative data considered primary and quantitative secondary or vice versa; or are both data types equal in importance); and *timing*, whether qualitative and quantitative are collected at the same time (simultaneous or concurrent) or sequentially (qualitative before quantitative or vice versa). Morse (2003) developed a notation system to facilitate communication among mixed methods researchers, which included (a) types of methods, Qual (qualitative) or Quan (quantitative); (b) priority or dominance of methods, QUAL (dominant) or qual (supplemental); and (c) timing of methods, qual + quan (simultaneous) or qual → quan (sequential). Thus, an MMR study whose research questions call for dominant focus on qualitative methods, using sequential timing with quantitative data collection following qualitative, is depicted as QUAL → quan.

Decisions about types of data, priority given to different types, and timing are dependent on the study purpose. The complexity of decision making related to Type II typology is reflected in the diversity of schemes for classifying design types, ranging from a continuum of qualitative–mixed methods–quantitative (Johnson, Onwuegbuzie, & Turner, 2007) to a scheme of eight types of designs representing all the variations in data type, timing, and priority (Leech & Onwuegbuzie, 2009). You might find the scheme proposed by Creswell and Plano Clark (2007) to be the most useful, which includes four design types linked to study purpose: (1) *triangulation*, with equal weight and timing of qualitative and quantitative data, QUAN + QUAL; (2) *embedded*, with dominance given to simultaneous data collection, QUAL [quan] or QUAN [qual]; (3) *explanatory*, in which qualitative data are collected subsequently to explain dominant quantitative findings, QUAN → qual; and (4) *exploratory*, in which the primary data collected first are qualitative, followed by quantitative data collection for confirmation, QUAL → quan. (For information about more complex schemes, see Leech and Onwuegbuzie, 2009; Nastasi et al., 2010.)

Type III typologies refer to the categorization of MMR designs based on the phase of the research strand in which mixing occurs—that is, the specific phases related to conceptualization, experiential, and inferential. Most important to these distinctions is (a) whether qualitative and quantitative methods are part of all phases of the research process—that is, pertaining to research questions, sampling, data collection, data analysis, inference, and so on; or (b) whether mixing is stage specific—for example, only applying to sampling, data collection, or inference. In planning a study, you will need to consider the following: Do the research questions require both qualitative and quantitative data collection? Do you need sampling procedures specific to both qualitative (purposive) and quantitative (random and representative sample) data collection? Do you need to include procedures for collection and analysis of both qualitative (e.g., interviews) and quantitative (e.g., structured survey instrument) data? Are your inferences based on both qualitative (what do interviews tell you) and quantitative (what are findings from surveys) data as well as the integration of both data sets (do data from interviews confirm or disconfirm survey data)? Researchers have proposed typologies that address mixing across all phases, including Johnson and Onwuegbuzie (2004), Ridenour and Newman (2008), and Teddlie and Tashakkori (2009). Other researchers have proposed typologies that are stage specific—for example, sampling (Kemper, Stringfield, & Teddlie, 2003; Onwuegbuzie & Collins, 2007; Teddlie & Yu, 2007), data collection (Johnson & Turner, 2003), data analysis (Onwuegbuzie & Teddlie, 2003), and data inference/representation (Erzeberger & Kelle, 2003; Sandelowski, 2003; see Nastasi et al., 2010, for full discussion). In the next section, I return to discussing the integration of qualitative and quantitative data.

INTEGRATION OF QUALITATIVE AND QUANTITATIVE METHODS IN MMR

Mixing or integration of qualitative (Qual) and quantitative (Quan) methods can occur at multiple points in the research process. Nastasi et al. (2010) proposed an inclusive framework to characterize mixing, in which questions regarding the inclusion of Qual and Quan are considered at each stage of the 10-stage research process: (1) existing theory, research, and practice/policy, describing the context for research; (2) worldview (theoretical or conceptual foundations); (3) research purpose and questions; (4) sampling; (5) data collection; (6) data analysis; (7) data inference; (8) inference quality; (9) data representation; and (10) application. Each stage is characterized by specific questions that guide decisions about mixing of qualitative and quantitative methods. This includes which methods to use, which are dominant, and the timing of the methods (Table 8.1). A full discussion of this inclusive framework can be found in Nastasi et al. (2010).

The published doctoral research by Woolley (2009) is an example of how the mixing of Qual and Quan happens throughout the research process. Notation of

TABLE 8.1 ● STAGE-SPECIFIC QUESTIONS TO GUIDE DECISIONS ABOUT QUAL–QUAN MIXING IN MMR

Stage	Questions	Application
Context	What context is the basis for your research? Is it existing theory, research, practice, and/or policy?	What are the implications of the context (e.g., theory or existing practice) for your choice of methods?
Worldview	What theory or conceptual framework guides your thinking about research?	How does your worldview influence the extent to which you take an inductive, deductive, or abductive approach to inquiry?
Purpose/question	What is the purpose of your research? What are your research questions?	What do your purpose and questions imply about selection of Qual, Quan, or MMR methods? Do different questions require different methods (e.g., some Qual, some Quan)? What are the implications of questions for timing, priority, and mixing of Qual and Quan?
Sampling	What types of sampling are appropriate to your research purpose and questions?	How are sampling decisions influenced by whether questions require Qual, Quan, or MMR? Are different sampling methods necessary for collecting Qual and Quan data?
Data collection	What data collection methods are appropriate for answering your research questions?	What qualitative and quantitative data collection methods (e.g., observation, interviews, surveys) are needed to answer your research questions? Do different questions require different methods (e.g., some Qual, some Quan)? What are the implications of questions for timing, priority, and mixing of Qual and Quan? For example, what types of data are dominant? In what order do you need to collect different types of data (e.g., sequential, concurrent)?
Data analysis	What are the implications of your theory, purpose, and questions for how you approach data collection in terms of choice of methods, priority, timing, and mixing? What data analysis approach is most appropriate to answer the research questions? How will you approach Qual and Quan data and their mixing? How will you make decisions about the need for more data collection (e.g., to achieve saturation or to make sure research questions are answered)?	Do your theory, purpose, and questions imply an inductive, deductive, or abductive approach to data analysis? How will you analyze Qual versus Quan data sets? Based on your purpose, how will you integrate the findings from Qual and Quan data analysis (e.g., Will Qual be used to explain Quan data)? Following integration of Qual–Quan, how will you decide if you need to collect more data?
Data inference	How will you interpret the different types of data as they relate to research purpose and questions? How does the priority of data type (e.g., QUAL, quan)	What is the process for interpreting data based on timing (concurrent vs. sequential), priority (dominance of data type), and mixing (complementary,

	influence your interpretation of the data? How does the timing of data collection influence your interpretation? How will you resolve discrepancies between Qual and Quan? How will you decide if you have answered the research questions, based on each type of data and their mixing?	explanatory, etc.)? For example, will the dominant data type have more weight in interpretation? If you engaged in qual → quan sequence of data collection, will you analyze the types of data in the same sequence, and will findings from Qual influence how you interpret Quan? How will you make decisions when integrating data, based on your conceptual framework and purpose? For example, a transformative paradigm would imply that data are mixed to facilitate social or political change. If the purpose of your study is to generate and test theory, would this require that you use QUAL for generating and QUAN for testing, or can you use both Qual and Quan to inform both generation and testing of theory?
Inference quality (validity)[a]	What techniques are necessary to promote inference quality of Qual, Quan, and their integration? How will findings related to inference quality influence decisions about additional data collection?	Based on your study purpose and design, what are the inference quality techniques for Quan data? For Qual data? For mixing Quan and Qual? How is that influenced by priority and timing of data types? What if one or both types of data have low inference quality? How can the integration of Qual and Quan enhance inference quality?
Data representation	What is the best way to represent the data types? How will you present Qual, Quan, and their integration for different audiences? How will presentation of data potentially inform subsequent research?	If you operate from a transformative paradigm, what is the best way to represent findings so that stakeholders can use the information to inform social or political change? How would you represent data differently for lay and professional audiences?
Application	What are the potential applications of research findings? What do the context, worldview, and purpose imply about the use of findings?	To what extent can research findings be used for the following purposes: (a) to extend existing knowledge; (b) to facilitate social change; (c) to generate new research questions; (d) to provide direction within a program of research; (e) to validate an assessment instrument or intervention program, which could then be used in practice; or (f) to generate a new conceptual framework? Are these applications justified based on the study design, findings, and inference quality?

Note: An expanded discussion of these questions can be found in Nastasi et al. (2010). MMR = mixed methods research; Qual = qualitative; Quan = quantitative.

a - Inference quality (validity) is addressed in Chapter 12.

relevant stages is provided in Table 8.1. He wanted to investigate the interaction of personal agency and sociocultural contexts (i.e., gender and institutional setting) and explore both the variations and importance in development of young adults, ages 18 to 25, living in Derby, England. He generated related research objectives and questions (Stages 1 and 3). His work was informed by a sociological perspective that required adopting MMR to generate a conceptualization of the agency–context interplay through the integration of qualitative and quantitative methods (Stage 2). The study's sequential design included initial data collection of quantitative survey with 300 participants (using quota sampling related to objectives), followed by focus group interviews with 47 participants (a subset of the 300; purposive sampling), and subsequently individual interviews with a subset of 8 participants (4 male and 4 female; purposive sampling) (Stages 4 and 5). Data analysis of the quantitative data (factor analysis, analysis of variance, descriptive statistics) informed focus group questions. Data from focus groups were used to elaborate on quantitative findings. Subsequent biographical interviews were used to further explicate the interplay of agency and context, initially established through surveys and focus groups (Stage 6). The integration of data from surveys, focus groups, and individual interviews informed the inferences drawn from the study. In the process of integration, Woolley also addressed apparent discrepancies, in part drawing on knowledge of the context from which the sample was drawn and discussed how this process influences data representation for dissemination (Stages 7, 9, and 10). Woolley did not explicitly address inference quality, although you might conclude that the systematic interplay of qualitative and quantitative data as described enhanced quality (Stage 8). Woolley (2009) described the process as "linking the quantitative and qualitative components effectively [as] the basis for producing integrated findings that are greater than the sum of their parts" (p. 23).

CONCLUSION

What is most promising about the field of MMR is the potential to explore more complex research questions such as those posed in implementation science, an interdisciplinary field focused on enhancing the translation of research to practice and policy. MMR is the integration of qualitative and quantitative methods. However, the field of MMR has expanded into a complex system in which the mixing of qualitative and quantitative research methods influences every stage of the research process. Whereas your initial decision about choice of methods—qualitative, quantitative, or mixed—must always follow from your study's purpose, this choice will lead to questions at every step of the research process. Ideally, your choice of MMR would result in mixing of qualitative and quantitative throughout the research process. In practice, you might only choose to mix or integrate in select phases—for example, only in data inference. Ultimately, the value of your research depends on the extent to which consumers, such as other researchers, practitioners, and policymakers, can be confident in research findings.

Questions for Reflection

1. For what purposes might the researcher choose to use MMR rather than qualitative or quantitative research designs alone?

2. Identify a published MMR study in your area of interest and answer the following questions:

    a. To what extent do the research purpose and/or research questions align with the use of MMR? Was MMR the best choice given the researcher's purpose or could qualitative or quantitative alone been sufficient? Why or why not?

    b. What type of MMR design was used? What other MMR design types could the researcher have used? Explain your answer.

3. To what extent did the researchers integrate qualitative and quantitative data to answer the research questions? Moreover, to what extent did the researcher integrate inductive (emic) and deductive (etic) perspectives in the analysis and interpretation of data?

4. How can MMR be used to facilitate the translation of research to practice—for example, helping teachers to apply educational research findings to their classrooms?

Key Sources

Creswell, J. W., & Plano Clark, V. L. (2010). *Designing and conducting mixed methods research* (2nd ed.). Thousand Oaks, CA: SAGE.

Johnson, R. B., & Onwuegbuzie, A. J. (2004). Mixed methods research: A research paradigm whose time has come. *Educational Researcher, 33*(7), 14–26. doi:10.3102/0013189X033007014

Mertens, D. M. (2007). Transformative paradigm: Mixed methods and social justice. *Journal of Mixed Methods Research, 1,* 212–225. doi:10.1177/1558689807302811

Tashakkori, A., & Teddlie, C. (Eds.). (2010). *Handbook of mixed methods in social and behavioral research* (2nd ed.). Thousand Oaks, CA: SAGE.

Teddlie, C., & Tashakkori, A. (2009). *Foundations of mixed methods research: Integrating quantitative and qualitative approaches in the social and behavioral sciences.* Thousand Oaks, CA: SAGE.

References

Beidas, R. S., Aarons, G., Barg, F., Evans, A., Hadley, T., Hoagwood, K., . . . Mandell, D. S. (2013). Policy to implementation: Evidence-based practice in community mental healh—study protocol. *Implementation Science, 8,* 38. doi:10.1186/1748-5908-8-38.

Bryman, A. (2006). Integrating quantitative and qualitative research: How is it done? *Qualitative Research, 6,* 97–113. doi:10.1177/1468794106058877

Creswell, J. W. (2009). Editorial: Mapping the field of mixed methods research. *Journal of Mixed Methods Research, 3,* 95–108. doi:10.1177/1558689808330883

Creswell, J. W., & Plano Clark, V. L. (2007). *Designing and conducting mixed methods research*. Thousand Oaks, CA: SAGE.

Creswell, J. W., & Tashakkori, A. (2007). Editorial: Differing perspectives on mixed methods research. *Journal of Mixed Methods Research, 1,* 303–308. doi:10.1177/1558689807306132

Denscombe, M. (2008). Communities of practice: A research paradigm for the mixed methods approach. *Journal of Mixed Methods Research, 2,* 270–283. doi:10.1177/1558689808316807

Eade, D. (1997). *Capacity-building: An approach to people-centred development*. Oxford, UK: Oxfam.

Erzeberger, C., & Kelle, U. (2003). Marking inferences in mixed methods: The rules of integration. In A. Tashakkori & C. Teddlie (Eds.), *Handbook of mixed methods in social and behavioral research* (pp. 457–490). Thousand Oaks, CA: SAGE.

Fixsen, D. L., Naoom, S. F., Blase, K. A., Friedman, R. M., & Wallace, F. (2005). *Implementation research: A synthesis of the literature*. Tampa, FL: University of South Florida, Louis de la Parte Florida Mental Health Institute, The National Implementation Research Network (FMHI Publication No. 231). Retrieved from http://nirn.fmhi.usf.edu

Goldstein, N. E. S., Kemp, K. A., Leff, S. S., & Lochman, J. E. (2013). Guidelines for adapting manualized interventions to new target populations: A step-wise approach using anger management as a model. *Clinical Psychology Science and Practice, 19*(4), 385–401. doi:10.1111/cpsp.12011

Greene, J. C. (2007). *Mixed methods in social inquiry*. San Francisco, CA: Jossey-Bass.

Greene, J. C., Caracelli, V. J., & Graham, W. F. (1989). Toward a conceptual framework for mixed method evaluation designs. *Educational Evaluation and Policy Analysis, 11,* 255–274. doi:10.3102/01623737011003255

Harkness, S., Moscardino, U., Bermúdez, M. R., Zylicz, P. O., Welles-Nyström, B., Blom, M., . . . Super, C. M. (2006). Mixed methods in international collaborative research: The experiences of the International Study of Parents, Children, and Schools. *Cross-Cultural Research, 40*(1), 65–82. doi:10.1177/1069397105283179

Hausman, A. J., Baker, C. N., Komaroff, E., Thomas, N., Guerra, T., Hohl, B. C., & Leff, S. S. (2013). Developing measures of community-relevant outcomes for violence prevention programs: A community-based participatory research approach to measurement. *American Journal of Community Psychology, 52,* 249–262. doi:10.1007/s10464-013-9590-6

Hitchcock, J., & Nastasi, B. K. (2011). Mixed methods for construct validation. In P. Vogt & M. Williams (Eds.), *Handbook of methodological innovation* (pp. 249–268). Thousand Oaks, CA: SAGE.

Hitchcock, J. H., Nastasi, B. K., Dai, D. C., Newman, J., Jayasena, A., Bernstein-Moore, R., . . . Varjas, K. (2005). Illustrating a mixed-method approach for identifying and validating culturally specific constructs. *Journal of School Psychology, 43*(3), 259–278. doi:10.1016/j.jsp.2005.04.007

Hitchcock, J. H., Sarkar, S., Nastasi, B. K., Burkholder, G., Varjas, K., & Jayasena, A. (2006). Validating culture- and gender-specific constructs: A mixed-method approach to advance assessment procedures in cross-cultural settings. *Journal of Applied School Psychology, 22,* 13–33. doi:10.1300/J370v22n02_02

Johnson, R. B., & Onwuegbuzie, A. J. (2004). Mixed methods research: A research paradigm whose time has come. *Educational Researcher, 33,* 14–26. doi:10.3102/0013189X033007014

Johnson, R. B., Onwuegbuzie, A. J., & Turner, L. A. (2007). Toward a definition of mixed methods research. *Journal of Mixed Methods Research, 1,* 112-133. doi:10.1177/1558689806298224

Johnson, B., & Turner, L. A. (2003). Data collection strategies in mixed methods research. In A. Tashakkori & C. Teddlie (Eds.), *Handbook of mixed methods in social and behavioral research* (pp. 297–320). Thousand Oaks, CA: SAGE.

Kemper, E. A., Stringfield, S., & Teddlie, C. (2003). Mixed methods sampling strategies in social science research. In A. Tashakkori & C. Teddlie (Eds.), *Handbook of mixed methods in social and behavioral research* (pp. 273–296). Thousand Oaks, CA: SAGE.

Kuhn, T. S. (1962). *The structure of scientific revolutions.* Chicago, IL: University of Chicago Press.

Lee, S. J., Altschul, I., & Mowbray, C. T. (2008). Using planned adaptation to implement evidence-based programs with new populations. *American Journal of Community Psychology, 41,* 290–303. doi:10.1007/s10464-008-9160-5

Leech, N. L., & Onwuegbuzie, A. J. (2009). A typology of mixed methods research designs. *Quality and Quantity, 43,* 265–275. doi:10.1007/s11135-007-9105-3

Maxcy, S. J. (2003). Pragmatic threads in mixed methods research in the social sciences: The search for multiple modes of inquiry and the end of the philosophy of formalism. In A. Tashakkori & C. Teddlie (Eds.), *Handbook of mixed methods in social and behavior research* (pp. 51–90). Thousand Oaks, CA: SAGE.

Mertens, D. M. (2003). Mixed methods and the politics of human research: The transformative-emancipatory perspective. In A. Tashakkori & C. Teddlie (Eds.), *Handbook of mixed methods in social and behavioral research* (pp. 135–166). Thousand Oaks, CA: SAGE.

Mertens, D. M. (2007). Transformative paradigm: Mixed methods and social justice. *Journal of Mixed Methods Research, 1,* 212–225. doi:10.1177/1558689807302811

Morgan, D. L. (2007). Paradigms lost and pragmatism regained: Methodological implications of combining qualitative and quantitative methods. *Journal of Mixed Methods Research, 1,* 48–76. doi:10.1177/2345678906292462

Morse, J. M. (2003). Principles of mixed methods and multimethod research design. In A. Tashakkori & C. Teddlie (Eds.), *Handbook of mixed methods in social and behavioral research* (pp. 189–209). Thousand Oaks, CA: SAGE.

Nastasi, B. K., Hitchcock, J. H., & Brown, L. M. (2010). An inclusive framework for conceptualizing mixed methods design typologies: Moving toward fully integrated synergistic research models. In A. Tashakkori & C. Teddlie (Eds.), *Handbook of mixed methods in social and behavioral research* (2nd ed., pp. 305–338). Thousand Oaks, CA: SAGE.

Nastasi, B. K., Hitchcock, J. H., Burkholder, G., Varjas, K., Sarkar, S., & Jayasena, A. (2007). Assessing adolescents' understanding of and reactions to stress in different cultures: Results of a mixed-methods approach. *School Psychology International, 28*(2), 163–178. doi:10.1177/0143034307078092

Nastasi, B. K., Hitchcock, J., Sarkar, S., Burkholder, G., Varjas, K., & Jayasena, A. (2007). Mixed methods in intervention research: Theory to adaptation. *Journal of Mixed Methods Research, 1,* 164–182. doi:10.1177/1558689806298181

Nelson, G., & Prilleltensky, I. (2005). *Community psychology: In pursuit of liberation and well-being*. New York, NY: Palgrave Macmillan.

Newman, I., Ridenour, C. S., Newman, C., & DeMarco, G. M. P., Jr. (2003). A typology of research purposes and its relationship to mixed methods. In A. Tashakkori & C. Teddlie (Eds.), *Handbook of mixed methods in social and behavioral research* (pp. 167–188). Thousand Oaks, CA: SAGE.

Onwuegbuzie, A., & Teddlie, C. (2003). A framework for analyzing data in mixed methods research. In A. Tashakkori & C. Teddlie (Eds.), *Handbook of mixed methods in social and behavioral research* (pp. 351–384). Thousand Oaks, CA: SAGE.

Onwuegbuzie, A. J., & Collins, K. M. T. (2007). A typology of mixed methods sampling designs in social science research. *Qualitative Report, 12,* 281–316. Retrieved from http://www.nova.edu/ssss/QR/QR12-2/onwuegbuzie2.pdf

Ridenour, C. S., & Newman, I. (2008). *Mixed methods research: Exploring the interactive continuum*. Carbondale, IL: Southern Illinois University Press.

Sandelowski, M. (2003). Tables or tableaux? The challenges of writing and reading mixed methods studies. In A. Tashakkori & C. Teddlie (Eds.), *Handbook of mixed methods in social and behavioral research* (pp. 321–350). Thousand Oaks, CA: SAGE.

Tashakkori, A., & Teddlie, C. (1998). *Mixed methodology: Combining quantitative and qualitative approaches.* Thousand Oaks, CA: SAGE.

Tashakkori, A., & Teddlie, C. (Eds.). (2003). *Handbook of mixed methods in social and behavioral research.* Thousand Oaks, CA: SAGE.

Tashakkori, A., & Teddlie, C. (Eds.). (2010). *Handbook of mixed methods in social and behavioral research* (2nd ed.). Thousand Oaks, CA: SAGE.

Teddlie, C., & Tashakkori, A. (2006). A general typology of research designs featuring mixed methods. *Research in the Schools, 13,* 12–28.

Teddlie, C., & Tashakkori, A. (2009). *Foundations of mixed methods research: Integrating quantitative and qualitative approaches in the social and behavioral sciences*. Thousand Oaks, CA: SAGE.

Teddlie, C., & Yu, F. (2007). Mixed methods sampling: A typology with examples. *Journal of Mixed Methods Research, 1,* 77–100. doi:10.1177/2345678906292430

Thomas, V. G. (2004). Building a contextually responsive evaluation framework: Lessons from working with urban school interventions. In V. G. Thomas & F. I. Stevens (Eds.), *Co-constructing a contextually responsive evaluation framework: New directions in evaluation* (No. 101, pp. 3–24). Hoboken, NJ: Wiley Periodicals.

Woolley, C. M. (2009). Meeting the mixed methods challenge of integration in a sociological study of structure and agency. *Journal of Mixed Methods Research, 3*(1), 7–25. doi:10.1177/1558689808325774

MIXED METHODS ANALYSIS

Sarah E. P. Munce and Anthony J. Onwuegbuzie

OVERVIEW

Integration at the data analysis stage of the research process of mixed methods research studies (also more appropriately known as mixed research studies[1]) typically is more complex than integration at any other stage of the mixed methods research process. Thus, clear frameworks are needed to help researchers who are new to conducting mixed research (i.e., novice and emerging mixed researchers) appropriately negotiate the data analysis integration challenge in a way that leads to the underlying research question(s) being addressed comprehensively. Therefore, the purpose of this chapter is to introduce the concept of data integration and common levels of integration, to provide a practical example of the application of data integration, and to outline some of the challenges that arise when conducting mixed research. The specific topics covered will include a definition and description of integration; a rationale for integration in mixed methods; key considerations in mixed methods data analysis (i.e., mixed analysis); common levels of integration, including integration at the data analysis levels and integration at the interpretation and reporting levels; and fit of data integration, including addressing discordant findings. The chapter concludes with an example of a mixed methods dissertation that demonstrates the application of data integration as well as some of the challenges/ considerations when conducting mixed research.

Definition and Description of Integration

In the context of mixed research, *integration* refers to the systematic and considered combination or interfacing of quantitative and qualitative methods, methodologies, paradigms, analyses, results, and/or the like. Approaches to integration at the analysis and results phases include merging, embedding, and connecting data sets (Creswell & Plano Clark, 2017; Fetters, Curry, & Creswell, 2013). At the analysis and results phases of the mixed research process, the purpose of integration is to enhance the findings and/or the application of the quantitative and qualitative results so that the "whole is greater than the sum of the individual parts" (Barbour, 1999, p. 40). Such synergy has been expressed as the 1 + 1 = 3 integration challenge in mixed research (Fetters & Freshwater, 2015); this challenge

---

[1] As contended by Johnson, Onwuegbuzie, and Turner (2007), the term mixed research is more appropriate than is the term mixed methods research, especially as it pertains to the concept of integration, because the term mixed methods research might falsely suggest that, in its optimum form, the underlying research process involves only the mixing of methods, when it really involves the integration of quantitative and qualitative methods, methodologies, paradigms, analyses, results, and/or the like.

is meant to encourage the investigation of quantitative, qualitative, and mixed disciplinary boundaries. However, Onwuegbuzie (2017) argued that the characterization of the benefits of integration in mixed research in this way emphasizes a quantitative/qualitative separation that can prevent a more complete kind of integration. Instead, he asserted that a $1 + 1 = 1$ integration formula denotes a more comprehensive and dynamic characterization of integration that involves the data collection and data analysis phases as well as the data interpretation phase (Onwuegbuzie, 2017). Moreover, Onwuegbuzie (2017) asserted that at its optimum level, integration involves not only the product (e.g., integration of findings) but also the process (e.g., integration of [disciplinary, methodological, etc.] teams). The mathematics of integration in mixed research (i.e., $1 + 1 = 1$ vs. $1 + 1 = 3$) reflect an attempt to go beyond merely adding the findings stemming from a qualitative analysis of qualitative data and the findings stemming from a quantitative analysis of quantitative data (which would represent a nonoptimal $1 + 1 = 2$ mixed research process). Therefore, if you would like to get more out of your qualitative and quantitative data when conducting mixed research, we encourage you to consider subscribing to the *mathematics of integration in mixed research*.

Rationale for Integration in Mixed Methods

There are several reasons for and benefits of using integration in mixed methods research. To illustrate some of these reasons, we will use a few simple formulae. For example, you can use qualitative data to generate hypotheses that can be tested in the quantitative component or phase. Using the notation of Morse (1991, 2003), this example can be represented as follows:

$$QUAL \rightarrow QUAN \quad (1)$$
$$\text{or}$$
$$Qual \rightarrow QUAN \quad (2)$$

depending on whether you want to give the qualitative and quantitative phases approximately equal weight or priority (i.e., both capitalized) or the quantitative phase more weight, as in Notation 2.

You can use qualitative data to gauge the validity of the quantitative results, as follows:

$$QUAN \rightarrow Qual \quad (3)$$

Furthermore, you can use qualitative results to develop or refine a survey or an intervention (Fetters et al., 2013; cf. Notations 1 and 2). As a final example, you can use quantitative data to create the qualitative sample or to explain the results from the qualitative data (Fetters et al., 2013), represented, respectively, as follows:

$$Quan \rightarrow QUAL \quad (4)$$
$$\text{or}$$
$$QUAL \rightarrow Quan \quad (5)$$

You can also integrate quantitative and qualitative data and analyses in a concurrent manner. That is, the data and analyses representing all quantitative and qualitative strands can simultaneously be merged, embedded, and/or connected, such as when you use the same analysis to analyze both qualitative and quantitative data simultaneously. This can be represented as follows:

$$QUAL + QUAN \qquad\qquad (6)$$

$$QUAL + Quan \qquad\qquad (7)$$
$$and$$
$$Qual + QUAN \qquad\qquad (8)$$

For additional reasons for and benefits of using integration in mixed research, we refer you to Collins, Onwuegbuzie, and Sutton (2006), who developed what they referred to as the RaP (i.e., *r*ationale and *p*urpose) model for conducting mixed research. Specifically, these authors present a typology that contains broad reasons for integration in mixed research. These include *participant enrichment* (i.e., mixing quantitative and qualitative approaches for the rationale of optimizing the sample), *instrument fidelity* (i.e., mixing quantitative and qualitative approaches to obtain data that have characteristics such as trustworthiness, credibility, dependability, legitimation, validity, generalizability, or transferability), *treatment integrity* (i.e., mixing quantitative and qualitative approaches for the rationale of assessing the fidelity of interventions, treatments, or programs), and *significance enhancement* (i.e., mixing quantitative and qualitative approaches for the rationale of enhancing researchers' interpretations of data).

Despite the significant benefits of integration, researchers have reported that the use of integration is limited (Fetters et al., 2013; Guetterman, Fetters, & Creswell, 2015). As such, we encourage and challenge you to make use of integration (and at various levels) in your own studies so that the true benefits of mixed research can be derived!

Key Considerations in Mixed Analysis: Linking to Other Design Components, Prioritizing of Analytical Components, and Determining the Level of Interaction Between Quantitative and Qualitative Analysis

There are numerous considerations or decisions that you should make when conducting a mixed analysis. In particular, Onwuegbuzie and Combs (2010) identified 13 criteria or decisions that researchers should make before and/or during the mixed analysis process. These criteria are as follows:

1. Rationale/purpose for conducting the mixed analysis

2. Philosophy underpinning the mixed analysis

3. Number of data types that will be analyzed

4. Number of data analysis types that will be used

5. Time sequence of the mixed analysis

6. Level of interaction between quantitative and qualitative analyses

7. Priority of analytical components

8. Number of analytical phases

9. Link to other design components

10. Phase of the research process when all analysis decisions are made

11. Type of generalization

12. Analysis orientation

13. Cross-over nature of analysis

In this chapter, we focus on linking to other design components (Criterion 9), prioritizing of analytical components (Criterion 7), and determining the level of interaction between quantitative and qualitative analysis (Criterion 6). We have selected these three criteria because, among them, they are determined by or determine all the other criteria.

Linking to Other Design Components. As with all types of research, in mixed research, the research objective(s) must be aligned with the research methods. Research methods, in turn, must be aligned with the analysis/integration of data (Criterion 1). Thus, the rationale and/or purpose for conducting the mixed analysis and its associated analysis/integration must be clear and sound (Collins et al., 2006; Johnson & Christensen, 2017), and the philosophy underpinning the mixed analysis must be explicated (Criterion 2; Onwuegbuzie, Johnson, & Collins, 2009).

Curry and Nunez-Smith (2015) outlined several key questions when thinking about the overall analysis plan for the study, including the following: (a) Will you use a concurrent or sequential approach? (Criterion 5); (b) How many and what types of sources of qualitative and quantitative data will you have? (Criterion 3); (c) Are the data interconnected or independent? (Criteria 6 and 13); (d) What data need to be analyzed to inform future phases and their associated data collection? (Criteria 3, 4, 8, 10, and 13); (e) What concepts are present in both sets of data and, therefore, can be the focus of analysis in the two sets of data? (Criteria 4, 10, 11, and 12); and (f) What are the plans for assessing divergent and convergent results? (Criteria 5, 6, 10, and 13). For a dissertation proposal or grant application, we suggest including a detailed analysis plan that includes one for the quantitative data, one for the qualitative data, and, finally, one for the integration and interpretation of both data types.

Priority of Analytical Components. There are three scenarios when considering the priority or weighting of study elements in a mixed research study: (1) the qualitative and quantitative components are of approximately equal priority,

(2) the quantitative component has more priority or weight than the qualitative component, and (3) the qualitative component has more priority or weight than the quantitative component (Curry & Nunez-Smith, 2015). Whatever the scenario, even if one component has less priority, it must still be conducted with a high degree of attention and rigor (Morse, 2010). To provide a sense of prioritization, or weighting, we provide an example later in this chapter that describes a study used to guide the development of a self-management program for individuals with a spinal cord injury (SCI). In this example, the qualitative component of the study was emphasized more heavily than the quantitative component that followed it, given the exploratory nature of the overall research objective.

Determining the Level of Interaction Between the Quantitative and Qualitative Analyses. There are numerous points of integration during the mixed research process. These points of integration occur at the research conceptualization, planning, and implementation phases of the mixed research process. In the following sections, we will go into more detail about some of these individual types of integration.

Fetters and Freshwater (2015) indicated that integration can occur at multiple, non-traditional levels, including theory, conceptual models, publication, and teams. For example, integration during sample selection can occur when the results of a first component are used to inform the selection of participants for a subsequent component. For example, based on the results of a survey, high versus low implementation (e.g., of a clinical practice guideline) might be identified. Targeted individual interviews or focus group interviews could be conducted with high versus low implementation sites to gain a deeper understanding as to why implementation varies. Alternatively, integration during sample selection can occur when the same participants are used for both/all components, which Onwuegbuzie and Johnson (2006) referred to as *sample integration*.

Integration during data collection can involve the use of the findings from one component to inform the tools that are used for data collection in the subsequent component (as is the case with the dissertation example). At its optimum level, integration during data collection involves collecting data that represent *both* quantitative data and qualitative data, for example, spirituality (i.e., noös) data, which "includes a sense of 'being present with' and empathy . . . [that] is not as easily defined, qualified, or quantified" (McLafferty, Slate, & Onwuegbuzie, 2010, p. 58)—what Onwuegbuzie, Gerber, and Abrams (2017) referred to as *multidata*, wherein the qualitative data and quantitative data cannot be separated (i.e., both data types coexist), thereby making integration unavoidable. At its most basic level, integration during data analysis involves the effort to bring together the two (or more) separate components into one single database, after the data from each component have been analyzed separately. At a more complex level, integration during data analysis involves analyzing the data from each component simultaneously.

Data interpretation represents the synthesized understanding of/conclusions drawn from the quantitative and qualitative findings of a study, yielding an outcome known as *meta-inferences* (Tashakkori & Teddlie, 1998). The integration of quantitative and qualitative results for the purposes of interpretation is considered to be extremely important, if not mandatory (Curry & Nunez-Smith, 2015).

Fetters and Freshwater (2015) advised readers to plan their studies so that integration can be leveraged across many of the points previously described. A good addition to a proposal or grant application would be a schematic or figure that includes your research objectives and shows how integration will occur across the objectives and/or quantitative and qualitative components. A good example of such a schematic is presented by Fetters et al. (2013). Two of the most common levels of integration, at the methods and the interpretation and reporting levels, are described in more detail in the following sections.

Integration at the Methods Level, Including Connecting, Embedding, and Merging

Connecting. Connecting occurs when one type of data builds on the other type of data (Creswell & Plano Clark, 2017). This type of integration can occur with respect to the sampling or the content of the data collection tools. With respect to sampling, you can use the results gleaned from one component to determine the sample for the other component. For example, in an explanatory sequential design, the results of a survey may be used to identify potential participants for the subsequent qualitative component (Curry & Nunez-Smith, 2015). Connecting also can occur when the first data collection procedure informs the second data collection protocol. An example of this type of connecting is the use of the exploratory sequential design, where the results of the qualitative component are used to develop a survey for the subsequent quantitative component (this is also referred to as *building*; Onwuegbuzie, Bustamante, & Nelson, 2010). With this form of connecting, the qualitative data are analyzed, in part, with the intention of creating conceptual domains or dimensions that can be carried over to the quantitative phase, in the survey (Curry & Nunez-Smith, 2015). Alternatively, you could use the results of the quantitative component to develop a qualitative instrument (e.g., interview guide, observation schedule).

Embedding. Embedding can occur when data collection and analysis are linked at numerous points during the study. An example of this is when qualitative data are used to adapt or select the measures for use in pilot testing ahead of a randomized controlled trial and a qualitative component is then subsequently used to understand the contextual factors that could explain the quantitative results of the trial (Curry & Nunez-Smith, 2015). This approach usually occurs in studies with both primary and secondary questions, in which different methods are used to address each question. Thus, embedding can be characterized as occurring when the secondary question (and method) is devised to support the primary question (Greene, 2007) and, therefore, the secondary method is nested within the framework of the primary method (Creswell & Plano Clark, 2017). Note that the secondary role of one objective (and method) does not permit a less rigorous or attentive approach (Morse & Niehaus, 2009).

In the health sciences, the most common example is the embedding of one or more qualitative components within a randomized controlled trial. However, in other fields, it is not unusual for the quantitative component to be embedded within the qualitative component, such as may occur in a case study—yielding what is referred to as a *mixed methods case study* (Onwuegbuzie & Leech, 2010). In an embedded approach, you can analyze the data associated with the secondary objective at various points in the larger study (Curry & Nunez-Smith, 2015).

Merging. Merging occurs after the collection and initial analysis of both quantitative and qualitative data have been completed. The results are then interpreted collectively, and this provides an opportunity to identify complementarity, convergence, and/or divergence between/among the data sets. Fetters et al. (2013) emphasized that, ideally, at the design phase, researchers should create a protocol for collecting both forms of data in a way that will be advantageous for merging the databases. The approach to interpretation is often guided by the data collection tools, for example, interview guides and surveys that yield data on the specific dimensions of the phenomenon of interest. Merging can be guided by a process whereby the main dimensions are known in advance and then the quantitative and qualitative results are combined to characterize each dimension. Alternatively, the data may yield related but distinct aspects of the phenomenon of interest.

Integration at the Interpretation and Reporting Levels, Including Narrative, Data Transformation, and Joint Displays

Three approaches to integration at the interpretation and reporting levels involve integrating through (a) narrative, (b) data transformation, and/or (c) joint displays. These approaches do not represent an exhaustive list of ways of integrating at the interpretation and reporting levels, but they are highlighted here because they are among the most common techniques.

When using a *narrative* approach, the quantitative and qualitative results are presented in a single report or a series of reports. There are a few techniques that facilitate narration. In the *weaving technique*, the quantitative and qualitative results are presented together, by concept or by theme. In the *contiguous technique*, the quantitative and qualitative results are presented in a single report but in separate sections. Finally, in the *staged technique*, the results of each stage are presented or published separately. This approach is often used in dissertations/theses.

In its most basic form, the *transformation approach* can involve two scenarios. Specifically, you can convert qualitative data into quantitative data (i.e., *quantitizing*; Tashakkori & Teddlie, 1998) or you can convert quantitative data into qualitative data (i.e., *qualitizing*; Tashakkori & Teddlie, 1998). An example of quantitizing is counting the number of times a particular theme or themes occurred across a selection of transcripts. Contrastingly, an example of qualitizing is assigning narrative labels or descriptors to quantitative data that emerge from survey responses—for instance, you could construct a narrative profile based on these quantitative survey responses much like elements of the Federal Bureau of Investigation's method of profiling used to identify and classify the major personality and behavioral characteristics of a criminal based on an analysis of the crime(s) committed by that person.

Data transformation often is a two-step process. First, you convert one type of data into another type of data (i.e., quantitative data into qualitative data or qualitative data into quantitative data). Then, you combine or integrate the transformed data, in some way, with data that have not been transformed. An example of this approach is content analysis, which involves the transformation of qualitative themes into counts (i.e., transformation of qualitative data into quantitative data; Krippendorff, 2013). These counts could then be integrated with a quantitative database. It is important to note that you do not have to use the transformed data to *replace* the original data; rather, you present the transformed data alongside the original data in some manner (i.e., connected, embedded, and/or merged). In this way, the data transformation *expands* the data rather than *reduces* the data, thereby leading to the creation of a new whole (i.e., $1 + 1 = 1$ or $1 + 1 = 3$).

Integration at the interpretation and reporting levels can be performed using a *joint display*. A joint display is defined as a technique to "integrate the data by bringing the data together through a visual means to draw out new insights beyond the information gained from the separate quantitative and qualitative results" (Fetters et al., 2013, p. 2143). Joint displays can be matrices, figures, or graphs (O'Cathain, Murphy, & Nicholl, 2010). In matrix/table form, the rows can represent the cases (e.g., individual participants, individual sites/organizations) or major constructs/themes of the topic derived from both quantitative and qualitative data, and the columns display the individual quantitative and qualitative results for each case or theme. Furthermore, the joint display can include another column that presents the integrated interpretation of the individual quantitative and qualitative results.

Thus, the joint display is not only a technique used for *reporting* the integrated findings but also a tool used for the process of *interpreting* the integrated quantitative and qualitative results. Despite the advantages of joint displays and the fact that they are increasingly considered an area of innovation for advancing integration in mixed research, they are still underutilized (Onwuegbuzie & Dickinson, 2008). Guetterman et al. (2015) have called for their increased application in mixed research so that the synergy of integrating quantitative and qualitative methods and results can be achieved.

Fit of Data Integration, Including Addressing Discordant Findings

An important consideration of data integration is the degree of consistency or fit between the quantitative and qualitative findings. The evaluation of fit can involve outcomes that include confirmation, expansion, and discordance. In *confirmation*, both types of data confirm the results of the other (i.e., yield similar conclusions), providing greater credibility to the findings. In *expansion,* the two types of data expand the understanding of the phenomenon of interest by describing complementary aspects. For example, the quantitative results may indicate the strength of the association, whereas the qualitative results may provide an understanding of the mechanism of the association.

In *discordance*, the results of the quantitative and qualitative results are inconsistent with or contradict each other. If you have discordant findings, then you should examine the potential sources of bias to determine whether they affected the data in any way. The options for addressing discordant findings include reanalyzing the data, seeking understanding from conceptual frameworks or theory, collecting more data, and considering the soundness of the constructs (Fetters et al., 2013). Experts assert that discordant findings should be expected given that mixed research is often used to address complex phenomena (Teddlie & Tashakkori, 2010). Furthermore, it is important to be transparent about these discordant findings and discuss possible rationales for these overall results. Last, as joint displays evolve and are used more commonly, there might also be a place in these tables to highlight such discrepant findings.

Bringing It All Together: Practical Example of Mixed Methods Integration at the Methods and Interpretation and Reporting Levels

As noted in the introduction, this chapter concludes with an example of a mixed methods dissertation that demonstrates the application of data integration as well as some of the challenges/considerations when conducting mixed research. The *overall research objective* of the PhD dissertation of the lead author was to understand the phenomenon of self-management among individuals with traumatic SCI and then, based on this understanding, to determine the specific implementation considerations (i.e., components) for a targeted self-management program for individuals with SCI. The *specific research objectives* were to (a) understand the meaning of self-management in traumatic SCI from the perspectives of individuals with traumatic SCI and their caregivers as well as managers; (b) understand the perceived facilitators and barriers to self-management to prevent secondary complications from the perspectives of individuals with traumatic SCI, their caregivers, and managers; (c) determine the relevant components of a self-management program for individuals with traumatic SCI; and (d) identify some of the psychological characteristics (e.g., self-efficacy, mastery, patient activation) in self-management that are associated with depression in individuals with traumatic SCI.

To accomplish this, an *exploratory sequential design* was adopted (i.e., a qualitative approach using telephone interviews followed by the administration of a survey that was developed from the themes gleaned from the qualitative phase). This approach was judged to be appropriate because it is a design that is particularly useful for the development of an intervention, as was the case in this dissertation study (i.e., the considerations revealed in this research study would be used for the piloting, evaluation, and implementation of a tailored self-management support program for individuals with SCI). Furthermore, this design also was used because it can increase the relevance and feasibility of a future intervention by tailoring the intervention to the patient population, thereby increasing the likelihood of successful implementation and uptake.

For integration at the methods level, *building* (i.e., the results of the qualitative component are used to develop a survey for the subsequent quantitative component) was used to develop the survey from the results of the two studies from the qualitative phase. *Merging* (merging occurs after the collection and initial analysis of both quantitative and qualitative data have been completed) was then used to integrate the findings of both the qualitative and the quantitative results. Collectively, the findings from all four specific research objectives contributed to a better understanding of self-management for individuals with traumatic SCI and the patient preferences/key implementation considerations for a self-management program.

In terms of integration at the interpretation and reporting levels, this dissertation was an "article-based dissertation," and therefore, four individual articles (two qualitative articles addressing the first two objectives and two quantitative articles addressing the last two objectives) were included in the dissertation and later published (i.e., *staged* approach). A synthesis chapter was included in the dissertation, which involved a *weaving* approach. Furthermore, *a joint display* was created using the major constructs/themes that were evident in both the quantitative and the qualitative components, including caregiver involvement/needs and peer support and feedback, among others (see Table 9.1). In a traditional dissertation, a narrative approach also may be used, whereby either the *weaving approach* (i.e., the quantitative and qualitative results are presented together by concept or by theme) or the *contiguous approach* (i.e., the quantitative and qualitative results are presented in a single report but in separate sections) is used to report the data. One or more *joint displays* also could be employed to complement the narrative. Integration at the methods and interpretation and reporting levels should be very specific and purposive, such that these plans are outlined a priori in a research proposal and represented in a figure, as previously discussed.

The great value of conducting mixed research that includes integration must be highlighted along with its inherent implementation challenges, which might be particularly relevant during graduate studies/early career stages. Time and associated resources can be a consideration, particularly when adopting a sequential approach and completing the necessary step of data integration. Furthermore, conducting a series of mixed research studies might present some challenges when attempting to secure the publication of an integrated article. For example, in the experience of the lead author, four individual articles (two qualitative works and two quantitative works) were published that stemmed from the PhD dissertation, previously described. The dissertation document itself also required a synthesis/integration chapter that included narrative approaches and joint displays, which formed the basis of the final manuscript. However, the unique contribution of this integrated manuscript needed to be sufficiently clear to journal editors and reviewers, and this can be challenging when the individual quantitative and qualitative articles have been previously published. Finally, another key consideration when conducting mixed research is to ensure adequate mixed research expertise on your team. It is

TABLE 9.1 ● EXAMPLE OF A JOINT DISPLAY ON SELF-MANAGEMENT PROGRAM CONSIDERATIONS FOR INDIVIDUALS WITH SPINAL CORD INJURY (SCI)

Self-Management Program Consideration	Results From Phase I (QUAL): Facilitators (F), Barriers (B), Meaning of Self-Management (M)	Results From Phase II (quan)	Combined Summary and Program/Implementation Considerations Based on the Results of QUAL Phase I and quan Phase II
Caregiver involvement/ needs	Physical support from the caregiver (F) Emotional support from the caregiver (F) Caregiver burnout (B) Directing someone else to provide your care (M) Importance of caregiver skill set (M)	36.4% of the participants stated that a module on "communicating with family" was "very important." The caregiver perspective was not sought in Phase II.	Given the high physical and emotional contributions and demands of caregivers of individuals with traumatic SCI, support for caregivers is warranted. This support for the caregiver would be in the form of emotional support and ongoing training to prevent/manage the secondary medical complications of individuals with traumatic SCI. This support needs to be responsive to the evolving needs of individuals with traumatic SCI (i.e., as they age and/or develop chronic conditions) and the similar evolving needs of the caregivers (i.e., aging, chronic conditions). The sustainability of caregiver activities and support required for SCI (i.e., facilitators of self-management) may be affected by aging and/or the chronic health conditions of the caregivers themselves. A program module on "communicating with family" (e.g., directing someone in the provision of your care) and/or including caregivers/family members in a self-management program for individuals with traumatic SCI could serve to reduce some of this burden.
Peer support and feedback (peer leader)	Peer support and feedback (F) Matching peer mentors (peer leaders) and mentees (program participants) by specific demographic and clinical/injury characteristics (age, sex, etiology of injury) should be considered.	In terms of program makeup, almost 75% of the participants indicated that having individuals with a similar level of injury was important. A preference for a program composed of individuals of a similar age was also noted.	Matching peer leaders to participants in a self-management program should consider, at a minimum, the level of injury and age.

insufficient to have individual *quantitative* and *qualitative* expertise on a research team or committee. Finding this mixed research expertise might be challenging but, hopefully, becomes easier as more and more investigators become familiar with/develop expertise in mixed research.

CONCLUSION

Considerations and challenges in mixed research include the need for increased time and resources, publishing individual studies from the quantitative and qualitative components of your mixed research as well as the integrated findings, and adding adequate mixed research expertise to your team. We encourage you to strive toward full integration (i.e., the 1 + 1 = 1 formula), yielding integration that involves the data collection and data analysis phases as well as the data interpretation phase (Onwuegbuzie, 2017).

- *Integration* refers to the systematic and considered combination or interfacing of quantitative and qualitative methods, methodologies, paradigms, analyses, results, and/or the like.

- Key considerations in mixed methods analysis include linking to other design components, prioritizing of analytical components, and determining the level of interaction between quantitative and qualitative analysis.

- Integration at the methods level can include connecting, embedding, and merging.

- Integration at the interpretation and reporting levels includes narrative, data transformation, and joint displays.

- A joint display not only is a technique used for reporting the integrated findings but also is a *tool* used for the process of interpreting the integrated quantitative and qualitative results. The increased application of joint displays in mixed research is encouraged so that the synergy of integrating quantitative and qualitative methods and results can be achieved.

- Fit of data integration, including discordant findings, should be addressed.

Questions for Reflection

1. At what levels will you be using integration in your research? At the methods level and/or at the interpretation and reporting levels? What other levels?

2. What approach(es) will you use in terms of integration at the interpretation and reporting levels: a narrative approach, data transformation, and/or a joint display? What is your rationale for using the selected approach(es)?

3. To what extent have you addressed the fit of integration, including confirmation, expansion, and discordance? How will you identify discordant findings?

4. What are some of the challenges that arise when conducting mixed methods research? Which challenges apply to your research? How will you mitigate these challenges?

Key Sources

Creswell, J. W., & Plano Clark, V. L. (2017). *Designing and conducting mixed methods research* (3rd ed.). Thousand Oaks, CA: SAGE.

Curry, L., & Nunez-Smith, M. (2015). *Mixed methods in health sciences research: A practical primer.* Thousand Oaks, CA: SAGE.

Fetters, M. D., Curry, L. A., & Creswell, J. W. (2013). Achieving integration in mixed methods designs: Principles and practice. *Health Services Research, 48*(6, Pt. 2), 2134–2156. doi:10.1111/1475-6773.12117

Guetterman, T. C., Fetters, M. D., & Creswell, J. W. (2015). Integrating qualitative and quantitative results in health science mixed methods research through joint displays. *Annals of Family Medicine, 13,* 554–561. doi:10.1370/afm.1865

Johnson, R. B., & Onwuegbuzie, A. J. (2004). Mixed methods research: A research paradigm whose time has come. *Educational Researcher, 33*(7), 14–26. doi:10.1177/1558689806298224

O'Cathain, A., Murphy, E., & Nicholl, J. (2010). Three techniques for integrating data in mixed methods studies. *British Medical Journal, 341,* c4587. doi:10.1136/bmj.c4587

Onwuegbuzie, A. J., & Johnson, R. B. (2006). The validity issue in mixed research. *Research in the Schools, 13*(1), 48–63.

Teddlie, C., & Tashakkori, A. (2010). Overview of contemporary issues in mixed methods research. In A. Tashakkori & C. Teddlie (Eds.), *SAGE handbook of mixed methods in social and behavioral research* (2nd ed., pp. 1–44). Thousand Oaks, CA: SAGE.

References

Barbour, R. S. (1999). The case for combining qualitative and quantitative approaches in health services research. *Journal of Health Services Research & Policy, 4,* 39–43. doi:10.1177/135581969900400110

Collins, K. M. T., Onwuegbuzie, A. J., & Sutton, I. L. (2006). A model incorporating the rationale and purpose for conducting mixed methods research in special education and beyond. *Learning Disabilities: A Contemporary Journal, 4,* 67–100.

Creswell, J. W., & Plano Clark, V. L. (2017). *Designing and conducting mixed methods research* (3rd ed.). Thousand Oaks, CA: SAGE.

Curry, L., & Nunez-Smith, M. (2015). *Mixed methods in health sciences research: A practical primer.* Thousand Oaks, CA: SAGE.

Fetters, M. D., Curry, L. A., & Creswell, J. W. (2013). Achieving integration in mixed methods designs: Principles and practice. *Health Services Research, 48*(6, Pt. 2), 2134–2156. doi:10.1111/1475-6773.12117

Fetters, M. D., & Freshwater, D. (2015). The 1 + 1 = 3 integration challenge. *Journal of Mixed Methods Research, 9,* 115–117. doi:10.1177/1558689815581222

Greene, J. C. (2007). *Mixed methods in social inquiry* (1st ed.). San Francisco, CA: Jossey-Bass.

Guetterman, T. C., Fetters, M. D., & Creswell, J. W. (2015). Integrating qualitative and quantitative results in health science mixed methods research through joint displays. *Annals of Family Medicine, 13,* 554–561. doi:10.1370/afm.1865

Johnson, R. B., & Christensen, L. (2017). *Educational research: Quantitative, qualitative, and mixed approaches* (6th ed.). Thousand Oaks, CA: SAGE.

Johnson, R. B., Onwuegbuzie, A. J., & Turner, L. A. (2007). Toward a definition of mixed methods research. *Journal of Mixed Methods Research, 1,* 112–133. doi:10.1177/1558689806298224

Krippendorff, K. (2013). *Content analysis: An introduction to its methodology* (3rd ed.). Thousand Oaks, CA: SAGE.

McLafferty, C. L., Slate, J. R., & Onwuegbuzie, A. J. (2010). Transcending the quantitative–qualitative divide with mixed methods: A multidimensional framework for understanding congruence, coherence, and completeness in the study of values. *Counseling and Values, 55*(1), 46–62. doi:10.1002/j.2161-007X.2010.tb00021.x

Morse, J. (1991). Approaches to qualitative–quantitative methodological triangulation. *Nursing Research, 40,* 120–123. doi:10.1097/00006199-199103000-00014

Morse, J. (2003). Principles of mixed methods and multimethod research design. In A. Tashakkori & C. Teddlie (Eds.), *Handbook of mixed methods in social and behavioral research* (pp. 189–208). Thousand Oaks, CA: SAGE.

Morse, J. M. (2010). Procedures and practice of mixed method design: Maintaining control, rigor, and complexity. In A. Tashakkori & C. Teddlie (Eds.), *SAGE handbook of mixed methods in social and behavioral research* (2nd ed., pp. 339–352). Thousand Oaks, CA: SAGE.

Morse, J. M., & Niehaus, L. (2009). *Mixed methods design: Principles and procedures.* Walnut Creek, CA: Left Coast Press.

O'Cathain, A., Murphy, E., & Nicholl, J. (2010). Three techniques for integrating data in mixed methods studies. *British Medical Journal, 341,* c4587. doi:10.1136/bmj.c4587

Onwuegbuzie, A. J. (2017, March). *Mixed methods is dead! Long live mixed methods!* Invited keynote address presented at the Mixed Methods International Research Association Caribbean Conference at Montego Bay, Jamaica.

Onwuegbuzie, A. J., Bustamante, R. M., & Nelson, J. A. (2010). Mixed research as a tool for developing quantitative instruments. *Journal of Mixed Methods Research, 4,* 56–78. doi:10.1177/1558689809355805

Onwuegbuzie, A. J., & Combs, J. P. (2010). Emergent data analysis techniques in mixed methods research: A synthesis. In A. Tashakkori & C. Teddlie (Eds.), *SAGE handbook of mixed methods in social and behavioral research* (2nd ed., pp. 397–430). Thousand Oaks, CA: SAGE.

Onwuegbuzie, A. J., & Dickinson, W. B. (2008). Mixed methods analysis and information visualization: Graphical display for effective communication of research results. *Qualitative Report, 13,* 204–225.

Onwuegbuzie, A. J., Gerber, H. R., & Abrams, S. S. (2017). Mixed methods research. In *The international encyclopedia of communication research methods* (pp. 1–33). doi:10.1002/9781118901731.iecrm0156

Onwuegbuzie, A. J., & Johnson, R. B. (2006). The validity issue in mixed research. *Research in the Schools, 13*(1), 48–63.

Onwuegbuzie, A. J., Johnson, R. B., & Collins, K. M. T. (2009). A call for mixed analysis: A philosophical framework for combining qualitative and quantitative. *International Journal of Multiple Research Approaches, 3,* 114–139. doi:10.5172/mra.3.2.114

Onwuegbuzie, A. J., & Leech, N. L. (2010). Generalization practices in qualitative research: A mixed methods case study. *Quality & Quantity, 44,* 881–892. doi:10.1007/s11135-009-9241-z

Tashakkori, A., & Teddlie, C. (1998). *Mixed methodology: Combining qualitative and quantitative approaches: Vol. 46. Applied social research methods series.* Thousand Oaks, CA: SAGE.

Teddlie, C., & Tashakkori, A. (2010). Overview of contemporary issues in mixed methods research. In A. Tashakkori & C. Teddlie (Eds.), *SAGE handbook of mixed methods in social and behavioral research* (2nd ed., pp. 1–44). Thousand Oaks, CA: SAGE.

DATA
COLLECTION

PART III

INTERVIEWING ESSENTIALS FOR NEW RESEARCHERS

Linda M. Crawford and Laura Knight Lynn

Interviews are a predominant form of data collection, providing rich information from study participants, including the text of responses, vocal tone and inflection, and body language. However, along with these benefits, there are risks in interviewing of which new researchers are typically not aware. If the researcher is not careful, much can happen during the data collection, analysis, and interpretation processes to impair the integrity of interview data. In this chapter, we define the types of interviews, provide information regarding the choice of individual or focus group interviews, describe the interview process, examine some interviewing pitfalls and solutions, and describe the important role of culture and power in interviewing.

TYPES OF INTERVIEWS

Interviews fall into two classifications. One classification relates to the *form* of the interview as structured, semistructured, or unstructured. The second classification addresses the *members* of the interview, including individual or group interviews.

Interview Form

There are three basic forms of interviews: (1) structured, (2) semistructured, and (3) unstructured. Each form is progressively less rigid in its questioning format and process. For a structured interview, the researcher composes a script of questions and asks the questions of each participant exactly as stated and in the exact sequence. The researcher records the responses but does not probe for clarification or additional information. Structured interviews are often conducted as quantitative, Likert-type scale surveys. One example is the researcher who stops participants in a mall and asks for answers to a few questions. Another example is the structured phone interview. In qualitative research, structured interviews are used when the intent is to precisely compare participant responses. For example, for a study of the problem of low minority enrollment in talented and gifted educational programs, the researcher might ask each participant about satisfaction with the program admittance procedures without probing for details.

For semistructured interviews, the researcher constructs interview questions related to the research question(s) and also anticipates probes that might be used to explore participant responses (Rubin & Rubin, 2012). The interview questions are posed to each participant, and probes are used as needed to gather deeper information from the participant. The research plan suggests an order for the interview questions, but probes might alter that order. For example, for a study of the problem of low minority enrollment in talented and gifted educational programs, the following might hold:

- *Research question:* How do minority parents perceive the relevance of talented and gifted programs for their children?

- *One interview question:* From what you know of the talented and gifted programming that has been provided for your child, how well do you think the program meets your child's needs?

- *Probe:* Tell me more about how your child has talked about his or her experience in the talented and gifted program.

Probes would be used in relation to the initial response from the participant and may or may not be used with all participants or for each question. Although probes can be anticipated, they also might be developed during the course of an interview, in which case the researcher must record the newly created probes.

In unstructured, or open, interviews, the interviewer constructs questions "on the fly" in response to participant contributions. For example, in relation to the previous example of minority participation in talented and gifted programs, an open interview might begin with a very broad question to a parent, such as "How do you feel the talented and gifted program fits your child's needs?" The next interview question would be constructed in relation to what the participant said. With unstructured interviews, the line of questioning may vary among participants depending on their responses.

Semistructured interviews are typical in qualitative research and are recommended for novice researchers. Structured interviews may not offer the researcher sufficient opportunity to probe participant responses. Without extensive experience as a qualitative researcher, unstructured interviews may not offer sufficient focus to answer the research question.

Interview Members

There are two membership groups for interviews: individual interviews and group interviews, known as focus groups. Individual interviews are conducted in a one-on-one situation with the interviewer, who asks questions, and the interviewee, who responds to them. For a focus group interview, the researcher assembles about 6 to

10 persons relevant to the study topic and moderates a discussion among them that is guided by the interview questions (Brinkmann & Kvale, 2015).

The choice between conducting individual or focus group interviews requires you to consider the following:

1. Study design (whether the design itself requires individual or group interviews)

2. Availability and time constraints (whether it is easier to schedule individuals or groups)

3. Location (whether there is a place to conduct individual interviews or focus groups in which audio and/or video recording is feasible)

4. Influence of group talk over individual talk in relation to the research questions (whether the focus group discussion enhances or unduly influences individual responses)

Study Design. Certain qualitative designs stipulate a requirement for individual or focus group interviews. Phenomenological studies require individual interviews because they intend to derive composite themes from individual experiences. Because the unit of analysis for narrative studies is at the individual level, narrative studies also require individual rather than focus group interviews. Individual interviews are usually used in grounded theory studies, but focus group interviews could also be used, and both individual and focus group interviews are commonly used for case and ethnographic studies. In the context of grounded theory, case study, and ethnographic research, focus groups may draw out a variety of viewpoints stimulated by the interaction among group participants (Brinkmann & Kvale, 2015).

Availability and Time Constraints. Study design is the major consideration in deciding between individual and group interviews, but the practical considerations of availability and time constraints are important as well. If participant availability is limited, then a group interview might be preferred, particularly if the researcher also has time constraints in accessing participants.

Location. Interviews need to be conducted in a location that provides accessibility, visual privacy, freedom from distractions, and audio/video recording capability. The location of the interview needs to be convenient to and permissible for the participants, in both time and location. For example, if the interview is conducted on the job site and during work time, the researcher needs to obtain permission to use the job site and time for the study. In addition, the space must be large enough to seat all the participants comfortably. Privacy is also essential, with the interview to be conducted in a closed-door area. The location needs to allow for clear audio/video recording without feedback or distortions and have sufficient access to electrical outlets. Video recording is especially important in focus group interviews to identify who is talking and to whom.

Group Talk Influence. When determining if individual interviews or focus group interviews are better for a study, you must consider the influence of group talk over individual responses. In a focus group, the responses of one person might influence the responses of others. This influence can be beneficial in that it can stimulate ideas in individuals, but it can also be detrimental in that it can bring the conversation in directions not associated with the research questions, prevent individuals from speaking in opposition to others, or result in group-think (Brinkmann & Kvale, 2015). Furthermore, sensitive topics, such as a personal abuse history, might not be appropriate for a focus group.

THE INTERVIEW PROCESS

Interviewing is not a simple task and requires attention to details. Such details include constructing an interview protocol as well as preparing for, conducting, and transcribing interviews. This section will focus on these aspects of the interview process.

Constructing an Interview Protocol

An interview protocol is a tool used to ensure interviewing consistency. It is a form with places to record the following:

1. Logistical details such as
   a. Date
   b. Location
   c. Start and end times
   d. Name and, if applicable, position/role of the interviewee
   e. Name of the interviewer
   f. Recording mechanism

2. Introductory explanation of the study purpose, informed consent, and how the interview will be conducted

3. Interview questions, with possible probes

4. A closing statement that thanks the participant, details what will happen next, and asks permission for further contact to gain clarification as needed

The interview protocol may include a section to record subjective interviewer observations of the participant or reactions to the participant's responses. As advised by Josselson (2013), the interview protocol is not intended for verbatim notation of the participant's responses, although the interviewer may make some brief notations for review during analysis.

Figure 10.1 shows a sample interview protocol.

FIGURE 10.1 ● SAMPLE INTERVIEW PROTOCOL

INTERVIEW PROTOCOL

Date of interview:

Location of interview:

Start time: End time:

Name of interviewee:

Name of interviewer:

Recording mechanism:

Introduction:

Thank you for taking your time to meet with me today. As you know, this interview will contribute information for a research study intended to [state purpose of the study]. You have signed an informed consent form, but, as a reminder, you may decline to answer any question you do not wish to answer or withdraw from the interview at any time. This interview will take approximately [X] minutes. With your permission, I will be making an audio recording of the interview and may take notes. Do you have any questions before we begin?

Interview Questions	Interviewee Responses	Interviewer Observations/Reactions
1. [List the interview questions, one per row.]	[Do not notate verbatim response, but notate some thoughts that jump out at you.]	[Notate observations, such as "The interviewee has drawn back in her chair and crossed her arms," and personal reactions, such as "I'm wondering if my question has offended or challenged her."]
2.		
3.		
Etc.		

Potential probes:

- Please tell me more about . . .

- How did you know . . . ?

- What kind . . . ?

- What was the best approach among those you named?

Conclusion:

Thank you for your time today. I very much appreciate your contributing to this study. [State the next steps, such as member checking.] May I contact you if I need any clarifications?

Clear protocols are important in all cases but especially when there is more than one interviewer. In that case, the additional interviewer should use the same protocol and be trained in interview implementation for consistency.

Preparing for Interviews

When preparing for interviews, you must consider the site, the recording mechanism, the participants, and yourself. Be sure that all relevant parties at the site are informed of the time, dates, and locations of the interviews. For example, if the interviews are to take place in a conference room during the work day, be sure to schedule the conference room for the required times. Think about small details, such as putting the trash can outside the door so that a custodian does not interrupt the interview to collect it.

Test audio equipment to ensure that it is positioned to record voices clearly, and if using video, ensure that the video frame includes all the participants. Bring spare batteries and a backup system for both audio and video recording in the event of equipment failure.

Confirm the scheduled dates and times with the participants. Ensure that the participants have received the informed consent materials and that you have previously obtained any required signatures or have a clear plan to obtain the required signatures at the time of the interview. If, during the interview, it seems that the session might go over the set time, ask for permission to continue but also have a plan for adjusting the interview to fit into the time frame without exceeding the schedule.

Practice interviewing with a friend or colleague, and record the practice sessions on videotape. Obtain feedback and conduct a self-critique with regard to your posture, your manner of asking questions, and any subtle facial expressions or voice tone that might influence participant responses. The goal here is to learn if, for example, you are asking questions too quickly or using body language to communicate judgment. The goal can also be to learn if you are missing opportunities to probe more deeply into responses.

Conducting Interviews

You must decide who is going to conduct the interview. It is preferable for the researcher to conduct the interview to bring the interviewer closer to the participants and the data. However, if you have a personal or professional relationship with the interviewee, then it may be advisable to have someone else conduct the interview. Certainly, if you have any supervisory or other power over the interviewee, you should seek someone else to conduct the interview. If someone other than yourself conducts the interview, then you must determine the qualifications of the interviewers, provide any necessary training, address any bias, and disclose such in the research report.

A question sometimes arises as to whether interviews must be conducted face-to-face or whether they can be conducted using audio/video conferencing tools or by telephone. We consider it preferable to conduct interviews face-to-face because the personal presence enhances the establishment of rapport, allows the researcher greater access to subtle body language cues from the interviewee, and permits the researcher greater control over the interview environment. However, technological tools expand the geographic area from which participants may be drawn and thus can be useful in studies for which the researcher cannot physically meet with the participants. Given a choice of technological tools, we advise using a tool with a video element. With such conferencing tools come problems with the stability of the tool, internet bandwidth, and avoidance of "breaking up" when recording the interview. Telephone interviews can be more stable but, of course, lack the video capability.

When conducting the interview, the researcher must avoid body posture, body language, voice tone, and linguistic constructions that communicate judgment or lead the participant. For example, a physical response that communicates "I like what you said" would inject researcher bias into the interview. Likewise, asking a follow-up probe such as "Don't you think people would be better off if . . . ?" communicates an opinion on the part of the researcher, whereas a more open question such as "What do you think would be better for . . . ?" allows the respondent to more freely express opinion.

You may find yourself overwhelmed with input when conducting an interview. You are hearing words from the participant(s), seeing body language, and reacting yourself. Josselson (2013) suggests not taking notes during interviews. The interviews are recorded so you have access to them, and taking notes can distract both you and the interviewee(s).

Transcribing Interviews

Transcription is the process of transferring audio-recorded statements from the recording to a printed text. This is a time-intensive process that requires concentration to accurately represent the participants' words and meaning. There are three options for transcribing interviews: (1) the researcher can transcribe them, (2) the researcher can hire someone to transcribe them, or (3) the researcher can use software to transcribe them. There are pros and cons to each choice.

The benefit of transcribing the interviews yourself is that you hear the participants' voices and become more intimately acquainted with their utterances. However, accurate transcription is quite time-consuming and requires listening and relistening to recordings to capture the utterances accurately—including filler words, such as *um*—as well as a good-quality recording from which to transcribe. You will need a tool that allows you to start, stop, and repeat sections, as well as sound-typing skills (Brinkmann & Kvale, 2015). A 30-minute interview can take approximately 180 minutes to transcribe; a 90-minute interview can take 4 to 6 hours to transcribe (Seidman, 2013).

There is the choice of using professional transcribers. However, hiring professionals takes you a step away from the data. Even if you hire a transcriber, you still should listen to the interviews while reading the transcripts to verify transcript accuracy. Furthermore, you should give the transcriber explicit instructions, such as how to indicate pauses in responses, how to indicate inflections, and how to punctuate to convey meaning. If more than one transcriber is employed, issues of consistency among transcriptions can arise. Using an experienced transcriber, though, can be a benefit in that the transcriber may be versed in conventions that communicate the meaning of utterances. You, then, must become versed in how to read those conventions.

There are software programs that can be used both to record and to transcribe interviews. Using software for transcription can be efficient, but to understand specific voices, the software might need to be trained for each interviewee. Using such software can be cumbersome when conducting group interviews because the program may be unable to distinguish among the multiple voices. Given these issues, we do not recommend using voice recognition/transcription software. We recommend audio recording of interviews and manual transcription. Manual interview transcription is a time-intensive process for individual interviews and even more so for group interviews. It is imperative to have start, stop, and repeat capability when listening to and transcribing interviews, and software packages and transcription tools generally provide that capability.

Group interviews present a unique transcription challenge in that people sometimes talk over each other, and it may be difficult to discern who is talking from just an audiotape. A video recording of group interviews will assist in overcoming these challenges; however, use of video recording presents a challenge in and of itself in that the transcriber must attend to both audio and video input. Transcription conventions, such as using a bracket to indicate overlapped utterances, can clarify the flow of conversation within a group interview (Brinkmann & Kvale, 2015).

INTERVIEWING PITFALLS AND SOLUTIONS

The reason there are pitfalls with interviews as the data collection approach is simple: The primary interview tool is *you*, and you are *human*.

What does this mean? It means you are subject to the influence of your collection of human experiences, memories, impressions, and feelings. These serve you well in daily life, but during interviews, your recollections, memories, and impressions can "muddy the waters." The aspects of yourself that help you navigate from point A to point B when moving through a crowded conference or shopping mall are the same aspects that can hinder you as a qualitative researcher and interviewer. How so? Your experiences, feelings, and filters color

- what you see in interviews,
- what you hear in interviews, and
- what you find important in interview utterances.

It is important to understand that what is not part of your mental and emotional background is often filtered out. You are primed to your hunches and notions, which facilitate attaching your biases to the data.

With this subjectivity in mind, Table 10.1 describes some common pitfalls in interviewing, why they are problematic, and some ways to avoid the pitfalls.

TABLE 10.1 ● INTERVIEWING PITFALLS AND POTENTIAL SOLUTIONS

Interviewing Pitfall	Why Problematic	Ways to Avoid This Pitfall
Rushing the informed consent/ explanation of steps process	Interviewees feel confused and pressured to complete the interview	Carefully plan the informed consent process. Be sure to present information in a calm and relaxed way. Be sure it is clear to interviewees that it is their choice to participate and they can withdraw at any time.
Rushing the interview	Limited data lacking rich information to answer the research questions	Continue the calm, relaxed, and pleasant approach. Because many people tend to talk quickly, overtly trying to slow down a bit can be helpful.
Too many facial expressions/ reactions	May close responses or influence the nature of responses	Find a comfortable, neutral facial expression and maintain it. If you tend to be naturally facially expressive, practice managing that in practice interviews. You want to be very careful not to express surprise, agreement, pleasure, or offense in reaction to the interviewee.
Frequent nodding	May influence the nature of responses as it indicates agreement	Limit nodding.
Lack of probes and follow-up questions	Limits the richness of data	Plan possible probes and use them to urge a participant to expand or more directly answer the question.
Only hearing and documenting part of the responses	Affects the integrity and validity of data	Audiotape or document verbatim. Listen to transcripts following the interview and/or review the notes.
Being unprepared for emotional responses	Unethical to have participants feeling vulnerable without follow-up or support	Have references available for counseling for emotionally laden interviews.
Too connected to the interviewee	Interviewees could be eager to please, and this can affect the integrity and truth of data	It is best not to interview people you are connected to in some way.
No rapport with the interviewee; being distant or robotic	Can limit responses	Make sure you are natural, with normal eye contact and responses, so the interviewee is comfortable.
Ordering of questions not well planned	If more intrusive questions are asked first, can limit responses	Start with more innocuous questions—such as demographic, factual-type questions—and build to the deeper questions.
Questions include presuppositions	Can be leading and influence the integrity of data	Use a direct preface. For example, instead of "How has this changed your life?" first ask, "Has this had an impact on your life?" Then ask, "How?"
Inappropriate use of "why" questions	Can be leading because there may not be a known "why"; "why" questions can lead to defensiveness	Make sure that the interviewee is likely to have an explanation of why. For example, with children, why questions are often confusing. Reword the question to avoid the use of "why."

(Continued)

TABLE 10.1 ⬡ (Continued)

Incompletely transcribing interviews	Makes data invalid and biased	Use software to slow down recording and transcribe completely. Consider hiring a transcriptionist.
Not audio recording interviews or documenting verbatim	If verbatim information is not available, can cause data to be limited and invalid	Audio record interviews, and be prepared to document verbatim on site if the interviewee refuses to be audiotaped.
Issues of power not considered	If the interviewee perceives the interviewer as a person of "power," can influence or limit what is reported	When meeting with the site contact, be sure to describe your role and background. Inquire as to whether the site contact foresees any issues. This information helps in protocol preparation and planning the data collection process.
Issues of culture not considered	Every environment has a culture, and specific people have cultures. If this is not considered, the researcher can intrude or offend unintentionally and limit the nature of the data reported.	The interviewer needs to gather information from the site on cultural considerations for both the environment and the people interviewed. Special consideration for ethnic norms should be made (e.g., eye contact, appropriateness of shaking hands).

In summary,

1. be sure, be calm, and go slow;

2. have a clear protocol, with a list of possible probes;

3. have a thorough plan for recording the interview; and

4. reflect on your own worldview and assumptions.

The fourth point, reflection on personal worldview and assumptions, is important enough to discuss further (see Chapter 2 for more information on worldview). You bring to the interview the person you are, with all your past experiences and assumptions. Although you try to create an open mind in order to receive the participant's experiences without bias, your own worldview and experiences can color how you hear the words of the interviewee. That is reality (Josselson, 2013). The researcher needs to recognize those personal influences and to *bracket* them. *Bracketing* is "a method used in qualitative research to mitigate the potentially deleterious effects of preconceptions that may taint the research process" (Tufford & Newman, 2010, p. 80). There are several ways to bracket, including memoing, reflexive journaling, and external interviews (Tufford & Newman, 2010).

Memos are notes written primarily to the self during the course of data collection and analysis. The notes may comprise descriptions of some aspect of the study as the researcher is seeing it, meanings the researcher attributes to analytical categories, and/or explanations of patterns emerging among the categories (Schwandt, 2015).

Reflexive journaling is an ongoing narrative of the researcher's rationale for the study, assumptions, values, and relationships to the participants in terms of culture and power. Reflexive journaling begins before even writing the research questions. Whereas memoing is the researcher's understanding of the data, reflexive journaling reveals the researcher's presuppositions in relation to the study and his or her relationships with the participants (Tufford & Newman, 2010).

A third way to bracket researcher bias is to engage in *external interviews*, that is, interviews with those not participating in the study but who may allow the researcher to discern biases in questions, probes, or judgmental reactions to participant responses. Such interviews allow the researcher to recognize, and correct, unintentional physical or verbal responses to participants that communicate judgment, closing off the flow of information (Tufford & Newman, 2010).

In addition to the pitfalls described earlier, issues of culture and power are often overlooked in interviewing. Because interviewing involves a one-on-one (or one-to-group) relationship, these issues can affect data collection.

CULTURE AND POWER IN THE INTERVIEW PROCESS

In addition to attending to the ethical considerations discussed in Chapter 13, researchers must be cognizant of culture and power in the interview process. Culture is everywhere. A business team has a culture, a university department has a culture, a K–12 school has a culture, and a hospital floor has a culture. Before entering the environment in which you will conduct interviews, you should find a way to understand its culture. Talk to your site contact; this contact is an insider who can provide valuable insight into particular nuances of the culture. He or she can give you tips on limiting intrusiveness by your presence and useful approaches for engaging in the interview. Many important questions can be answered, such as the following: What should you be sensitive to? Are employees time pressured? Are they fearful of exposure?

There are also ethnic and religious considerations. Some of your interviewees could be uncomfortable being interviewed by a woman, engaging in eye contact, or shaking hands. Some questions that seem okay within American culture could be offensive to those from a different culture. Try to acquire an understanding of your site population and the possibility of diverse national origins. Be careful to understand but not stereotype (Seidman, 2013). When unsure, simply ask the interviewee for permission or about his or her comfort level.

In addition to culture, power or perceived power can make a difference in data collection. A participant can perceive you to be a person of power without your knowing it. Do you hold an advanced position in your field? Do you have a college degree? Do you have a master's degree? Are you a doctoral student? Are you known for something in your field? Some participants may look up to you for these reasons and want to please you. You should consider your setting, make sure you encourage candid responses, and explain the purpose of your research and the usefulness of honest, candid answers. In some cases, perceived power differentials cannot be overcome. You need to be perceptive of clues that an interviewee is modifying responses to please you. For example, notice if the interviewee looks to you for affirmation of responses or expresses undue admiration of your position. In such situations, you might want to have a person other than yourself conduct the interview, or it might be that the participant's data become marginal to the study.

CONCLUSION

Interviewing can be a dynamic way to collect rich, in-depth qualitative data. Becoming a qualitative interviewer requires practice and also studying some of the key sources offered below. Remember that just as you would perfect a survey or select the best quantitative assessment for your study, when collecting interview data, you are the research tool that needs to be perfected and sharpened. You need to make sure you are prepared and practiced to limit the ways you could unintentionally invalidate your data. Novice researchers often make the mistake of thinking that interviewing is easy. It is not. Anyone conducting interviews should gain some training in interviewing skills, preferably in a class on interviewing. At the very least, read one of the many resources available on interviewing skills, and practice before conducting your first interview. Colleagues will be happy to provide feedback on your style and presence during the interview, as well as on the data you receive.

Questions for Reflection

1. How do study design and researcher skills influence the selection of interview format and the use of individual or focus group interviews?

2. How can a researcher manage preparation and attention to logistical details in support of a successful interview process?

3. How might a researcher mitigate the influence of personal worldview and assumptions on the conduct of interviews?

Key Sources

Brinkmann, S., & Kvale, S. (2015). *Interviews: Learning the craft of qualitative research interviewing* (3rd ed.). Thousand Oaks, CA: SAGE.

Gubrium, J. F., Holstein, J. A., Marvasti, A. B., & McKinney, K. D. (2012). *The SAGE handbook of interview research: The complexity of the craft* (2nd ed.). Thousand Oaks, CA: SAGE.

Josselson, R. (2013). *Interviewing for qualitative inquiry: A relational approach.* New York, NY: Guilford Press.

Rubin, H. J., & Rubin, I. S. (2012). *Qualitative interviewing: The art of hearing data.* Thousand Oaks, CA: SAGE.

Seidman, I. (2013). *Interviewing as qualitative research: A guide for researchers in education and the social sciences* (4th ed.). New York, NY: Teachers College Press.

References

Brinkmann, S., & Kvale, S. (2015). *Interviews: Learning the craft of qualitative research interviewing* (3rd ed.). Thousand Oaks, CA: Sage.

Josselson, R. (2013). *Interviewing for qualitative inquiry: A relational approach.* New York, NY: Guilford Press.

Rubin, H. J., & Rubin, I. S. (2012). *Qualitative interviewing: The art of hearing data.* Thousand Oaks, CA: SAGE.

Schwandt, T. A. (2015). *The SAGE dictionary of qualitative inquiry* (4th ed.). Thousand Oaks, CA: SAGE.

Seidman, I. (2013). *Interviewing as qualitative research: A guide for researchers in education and the social sciences* (4th ed.). New York, NY: Teachers College Press.

Tufford, L., & Newman, P. (2010). Bracketing in qualitative research. *Qualitative Social Work, 11*(1), 80–96. doi:10.1177/1473325010368316

SURVEY RESEARCH

Kimberley A. Cox

Survey research is a descriptive, nonexperimental method used to collect information through interviews and/or questionnaires. It can be used alongside other methods in quantitative, qualitative, and mixed methods research to explore, describe, and explain a multitude of constructs, characteristics, attitudes, and behaviors. For this reason, survey research is a popular method in the social, behavioral, management, and education sciences.

In this chapter, I present an overview of survey research, including its origins, purpose, and methods. I discuss common types of survey instruments, their respective advantages and disadvantages, and the types of information you can collect. Last, I present a brief overview of some key considerations in designing a survey instrument, including common types of survey items and response scales as well as reliability and validity of measurement.

ORIGINS OF SURVEY RESEARCH

Contemporary survey research has been shaped by social and political events and influenced by various academic disciplines and organizations such as the National Opinion Research Center. As a tool for research, the survey was an outcome of efforts by business and government sectors in the 20th century. For example, by the 1940s, federal agencies were using polls, such as the Gallup Poll, and surveys, such as the U.S. Census, to gather information about the public and to measure people's opinions about national problems (Converse, 1987). As the U.S. Postal Service expanded and telephones became commonplace, larger samples of the population could be surveyed (Converse, 1987). It was not until the 1960s, however, that survey research firmly established itself in academia. With the emergence of the internet in the 1980s and subsequent technological advances in the 21st century, new modes of collecting survey data, such as web-based surveys, have become increasingly popular. Today, numerous disciplines, such as psychology, political science, public policy, public health, marketing, and education, make extensive use of surveys to collect information.

TYPES OF SURVEY INSTRUMENTS

A *survey* is a method of collecting data from and about people (Fink, 2009). A *survey instrument* is the tool used to gather data—this term is typically used to differentiate the tool from the survey research it supports. There are two general tools for collecting data through survey research: (1) verbal surveys (or interviews) and (2) written surveys (or questionnaires). A verbal survey or interview refers to a survey instrument that can be administered in person, over the telephone or internet, or a combination of these methods. A written questionnaire refers to a survey instrument that contains items that the respondent is expected to read and then report his or her own answers. There are three main types of questionnaires: (1) self-administered mail questionnaires, where respondents provide their answers to the survey items and return the questionnaire by mail in a self-addressed stamped envelope that is provided; (2) in-person individual or group-administered questionnaires, which are administered to a single respondent or a group of respondents, respectively; and (3) self-administered web-based questionnaires, which are administered online through a website or a commercial web-based survey host.

In survey research, your role as the researcher will vary depending on how the survey is administered. For example, in a self-administered mail or web-based questionnaire, you will have little to no direct contact with respondents. Your only contact with respondents is likely to occur through an introductory email or letter describing the study and instructions for its completion. In survey research conducted through interviews by telephone, on the internet (e.g., Skype™), or in person, you will have direct contact with respondents as you ask questions or present statements and the respondents provide their answers. It is this characteristic of engagement with participants that distinguishes survey research from other kinds of descriptive research, such as observational research, which is characterized by observations of individuals in their natural environment without researcher involvement.

Advantages and Disadvantages of Survey Instruments

Each type of survey instrument has advantages and disadvantages. Therefore, you must weigh the costs and benefits of each type with consideration of your study's purpose, research question, sampling strategy, and data analysis plans.

Interviews. Interviews generally yield quality responses from respondents and high response rates because the interviewer is present to clarify survey items and answer questions. However, interviews can be costly, and they typically require more time, especially if multiple interviewers need to be recruited and trained. Interviews may pose a risk for unintentional coercion or interviewer bias, and they may offer less privacy than other types of surveys. A lack of privacy may influence respondents' willingness to answer questions truthfully.

Self-Administered Questionnaires. Self-administered questionnaires are typically an inexpensive and quick method of reaching a large sample. Self-administered questionnaires may offer more privacy than interviews, if they are anonymous. As a result, respondents may be more willing to answer sensitive questions. Because there is no interviewer present, there is minimal concern about interviewer bias or coercion. However, without the researcher present, self-administered questionnaires generally yield lower response rates than interviews. To improve the response rate, self-administered questionnaires should be easily understood and clear because there is no interviewer present to answer questions or provide clarification. Self-administered questionnaires delivered by postal mail may cost more and require more time to collect data than those administered by telephone or in person.

Self-Administered Web-Based Questionnaires. Self-administered web-based questionnaires may be faster and less costly to administer than other types of surveys. They also tend to provide respondents with a greater sense of privacy, if personal identifying information is not collected. The data collected through some commercial web-based survey hosts can be exported directly into the Statistical Package for Social Sciences® (IBM® Corp., Armonk, NY) or Microsoft® Excel, and thus, time devoted to manual data entry is eliminated. Web-based questionnaires have unique ethical and security concerns compared with other types of surveys, including, but not limited to, issues around the storage of data and the possibility of a breach of respondents' data (Nosek, Banaji, & Greenwald, 2002).

Although many people have access to the internet and email, those without access will not be able to participate in a web-based survey. People also possess varying degrees of technical skill that may hinder their ability to complete a web-based survey. Therefore, the targeted population must have access to and competence in using the internet and/or email.

PURPOSES OF SURVEY RESEARCH

Survey research generally serves one or more of three main purposes: (a) exploration, (b) explanation, and (c) description (Martella, Nelson, & Marchand-Martella, 1999). First, a survey can be used to explore a topic that has not been previously examined. For example, Duan, Brown, and Keller (2010) conducted an exploratory study on the experiences of male faculty in academia. The researchers designed a self-administered questionnaire that was distributed by mail to collect information on male faculty members' perceptions of their academic career, their values toward family and work, and their experiences in meeting their roles and expectations.

Second, when a survey is used to explain the relationship between two or more variables of interest, its purpose is explanation (Martella et al., 1999). For example, Farc and Sagarin (2009) conducted a study to investigate the relationship between attitude strength and voter behavior in the 2004 U.S. presidential election. The researchers used an in-person group-administered questionnaire to collect data on college students' voting behavior and attitudes toward the presidential candidates before and after the election.

Third, when a survey is used to describe the characteristics or attributes of a population, its purpose is description (Martella et al., 1999). The goal in descriptive survey research is to describe a population rather than understand why a relationship may exist between variables. For example, Barusch and Wilby (2010) conducted a study to describe how older adults experience and cope with depression. The researchers used in-person interviews to collect information on older adults' coping strategies and coping effectiveness.

TYPES OF INFORMATION RESEARCHERS COLLECT WITH SURVEYS

The purpose of a survey will determine the type of information you collect, and the type of information should be aligned with your study's research question and data analysis plan. For example, will groups be compared? Will a relationship between variables be examined? Will the frequency of behaviors be described? Alignment in this regard is critical for collecting information that will produce meaningful data that can answer your research question.

The three main types of information commonly collected with surveys are (1) descriptive, (2) attitudinal, and (3) behavioral. Most surveys include a combination of these types of information. Surveys that collect descriptive information often ask questions to gather information that describes respondents' characteristics, such as education and age. This descriptive information is important in most survey research because it will permit you to better understand your sample and make inferences about its representativeness to the target population. For example, in Farc and Sagarin's (2009) study of university students' attitudes toward presidential candidates, the researchers asked respondents, "Which political party do you usually feel closest to?" in order to describe their political affiliation (Barnes, Jennings, Ingelhart, & Farah, 1988, as cited in Farc & Sagarin, 2009).

Researchers are also often interested in using surveys to gather information about respondents' attitudes toward various objects, events, things, or people. For example, in Duan et al.'s (2010) study of male faculty members' perceptions of their academic careers, the researchers asked respondents, "What do you like about your career in academia?" in order to gather information about their attitude toward their career.

Last, researchers are also frequently interested in using surveys to gather information about respondents' behaviors, such as how often one engages in a particular action or activity. For example, Barusch and Wilby (2010) used an open-ended question that asked older adults, "How do you cope with this [depressive symptom]?" in order to gather information about their coping behavior.

After you decide on a type of survey, its purpose, and the information it will collect, your sampling strategy should be considered. The term *sampling plan* is typically used in survey research to refer to the strategy used to select the sample from a population (Levy & Lemeshow, 2009). In determining the sampling plan, you must decide whether to use a probability or nonprobability sampling strategy. In probability sampling (also called random sampling), the selection of participants is determined by chance, with each member of a population having an equal chance of being selected. In nonprobability sampling (also called nonrandom sampling), the probability of selection is not known. That is, each member of a population does not have an equal chance of being selected. See Chapter 4 for an overview of common types of sampling strategies.

BENEFITS AND LIMITATIONS OF SURVEY RESEARCH

Survey research can help you gather information directly from people about how they act and what they think, know, and believe as well as their descriptive characteristics, which can be challenging to measure with other methods. For example, the measurement of attitudes, which cannot be directly observed, is possible with survey research. Survey research is also useful for collecting information from a geographically dispersed sample of individuals.

Although surveys have numerous benefits, there are some limitations to their use. For example, they may not provide exact measurements; rather, they typically supply estimates of the population under study (Salant & Dillman, 1994). Therefore, you should generally exercise caution in generalizing your findings to a larger population.

The response rate or rate of return on self-administered questionnaires is another potential limitation that can cast doubt on the validity of a study's results. A low response rate could signal that respondents who returned the questionnaire are different in important ways from respondents who did not. A low response rate can also limit your ability to generalize findings to the target population. Therefore, it is important to consider strategies for improving rates in advance to reduce these challenges; for recommendations, see Dillman, Smyth, and Christian (2014).

The accuracy of survey data often rests on the ability of respondents to accurately interpret the meaning of survey items and correctly and honestly report their attitudes and behaviors. Respondents may also have difficulty recalling information or may misinterpret a survey item. Therefore, surveys are susceptible to bias due to their self-report nature. Bias may also occur because of a respondent's intentional or unintentional misreporting of information.

DESIGNING A SURVEY INSTRUMENT

Many phenomena have been studied to such an extent that there exist reliable and valid survey instruments for their measurement. Therefore, it is important that you conduct a thorough review of the literature and search reference materials, online resources, and databases to determine whether a survey instrument is already available before designing one. For example, reference materials like the *Mental Measurements Yearbook* (Buros Center for Testing, n.d.) and databases such as the *Test Collection* (Educational Testing Services, n.d.), PsycTESTS® (American Psychological Association, n.d.), and Health and Psychological Instruments (Behavioral

Measurement Database Services, n.d.) provide access to existing survey instruments in numerous disciplines.

If you locate an existing survey instrument that is suitable for your study, the next step is to obtain permission to use it for your own research. First, check the instrument for any copyright restrictions. Many journals hold the copyright for published tests or measures. Second, you may need to contact the publisher or author of the instrument to request permission. Be sure to retain copies of any communications you receive granting permission. Although there may be situations where it is acceptable to use an instrument that is published in a journal without permission, confirmation from the author is typically advised.

Some circumstances may call for you to modify or use only certain items from an existing survey instrument. For example, Barusch and Wilby (2010) modified the Center for Epidemiological Studies Depression Scale (CES-D; Radloff, 1977) to include two additional questions about coping behavior and coping effectiveness. If a participant reported that he or she experienced any of the depressive symptoms assessed by the CES-D, then the interviewer asked, "How do you cope with this?" followed by, "How effective has this been for you?" Permission is typically needed from the instrument's author to make modifications, and it is important to keep in mind that modifications of survey items may raise potential issues about the instrument's reliability and validity because changes can affect its psychometric properties.

If a survey instrument does not already exist to measure the construct or phenomenon of interest, and modification is not appropriate, you may need to design a survey instrument. Deciding whether to do so involves consideration of several important steps:

- Determining the factors associated with the construct or phenomenon of interest

- Selecting a method of administration

- Determining the sample to be studied

- Selecting a sampling plan

- Writing questions or statements

- Writing response scales

- Pilot testing

In the sections that follow, some of these steps will be described in more detail.

Writing Survey Questions and Statements

Good survey questions and statements share some common characteristics: They are free of biased language, easy to understand, and presented one at a time. As a result, they yield responses that are valid and reliable measures of the construct or phenomenon of interest. Survey questions and statements should also be written with knowledge of your plans for data analysis. A good place to begin is identifying the most appropriate scale or level of measurement—nominal, ordinal, interval, or ratio—for the type of data to be collected according to the statistical analysis that will be performed. See Chapter 4 for an overview of levels of measurement.

There are two main types of survey questions: open-ended and closed-ended. Open-ended questions are survey items that ask respondents to provide an answer, such as a small amount of text or a number, in their own words; that is, response options are not provided to respondents. For example, Duan et al. (2010) asked male faculty, "What do you like about your career in academia?" and "What do you dislike about your career in academia?" Open-ended questions such as these are most appropriate when (a) you are exploring a new topic of study, (b) the list of potential response options is too lengthy for a closed-ended format, and (c) the aim of the study is to obtain diverse responses. Open-ended questions often require more cognitive thought for respondents to answer than closed-ended questions (Tourangeau, Rips, & Ransinki, 2000). Content analysis is typically required for analyzing responses from open-ended questions, which can be time-consuming and complex, because it involves determining coding categories and then categorizing responses into themes.

Closed-ended questions are survey items presented with a specified set of response options. These response options can be presented in a dichotomous, multiple-choice, ranking, or rating format. For example, using a closed-ended question on marital status, Duan et al. (2010) presented male faculty respondents with the response options of single, married, divorced, and living together. Closed-ended questions require that the response options include all the possible answers that could be expected from respondents. Researchers often include an "Other" category as a response option to capture a response that is not listed, but doing so means that such responses may need to be analyzed similar to those in an open-ended question.

Response options are typically formatted to either the right of the question or statement or directly below it. Response options for rating scale questions are generally displayed horizontally, whereas response options for multiple-choice and ranking scale questions are generally listed vertically.

Some common errors in writing survey questions and statements include the following:

- *Ambiguity:* Ambiguity refers to questions and statements that are vaguely written. Ambiguous questions and statements lead to confusion because respondents must try to make sense of the researcher's meaning of a survey item.

- *Biased wording:* Biased wording refers to words within a question or statement that may trigger an emotional reaction. Biased words may influence a respondent's answer in a way that is not intended by the survey item.

(Continued)

(Continued)

- *Leading questions and statements:* To lead a question or statement refers to words that lead a respondent to favor or disfavor a particular perspective. For example, a question such as "Don't you agree that recycling plastic is important?" may lead a respondent to expect that a particular response is desired from the researcher.

- *Double-barreled questions and statements:* Double-barreled refers to questions and statements that ask for responses to two or more things or constructs within the same item. For example, the statement "I think it is important to recycle plastic and conserve water" reflects two different topics: (1) recycling plastic and (2) conserving water. A respondent may wish to answer one way about one of the topics and differently for the other topic.

- *Complicated skip patterns:* Skip patterns are instructions that direct respondents to skip questions or statements that do not apply and proceed to items elsewhere within the survey. If the skip patterns are overly complex, it may be difficult for respondents to follow them.

Some tips to avoid common errors in writing survey questions and statements include the following:

- Provide respondents with clear instructions.

- Write questions and statements that are clear, simple, and as short as possible.

- Write in complete sentences; for example, write "What is your gender?" and not "Gender?"

- Avoid using biased or leading words that may cause an emotional response or lead a respondent to favor or disfavor a particular perspective.

- Avoid using double negatives.

- Avoid using "and" in questions and statements to ensure that only one topic is being measured in each item.

- Avoid complicated skip patterns that can be difficult for respondents to follow.

- Pretest questions and statements for clarity by asking others to read them aloud and record any issues that arise to inform potential revision.

Another consideration to keep in mind when writing survey questions and statements, especially those that are sensitive in nature, is response bias. One type of response bias is *social desirability*, which refers to the tendency for people to make themselves appear positively or socially desirable by responding to items in a certain way. There are several different ways to reduce social desirability (see Nederhof, 1985), such as designing the survey so that it ensures anonymity and communicating to respondents the privacy protections you have put in place. Another type of response bias is the tendency for people to only provide extreme answers on a scale (e.g., on a Likert scale, selecting "strongly agree" for every item). In this case, formatting items so that some are worded for disagreement and some are worded for agreement may help reduce this bias.

Writing Rating Scales

Rating scales are used in survey research to quantify a respondent's answer to a survey item. Two main types of rating scales are Likert and semantic differential. A Likert scale presents a range of adjective options along a continuum, such as "strongly disagree," "disagree," "undecided," "agree," and "strongly agree." Respondents are asked to indicate their agreement or disagreement to a statement by selecting the numerical value that corresponds to their selection. For example, Duan et al. (2010) asked male faculty to respond to statements such as "My self-worth is determined more by my family and personal life than my career" on a 4-point Likert-type scale with 1 = *strongly disagree*, 2 = *disagree*, 3 = *agree*, and 4 = *strongly agree.*

A semantic differential scale presents response items with bipolar adjectives following a word, such as in the item, Good _._._._._ Bad. Respondents place a mark on the continuum between the set of adjectives that best represents the meaning they associate with the word presented. For example, Farc and Sagarin (2009) used a semantic differential scale as one measure of college students' attitudes toward candidates in the 2004 U.S. presidential election. The participants were presented with the candidates' names followed by response items, such as "Positive _._._._._ Negative" and "Wise _._._._._ Foolish."

Pilot Testing a Survey Instrument

A pilot test is the final step in designing a survey instrument (Martella et al., 1999). A pilot test allows you to gain preliminary information about how a survey instrument performs under realistic conditions (Martella et al., 1999). You should administer the survey instrument to respondents from the same or similar population of interest in a setting that is as similar as possible to your actual study. The size of the pilot sample may range from as few as 10 respondents to as many as several hundred depending on various factors, such as the purpose of your pilot study (Hertzog, 2008; Johanson & Brooks, 2010), the size of the target population, your access to a representative sample of the target population, the number of items in the survey, and sufficient power for determining statistical significance (Johanson & Brooks, 2010).

You should use the information obtained from a pilot test to evaluate the reliability and validity of your survey instrument (Martella et al., 1999). You can also use the pilot test as an opportunity to ask respondents questions regarding the survey, such as how easily they understood the items, how they arrived at their responses, and their opinions about its user-friendliness, all of which can help inform potential revisions to the instrument before your actual study begins.

Reliability and Validity of Measurement

In survey research, *reliability* is the consistency of responses over time. *Test–retest reliability* refers to whether or not the survey instrument yields the same result with repeated administration. To determine test–retest reliability, researchers calculate the correlation of scores (called the reliability coefficient) from participants who completed the survey at two different points in time. *Split-half reliability* refers to the method of evaluating the internal reliability of a survey instrument by correlating one half of the items with the other half. To determine split-half reliability, researchers might score the odd-numbered items and even-numbered items separately, thus yielding two scores for each respondent. A correlation coefficient (called the split-half reliability coefficient) is then computed on these scores to provide the instrument's reliability.

To assess internal consistency among items in a survey instrument, Cronbach's alpha (also called coefficient alpha) can be calculated. This test yields an alpha, α, ranging in value from 0 to 1, with higher levels reflecting relatively high internal consistency among items. That is, the items in the instrument provide a consistent measure of the underlying construct. For a discussion on interpreting coefficient alpha and issues with its use, see Schmitt (1996).

Validity refers to the degree to which a survey instrument measures what it was designed to measure. There are three main types of validity in survey research: (1) face validity, (2) construct validity, and (3) criterion validity. *Face validity* refers to whether a survey instrument appears to reasonably measure what it intends to measure. *Construct validity* refers to whether a survey instrument measures the issue it was intended to measure, typically in relation to a particular theory. *Criterion validity* refers to how well an instrument correlates with another instrument that measures a similar construct, called a criterion measure. To assess criterion validity, you would compare scores from the new survey instrument to those from an established instrument known to measure a similar construct to the one being studied. For further discussion of validity, see Chapter 12.

CONCLUSION

If you are considering survey research for your research project, ask yourself, "Is my topic appropriate for survey research?" "Will I be able to gather information from participants?" "Is there an existing reliable and valid survey instrument available to measure my phenomenon or construct of interest?" "Will I need to design my own survey instrument?" Your answers to these questions may lead you toward using the survey research method to explore, describe, and explain a phenomenon or construct that will contribute to understanding people's attributes, attitudes, and/or behaviors.

Questions for Reflection

1. How is survey research different from other methods of research?

2. What are the strengths and limitations of survey research methods?

3. In what way is the purpose of a survey related to the type of information it collects?

4. What are the characteristics of reliable and valid survey questions and statements?

Key Sources

Dillman, D. A., Smyth, J. D., & Christian, L. M. (2014). *Internet, phone, mail, and mixed-mode surveys: The tailored design method* (4th ed.). Hoboken, NJ: Wiley.

Fowler, F. J., Jr. (1995). *Improving survey questions: Design and evaluation.* Thousand Oaks, CA: SAGE.

Fowler, F. J., Jr. (2009). *Survey research methods* (4th ed.). Thousand Oaks, CA: SAGE.

Johanson, G. A., & Brooks, G. P. (2010). Initial scale development: Sample size for pilot studies. *Educational and Psychological Measurement, 70,* 394–400. doi:10.1177/0013164409355692

Rossi, P. H., Wright, J. D., & Anderson, A. B. (Eds.). (1985). *Handbook of survey research* (pp. 195–230). New York, NY: Academic Press.

Schuman, H., & Presser, S. (1996). *Questions and answers in attitude surveys: Experiments on question form, wording, and context.* Thousand Oaks, CA: SAGE.

Sue, V. M., & Ritter, L. A. (2011). *Conducting online surveys* (2nd ed.). Thousand Oaks, CA: SAGE.

References

American Psychological Association. (n.d.). *PsycTESTS®.* Retrieved from https://www.apa.org/pubs/databases/psyctests/

Barusch, A. S., & Wilby, F. (2010). Coping with symptoms of depression: A descriptive survey of community-dwelling elders. *Clinical Gerontologist, 33,* 210–222. doi:10.1080/07317111003773650

Behavioral Measurement Database Services. (n.d.). *Health and psychosocial instruments (HaPI).* Retrieved from http://bmdshapi.com/

Buros Center for Testing. (n.d.). *Mental measurements yearbook.* Retrieved from http://buros.org/mental-measurements-yearbook

Converse, J. M. (1987). *Survey research in the United States: Roots and emergence (1890–1960).* Berkeley: University of California Press.

Dillman, D. A., Smyth, J. D., & Christian, L. M. (2014). *Internet, phone, mail, and mixed-mode surveys: The tailored design method* (4th ed.). Hoboken, NJ: Wiley.

Duan, C., Brown, C., & Keller, C. (2010). Male counseling psychologists in academia: An exploratory study of their experience in navigating career and family demands. *Journal of Men's Studies, 18*(3), 249–267. doi:10.3149/jms.1803.249

Educational Testing Services. (n.d.). *About the test collection at ETS*. Retrieved from https://www.ets.org/test_link/about

Farc, M., & Sagarin, B. J. (2009). Using attitude strength to predict registration and voting behavior in the 2004 U.S. presidential elections. *Basic and Applied Social Psychology, 31,* 160–173. doi:10.1080/01973530902880498

Fink, A. (2009). *How to conduct surveys: A step-by-step guide* (4th ed.). Thousand Oaks, CA: SAGE.

Hertzog, M. A. (2008). Considerations in determining sample size for pilot studies. *Research in Nursing & Health, 31*(2), 180–191. doi:10.1002/nur.20247

Johanson, G. A., & Brooks, G. P. (2010). Initial scale development: Sample size for pilot studies. *Educational and Psychological Measurement, 70*(3), 394–400. doi:10.1177/0013164409355692

Levy, P. S., & Lemeshow, S. (2009). *Sampling of populations: Methods and applications* (4th ed.). New York, NY: Wiley.

Martella, R. C., Nelson, R., & Marchand-Martella, N. E. (1999). *Research methods: Learning to become a critical research consumer*. Needham Heights, MA: Allyn & Bacon.

Nederhof, A. J. (1985). Methods of coping with social desirability bias: A review. *European Journal of Social Psychology, 15*(3), 263–280. doi:10.1002/ejsp.2420150303

Nosek, B. A., Banaji, M. R., & Greenwald, A. G. (2002). E-research: Ethics, security, design, and control in psychological research on the Internet. *Journal of Social Issues, 58*(1), 161–176. doi:10.1111/1540-4560.00254

Radloff, L. S. (1977). The CES-D scale: A self-report depression scale for research in the general population. *Applied Psychological Measurement, 1,* 385–401. doi:10.1177/014662167700100306

Salant, P., & Dillman, D. A. (1994). *How to conduct your own survey*. New York, NY: Wiley.

Schmitt, N. (1996). Uses and abuses of coefficient alpha. *Psychological Assessment, 8*(4), 350–353. doi:10.1037/1040-3590.8.4.350

Tourangeau, R., Rips, L. J., & Ransinki, K. (2000). *The psychology of survey responses*. New York, NY: Cambridge University Press.

RESEARCH QUALITY AND ETHICS

PART IV

QUALITY CONSIDERATIONS

Molly S. Stewart and John H. Hitchcock

If you want to have an impact in academic, policy, business, and program evaluation settings, you must be able to conduct high-quality research. You must also have the skills to assess the quality and rigor of other published research. One way to think about quality in research is to consider certain indicators that demonstrate research findings accurately represent the subject, phenomenon, or process being studied. Failure to meet standards of quality may result in research that is misleading or inaccurate. For example, suppose that a study examined the effectiveness of a reading intervention by analyzing the test results of first graders before and after the implementation of the intervention. However, the study was done in a way that did not allow the researchers to be reasonably sure that the intervention exposure was the best explanation for any observed improvement. The findings of such a study would have limited use for educators and administrators because they would not know if they should use the intervention in question. Hence, it is important to be able to develop and critique studies that yield findings that can clearly inform decision making. This chapter introduces and offers examples of commonly used quality indicators in the context of different approaches to inquiry.

The typical approach through which researchers and scholars address quality is to consider the degree to which findings (and the data and inferences that form the basis of findings) are *valid*; in other words, they must reflect the actual phenomenon under study rather than reflecting coincidental relationships, the biases of the researcher, or the limitations of the study design (e.g., see Cook & Campbell, 1979). One aspect of validity is *reliability*, which refers to the consistency of results from a research instrument, strategy, or approach. That is, a reliable research instrument would be one that, when administered multiple times on the same subject, yields the same findings. In this chapter, we provide a conceptual overview of these two specific quantitative quality considerations—validity and reliability—as well as their qualitative counterparts—credibility, transferability, and dependability—because these are the primary yardsticks by which research quality is gauged (Creswell & Miller, 2000).

The purpose of this chapter is to make you aware of the conceptual bases of *quality* in social science research and some of the broad debates that shape these concepts. In this chapter, we do not go into great detail on method-specific issues related to validity and reliability or the philosophical orientations aligned with different epistemologies; rather, our aim is to describe how your increased attention to research design, execution, and analysis can yield higher quality findings. Finally, although validity and reliability are two of the most central quality indicators, they are certainly not the only important indicators. This chapter is thus not a one-stop source for what you need to know but, rather, a starting point to understanding the quality considerations involved in every step of the research process (Guest & MacQueen, 2008).

This chapter begins by providing an overview of the basic concepts underlying validity and reliability. Then, using experimental design as a concrete example, we show how validity can be undermined or enhanced as a function of design choice. This discussion includes detailed sections on both internal and external validity and their respective threats. In the second half of the chapter, we discuss the concepts of validity and reliability as they relate to qualitative inquiry, and we provide several techniques that can be used to mitigate possible issues with each of those areas.

VALIDITY AND RELIABILITY

Validity

The meaning of *validity* is related to the concept of truth; in research, *valid* findings accurately describe or reflect the phenomenon under study, with the understanding that validity is not an either/or dichotomy but instead a continuum wherein a set of findings might be supported by poor to excellent validity evidence. The concept of truth is also reflected in the qualitative term *trustworthiness*, which some scholars approximate to the quantitative notion of validity. There are several considerations in the research process that are necessary to promote valid findings, and all these relate to designing a study that is appropriate for the research question. Such considerations include understanding whether (a) the method of data collection enables you to answer the specific research question, (b) the types of data collected enable you to answer the research question, (c) the sample of data collected enables you to address a target question (i.e., did you question or test the appropriate types of people or other subjects?), (d) you asked the participants questions that were appropriate to the research question, and (e) you included enough participants such that results can be applied beyond the study. These are just a few of the details that you must consider when thinking about the quality of a study.

Although the concept of validity broadly reflects the idea that research findings reflect the true phenomenon, causal mechanism, or attitudes under study, different types of studies and methods necessitate different approaches to promote validity. Many qualitative and mixed methods scholars use different terminology for concepts related to validity, such as *credibility, trustworthiness* (e.g., Lincoln & Guba, 1985; see also Guest & MacQueen, 2008; Onwuegbuzie & Johnson, 2006), *legitimation* (e.g., Johnson & Onwuegbuzie, 2004), and *inference quality* (e.g., O'Cathain, 2010). Some qualitative methodologists even reject the concept of qualitative validity altogether (e.g., Wolcott, 1990). Some of these disagreements are rooted in philosophical differences. For example, some postmodernist researchers question the assumption that there can be one reality to portray a finding or that even primary data, such as informant interviews, test results, or survey responses, are able to fully describe reality (cf. Lofland, Snow, Anderson, & Lofland, 2009; Onwuegbuzie & Johnson, 2006). However, for the purposes of this chapter, we operate from the assumption that certain aspects of reality can be observed and/or measured by researchers.

You must consider what kind of study design and methods are appropriate to address your research questions. Fortunately, for most design types, there is an existing framework[1] for thinking through validity. Methodological guidelines, or frameworks, are available when doing surveys, case studies, psychometric studies, experiments, ethnographies, phenomenological studies, mixed methods investigations, and so on (see Table 12.1).

A framework is an established structure for the design and execution of a given type of study, including data collection methods, data management, and analytic methods. Frameworks include components for checking for quality, whether in terms of validity (quantitative) or trustworthiness (qualitative). Validity should not be considered a one-dimensional goal. It is not only an outcome but also an iterative process that continually helps us understand the truth of whatever is being studied. Again, validity is best thought of as a kind of continuum. As Cook and Campbell (1979) stated, "We should always use the modifier 'approximately' when referring to validity, since one can never know what is true. At best, one can know what has not yet been ruled out as false" (p. 37).

Quality of Data Sources and Methods

The quality of data sources and data collection methods has implications for validity. In both qualitative and quantitative studies, there may be inconsistencies among data sources. For example, a participant's actions may not match what the participant says he or she does, or the topic of a given survey question, such as drug use or other illegal activities, may incentivize participants to answer items inaccurately (Cronbach, 1946; Groves et al., 2009; Lofland et al., 2009). For example, if you wanted to study the prevalence of cheating, how might you gather such information? Would you conduct interviews to ask participants to confess their tendency to cheat? The chances are fairly high that your participants would underreport their behavior. If you chose a different approach such as allowing them to self-disclose their cheating behavior via an anonymous survey, you might get a more accurate—or valid—portrayal of their behavior. You must therefore examine your data sources and data collection methods for problems that may undermine validity. For this reason, triangulating data sources and using mixed methods are often done to bring to

---

[1] By *framework*, we refer to a set of ideas that can help us think through research processes and findings. Shadish et al. (2002), for example, describe four facets of experimental validity and ways in which validity can be undermined during the course of an experiment. Lincoln and Guba (1985) offer one of the earlier sets of guidelines for strengthening qualitative inquiry. As another example, O'Cathain (2010) describes a framework for assessing the quality of mixed methods studies.

TABLE 12.1 ● LIST OF DIFFERENT FRAMEWORKS AND SUGGESTED READINGS		
Type of Inquiry	**Description**	**Suggested Readings**
Case studies	Used when trying to learn about phenomena in the context of a particular case (e.g., a community, school, etc.)	Yin (2009)
Experimental design	To be used when a central question is causal in nature, such as when obtaining evidence that a new teaching technique might yield better learning outcomes compared with another technique	Shadish, Cook, and Campbell (2002)
Ethnography	Tends to be used when studying a particular cultural group	LeCompte and Schensul (2010)
General qualitative inquiry	For studies where the aim is to explore and learn about phenomena in natural settings	Brantlinger, Jimenez, Klingner, Pugach, and Richardson (2005), Denzin and Lincoln (2005), Lincoln and Guba (1985), Nastasi and Schensul (2005), and Patton (2014)
General statistical guidance	There is a lot of guidance around application of the general linear model, which is used in most statistical analyses readers of this text are likely to run into. We offer one text because we find it to be accessible and amusing	Field (2013)
Meta-analysis	For use when synthesizing the results of multiple existing studies to learn about aggregated levels of evidence	Hedges and Olkin (1985) and Lipsey and Wilson (2001)
Mixed methods	Combining both qualitative and quantitative design elements	Creswell and Plano Clark (2010), O'Cathain (2010), and Tashakkori and Teddlie (2010)
Psychometrics	To be used when the central purpose of a study is to develop or refine a test/measurement instrument	American Education Research Association, American Psychological Association, and National Council on Measurement in Education (2014) and Crocker and Algina (1986)
Phenomenology	A particular variant of qualitative inquiry that focuses on understanding the experiences of research participants	Moustakas (1994)
Single-case (single-subject) designs	For studies that aim to test intervention effects on small numbers of people (e.g., ABAB and multiple-baseline designs)	Horner et al. (2005), Kratochwill et al. (2010), Kratochwill et al. (2013), and Kratochwill and Levin (2014)
Surveys	Typically used when working with a sample and when the intent is to learn more about some population of interest	Dillman, Smyth, and Christian (2009), Fowler (2009), and Groves et al. (2009)

Note: This list is not meant to be complete, because there is such wide variation in the types of studies and designs within the broad arena of the social sciences. We selected a few that we think are commonly used. The citations can be considered as a beginning set of resources to learn more. Later in the chapter, we cover ideas from experimental and qualitative frameworks in more detail. Finally, note that some of the citations we offer use the term *framework* and others do not, but we are otherwise confident that the authors intended to offer guidance on how to carry out that particular form of inquiry.

light inconsistencies among qualitative sources (Denzin, 1989; Guest & MacQueen, 2008; LeCompte & Goetz, 1982; Onwuegbuzie & Johnson, 2006), and there are statistical methods for designing and checking the validity of specific survey and assessment questions (see, e.g., Borgers, Hox, & Sikkel, 2004).

The validity of a research instrument depends in part on its intended purpose and whether it is used for that purpose. In other words, when thinking about data quality, you should consider the evidence for using a specific instrument in a particular situation, rather than thinking of the instrument as valid or not (see Kane, 2013). Consider, for example, standard college or graduate school entrance examinations designed to assess achievement, such as the Scholastic Aptitude Test (SAT), American College Testing (ACT), and Graduate Record Examinations (GRE). There may be some evidence that these assessments have a valid application in terms of deciding which students are likely to perform well if admitted to given schools (cf. Brewer, Knoeppel, & Clark Lindle, 2015; Hamilton, Stecher, & Klein, 2002; Heubert & Hauser, 1999; Messick, 1994, 1995), but the evidence to support their use for assessing intelligence is far weaker.

Therefore, it is critical to always think of a research instrument as a tool, and then consider whether the tool is being used for its intended purpose (Shadish, 1995). Using the tool analogy, a particular hammer may be one of the very best ones ever made, but it still would be a poor tool to use when you need a screwdriver. This analogy applies equally well when thinking about what instruments to use when gathering data. If, for example, we hoped to assess whether some new teaching technique yielded improvements in reading scores, we would not logically choose a mathematics test to use for the outcome measure. But reading is a complex skill with many subcomponents—such as fluency versus comprehension—and we must be able to distinguish the specific skills being tested and which assessments will measure those specific skills. Above all, it is important to make sure you are using the right tool for the job.

A related aspect of understanding validity entails thinking about the *contextual variables* of the study, including local cultures, time period, and environment (Onwuegbuzie & Johnson, 2006). Every variable, even in quantitative work, represents an attribute that is situated within a specific time and place, and depending on the focus of a given study, certain aspects of variables may be relevant to the defensibility of findings. It is therefore important to always consider the context in which data were collected and interpreted. For example, if you were to do a study on political values, you would need to note the current political climate in which you are doing the study. Alternatively, if you were to read a study on political values, you would need to note the publication date of that study and consider the political climate of that time period. Consider the two largest political parties in the United States: Democrats and Republicans. In this example, *time* is a relevant type of context, because there has been a shift in the overarching political beliefs of these two parties over time. Decades ago, Republicans would have been thought of as being the more socially liberal of the two political parties.

A related issue is the concept of social construction of variables, or the fact that the common understanding of a variable may be defined by the society in which it is situated, as opposed to being defined by scientific differences. Race is a well-known example of a socially constructed variable, in which racial identity has very little to do with biological differences. However, the experiences of people from different races tend to be systematically different within certain societies. One example of how race can be socially constructed in multiple ways is the construction of *white* in the United States. Several immigrant groups who are now considered white, including the Irish and eastern Europeans, were once considered racially different from immigrant groups from other western and northern European areas (Jacobson, 1998). Racial identities can change as demographic groups assimilate with or differentiate themselves from other groups, and there are often social, economic, and political benefits and/or drawbacks to these changes. As a researcher, you must be aware of the possibility that an attribute has been socially constructed and, if so, whether and how that social construction affects the meaning of the variable. The ways in which variables are constructed will have considerable influence on study validity (cf. Reynolds et al., 2014; Spillane et al., 2010; Wells, Williams, Treweek, Coyle, & Taylor, 2012). You can enhance validity by providing clear, straightforward definitions of each variable *as applied in your study*.

In summary, we reiterate that *validity* is somewhat synonymous with *truth*. And just as your definition and understanding of *truth* can be individually subjective as well as based on cultural and social interpretations, so it is with the concept of validity. When thinking in terms of research quality, consider how to design studies that can yield defensible evidence that can be used to make a reasonably accurate inference or proposition. Being detailed, specific, and thoughtful in all of your design elements and analysis will help you enhance validity and the defensibility of your findings.

Reliability

Reliability refers to the extent to which findings and results are consistent across researchers using the same methods of data collection and analysis. The heart of the concept is synonymous with the notion of consistency (Crocker & Algina, 1986), and it is related to validity. You must consider the importance of data and methodological consistency (reliability), because consistency increases the likelihood that your interpretation of data has validity. On the other hand, findings might also be reliably wrong, and this is a critical difference between reliability and validity. To illustrate reliability, consider a scale used to measure a person's weight. If the scale yields a close approximation of the person's actual weight, then one would say that the scale's measure is accurate, a key aspect of validity. But now consider the idea of consistency. Suppose a person is weighed once a day for a week, and the scale indicates values of 130, 150, 170, 110, 190, 145, and 155 pounds, respectively. Since the weight of one person will not vary so much in the span of a week, the conclusion to be drawn is that the scale is broken. Because of the lack of consistency, or reliability, there is little reason to trust the validity of any single measurement. *Valid estimation requires consistent, or reliable, scores.*

It is also instructive to see that just because measurements are reasonably reliable, they might also be characterized by poor evidence validity. A person may weigh 150 pounds, but suppose that the measurements produced by the scale across 1 week are 191, 189, 190, 191, 190, 190, and 189 pounds, respectively. These scores consistently indicate that the person weighs about 190 pounds, but the estimates are consistently wrong. *Reliability is a necessary aspect of validity, but it is insufficient if used alone as a measure of quality.* When using tests and surveys to measure a phenomenon, it is thus critical to understand the properties of the measurement tool and consider whether the measurement tool has been well designed and is suited for the job at hand. When engaging in qualitative tasks such as observations and interviews, think of strategies for assessing whether any conclusions to be drawn from these data collection approaches are likely to be reasonably consistent (reliable) and accurate (valid).

Reliability Issues in Data Collection and Analysis. Reliability checks can take place at two stages of research: during data collection and during analysis. To test reliability at the data collection stage, another researcher could collect data using the same methods to see if consistent data are being collected. It is also possible to have two groups analyze the same set of data with the same analytical methods to see if the two groups come to the same understanding of the data.

The types of data collected have significant influence over the reliability and replicability of a study (Peräkylä, 1997). Quantitative data sets are often easily accessible and transferable among researchers. Furthermore, quantitative data, once collected and recorded, are not usually subjected to any detailed interpretation beyond understanding what a number is supposed to represent. For example, consider a 5-point response scale, where 5 = *strongly disagree*, 4 = *disagree*, 3 = *neutral*, 2 = *agree*, and 1 = *strongly agree*. The number 4 is understood to have one meaning (*disagree*), and researchers tend not to conjecture further without having special reason to do so. In contrast, qualitative data are often products of the researcher's filtering and interpreting of information during data collection via observation and interview notes. For example, a researcher creates notes about an observed lesson, and these notes become part of the data set. However, the researcher cannot observe, or record, every detail of the lesson, due to the limited capacity of human observation as well as the choices—conscious or unconscious—the researcher makes about which details to notice and record. In contrast, data that are not filtered by the researcher at the time of collection include documents, tape-recorded interviews, and videos of observations. The researcher does not have to transfer such heard or observed data into a tangible record, such as drawings or notes, because the data are already in a tangible format. Qualitative researchers generally agree that a combination of machine-recorded and interpretive data is ideal to achieve a full understanding of the phenomenon under study (see, e.g., Lofland et al., 2009). Research design conceptualization, whether qualitative, quantitative, or mixed method, should entail examining the trade-offs of different kinds of data collection and should incorporate plans for increasing the reliability of the research, such as by using multiple researchers or multiple data sources, or other strategies.

LeCompte and Preissle (1993) discussed the challenges inherent in trying to replicate the data collection phase of a qualitative study, comparing it with quantitative methods:

> Unique situations cannot be reconstructed precisely because even the most exact replication of research methods may fail to produce identical results. Qualitative research occurs in natural settings and often is undertaken to record processes of change, so replication is only approximated, never achieved. . . . Moreover, because human behavior is never static, no study is replicated exactly, regardless of the methods and designs used. (p. 332)

Discussions of reliability are still fairly new to qualitative methodologists, as demonstrated by the diversity of opinions regarding theory and standardized practices for achieving reliability in qualitative studies.

In summary, you will need to consider whether your data are collected in a consistent manner and whether the type(s) of data collected will help you develop inferences and propositions that approximate the reality of your studied phenomenon. These are not the only important considerations, however. Even when your data are of high quality and are appropriate for the research questions, there are additional considerations to keep in mind when making analytic inferences from these data. That is, you must choose the most appropriate methods to analyze and interpret data in order to reach valid conclusions about your object of study. We use the methodology of experimental design as one example to demonstrate how analytic methods can positively or negatively affect the validity of conclusions.

VALIDITY CONSIDERATIONS IN EXPERIMENTAL DESIGN

Shadish and colleagues (2002) provided an overview of a four-component framework that focuses on validity in the context of experimental designs: internal, external, statistical-conclusion, and construct validity. Each type of validity is briefly reviewed in this section, though we focus on internal and external validity because these offer relatively concrete examples of how the truth of a proposition can be defended or undermined. This particular validity framework was developed to help researchers assess *causal mechanisms* specifically; that is, it is used to determine whether a particular condition or treatment causes better outcomes compared with some alternative. This is one example of a framework that provides researchers with standards by which to judge the validity of conclusions. The following discussion of internal validity prompts the use of the experimental design framework, due to the element of causation.[2]

Internal Validity of Experimental Findings

Consider the following statement: *I took some aspirin, and my headache went away; therefore, aspirin reduced my pain.* This statement contains a causal inference: Taking aspirin caused the reduction in pain. The degree to which this inference is valid reflects the degree of *internal validity*. In experimental designs, researchers examine whether some variable (the *independent* variable), rather than others, produces some result or change (the *dependent* variable; Shadish et al., 2002). Consideration of *internal validity* begs the question "How truthful is the proposition that a change in one variable, rather than changes in other variables, causes a change in outcome?"

Causal inference, and thus internal validity, can be surprisingly tricky. For any given proposition about a causal inference, there are rival explanations; these explanations are referred to as *threats* to a statement's validity. For our example, we might assume that you usually take aspirin with water; if the headache had been caused by dehydration, then it is possible that hydration—not the aspirin—was the actual cause of pain relief. Alternatively, it is possible that the headache eventually subsided on its own, and thus it was the natural recovery processes—not the aspirin—that yielded the improvement. In short, just because the pain subsided after taking aspirin, it does not mean that the drug was the causal agent. We must consider whether the aspirin explanation is better than the rival explanations.

To test causal inference, we must assess the various threats (or alternative explanations) to internal validity. The experimental validity framework identifies a number of common threats to internal validity; the following discussion draws on examples of these threats in order to illustrate the process of identifying and eliminating rival explanations (see Shadish et al., 2002, for a complete list and description of threats; see also Table 12.2). One example is the *history* threat, or the possibility that other events may have occurred during the experiment that could explain the change in outcome. In the case of aspirin, the fact that common headaches eventually subside on their own is an example of a history threat.

Many internal validity threats can be addressed by including a comparison (or *control*) group that does not receive the treatment being studied. If a treatment effect is observed by comparing performance across both groups (e.g., students who received counseling show better outcomes than those who did not), then it becomes clear that the independent variable—that is, *treatment exposure*—is the best overall explanation for the difference in outcomes between the groups. Many threats to internal

---

[2] A broader notion of internal validity can be conceptualized as the degree to which interpretations of a particular data set are reasonable inferences, causal or otherwise. But for now, we apply the narrower idea as used in an experimental framework, where one has a research question related to causation.

TABLE 12.2 ● OVERVIEW OF INTERNAL VALIDITY THREATS		
Threat	**Definition**	**Example**
History	Other events may have occurred during the duration of the study that could explain the improved behavior	During the course of treatment, the children in the counseling treatment group were also assigned to a new teacher who is excellent at managing behavioral concerns. In this scenario, was the improvement due to the treatment, the presence of the new teacher, or both?
Maturation	The fact that people, including study participants, change over time	During a 1-year study, the treatment students could have simply outgrown their initial behavior problems; their personal development, unrelated to the counseling, may have contributed to or even been solely responsible for the improved behavior scores.
Testing	The possibility that repeated exposure to a measurement instrument could, by itself, affect test-taking behavior and test scores	The children who took the baseline measurement test reflected on what the test was measuring and at posttest offered socially desirable responses that resulted in higher scores; yet their overall classroom behavior may not have actually improved.
Instrumentation	(1) A testing instrument may change or may be used in a way that does not correctly measure the treatment effect	This might happen if there are two versions of a test (Form A and Form B) that are incorrectly assumed to be equivalent. In this case, it could be that behavior as measured by Form A looks more problematic as compared with Form B. If Form B was used at posttest, then any apparent improvement cannot be attributed to the treatment; rather, differences in the test could be responsible for the change.
	(2) There may be unknown contextual factors that can impact testing	Perhaps baseline measurement was done in the morning and posttest measurement was done in the afternoon, and for some reason, the children in the study were more likely to demonstrate better behavior after lunch.
Statistical regression to the mean	The phenomenon that extreme scores tend to not be repeated	Suppose someone is not normally depressed but we measure this trait after some sad event that occurred, and the score suggests that the individual needs counseling. Six months later, we see improved mood. Is this because the counseling worked, or did the person simply revert back to his or her typical emotional status and this would have happened irrespective of counseling? Over time, extreme scores—both positive and negative—tend to move closer to the average for that particular measure.
Researcher bias	Changes in research design or analysis that are a result of the researcher's subjective views regarding the study topic, participants, theory of change, etc.	The researchers may be so convinced that the new counseling approach works that they unintentionally modify aspects of the original study design to show that the treatment makes a difference.

Selection	The process of creating participant groups in a study—nonrandom selection might yield two groups that are not equivalent at the beginning of the study. If there are key differences between the two groups, one cannot know if any posttest differences are due to a treatment effect or due to prior group differences	Due to legal restrictions about research, students in a treatment group may have to be volunteered by their parents/guardians; the requirement that participants actively volunteer and have parent permission introduces the possibility that the characteristics of students in the treatment group are systematically different from those in the control group. In such an example, if we see that children who were treated appear to perform better on a posttest, is it because the treated children have more involved parents (i.e., they would have been better off anyway) or is it because the treatment worked? The selection threat is not a concern if study participants are assigned randomly to study groups because, on average, there should be no differences between participants in the treatment and control conditions.
Overall mortality (attrition)	Loss of members in the study sample	A study compares pre- and posttest scores on an assessment to measure participant change. Some students drop out before completing the posttest. The loss of part of the sample creates the possibility that the students who remained in the study and completed the posttest have systematically different characteristics from the students who left the study.
Differential mortality	Members of sample groups (e.g., treatment and control) drop out at different rates and nonrandomly—in one group more than the other	Some students in the treatment sample drop out because they no longer wish to receive the counseling and miss out on other activities during the school day. These students may be differently motivated or have systematically different behavioral characteristics from the students who are willing or happy to miss other school activities.

validity can be addressed by adding a control group when the intent is to make a causal inference. A basic quality indicator for studies that set out to address a causal question is to look for the presence of a control condition (Shadish et al., 2002).

By adding a control group, we also potentially introduce new threats to internal validity. One such threat is *selection*, which refers to how groups in a study were formed. There are many ways to form groups. People can volunteer to be treated, students might be picked by a teacher, a researcher may decide who is most in need of treatment, and so on. Of the many options, one approach to selecting who is treated and who is in a control group is to use random assignment to treatment and control groups. Such assignment is essentially based on chance: If you use random procedures (e.g., coin flips or computer algorithms), you can expect that, on average, there will be no systematic differences between groups.

When assignment is nonrandom, such as when participants in groups are purposefully selected based on certain characteristics, there may be key differences between the treatment and control groups (see the *selection* example in Table 12.2). Thus, the manner in which selection was done can threaten later attempts to make causal inferences. It is possible that students in the treatment group from the *selection* example might have done better than those in the control group even if the treatment was not the cause of the students' improvements. In other words, the way the groups were formed may have made it look like the new counseling technique made a difference, even if it did not. Researchers can prevent selection bias by using random assignment to treatment and control groups when possible. When random assignment is not an option, researchers may statistically "control" for other variables, such as socioeconomic status, gender, race, age, and disability status, in statistical models to decrease the systematic differences between groups.

The broader point here is that, in general, not all designs are equal in terms of their inherent capacity to address the internal validity of target research questions. If you are conducting an experiment, it will behoove you to design studies to have stronger validity because doing so will result in better quality. Without certain design features put into place, the improvement in behavior may indeed be due to the treatment but may also be due to any of the threats listed. Fortunately, in the context of an experiment, as with many other methodologies, there is guidance that you can consult to assist with recognizing and addressing these threats. Unless these threats can be removed as plausible explanations, the study quality must be considered questionable.

External Validity of Experimental Findings

External validity—the extent to which findings hold true across contexts—and its threats are also major considerations in research design quality. Suppose you have produced a study with high internal validity; that is, none of the previously discussed threats are plausible explanations for the observed improvements in a treated group. The best explanation for the outcome of the study is that the treatment worked. This high level of internal validity leads other researchers to want to know whether this finding is likely to hold true across other students in other places, times, contexts, cultures, and so on. As with internal validity, there are several common threats to external validity (Shadish et al., 2002; see Table 12.3).

One such threat is *treatment variation*. To elaborate on the example given in Table 12.3, one example would be inconsistency in dosage levels. Consider for example a case in which one teacher delivering the intervention has excellent classroom management skills, and the second teacher does not. The second teacher's students receive a smaller dosage of the intervention because one third of class time is spent on classroom management issues.

Threats to external validity present a number of concerns, and researchers must find ways to account for these threats. There are two broad strategies for addressing threats to external validity. The first is to engage in thorough literature reviews and to build on previous related studies. External validity can be strengthened by limiting the research focus and by comparing the new findings with existing studies in the literature. A careful review can highlight gaps in the existing literature; these

TABLE 12.3 ● OVERVIEW OF EXTERNAL VALIDITY THREATS

Threat	Definition	Example
Interactions of the observed causal relationship with sample units	The possibility that whatever was observed with one particular sample may not hold true for different samples	The treatment may work well with students in suburban schools but not in rural schools.
Treatment variations	The effect of a treatment reflects variations in how it was administered, as opposed to the effect of the treatment itself	Treatment variation might be a function of human error in administering a treatment or a function of how a program is implemented (e.g., dosage levels, time of day the treatment is delivered, or failure to correctly implement some element of the treatment).
Types of outcome measures used	Treatment effects may be found with one kind of test but not another	One might see an effect with a particular type of test but not another, such as measuring reading fluency with tests from two different publishers.
Settings in which the treatment was delivered	The possibility that the observed effects are due to contextual factors, as opposed to the treatment itself	Treatment effects in a school that is located in a high-income community might be different from effects in more impoverished settings.
Context-dependent mediation	The influence of a mediating factor in one setting versus another setting	A common mediating factor is treatment dosage; other factors may include staff skill or availability. For example, is it possible to fully implement an intended treatment in the form of intense counseling in an overcrowded school setting where there are extensive demands on a counselor's time?

gaps then justify a specific focus that is situated within an existing framework of studies. For example, a specific counseling technique may have been thoroughly studied in residential treatment settings, and so your focus might be on the first effort to try it in a public school. The design of your study will be strengthened by the evidence available from other, related studies, and the threats to external validity will be minimized by limiting the focus to a very specific area.

The second strategy is to think carefully about ways in which your findings may apply, or generalize, to other settings. Shadish (1995) listed a number of principles that can help you think about generalization when doing experiments, ethnographies, or other types of studies. You must consider how applicable the findings from your study might be to another setting, such as similarities in the sample and how it was obtained, the measurements used, the duration, and other treatment details. Above all, claims of generalizability are most appropriate when there is evidence that a very specific aspect of a treatment yields an exact outcome. Knowing what aspects of a study are likely to generalize and what aspects are likely to be highly context specific is the key to thinking through considerations that might threaten the generalizability of a finding to some new scenario.

To illustrate these issues around generalizability, we use an example from a study by Paino, Renzulli, Boylan, and Bradley (2014), which examined, not the effect of a treatment, but rather, charter school closings in North Carolina (this is to show that generalization can and should be pondered not only when dealing with treatment effects but also when dealing with other issues, e.g., state policy). The authors performed a quantitative analysis of data on charter schools and the nearby public districts. Data included financial information, local market variables, density of charters in the area, school demographics, enrollment, age of the school, and academic performance information. This quantitative analysis allowed the researchers to examine the probability of a charter school closing at a given point in time. The findings suggested that charter schools were less likely to close with increases in school enrollment, compliance with federal desegregation orders, and state and federal funding of charters. However, because the location of this study was in one state, its findings may not generalize well to another state that may have different policies. Here, the authors' inclusion of a qualitative case study analysis could help them better understand the degree to which these findings might generalize to other states and contexts. Suppose a state has conditions similar to that of North Carolina—contextual conditions that have been rigorously analyzed in relation to the quantitative findings. As a reviewer of the study, you may feel more confident in applying the study findings to that new context. On the other hand, if the case studies in North Carolina show major differences in state charter policies, funding, or enrollment patterns, you may not feel confident in using the findings of this study to understand patterns in the other state.

Statistical-Conclusion and Construct Validity

There are two remaining types of validity from Cook and Campbell's (1979) framework. *Statistical-conclusion validity* refers to the degree to which researchers are correct about the relationship between two variables. This type of validity requires not only that researchers know which kind of statistical models or techniques are appropriate for a given data set and research question but also that they can accurately test those models and apply those techniques. Shadish and colleagues (2002) identified nine distinct threats, which is helpful; if you are doing experimental research, we highly encourage you to review this resource in depth. Other concepts and techniques that relate to statistical-conclusion validity include statistical power, data cleaning, and outlier analyses. Measurement reliability, or its lack thereof, is classified as a threat to this form of validity.

Construct validity refers to the degree to which underlying ideas (e.g., treatments, behaviors, behavior problems, cooperative learning, and socioeconomic status) are properly conceptualized and operationalized in a study. Every study is based on a set of concepts that underlie the theory being tested. In our ongoing example, the theory being tested in the experiment is that a certain type of counseling intervention will improve problematic behavior issues. If the measurement of this improvement is completed through a student pre- and postintervention assessment, we must ensure that (a) the intervention addresses the behaviors under study and (b) the questions on the assessment correctly represent the behaviors under study. An intervention or measurement that does not accurately represent the constructs being studied cannot result in reasonable, valid findings about the constructs.

CONSIDERATIONS IN QUALITATIVE INQUIRY

Earlier, we presented aspects of the experimental validity framework to demonstrate the point that your design choices can affect the validity of the inferences you make at the end of your study. We also demonstrated this point because causal questions tend to be of wide interest. Moving forward, we focus on another broad arena—qualitative research. Some of the challenges, or threats, to reaching validity and reliability in quantitative and qualitative research are similar, although they must be observed or measured using different techniques (Creswell & Miller, 2000). For example, whereas quantitative researchers attempt to statistically control for variables that may influence the outcome, qualitative researchers attempt to understand the influence of variables through careful observation and recording of phenomena (Cook & Campbell, 1979; LeCompte & Goetz, 1982). In the next section, we provide an introduction to validity and reliability issues with regard to qualitative research methods.

Trustworthiness

Trustworthiness is the qualitative term that is often used in place of the quantitative term *validity*. Trustworthiness is the degree to which you, as a researcher, can have confidence in your sources as well as the methods used to gather your sources. Steps taken in the earliest stages of research—study purpose and design—can help you decide which collection methods will result in the most relevant, trustworthy data for your research questions. Ethnographic field notes, formal and informal interviews, formal and informal observations, video recordings, photographs, and archival records offer different strengths and weaknesses (LeCompte & Goetz, 1982). For example, Peräkylä (1997) discussed the specific benefits and drawbacks of tape-recorded and transcribed (audio and/or visual) data as compared with ethnographic field notes. Field notes filter observations at the time of data collection through the researcher's particular frameworks; in contrast, audio/visual recordings capture all of the data from one particular angle and/or sense (e.g., visual vs. audio). Downsides to audio/visual recordings are the inability to see gestures and movements (audio) or to see the observation from multiple angles or perspectives. Ethnographers can take in an entire observation site through all of the senses, but they are limited in what they can record in words or pictures. Using a combination of these data collection methods allows you to compare two or more data sources; such comparisons can highlight areas of inconsistency that need further inquiry or patterns/themes that have a high degree of consistency (i.e., they surface in multiple types of sources and in ways that do not conflict).

There are a variety of ways in which you as a qualitative researcher can check the trustworthiness of emerging themes in your data (Tracy, 2010). During data collection and analysis, researchers can attend to potential *observer effects*, employ *multiple researchers*, and use *member checks*. Also, see Lincoln and Guba (1985) and Nastasi and Schensul (2005) for more in-depth discussion on trustworthiness.

Observer Effects. *Observer effects* refers to the possibility that the collected data have been contaminated, or influenced, by your presence or your research instruments. One example of observer effects is a change in participant behavior during observations due to your presence (LeCompte & Goetz, 1982). Depending on the type of activity and individuals under observation, your demographic characteristics, and the methods by which you are recording data, participants may consciously or unconsciously change their behavior. If participants change their behavior, then you cannot report that their observations are typical of their natural or normal behavior.

We can use the example of a counseling intervention to illustrate this issue. Imagine this scenario. Suppose there is a qualitative observation element to the study, in which you observe a group counseling session for student participants. The majority of the students in the session speak English as a second language, and about half of them have parents who are not U.S. citizens. The majority of the students in the group also receive free or reduced-price lunch. In comparison, you, the researcher, are white, are well dressed, and speak only English. The demographic differences between you and the student participants include social class, first language, age, and, in some cases, race/ethnicity and/or citizenship. These differences may lead students to behave differently in front of you than they would with only the counselor present.

You can take two precautions against observer effects. First, you can note all of the potential effects that your presence may have on the participants or their behavior; getting a second opinion on these potential effects can dually strengthen this precautionary strategy. Second, you can follow up with members of the group—in this case, the counselor or one of the participants—to ask whether the observed session was typical or uncommon in any way. This type of member check with a member of the group can help you put your observations in perspective.

Multiple Researchers. Although not always feasible in qualitative studies, using multiple researchers in data collection has benefits as well as challenges for validity. When multiple researchers collect data, they are able to demonstrate that they are recording data in comparable ways; this is vital to study validity. Similar to interrater reliability (see later discussion), multiresearcher data collection procedures must be uniform to collect valid and trustworthy data across an entire study. One example of aligning data collection procedures relates to level of detail; all the researchers should know how much detail to include in field notes or observation rubrics. This is true for all methodologies; just as tests producing quantitative data must be administered and recorded consistently, interview and observation data must be recorded using the same techniques.

Member Checks. Member checking involves sharing emergent patterns and findings with members of participant groups to get feedback on the accuracy of those findings. Although the purpose of independent research is to create and implement an unbiased research design, there are also limitations to conducting research as an outsider. Outside researchers rarely have the insider cultural perspective or organizational knowledge that is needed to fully understand the phenomena being observed. Member checking allows the outside researcher to share his or her ideas with an insider and develop an ongoing, increasingly accurate understanding of the phenomena (LeCompte & Goetz, 1982; Lofland et al., 2009). The dual use of insider and outsider perspectives is crucial to achieving this accuracy because both perspectives tend to have particular types of biases, such as ingrained cultural or social beliefs (Bloor, 1978; Turner & Coen, 2008). Such beliefs can include views on gender/sex, racial or ethnic groups, or age-appropriate behaviors.

Reliability in Qualitative Research

The concept of reliability, sometimes called *dependability*, is relevant in some ways for qualitative methods and problematic in other ways. The definition of reliability as "replicability" is problematic for qualitative, especially naturalistic, methodologies. As LeCompte and Goetz (1982) explained, "Because human behavior is never static, no study is replicated exactly, regardless of the methods and designs employed" (p. 35). However, there are ways in which the larger concept of reliability has been adapted to apply to qualitative, naturalistic fields of study. Areas of focus within the umbrella of qualitative reliability include the replicability of data collection and analysis (e.g., understanding how much of the analysis is specific to an individual researcher's interpretations) and intercoder reliability or interrater agreement, which refers to the degree to which multiple researchers within the same study agree on how to describe and categorize the observed data in terms of the study's theoretical framework. These issues of reliability can be found in many qualitative studies, and researcher subjectivity plays an important, if sometimes overlooked, role in these processes. The following sections examine challenges to and strategies for strengthening qualitative reliability.

Researcher Subjectivity. Researcher subjectivity refers to the unique perspective that each researcher brings to a given study; this uniqueness poses a reliability challenge for qualitative studies at the stages of both data analysis and data collection because the interpretations of two or more unique researchers are unlikely to be identical or replicable (Carey & Gelaude, 2008). For example, in an empirical study of qualitative thematic coding, Armstrong, Gosling, Weinman, and Marteau (1997) found that a sample of trained, experienced experts in qualitative coding, looking at the same data set, did not reach the exact same conclusions about the data. The study demonstrated that when multiple researchers analyzed the same data, the themes that emerged were similar enough to be considered common but different enough to highlight the role of researcher discipline, training, and cultural background. The findings of this study suggested that the inherent nature of subjective analysis in qualitative methods will result in some degree of agreement and some degree of disagreement. See Glaser and Strauss's (1967) description of the constant-comparison method for a specific example of how to systematically code qualitative data.

Reflexivity. The findings of this study also point to the need for individual researchers to be *reflexive*, or transparent and forthcoming, about their demographics, their discipline, their training, and any other characteristics that may influence their collection or analysis of data. Toward this end, you should reflect on your position in relation to the study and examine the potential for bias based on your cultural or socioeconomic background, nationality, ability status, and other factors (LeCompte & Preissle, 1993; Onwuegbuzie & Johnson, 2006). Your explanation of methodology should also include the steps that you take to minimize the impact of your researcher bias on the research design, data collection, and analysis (Guest & MacQueen, 2008).

Interrater Reliability. When multiple researchers are used to analyze qualitative data, reliability issues arise. In addition to being reflexive about individual characteristics, the research team must also take steps to ensure that they are using the same criteria to analyze the same data set. *Interrater reliability* refers to the rate of agreement among multiple research team members applying the same analytic methods to the same data set; these methods typically involve some degree of researcher subjectivity, such as coding text or rating observed behaviors. Additional benefits of determining interrater reliability are twofold: The process allows the research team to examine both the team's understanding of codes and concepts as well as individual team member accuracy in using the coding or rating system (Carey & Gelaude, 2008). Like many phases of research, interrater agreement is an iterative process. If the independently coded data samples end up with substantially different results, the coding system must be reviewed and clarified or individual coders must be trained further. Interrater reliability testing must continue until the desired level of agreement among researchers has been achieved (MacQueen, McLellan-Lemal, Bartholow, & Milstein, 2008).

Transferability. A final point, related to reliability in qualitative research, is to consider the concept of *transferability.* Transferability is the degree to which a set of findings from one study will transfer to another particular situation (Lincoln & Guba, 1985). The idea is largely associated with qualitative inquiry but is similar to the concept of generalizability in quantitative work. The general challenge in transferability is describing the setting of a study with sufficient clarity and detail so that readers of that study can make their own judgments about what does and does not apply to other scenarios.

CONCLUSION

Research quality is important in all disciplines and fields and in program development and implementation because all knowledge—understanding human behavior, program designs, and effects of medical treatments—is influenced by the quality of the research on which it is based. If inaccurate research findings are used as the basis for products, program development, or policy improvements, these changes are unlikely to actually work as hoped, potentially wasting time and other valuable resources. Some areas of product or program development have a variety of parties with established financial or political stakes in the direction of development; here it is especially important that the cited research be independent and of high quality. Peer review is generally understood to be a hallmark in the research process because it entails review by multiple experts in the field; the experts are looking for indicators of research quality that provide confidence in the findings.

It is also important to note that there are particular aspects of mixed methods research that lend it to increasing validity, such as the ability to take advantage of the strongest tools of each framework (Onwuegbuzie & Johnson, 2006). Onwuegbuzie and Johnson (2006) discussed several sets of existing guidelines for making mixed methods research decisions (e.g., Collins, Onwuegbuzie, & Sutton, 2006; Greene, Caracelli, & Graham, 1989; Onwuegbuzie & Johnson, 2004). Some qualitative and quantitative methodologists, without purposefully using a mixed methods framework, have incorporated these tools organically to best answer their research questions (e.g., Reynolds et al., 2014; Wells et al., 2012).

This introduction should help you understand that threats to validity and reliability can surface at any point in the research project: design, data collection, data analysis, or even results reporting. To handle validity and reliability concerns, you first need to be aware of them. At every step, you should be looking out for possible threats to research quality, making sure that the design minimizes these threats as much as possible and clearly reporting the severity of existing threats. To facilitate this process, you should first have a clear understanding of your research question(s). Then, seek methodological frameworks or guidance that promote thinking through designs and generating the highest quality inferences. Finally, you should identify design choices that have the capacity to answer the question well. Table 12.1 is designed with that purpose in mind.

Our overriding advice for you is to appreciate the idea that design decisions can influence the quality of the data collected, later analyses, and the overall inferences drawn from your work. We recommend that you investigate further the wide range of specific strategies and techniques to address the threats to validity and reliability that were briefly introduced here.

Questions for Reflection

1. Do a quick search for a standard dictionary definition of the word *validity* (or *valid*). How does this definition fit with your use of the word in everyday conversation? How will it change the way you use this term going forward?

2. How does the definition of *validity* apply when thinking about research quality?

3. How is validity connected to the idea of reliability? According to the ideas presented in this chapter, describe an example where a measure yields reliable information but the validity of the information is still questioned.

4. Why is it important to think about the idea that an instrument is being used in a valid manner as opposed to just saying that an instrument is "valid"?

5. How are trustworthiness and validity different?

Key Sources

Brewer, C., Knoeppel, R. C., & Clark Lindle, J. (2015). Consequential validity of accountability policy: Public understanding of assessments. *Educational Policy, 29*(5), 711–745. doi:10.1177/0895904813518099

LeCompte, M. C., & Preissle, J. (1993). *Ethnography and qualitative design in educational research* (2nd ed.). San Diego, CA: Academic Press.

O'Cathain, A. (2010). Assessing the quality of mixed methods research: Toward a comprehensive framework. In A. Tashakkori & C. Teddlie (Eds.), *Handbook of mixed methods in social and behavioral research* (2nd ed., pp. 305–338). Thousand Oaks, CA: SAGE.

Shadish, W. R., Cook, T., & Campbell, D. (2002). *Experimental and quasi-experimental designs for generalized causal inference.* Boston, MA: Houghton Mifflin.

Tracy, S. J. (2010). Qualitative quality: Eight "big-tent" criteria for excellent qualitative research. *Qualitative Inquiry, 16*(10), 837–851. doi:10.1177/1077800410383121

References

American Education Research Association, American Psychological Association, & National Council on Measurement in Education. (2014). *Standards for educational and psychological testing.* Washington, DC: American Educational Research Association.

Armstrong, D., Gosling, A., Weinman, J., & Marteau, T. (1997). The place of inter-rater reliability in qualitative research: An empirical study. *Sociology, 31*(3), 597–606. doi:10.1177/0038038597031003015

Bloor, M. (1978). On the analysis of observational data: A discussion of the worth and uses of inductive techniques and respondent validation. *Sociology, 12*(3), 545–552. doi:10.1177/003803857801200307

Borgers, N., Hox, J., & Sikkel, D. (2004). Response effects in surveys on children and adolescents: The effect of number of response options, negative wording, and neutral mid-point. *Quality & Quantity, 38*(1), 17–33. doi:10.1023/B:QUQU.0000013236.29205.a6

Brantlinger, E., Jimenez, R., Klingner, J., Pugach, M., & Richardson, V. (2005). Qualitative studies in special education. *Exceptional Children, 71*, 195–207. doi:10.1177/001440290507100205

Brewer, C., Knoeppel, R. C., & Clark Lindle, J. (2015). Consequential validity of accountability policy: Public understanding of assessments. *Educational Policy, 29*(5), 711–745. doi:10.1177/0895904813518099

Carey, J. W., & Gelaude, D. (2008). Systematic methods for collecting and analyzing multidisciplinary team-based qualitative data. In G. Guest & K. M. MacQueen (Eds.), *Handbook for team-based qualitative research* (pp. 227–272). Lanham, MD: AltaMira Press.

Collins, K. M. T., Onwuegbuzie, A. J., & Sutton, I. L. (2006). A model incorporating the rationale and purpose for conducting mixed methods research in special education and beyond. *Learning Disabilities: A Contemporary Journal, 4*, 67–100.

Cook, T. D., & Campbell, D. T. (1979). *Quasi-experimentation: Design and analysis issues for field settings.* Boston, MA: Houghton Mifflin.

Creswell, J. W., & Miller, D. L. (2000). Determining validity in qualitative inquiry. *Theory Into Practice, 39*(3), 124–130. doi:10.1207/s15430421tip3903_2

Creswell, J. W., & Plano Clark, V. L. (2010). *Designing and conducting mixed methods research* (2nd ed.). Thousand Oaks, CA: SAGE.

Crocker, L. M., & Algina, J. (1986). *Introduction to classic and modern test theory.* New York, NY: Holt, Rinehart, & Winston.

Cronbach, L. J. (1946). Response sets and test validity. *Educational and Psychological Measurement, 6*(4), 475–494. doi:10.1177/001316444600600405

Denzin, N. K. (1989). *The research act: A theoretical introduction to sociological methods.* Englewood Cliffs, NJ: Prentice Hall.

Denzin, N. K., & Lincoln, Y. S. (2005). The discipline and practice of qualitative research. In N. K. Denzin & Y. S. Lincoln (Eds.), *The SAGE handbook of qualitative research* (3rd ed., pp. 1–32). Thousand Oaks, CA: SAGE.

Dillman, D. A., Smyth, J. D., & Christian, L. M. (2009). *Internet, mail and mixed-mode surveys: The tailored design method* (3rd ed.). Hoboken, NJ: Wiley.

Field, A. (2013). *Discovering statistics using IBM SPSS Statistics* (4th ed.). Thousand Oaks, CA: SAGE.

Fowler, F. J. (2009). *Survey research methods.* Thousand Oaks, CA: SAGE.

Glaser, B. G., & Strauss, A. L. (1967). *The discovery of grounded theory: Strategies for qualitative research.* New Brunswick, NJ: Transaction.

Greene, J. C., Caracelli, V. J., & Graham, W. F. (1989). Toward a conceptual framework for mixed-method evaluation designs. *Educational Evaluation & Policy Analysis, 11*, 255–274. doi:10.3102/01623737011003255

Groves, R. M., Fowler, F. J., Couper, M. P., Lepkowski, J. M., Singer, E., & Tourangeau, R. (2009). *Survey methodology* (2nd ed.). Hoboken, NJ: Wiley.

Guest, G., & MacQueen, K. M. (2008). Reevaluating guidelines in qualitative research. In G. Guest & K. M. MacQueen (Eds.), *Handbook for team-based qualitative research* (pp. 205–226). Lanham, MD: AltaMira Press.

Hamilton, L. S., Stecher, B. M., & Klein, S. P. (2002). *Making sense of test-based accountability in education.* Washington, DC: Rand Corporation.

Hedges, L. V., & Olkin, I. (1985). *Statistical methods for meta-analysis.* New York, NY: Academic Press.

Heubert, J. P., & Hauser, R. M. (1999). *High stakes: Testing for tracking, promotion and graduation.* Washington, DC: National Academies Press.

Horner, R. H., Carr, E. G., Halle, J., McGee, G., Odom, S., & Wolery, M. (2005). The use of single subject research to identify evidence-based practice in special education. *Exceptional Children, 71,* 165–179. doi:10.1177/001440290507100203

Jacobson, M. F. (1998). *Whiteness of a different color: European immigrants and the alchemy of race.* Cambridge, MA: Harvard University Press.

Johnson, R. B., & Onwuegbuzie, A. J. (2004). Mixed methods research: A research paradigm whose time has come. *Educational Researcher, 33*(7), 14–26. doi:10.3102/0013189X033007014

Kane, M. (2013). The argument-based approach to validation. *School Psychology Review, 42*(4), 448–457.

Kratochwill, T. R., Hitchcock, J., Horner, R. H., Levin, J. R., Odom, S. L., Rindskopf, D., & Shadish, W. R. M. (2010). *Single-case designs technical documentation.* Retrieved from https://ies.ed.gov/ncee/wwc/Docs/ReferenceResources/wwc_scd.pdf

Kratochwill, T. R., Hitchcock, J. H., Horner, R. H., Levin, J. R., Odom, S. L., Rindskopf, D. M., & Shadish, W. R. (2013). Single-case intervention research design standards. *Remedial and Special Education, 34,* 26–38. doi:0.1177/0741932512452794

Kratochwill, T. R., & Levin, J. R. (Eds.). (2014). *Single-case intervention research: Methodological and statistical advances.* Washington, DC: American Psychological Association.

LeCompte, M. D., & Goetz, J. P. (1982). Problems of reliability and validity in ethnographic research. *Review of Educational Research, 52*(1), 31–60. doi:10.3102/00346543052001031

LeCompte, M. D., & Preissle, J. (1993). *Ethnography and qualitative design in educational research* (2nd ed.). San Diego, CA: Academic Press.

LeCompte, M. D., & Schensul, J. J. (2010). *Designing and conducting ethnographic research: An introduction* (2nd ed.). Lanham, MD. AltaMira Press.

Lincoln, Y. S., & Guba, E. G. (1985). *Naturalistic inquiry.* Beverly Hills, CA: SAGE.

Lipsey, M. W., & Wilson, D. B. (2001). *Practical meta-analysis.* Thousand Oaks, CA: SAGE.

Lofland, J., Snow, D. A., Anderson, L., & Lofland, L. H. (2009). *Analyzing social settings: A guide to qualitative observation and analysis* (4th ed.). Belmont, CA: Wadsworth.

MacQueen, K. M., McLellan-Lemal, E., Bartholow, K., & Milstein, B. (2008). Team-based codebook development: Structure, process, and agreement. In G. Guest & K. M. MacQueen (Eds.), *Handbook for team-based qualitative research* (pp. 119–135). Lanham, MD: AltaMira Press.

Messick, S. (1994). The interplay of evidence and consequences in the validation of performance assessments. *Educational Researcher, 23,* 13–23. doi:10.2307/1176219

Messick, S. (1995). Validity of psychological assessment: Validation of inferences from persons' responses and performances as scientific inquiry into score meaning. *American Psychologist, 50,* 741–749. doi:10.1037/0003-066X.50.9.741

Moustakas, C. (1994). *Phenomenological research methods.* Thousand Oaks, CA: SAGE.

Nastasi, B. K., & Schensul, S. L. (2005). Contributions of qualitative research to the validity of intervention research. *Journal of School Psychology, 42,* 177–195. doi:10.1016/j.jsp.2005.04.003

O'Cathain, A. (2010). Assessing the quality of mixed methods research: Toward a comprehensive framework. In A. Tashakkori & C. Teddlie (Eds.), *Handbook of mixed methods in social and behavioral research* (2nd ed., pp. 305–338). Thousand Oaks, CA: SAGE.

Onwuegbuzie, A. J., & Johnson, R. B. (2004). Mixed method and mixed model research. In B. Johnson & L. Christensen (Eds.), *Educational research: Quantitative, qualitative, and mixed approaches* (pp. 408–431). Boston, MA: Allyn & Bacon.

Onwuegbuzie, A. J., & Johnson, R. B. (2006). The validity issue in mixed research. *Research in the Schools, 13*(1), 48–63.

Paino, M., Renzulli, L., Boylan, R., & Bradley, C. (2014). For grades or money? Charter school failure in North Carolina. *Educational Administration Quarterly, 50*(3), 500–536. doi:10.1177/0013161X13505289

Patton, M. Q. (2014). *Qualitative research and evaluation methods: Integrating theory and practice* (4th ed.). Thousand Oaks, CA: SAGE.

Peräkylä, A. (1997). Reliability and validity in research based on tapes and transcripts. In D. Silverman (Ed.), *Qualitative research: Theory, method, and practice* (pp. 201–220). London, UK: SAGE.

Reynolds, J., DiLiberto, D., Mangham-Jefferies, L., Ansah, E. K., Lal, S., Mbakilwa, H., . . . Chandler, C. I. R. (2014). The practice of "doing" evaluation: Lessons learned from nine complex intervention trials in action. *Implementation Science, 9*(75), 1–12. doi:10.1186/1748-5908-9-75

Shadish, W. R. (1995). The logic of generalization: Five principles common to experiments and ethnographies. *American Journal of Community Psychology, 23,* 419–428. doi:10.1007/BF02506951

Shadish, W. R., Cook, T., & Campbell, D. (2002). *Experimental and quasi-experimental designs for generalized causal inference.* Boston, MA: Houghton Mifflin.

Spillane, J. P., Pareja, A. S., Dorner, L., Barnes, C., May, H., Huff, J., & Camburn, E. (2010). Mixing methods in randomized controlled trials (RCTs): Validation, contextualization, triangulation, and control. *Educational Assessment, Evaluation, and Accountability, 22*(1), 5–28. doi:10.1007/s11092-009-9089-8

Tashakkori, A., & Teddlie, C. (Eds.). (2010). *SAGE handbook of mixed methods in social and behavioral research* (2nd ed.). Thousand Oaks, CA: SAGE.

Tracy, S. J. (2010). Qualitative quality: Eight "big-tent" criteria for excellent qualitative research. *Qualitative Inquiry, 16*(10), 837–851. doi:10.1177/1077800410383121

Turner, S., & Coen, S. E. (2008). Member checking in human geography: Interpreting divergent understandings of performativity in a student space. *Area, 40*(2), 184–193. doi:10.1111/j.1475-4762.2008.00802.x

Wells, M., Williams, B., Treweek, S., Coyle, J., & Taylor, J. (2012). Intervention description is not enough: Evidence from an in-depth multiple case study on the untold role and impact of context in randomised controlled trials of seven complex interventions. *Trials, 13*(95), 1–17. doi:10.1186/1745-6215-13-95

Wolcott, H. F. (1990). On seeking—and rejecting—validity in qualitative research. In E. W. Eisner & A. Peshkin (Eds.), *Qualitative inquiry in education: The continuing debate* (pp. 121–152). New York, NY: Teachers College Press.

Yin, R. K. (2009). *Case study research: Design and methods* (4th ed.). Thousand Oaks, CA: SAGE.

ETHICAL CONSIDERATIONS

Kimberley A. Cox

Many of the decisions researchers make are guided by consideration of research ethics, including, but not limited to, decisions about participant recruitment, instrumentation, data storage, data analysis, and dissemination. Although the research designs covered in previous chapters each carry specific ethical implications, they share some common considerations regarding the ethical treatment and protection of research participants. It is these commonalities that are the focus of this chapter.

In this chapter, I address ethical issues of relevance to and most commonly encountered by student researchers in the social, behavioral, management, and education disciplines. The modest coverage of ethics adopted in this chapter acknowledges that ethical issues are often context dependent. Therefore, you are encouraged to discuss your proposed research study with your institution's ethics review board and supervisory committee in the early stages of research planning.

I begin this chapter with a brief historical overview of the codes and regulations governing ethical conduct in research, followed by the role of professional associations in research ethics. I then cover the essential components of ethical research planning, such as assessing risks and benefits, the role of institutional review boards (IRBs), and the informed consent process. I discuss some common ethical challenges, such as conducting research with vulnerable populations, maintaining privacy, and using deception and debriefing techniques. Last, I address the unique ethical implications of internet-based research.

ETHICS CODES AND REGULATIONS

The first international code of protections for human research participants dates back to the first part of the 20th century, most notably the 1946–1947 Nuremberg medical trial. During this trial, it was revealed that German doctors and others conducted involuntary human medical experimentation in Nazi concentration camps and clinics (Weindling, 2001). The Nuremberg Code arose as a result of this trial.

The Nuremberg Code contained a set of basic ethical principles that have since influenced subsequent research ethics codes and regulations. These principles emphasized certain conditions to protect research participants, including voluntary informed consent, avoidance of harm, assessment of risk, right to withdrawal, and the researcher's responsibility to terminate an experiment if its continuation might pose harm to the participant ("Trials of War Criminals," as cited in U.S. Department of Health and Human Services [DHHS], 2016b).

A history of egregious research abuses in the United States, such as the Tuskegee and Willowbrook studies, led to the 1974 National Research Act (Public Law 93-348), which directed establishment of the National Commission for the Protection of Human Subjects of Biomedical and Behavioral Research (U.S. DHHS, 2016a) and included the requirement for ethics review boards at research institutions. This commission, through publication of the Belmont Report (U.S. Department of Health, Education, and Welfare, 1979), identified three ethical principles—respect for persons, beneficence, and justice—and established guidelines for conducting research to ensure that these principles are observed.

The ethical principle of *respect for persons* refers to respecting autonomy, which involves acknowledgment of an individual's autonomy to make personal choices and protections from harm for individuals with diminished or impaired ability to exercise autonomy. *Beneficence* refers to an obligation to do no harm and the need for research to maximize potential benefits and minimize possible harms. *Justice* refers to treating individuals in a way that is morally right, such that the selection of research participants and any potential benefits and burdens of participating in research are equitable among groups (U.S. Department of Health, Education, and Welfare, 1979).

The Belmont Report influenced the protections that are currently in place for human research participants in biomedical and behavioral research conducted in the United States. Its three ethical principles were translated in 1991 by the work of more than a dozen U.S. federal departments and agencies, such as the U.S. DHHS and the U.S. Food and Drug Administration, into the Federal Policy for the Protection of Human Subjects, commonly referred to as the Common Rule (U.S. DHHS, 2016a). The Common Rule describes the regulations for protecting individuals who participate in research, including the requirements for informed consent and the functions of IRBs.

On January 19, 2017, the U.S. DHHS and several other U.S. federal departments and agencies published a final rule revising the Common Rule and thus modernized the federal regulations originally disseminated in 1991; amendments followed on January 22, 2018, and June 19, 2018 (U.S. DHHS, 2017). The revised Common Rule, also called the "2018 Requirements" (see U.S. DHHS, 2018), took effect on January 21, 2019. For researchers in the social, behavioral, management, and education disciplines, the most notable changes in the 2018 Requirements are (a) in the informed consent process, such that it is more transparent and stringent in its requirements for communicating information about the research to prospective participants, and (b) in the expansion of exclusion and exemption categories for low-risk research (see Menikoff, Kaneshiro, & Pritchard, 2017, for a succinct overview of these changes).

Professional Codes of Ethics

In addition to the U.S. federal regulations, another source of guidance for designing ethically sound research are the ethics code and guidelines in your discipline.

Many disciplines with affiliated professional associations have developed a code of ethics that reflects the common issues faced by researchers in that discipline and sets standards for the protection of research participants. The American Educational Research Association, the American Political Science Association, the American Psychological Association (APA), and the American Public Health Association are a few examples of professional associations that have published a code of ethics to guide professionals in their respective fields. Many professional associations outside the United States have also established an ethics code and guidelines, and more than 100 countries have established regulations, laws, and/or guidelines for the protection of research participants.[1]

ASSESSING RISKS AND BENEFITS

Early in the research-planning stage, you should assess the possible risks and potential benefits of conducting your study. This assessment of possible costs or risks relative to the potential benefits or contributions of a research study is commonly referred to as the *cost–benefit ratio* or *risk–benefit ratio*. The nature of this assessment is often subjective, so it is especially helpful at this stage to consult the pertinent ethics code, regulations, and your institution's ethics review board for guidance.

A research study might provide potential benefits to participants, such as a sense of satisfaction, self-insight, or new knowledge or skills acquired through participation. In terms of costs or risks, all research involves some degree of risk; some research methods, such as observations of public behavior, and some types of secondary research are essentially low risk. Other research methods, such as surveys and experiments, might place research participants at *minimal risk* or *more than minimal risk*. Minimal risk is defined as when the "probability and magnitude of harm or discomfort anticipated in the research are not greater in and of themselves than those ordinarily encountered in daily life or during the performance of routine physical or psychological examinations or tests" (U.S. DHHS, 2018—see 45 CFR Section 46.102[j]). For example, participants might experience minor frustration or stress in a survey research study where they are asked about their spending habits or in an experimental research study where they engage in a timed performance task under observation. The discomfort that might arise in these research study examples would likely be considered minimal risk because it is probable that individuals may experience a similar magnitude of discomfort in the course of daily life, such as when delayed in traffic. If, however, participants' experience during a research study is such that the degree of physical or psychological discomfort might exceed what might be expected in daily life or from physical or psychological tests considered routine in nature, then they are considered to be at more than minimal risk; these experiences include research that might pose psychological and/or physical harm to participants. For example, participants might experience anxiety during

---

[1] For extensive lists of international regulations, laws, and guidelines, visit https://www.hhs.gov/ohrp/international/compilation-human-research-standards/index.html.

a research study that requests disclosure of sensitive aspects of their private lives. Although physical harm is less likely in research conducted in the social, behavioral, management, and education disciplines, stressful conditions could potentially lead to physical discomfort.

It is your responsibility then, as the researcher, to assess the cost–benefit ratio of your study and clearly articulate the ethical safeguards in place to protect participants from possible risks when submitting your research proposal to your institution's ethics review board. In the next section, I discuss the role of the ethics review board and highlight the process you can expect when submitting a research proposal for review.

INSTITUTIONAL REVIEW BOARDS

U.S. federal regulations require that institutions, including colleges and universities, private research firms, and governmental agencies, that receive federal funding for biomedical or behavioral sciences research with human participants have an IRB in place to assess the ethical compliance of research studies and oversee the conduct of research to protect participants, researchers, and institutions (U.S. DHHS, 2018). There are many institutions that neither seek nor receive federal funding for research but voluntarily apply federal regulations when assessing and overseeing research. Many institutions located outside the United States also have external bodies that review proposed research, such as Australia's human research ethics committee, Canada's research ethics board, and the United Kingdom's research ethics committee.

U.S. federal regulations stipulate that an IRB be composed of at least five members from various disciplines representing varied backgrounds. These members must include at least one individual from the outside community who is not affiliated with the institution, one from the sciences, and one who is considered a nonscientist or whose background falls outside of scientific areas (U.S. DHHS, 2018—see 45 CFR Section 46.107).

Before you can begin collecting data, you must submit your proposed research study to your institution's IRB for review. The IRB review process typically requires completion of an application that consists of a series of questions about your study, accompanied by copies of your research proposal, the informed consent form, and study materials, such as survey instruments and letters of agreement or cooperation from community research partners, if applicable. Community research partners are entities outside of one's institution that will be involved in participant recruitment or data collection. Most IRBs will also require confirmation of the researcher's completion of ethics education training on human research subjects' protections. Because an IRB may impose requirements that expand on federal regulations, you should seek information on the IRB review process and any ethics education training requirements at your institution early in the research-planning stage.

In conducting its review, the IRB is particularly concerned about the possibility of harm or risk to participants. The IRB therefore weighs the potential benefits or contributions of the research in relation to its possible risks. The IRB also evaluates the safeguards that you have proposed to minimize risk to your participants, such as the informed consent process.

There are various types of IRB reviews, including full, expedited, and exempt. The U.S. federal regulations establish the research categories that may qualify for an exempt or expedited review, and the 2018 Requirements established new exempt categories based on the proposed research study's risk profile (U.S. DHHS, 2018—see 45 CFR Section 46.110). An IRB, however, can set its own standards for what is exempt and expedited, and it may require more review than what is minimally required by federal regulations. Therefore, I recommend checking with your institution's IRB to determine the type of review that will apply to your proposed research study.

If you are proposing to conduct research in your place of employment or collect data from your employees, students, or clients, you might encounter potential ethical dilemmas, such as confidentiality concerns and conflicts of interest. For example, proposing to conduct research with employees in your workplace could mean that you will hold dual roles of both supervisor and researcher in the setting. Prospective participants might feel unduly pressured to participate in your research study because of their relationship to you or might respond in a biased manner, both of which can compromise the validity of the data collected. Two common methods for addressing such an ethical dilemma are to collect data anonymously or perform a secondary analysis on existing records, such as employee assessments or therapeutic records that have all information that could identify participants removed.

The outcome of an IRB's review can include notice of approval, required modifications, or disapproval (U.S. DHHS, 2018—see 45 CFR Section 46.109[a]). If your proposed study involves a community research partner, it will likely need to be reviewed by its own review board before your institution grants approval. Notice of approval from an IRB to begin a research study does not end your responsibility to comply with ethical standards and guidelines. You may also be required to renew your approval on a periodic basis, so consult with your institution on its policies.

INFORMED CONSENT

Informed consent is the ongoing process of communication of information between you, the researcher, and prospective participants. It begins at the recruitment stage of your study and continues for its duration (National Institutes of Health [NIH], 2018; U.S. DHHS, 1993). Informed consent is based on the notion that it is an individual's right to make an informed and voluntary decision about participating in a research study. The 2018 Requirements of the U.S. federal regulations included changes to the informed consent process and consent form such that there is more transparency and rigor with respect to communicating information about the research study to prospective participants than what was required in the pre–2018 Requirements regulations (U.S. DHHS, 2018—see 45 CFR 46.116).

Informed Consent Form

A *consent form* is a common method for informing prospective research participants about their potential involvement in a research study and documenting (often by written signature) their voluntary willingness to participate (U.S. DHHS, 2018—see 45 CFR 46.117). An informed consent form should reflect the three ethical principles identified in the Belmont Report, namely respect for persons, beneficence, and justice. The principle of respect for persons is reflected in a consent form that discloses sufficient information about the research study so that prospective participants can freely decide, without coercion, whether or not to participate (NIH, 2018). The principle of beneficence is reflected in a consent form that describes any anticipated risks and benefits associated with participation. Finally, the principle of justice is reflected in a consent form that explains who will benefit from the research study and discloses any alternative treatments or procedures, if applicable.

It is important for you to consider the different cultural perceptions and beliefs that may exist about research and decision making in the context of informed consent. For example, "in the United States, individuals are expected to make decisions for themselves. . . . However, in many places throughout the world, decisions are not necessarily made by the individual, but instead by family members or community representatives" (Citro, Ilgen, & Marrett, 2003, p. 96). Therefore, you should incorporate cultural norms in the informed consent process when applicable (NIH, 2018). Receiving permission from family or community members does not, however, replace an individual's consent, but such permission may be appropriate to obtain in advance of obtaining consent from the prospective research participant (NIH, 2018).

Many institutions provide a consent form template for their researchers. If a template is not available for you, the ethical principles found in your discipline's professional code of ethics are a good source to review for guidance. A list of content typically found in a consent form for research that poses minimal risk is provided below, followed by further explanation of some of the content; this list serves as a general example and is not a substitute for the requirements set forth in the federal regulations (U.S. DHHS, 2018—see 45 CFR 46.116) and an institution's policy. A consent form should

- begin with a concise initial presentation of key information about the study;

- briefly explain the purpose of the study;

- state the expected duration of participation in the study;

- describe the study's procedures in sufficient detail (i.e., what the participant will do);

- describe any experimental procedures and disclose any alternative treatments or procedures, if applicable;

- describe any anticipated discomforts or risks associated with participation;

- describe any anticipated benefits of participation;

- describe any incentives (e.g., monetary compensation) for participation, if applicable;

- state that participation is voluntary and refusal to participate or discontinuation of participation at any time will pose no negative consequences;

- describe how the confidentiality of data will be maintained; and

- state the names and contact information of individuals who can answer questions about the study and one's rights as a research participant and whom to contact if a research-related injury occurs to the research participant.

Tips for Writing an Informed Consent Form

- Avoid scientific jargon. Write clearly using language that is easily understandable (U.S. DHHS, 1993).

- Write at an appropriate reading level. It is common practice to write the consent form at an eighth-grade reading level. Word processing programs typically have a tool to check the grade level and readability (i.e., reading ease) of a document.

- Use headings in bold type to differentiate the main sections of the consent form as a means of organization.

- Use the active voice to address prospective participants directly. For example, write, "You will be asked to complete a survey . . ." rather than "A survey will be completed . . ."

- Show sensitivity to cultural differences by using language that is sensitive to the targeted research population (APA, 2017). Consult with your institution's IRB about when language translation and back-translation might be necessary.

In describing your study's procedures, it is best to keep the description focused on what participants will actually do, in language that is clear and easily understood by nonscientists. A detailed discussion of your study's research questions, hypotheses, theoretical framework, or statistical analysis is typically omitted to avoid potentially biasing participants' responses or weakening the effectiveness of the study.

Any benefits of participation should be realistically described within the bounds of your study. Often, the benefits for research participants fall within the domain of satisfaction and, in some cases, self-insight, such as when the results are shared with each participant. You should avoid making claims or setting expectations for a benefit that participation cannot genuinely deliver (Rosenthal, 1994).

If an incentive, such as monetary compensation, will be offered to participants, you should consider an appropriate amount that is not excessive, to avoid unduly influencing prospective participants' decision to voluntarily participate. If there are conditions whereby participants might receive no incentive or a partial incentive because of the study's design, you should clearly explain those conditions in the informed consent form. For example, if your study involves participation across multiple points of time, it is typically best to provide compensation at each time of participation to avoid unduly influencing participants' decision to continue in the study.

If your study will involve students as participants, it is a common and generally acceptable practice to offer extra credit, if the amount is reasonable and an alternative to research participation is also provided for extra credit. The alternative is offered to avoid unduly influencing students' decision to voluntarily participate. Subject pools at colleges and universities are growing in popularity as a means to recruit students who might be willing to participate in research. It is important to remember that registration with such a subject pool does not qualify as informed consent because the registrants do not yet have the information they need to make an informed decision about whether or not to participate in a particular study. Therefore, unless consent has been waived by your institution's IRB, you must obtain informed consent from prospective participants who are recruited from subject pools.

In stating the voluntary nature of participation, you should include in the consent form the assurance that an individual can refuse to participate or discontinue participation at any time without negative consequences, in such a way that it is tailored to your particular research setting. For example, for a research study proposed in a workplace setting, the statement would mention that one's decision to participate or not participate will have no effect on one's employment or treatment by the employer.

You should also address privacy measures in the consent form with a statement that describes how participants' identity and data will be protected. Anonymity and confidentiality are two methods for safeguarding privacy. *Authentic anonymity* (L. Endicott, personal communication, August 13, 2015) is only possible when the identities of participants are not known to anyone, including you, which means that no identifying information is collected from participants. This type of authentic anonymity differs from anonymizing the data so that they no longer contain identifying information (L. Endicott, personal communication, August 13, 2015). *Confidentiality* refers to the situation where the identities of participants are known but their identifying information is not shared without their consent or the reporting of data does not reveal their identities or permit their identities to be inferred. You should state in the consent form whether there are any limits or risks to confidentiality. For example, in some disciplines, such as psychology, confidentiality may be broken in some situations when mandated by law, such as to protect a participant from self-harm or harm to others (APA, 2017). You should also check for any local and state mandating laws that may apply to your discipline.

The names and contact information of individuals who can answer questions should be provided on the consent form. You, as the researcher, are typically listed as the contact for questions about the research study, and an ombudsperson, IRB representative, or administrative representative is typically listed as the contact for questions about the rights of research participants or should a research-related injury happen to the participant.

Under certain conditions, your institution's IRB may allow you to alter the components of or waive informed consent, per federal regulations (U.S. DHSS, 2018—see 45 CFR Sections 46.116[e] and 46.116[f]). These conditions are applicable to some research commonly conducted in the social, behavioral, management, and education disciplines. The IRB may also require the documentation of additional information that is not listed in the federal regulations, per its institutional policy and/or local law (U.S. DHHS, 1993, 2018—see 45 CFR Section 46.109[b]). Therefore, you should check with your institution's IRB for any requirements or guidelines for writing the consent form.

Common Methods for Protecting Privacy

When a study's design allows for it, anonymity protects the privacy of participants' data. The simplest way to protect privacy is to not request any identifying information from participants. The following examples reflect some of the common methods for collecting data anonymously:

- For an online survey research study, consent can be implied by participants' completion of the survey in some situations. If approved by an IRB, the initial webpage that greets participants would include the components of an informed consent form, but no written or electronic signature would be obtained that could reveal participants' names. To further safeguard participants' privacy, settings can be disabled within the survey software program so that it does not collect participants' unique Internet Protocol (IP) address.

- For a survey research study conducted by postal mail, participants' consent can be implied by their response to the survey and its return by mail in some situations. If approved by an IRB, a written statement provided with the study materials would include the components of an informed consent form, but no signature would be obtained that could reveal participants' names. The return envelope and study materials would not contain any information that could potentially identify a participant.

When anonymity is not possible due to the study's design, the following examples reflect some of the common methods for ensuring confidentiality of data:

- For an online survey research study that involves multiple time points of access for completion and, thus, the matching of participants' data across time, participants could be instructed to create a unique identifier only known to them to repeatedly gain access to the survey.

- For a survey research study conducted by postal mail that calls for matching participants with their data, the participants could be assigned an identification number. The master file with the identification numbers and the signed consent forms would be stored in a secure (i.e., locked)

(Continued)

(Continued)

location separately from the data. The same method could also be applied to research conducted in person.

- Computer data files should be password protected, and knowledge of the password and access to the data should be limited to authorized persons only.

- If your research is on a topic deemed highly sensitive, such as drug use or illegal behavior, you might be able to obtain a *certificate of confidentiality* to protect the release of identifying information about participants as a result of a court order or subpoena.

Research With Vulnerable Populations

Special protections are necessary during the informed consent process for research involving members of vulnerable populations, such as children, residents of nursing homes, prisoners, individuals with impaired decision-making ability, or individuals who are economically or educationally disadvantaged (U.S. DHHS, 2018—see 45 CFR Section 46.111[b]). Because informed consent implies the ability to understand information about a research study and the ability to freely decline participation, individuals who lack either are afforded extra protections during the recruitment and data collection processes. When an individual from a vulnerable group is not legally capable of giving informed consent, you must obtain informed consent from that individual's legal guardian while also obtaining the individual's assent, if he or she is capable. *Assent* refers to a verbal (or nonverbal) expression of agreement by the prospective participant to participate in the study (Roth-Cline & Nelson, 2013).

Children, for example, have not yet reached the legal age for consent (U.S. DHHS, 2018—see 45 CFR Part 46, Subpart D). Therefore, the child's parent(s) or legal guardian must give permission, and the child must have the opportunity to provide or withhold assent to the extent he or she is capable. The IRB considers the psychological state, maturity, and age of the children involved in the research study in determining their capability to provide assent and the requirements for obtaining it (U.S. DHHS, 2018—see 45 CFR Section 46.408[a]). More complex informed consent procedures exist for research with prisoners and individuals with impaired decision-making ability, which are beyond the scope of this chapter. I recommend consulting with your institution's IRB and reviewing applicable federal regulations for guidance on conducting research with any vulnerable population.

DECEPTION IN RESEARCH

In some circumstances, it may be permissible to intentionally withhold some information about a study from participants—a research technique that is referred to as *deception*. Deception involves not fully informing participants about a study's purpose or misleading participants about the true nature of a study's procedures. When it is used, deception is typically justified on methodological grounds as a means to obtain unbiased data on attitudes and behaviors that will be more true to real life than what could be expected in an artificial research setting if the participants were fully informed (Fisher & Fyrberg, 1994). In conjunction with guidance from the IRB, a forewarning statement can be included in the consent form to let participants know in advance that the study's purpose and/or some of its procedures will not be accurately described so they can consider whether or not to participate.

When participants are misled or not fully informed about a study's true purpose and/or procedures, this is typically done through a *cover story*, which refers to the presentation of a false description to lead participants into thinking that the study's purpose and/or procedures are different from their true intention. One of the most famous examples of a study that used deception and a cover story is Stanley Milgram's (1963) behavioral study of obedience. The participants in Milgram's study were told that its purpose was to examine the effects of punishment on their memory, and they were intentionally led to believe that they were delivering electric shocks of increasing intensity to a fellow participant, when in reality there were no shocks delivered. The fellow participant was a research confederate working with Milgram, and the true purpose of the study was to examine obedience to authority. Another example of deception is giving participants false feedback on a task, such as a quiz or activity, regardless of their true performance.

Deception has a history of generating considerable controversy within the research community (see Baumrind, 1964; Milgram, 1964) and among the public, and it remains ethically controversial (Fisher, 2005; Kimmel, 2012). If you are proposing a research study that involves deception, you assume considerable responsibility to weigh the possible risks associated with the deception against the potential benefits of conducting the study. The APA's (2017) *Ethical Principles of Psychologists and Code of Conduct* provides guidance to researchers on when deception might be justified— for example, if the study lacks the means for an alternative, nondeceptive technique and the deception is not expected to cause significant distress or pain, is justified by the study's importance, and is explained to participants as soon as possible, if appropriate (see Standard 8.07, Deception in Research). This latter condition, of explaining the deception to participants, is referred to as *debriefing*. To mitigate any possible negative effects of deception, participants should receive an explanation of the deception used, its rationale, and the true purpose of the study during a debriefing session as soon as possible, if such a session will not result in harm. When handled successfully, a debriefing session achieves two outcomes: postdeception dehoaxing and postdeception desensitizing (Holmes, 1976a, 1976b). *Dehoaxing* refers to explaining the true purpose of the study and correcting any misleading or false information, and desensitizing refers to reducing any negative effects participants might have experienced, such as stress (Holmes, 1976a, 1976b). Time should also be allotted in the debriefing session to address any questions or concerns. When research is conducted solely online, informed consent, deception, and debriefing can pose unique ethical challenges. An overview of these challenges is provided in the next section.

ETHICAL IMPLICATIONS OF INTERNET RESEARCH

According to national surveys, nearly 80% of American adults reported occasional use of a computer at school, work, and/or home (Pew Research Center, 2014), and almost 90% of American adults reported using the internet (Pew Research Center, 2018). The widespread use of computers and access to the web have contributed to the growing use of the internet as a mode for participant recruitment and data collection. Indeed, internet-based research has been growing in popularity because of the advantages and benefits it can afford researchers—such as access to large, diverse populations; reduced risk of researcher bias; and cost-effectiveness (Allen & Roberts, 2010; Kraut et al., 2004; Nosek, Banaji, & Greenwald, 2002). However, with these advantages and benefits come unique ethical challenges and responsibilities for researchers, including managing the online informed consent process, protecting participants' privacy, debriefing, and maintaining data security (Allen & Roberts, 2010; Emery, 2014; Hoerger & Currell, 2012).

Internet-based research is most commonly used for studies that employ online observations, surveys, and experiments, all of which require upholding the ethical principles of respect for persons, beneficence, and justice. The cost–benefit ratio, or assessment of possible risks relative to potential benefits, should also be conducted. The possibility of risks is often unique for any particular online study and, thus, must be considered in the context of the proposed research (Kraut et al., 2004), with safeguards tailored toward minimizing any possible harm.

Informed Consent

The ethical principle of respect for persons remains of upmost importance in internet-based research given the unique challenges that exist with the online informed consent process. Managing this process effectively requires thoughtful consideration of the design of the study and the format of the online materials, including, for example, how participants will proceed from one question or activity to the next and how they will contact you, the researcher, with any questions or concerns.

The consent form is often presented as the first webpage when a prospective participant gains access to the study's website. If the signature requirement is waived by the IRB, information about the study should still be presented on this introductory webpage, with sufficient description of the study's purpose followed by links or buttons for participants to click to indicate their decision to participate, such as *I agree* and *I decline*. When a signature is not required, a participant's consent is implied by his or her decision to complete the study.

For internet-based research that may place participants at risk, additional safeguards should be put in place to ensure that participants have read and understood all of the information presented in the informed consent form. Examples of such safeguards include strategies such as presenting a series of buttons that read *I agree* or *Click to accept* following each section within the form or including a brief quiz at the end of the form to confirm comprehension (Kraut et al., 2004). Another strategy is to include a "Frequently Asked Questions" document that covers possible concerns and questions regarding the consent form (Nosek et al., 2002).

If children or adolescents are the intended participants in an online study, it is important to be familiar with relevant laws and regulations. For example, internet-based research with minors is subject to the federal regulations of the Children's Online Privacy Protection Act (1998). When minors are not the intended participants of an online study, it is important to consider how to minimize and screen their potential access. One strategy, for example, is the use of a short quiz as described earlier (Hoerger & Currell, 2012; Kraut et al., 2004). Another strategy is to include a question that asks prospective participants if they are 18 years of age or older or asks for their date of birth; a response that indicates minor status would result in termination of the study for the participant (Alessi & Martin, 2010). A more reliable and robust technique is to have prospective participants use a trusted technology company's identification system to verify age.

To reinforce the voluntary nature of participation, participants should be permitted to skip any questions or items they wish rather than presenting them with forced answer choices (Fox, Murray, & Warm, 2003). It is also recommended that a link or button to exit the study be provided on each page to reinforce voluntariness (Emery, 2014; Hoerger & Currell, 2012; Keller & Lee, 2003; Nosek et al., 2002). It is also a good practice to design the online site to lead to a webpage containing contact information when a participant exits at any point within the study (in the case of early termination) or completes his or her participation (Emery, 2014); this practice can be accomplished with a "Thank you" page that is presented on exiting. You can also include a statement to encourage participants to print or write down the contact information should they have any questions or concerns. The aforementioned techniques are important in internet-based research because you are limited in your ability to know whether a participant had a negative experience. Thoughtful planning and designing of the online site and study materials serve as good preparation to maximize benefits and minimize negative outcomes.

Debriefing

Debriefing participants in an online study holds the same importance as it does in research that is not conducted online. You can use a variety of strategies for debriefing, such as (a) e-mailing participants a link to a webpage with debriefing content, (b) e-mailing participants debriefing content in the body of the message, or (c) directing participants to a debriefing webpage after they exit or complete the study (Kraut et al., 2004; Nosek et al., 2002). The study's design, including whether participants' identities are anonymous or not, will determine the strategy to use. In all such strategies, the debriefing content should be updated as necessary and tailored to the participants when appropriate (Kraut et al., 2004).

Privacy

Safeguarding online research participants' privacy poses unique ethical challenges. For example, you must consider the ways in which websites might identify and store information that could be used to potentially detect participants' identities, such as IP addresses (Nosek et al., 2002). Researchers have also drawn attention to the potential for threats to privacy when external commercial survey providers are used to collect and store (often temporarily) participant data (Allen & Roberts, 2010).

Most online survey software programs allow for disabling IP address tracking, and you can ask participants to create a unique code to be used for matching, if necessary, instead of collecting IP addresses (Hoerger & Currell, 2012). If you intend to use a commercial survey provider to host, collect, and/or store your data rather than an internal web server at your institution, you should familiarize yourself with the provider's policies, including in what situations (e.g., a court order) the provider might disclose identifying participant information. If you are planning to conduct international research, familiarize yourself with any possible regulations that pertain to online privacy and use of the internet to collect data in the country of interest.

CONCLUSION

Although it was not possible to provide comprehensive coverage of all the ethical issues you might encounter, the overview of research ethics topics presented in this chapter is intended to support your efforts in designing and implementing ethically sound research. The suggestions and best practices offered in this chapter are meant to serve as the start of a conversation among you, your institution's ethics review board, and your supervisory committee.

Questions for Reflection

1. How will federal regulations and ethics codes influence your research study, including its design, participant recruitment strategy, and data collection method?

2. What are the procedures for a research ethics review at your institution?

3. Why is informed consent best characterized as a process?

Author Note

I sincerely thank Leilani Endicott, PhD, for her helpful comments on an earlier draft of this chapter.

References

Alessi, E. J., & Martin, J. I. (2010). Conducting an Internet based survey: Benefits, pitfalls and lessons learned. *Social Work Research, 34*(2), 122–128. doi:10.1093/swr/34.2.122

Allen, P. J., & Roberts, L. D. (2010). The ethics of outsourcing online survey research. *International Journal of Technoethics, 1*(3), 35–48. doi:10.4018/jte.2010070104

American Psychological Association. (2017). *Ethical principles of psychologists and code of conduct.* Retrieved from https://www.apa.org/ethics/code/ethics-code-2017.pdf

Baumrind, D. (1964). Some thoughts on ethics of research: After reading Milgram's "Behavioral Study of Obedience." *American Psychologist, 19*(6), 421–423. doi:10.1037/h0040128

Children's Online Privacy Protection Act, 13 U.S.C. §§ 1301–1308 (1998). Retrieved from https://www.ftc.gov/enforcement/rules/rulemaking-regulatory-reform-proceedings/childrens-online-privacy-protection-rule

Citro, C., Ilgen, D., & Marrett, C. (2003). *Protecting participants and facilitating social and behavioral sciences research.* Retrieved from http://www.nap.edu/ catalog.php?record_id=10638

Emery, K. (2014). So you want to do an online study: Ethics considerations and lessons learned. *Ethics & Behavior, 24*(4), 293–303. doi:10.1080/10508422.2013.860031

Fisher, C. B. (2005). Deception research involving children: Ethical practices and paradoxes. *Ethics & Behavior, 15*(3), 271–287. doi:10.1207/s15327019eb1503_7

Fisher, C. B., & Fyrberg, D. (1994). Participant partners: College students weigh the costs and benefits of deceptive research. *American Psychologist, 49*(5), 417–427. doi:10.1037/0003-066X.49.5.417

Fox, J., Murray, C., & Warm, A. (2003). Conducting research using web-based questionnaires: Practical, methodological, and ethical considerations. *International Journal of Social Research Methodology, 6*(2), 167–180. doi:10.1080/13645570210142883

Hoerger, M., & Currell, C. (2012). Ethics issues in Internet research. In S. J. Knapp, M. C. Gottlieb, M. M. Handelsman, & L. D. VanderCreek (Eds.), *APA handbook of ethics in psychology: Vol. 2. Practice, teaching and research* (pp. 385–400). Washington, DC: American Psychological Association. doi:10.1037/13272-018

Holmes, D. S. (1976a). Debriefing after psychological experiments: I. Effectiveness of postdeception dehoaxing. *American Psychologist, 31*(12), 858–867. doi:10.1037/0003-066X.31.12.858

Holmes, D. S. (1976b). Debriefing after psychological experiments: II. Effectiveness of postdeception desensitizing. *American Psychologist, 31*(12), 868–875. doi:10.1037/0003-066X.31.12.868

Keller, H. E., & Lee, S. (2003). Ethical issues surrounding human participants research using the Internet. *Ethics & Behavior, 13*(3), 211–219. doi:10.1207/S15327019EB1303_01

Kimmel, A. J. (2012). Deception in research. In S. J. Knapp, M. C. Gottlieb, M. M. Handelsman, & L. D. VanderCreek (Eds.), *APA handbook of ethics in psychology: Vol. 2. Practice, teaching and research* (pp. 401–421). Washington, DC: American Psychological Association. doi:10.1037/13272-019

Kraut, R., Olson, J., Banaji, M., Bruckman, A., Cohen, J., & Coupler, M. (2004). Psychological research online: Report of Board of Scientific Affairs' Advisory Group on the conduct of research on the Internet. *American Psychologist, 59*(2), 105–117. doi:10.1037/0003-066X.59.2.105

Menikoff, J., Kaneshiro, J., & Pritchard, I. (2017). The common rule, updated. *New England Journal of Medicine, 376*(7), 613–615. doi:10.1056/NEJMp1700736

Milgram, S. (1963). Behavioral study of obedience. *Journal of Abnormal and Social Psychology, 67*(4), 371–378. doi:10.1037/h0040525

Milgram, S. (1964). Issues in the study of obedience: A reply to Baumrind. *American Psychologist, 19*(11), 848–852. doi:10.1037/h0044954

National Institutes of Health, Office of Extramural Research. (2018). *Protecting human research participants (PHRP)*. Retrieved from https://humansubjects.nih.gov/hs/phrp

Nosek, B., Banaji, M., & Greenwald, A. G. (2002). E-research: Ethics, security, design, and control in psychological research on the Internet. *Journal of Social Issues, 58*(1), 161–176. doi:10.1111/1540-4560.00254

Pew Research Center. (2014, February). *The Web at 25 in the U.S.* Retrieved from http://www.pewinternet.org/2014/02/27/the-web-at-25-in-the-u-s/

Pew Research Center. (2018, February). *Internet/broadband fact sheet*. Retrieved from http://www.pewinternet.org/fact-sheet/internet-broadband/

Rosenthal, R. (1994). Science and ethics in conducting, analyzing, and reporting psychological research. *Psychological Science, 5*(3), 127–134. doi:10.1111/j.14679280.1994.tb00646.x

Roth-Cline, M., & Nelson, R. M. (2013). Parental permission and child assent in research on children. *Yale Journal of Biology and Medicine, 86*(3), 291–301. Retrieved from https://medicine.yale.edu/yjbm/

U.S. Department of Health & Human Services, Office for Human Research Protections. (1993). *Informed consent tips (1993)*. Retrieved from http://www.hhs.gov/ohrp/policy/ictips.html

U.S. Department of Health & Human Services, Office for Human Research Protections. (2016a). *Federal policy for the protection of human subjects ("Common Rule")*. Retrieved from http://www.hhs.gov/ohrp/humansubjects/commonrule/index.html

U.S. Department of Health & Human Services, Office for Human Research Protections. (2016b). *The Nuremberg code*. Retrieved from http://www.hhs.gov/ohrp/archive/nurcode.html

U.S. Department of Health & Human Services, Office for Human Research Protections. (2017, January 19). *Revised Common Rule*. Retrieved from https://www.hhs.gov/ohrp/regulations-and-policy/regulations/finalized-revisions-common-rule/index.html

U.S. Department of Health & Human Services, Office for Human Research Protections. (2018). *Revised Common Rule regulatory text, 45 CFR 46 of the July 19, 2018 edition of the e-Code of Federal Regulations*. Retrieved from https://www.hhs.gov/ohrp/regulations-and-policy/regulations/revised-common-rule-regulatory-text/index.html

U.S. Department of Health, Education, and Welfare. (1979). *The Belmont Report: Ethical principles and guidelines for the protection of human subjects of research.* Washington, DC: National Commission for the Protection of Human Subjects of Biomedical and Behavioral Research, Office of the Secretary, Department of Health, Education, and Welfare. Retrieved from http://www.hhs.gov/ohrp/policy/belmont.html

Weindling, P. (2001). The origins of informed consent: The International Scientific Commission on Medical War Crimes, and the Nuremberg Code. *Bulletin of the History of Medicine, 75*(1), 37–71. doi:10.1353/bhm.2001.0049

SELECTED RESEARCH DESIGNS AND APPROACHES

PART V

PHENOMENOLOGY

Paula Dawidowicz

In this chapter, I provide an overview of an approach that is both a method and a methodology and has a rich philosophical tradition. I begin by discussing the origins and philosophical underpinnings of phenomenology. Examples highlight the use of phenomenology across a variety of disciplines and the research questions that are most appropriate. Issues related to sample size, the role of the researcher (which is unique to phenomenological data collection and analysis), and quality round out the chapter.

BACKGROUND

Phenomenology entails collection and analysis of people's perceptions related to a specific, definable phenomenon. Other phrases describing *perception* include lived experience, how people relate to a phenomenon, how people understand a phenomenon, and the meaning people give to a phenomenon. A *phenomenon* is a finite and definable event, an experience, or something that happens to someone. Some examples of a phenomenon include giving birth, losing a first tooth, or failing or passing a test.

As a research design, phenomenology can help you understand human factors involved in an experience and how people perceive a phenomenon to place it within a context to help you clearly understand human perceptions. Because meaning is filtered through your own interpretation of information, you can misunderstand the meaning of people's experiences. Phenomenology lets you avoid misunderstanding by focusing directly on people's experiences to understand clearly their perspectives and why they react in a specific way to an event or experience. Phenomenology also allows you to examine how transferable responses to experiences are from one participant to someone else. For example, phenomenology can help answer the question about whether the experiences of others with similar backgrounds or in similar circumstances are transferable or similar.

Origins of Phenomenology

Phenomenology originated as a philosophical movement founded by Edmund Husserl focused on the detailed description of consciousness from the first-person point of view (Husserl, 1962). Central to Husserl's philosophy is the concept of *epoché*, which means freedom from suppositions, that centers on the idea that people cannot feel they know something without reflecting on it and that only what people think about things gives them meaning (Welton, 1999). Applying epoché to studies requires researchers to recognize their own biases, recognize the impact those biases have on their analysis of data, and purposely set those biases aside.

Husserl's phenomenology began as a pure reporting process without analysis. Husserl wanted to capture how people perceived events or experiences, what they thought of phenomena, and how they lived through events or experiences. Over time, and with the help of others like Amedeo Giorgi (1991), Husserl's philosophy evolved into a variety of approaches. Today, these approaches are far from unified. However, there are commonly two main traditions in practice: (1) descriptive (or transcendental) phenomenology and (2) interpretive phenomenology.

Descriptive (transcendental) phenomenology looks at how to transcend individual experience by reducing individuals' reported experiences into patterns and themes to find the commonalities people shared about that phenomenon. Individuals such as Clark Moustakas (1994) and Max van Manen (1997) honed descriptive phenomenology. Interpretive phenomenology entails looking at the same experiences and collecting the same data as descriptive phenomenology but considers the psychological and/or sociological factors that influenced the response. Interpretive phenomenology stems from Martin Heidegger's philosophy (Heidegger & Krell, 2008).

Both schools of phenomenology pivot around the idea of intentionality—that humans intentionally choose the words they do to describe experiences and perceptions to convey specific meanings. Those meanings are what one needs to collect and analyze rather than inadvertently altering participants' meanings by inserting one's own biases (Vagle, 2013). Because phenomenology is based on the idea that individual perceptions guide actions and responses, both schools align with qualitative research. Thus, this analysis provides no absolute reality because people understand actions only in terms of their perceptions.

DISCIPLINE-SPECIFIC APPLICATIONS OF PHENOMENOLOGY

All disciplines can use phenomenology for specific purposes. For example, phenomenology can be used in the following:

- *Psychology:* To see how parents experienced the loss of a child from sudden infant death syndrome and why they experienced it the way they did (DeCanio, 2000)

- *Nursing:* To ask which parts of the nursing care experience resonate for the patient (Huguelet, 2014)

- *Epidemiology:* To find out how people experience the use of a specific drug (Ghaffari-Nejad, Ziaadini, Saffari-Zadeha, Kheradmand, & Pouya, 2014)

- *Public policy:* To determine how people experience voting in local elections (Renshon, 1975)

- *Education:* To understand how people experience teaching second language writing (Tsui & Ng, 2010)

Research Topics for Phenomenology

Not all research topics are appropriate for phenomenology. The best topics tend to be those that consider how and why people do what they do or how they feel or interact with a phenomenon.

> Examples of research topics explored using phenomenology include the following:
>
> - Personal expectations on the experience of being married and divorced (Friedman, Friedlander, & Blustein, 2005)
>
> - Parents/guardians and special education students' perceptions of the transition to life after high school (Stein, 2012)
>
> - Nursing program graduate experiences shifting from being practical to registered nurses (Rice, 2011)
>
> - How clinicians view their competency in treating transgender individuals (Johnson & Federman, 2013)

When formulating a phenomenological research question, be sure you ask a question that can be answered. For example, a phenomenological study cannot answer the question, "What is the best method of training nurses?" When asking this question, people will report on instructional methods based on their perceptions of personal efficacy. However, efficacy and actual skill development do not always align, so participants' perceptions cannot provide the level of accuracy on results that another method using a measured assessment could. A better question would be, "How do nurses perceive the quality of their training?"

Be sure you interview the right people. For example, interviewing nurses would not allow you to answer the question, "Why do patients respond better to nurses who explain everything than to nurses who do not?" Nurses do not have the perspective to be able to explain why patients respond the way they do. Be sure to go to the source rather than to a group of participants who can only provide their potentially faulty interpretations as responses.

Can Phenomenology Be Used With Other Methodologies?

Phenomenological approaches can be used as part of another research method, such as a case study or ethnography. A phenomenological case study examines how different groups of people experience a phenomenon in a specific case bounded by time and location. For example, you might examine how people experience the campaigning process for an election in a certain town by interviewing campaigners, politicians, and voters to get their perspectives. In a case study on the experiences of African American high school dropouts, researchers interviewed different groups of former students about their educational experiences and feelings of connection or disconnection from the process of education (West, 2013). Remember, your research should focus on participants' experiences and perceptions, not their beliefs or conclusions. Those types of questions should be addressed using a different research method.

Phenomenological ethnographies focus on using interviews with different groups of individuals to understand a phenomenon within a culture (Katz & Csordas, 2003). By collecting data through interviews, you gain deeper insight into how people experience and sometimes alter the culture being examined. The underlying assumption is that being outside a culture prevents understanding that culture's nature without collecting interview data from members of that culture (Maso, 2001). One example is a study on shame in the German criminal law system that allowed researchers to gain greater knowledge about the influence of participants' experiences and related law-relevant emotions (Kozin, Landweer, & Rosenmueller, 2016).

Although you can embed phenomenology within another qualitative design, you should not combine it with a quantitative design to create a mixed methods study. Doing so affects the integrity of the phenomenology and may even force you to conduct two separate studies instead of one cohesive study.

When a Phenomenology Is Not Really a Phenomenology

It is important to consider how you could mistakenly use the phenomenological method when another method is more appropriate. Phenomenology is limited to the examination of perceptions and experiences. Collecting information on the usefulness of, process of, or other aspects of the phenomenon violates the purpose of the design. Furthermore, interpolating from participants' experiences their beliefs about usefulness, process of, or other aspects of the phenomenon is not appropriate. Rather than designing either study as a phenomenology, these studies would be more appropriately designed as case studies or basic qualitative studies.

Reminders About Theoretical and Conceptual Frameworks

In designing a phenomenological study, remember that humanistic concepts inform phenomenology—people's perceptions both reflect and alter how people feel about a phenomenon. Therefore, you use a conceptual framework. You develop this framework from a combination of current research and, at times, a theory or two to create a lens or perspective—an angle or approach—to investigate the phenomenon. Some possible frameworks might include critical theory or critical race theory (giving voice to groups that are not normally heard) or a combination of key current research on the phenomenon that indicates why and how you believe the research questions (or interview questions used) are important.

Sample Size for Phenomenology

Phenomenology is about getting the depth, not the breadth, of people's perceptions. In determining an appropriate sample size, the goal should be to obtain enough data from a sufficient number and variety of individuals. Most often, participant numbers are between 5 and 15. Often, the sample size is between 8 and 12.

Here are some examples of sample size from contemporary studies:

- Studying how cooperative education could grow talent among South Africans, Groenewald (2004) used a sample size of 10 managers, 5 at educational programs and 5 at collaborating enterprises.

- Examining experiences of people with HIV/AIDS in China, Zhou (2010) used a sample size of 21 HIV-infected adults, 15 men and 6 women, ranging in age from 21 to 46 years.

- Studying women's experiences of prostitution and substance abuse, Sallmann (2010) used a sample size of 14 women, who identified as white, black, or biracial and ranged in age from 19 to 48 years.

Phenomenology is not meant to result in generalizations. The value of the results of a phenomenological study lies in their transferability (i.e., ability to apply the learning to another situation), and using larger numbers does not necessarily produce more insight into a phenomenon. Moreover, since an hour-long interview can yield a transcript of 20 to 30 pages, analyzing data for larger numbers of participants is impractical. As a result, the appropriate number of participants is smaller than in some other types of qualitative studies.

The Role of the Researcher

In phenomenology, you gather, organize, and analyze perceptions from people who have experienced a phenomenon while avoiding or controlling bias through reflexivity and appropriate interviewing during both the data collection and analysis processes. Participants can change their answers based on their perceptions of your bias, causing you to lose the integrity of their responses. To avoid researcher bias, do not imply by your questions, facial expressions, or gestures the perspective you want them to share. Do not push participants to answer questions they do not want to answer, share your own stories with participants, or share participants' stories with other participants. If you have assistants who collect data, carefully train them so they do not ask questions in a biased manner.

You should audio record interviews and use a researcher's journal to record your reflections, ideas, and thoughts about possible connections between data and participants. Be sure to conduct ongoing review of participant responses, including a review of your conclusions.

Make sure you understand the process of *bracketing*. In qualitative research, you bracket your personal experiences, biases, and perceptions prior to conducting research, so you can control how you might alter participants' responses and avoid that possibility. You also bracket your experiences during data collection, so you can analyze your perceptions separately from those of participants. In phenomenology, bracketing is particularly important so that participants' perceptions of a phenomenon remain intact. You should record any potentially biased comments that occur to you during interviews, so you can bracket them during data analysis, although this bracketing does not guarantee objective data collection or analysis. In fact, complete objectivity is recognized as impossible. Instead, the goal is to recognize bias through reflexivity and attempt to control its impact on data analysis or conclusions (Ahern, 1999).

You can approach bracketing from descriptive and interpretive perspectives, both of which can have strengths and weaknesses when used in phenomenology. In descriptive bracketing, you attempt to pull your thoughts as much as possible from data collection and analysis. In interpretive bracketing, after you record your biases, you interact with participants to probe those biases without allowing the biases to steer the conversation or to suggest responses to participants (Sorsa, Kiikkala, & Åstedt-Kurki, 2015). Having explored those biases during data collection, you use that exploration to better understand why participants had the experiences and perceptions they shared. One example of such a study, conducted by Vagle (2008), involved interviews with teachers to explore their perceptions of a phenomenon and gain greater understanding of the circumstances when perceptions formed specific patterns. This process can be tricky. For example, if a participant responds with an idea opposite to your beliefs, it is important to recognize that difference so the clash in beliefs will not result in interview questioning or data analysis that discounts the participant's thoughts. At the same time, it is important to remember that the goal is to understand perceptions and experiences, not opinions, beliefs, or other aspects of the phenomenon a researcher can inadvertently and inappropriately begin to probe.

DATA COLLECTION FOR PHENOMENOLOGY

Phenomenology requires direct responses from participants, so it has a limited range of data collection sources. Appropriate ways to collect data include interviews, focus groups, journals, or other similar products that capture individuals' responses to a phenomenon in their own words. You may use the internet and other technologies to collect data. For example, you can conduct interviews or do focus groups via online videoconferencing services such as Skype.

Most often, phenomenological researchers collect data by using interviews, although the length of the interviews may vary depending on the study's purpose. For example, McCormick (2011) interviewed each woman in her study four times for 1 to 1.5 hours per interview. Sallmann (2010) interviewed each of her participants for 45 minutes to 3 hours. Zhou (2010) interviewed each of the adults in her sample for 2 to 3 hours. The focus of phenomenology is to delve deeply into a phenomenon rather than gather shallow amounts of data from larger numbers of people; thus, the time spent with each person reflects a process of gaining that depth. The time required can vary depending on people's readiness to provide that depth and the speed with which they provide it in the interviews.

Whatever combination of collection methods you use, ensure that the same methods are used for each participant. If you interview a participant and give the person a journal in which to write, you must interview all your other participants using the same questions and administer the same journal to all participants. As an example, Groenewald (2004) interviewed each of his participants and asked them to write essays about their viewpoints; this was done in the same way for all study participants.

As researcher, you must develop a data collection protocol (a set of questions for prompting responses) to ensure complete and thorough data collection. The protocols for different types of data such as interviews, focus groups, and journals will be different, but they are basically a set of core open-ended questions or prompts to which people can respond. For example, Sallmann (2010) used prompts such as "Tell me more about that" "What was that like for you?" and "Please give me an example." Prompts can also be questions specific to the topic of discussion. The frequency of prompts during an interview will naturally vary, depending on how forthcoming and communicative each participant is.

How to Analyze Phenomenological Data

Once you collect data, how do you analyze it? Generally, data analysis involves reviewing the collected data, identifying themes, and synthesizing the results. Techniques vary based on the type of phenomenological study and its purpose. For example, McCormick (2011) transcribed her four recorded interviews of about 1.5 hours each with 15 women, which yielded about 3,000 pages of transcripts. She assembled the transcripts into a book for each participant, read the books several times, listened to the recorded interviews without reading the transcripts, and then listened to the interviews while reading the transcripts. She analyzed each book separately. Then, she analyzed the interviews across books. Her goal was to "allow the full array of themes to emerge." Rather than "fragment the transcripts through line-by-line coding," she read the books as whole texts, allowing themes to emerge "continuously, unexpectedly." She used the themes to develop "meaning-clusters," which formed the basis for her description of the phenomenon (McCormick, 2011, pp. 76–77).

Sallmann (2010) applied a hermeneutic analysis. She used a research team to read the interview transcripts for her interviews with her 14 participants, write summaries of them, and begin identifying themes. The team shared their summaries to reach consensus about themes and reviewed theoretical literature to clarify themes. Sallmann then reread the transcripts to examine the themes and produce new themes. She drafted the research manuscript, which she shared with the research team, other reviewers, and some of the study participants. She then integrated their feedback into the final manuscript.

Groenewald (2004) used a process of *explication* rather than *analysis*. Whereas analysis involves breaking data into parts, explication allows examining data in its whole context. Groenewald's explication began with conscious bracketing of his biases and perspectives so he could consciously attempt to exclude them from his examination of the data. He then listened repeatedly to the audio interviews to get a sense of each participant's perspective as a whole, extracted units of meaning from each interview, and clustered them to form themes. He integrated these with the essays each participant provided. He then summarized and validated each interview and essay and wrote a composite summary reflecting the common and individual themes.

Data analysis techniques for phenomenology can also be the same as those used in other qualitative research methods. Because the focus is on sharing participants' perspectives, an *emic* focus is used. In an *emic* focus, you present participants' perspectives rather than your own, letting their voices be heard, progressively honing and refining the focus of your conclusions (Schutt, 2014, p. 322). As data collection begins, so does data analysis. Such ongoing analysis allows you to evolve better and more detailed follow-up probes, so you can get data from each participant who best answers research questions.

You can code data using multiple strategies designed to identify themes and patterns existing within the data. You might find it useful to establish predetermined, a priori, codes to initially sort data based on potential participant responses identified in your literature review. At other times, you might use *open coding*, identifying conceptual categories for data as you begin your analysis. Open coding often leads to *axial coding*, where data previously clustered through open coding are examined more closely, separated, and coded again based on common characteristics, contexts, or conditions to provide clearer insights into the meanings of the data (Flick, 2013). Finally, you may use *selective coding*, in which you reintegrate the data to identify the underlying themes and the patterns that answer your research questions (Khiat, 2010). Be aware, though, that pulling lines or phrases out to code can result in losing the context or meaning of that line or phrase. For example, two people can say, "Wow, what a long day!" to describe two very different types of days—one long because it included many rough tasks and the other long because it included a lot of strenuous entertaining activities. Removing lines from context or searching for words or phrases without reviewing the context of those words or phrases for meaning can result in biased or incorrect results and study conclusions (see Figure 14.1).

Quality in a Phenomenological Research

In a phenomenological study, researchers look for trustworthiness, which is designing and conducting the research in a manner that guarantees the integrity and validity of the study and its results. Threats to trustworthiness can include too shallow a view of participants' experiences with the phenomenon, bias in interpretation, leading participants' responses, not collecting enough data, or reading into the data rather than letting the data speak for itself.

To ensure quality in a phenomenological study, be sure to record interviews and collect enough data. For example, interview participants several times in case their perspectives change from one session to the next. Let each session begin with the option for them to summarize their previous answers. You should also triangulate sources, which involves using multiple data sources to build a complete picture of participants' perceptions of a phenomenon.

FIGURE 14.1 ● SAMPLE CODING DETAIL

What perceptions do you have of your interactions with your mother, and why?

I hate my mother. She is a demon, and I would swear I am living in hell on earth!

Don't like	Negative treatment/comments

I love the way my mother always encourages me. She is my inspiration.

Encourages/supports

I think my mother hates me. She always has something bad to say to me.

Don't like	Negative treatment/comments

I find my mother confusing. What is it she wants from me? I can never figure it out.

Confusing	Negative treatment/comments

Sometimes my mother confuses me—I don't know what she wants, and she doesn't get me. But, you know what, she is always on my side and supports whatever I want to do.

Confusing	Encourages/supports

She puts up with me and leaves me alone. I guess she's okay, and I get to do whatever I want.

Okay	Neglectful

I really don't like her. She leaves me alone, but I never feel like she cares what I do.

Don't like	Neglectful

Themes:

Not like—negative	Confusing—encouraging/supportive
Encouraging/supportive—inspires	Okay—neglectful
Not like—negative	Not like—neglectful
Confusing—negative	

One method of triangulation can be member checks if they are conducted correctly. As participants reflect on their experiences and perspectives on a phenomenon during member checks, participants review the transcripts of their interviews to ensure that their thoughts on the topic remain the same as they have previously stated. This lets you ensure you have their most accurate thoughts on the phenomenon you are researching. Finally, member checking of your finalized analysis can allow you an opportunity to gain final insights from participants on what you have concluded. The insights they share can clarify the meaning of the data you have collected and the accuracy of your conclusions or can bring to light perspectives they share with you that you might not previously have considered. As a result of these discussions, the quality of your data analysis and related study conclusions can be improved.

To promote quality, do not overgeneralize in your research. Remember, the nature of qualitative research is one of transferability, not generalizability. The general characteristics of the group being examined should be shared, although specific details about individuals within the group should remain hidden, including during member checking of your finalized analysis.

APPROPRIATENESS OF PHENOMENOLOGY FOR YOUR RESEARCH DESIGN

If you are considering doing a phenomenological study, here are some questions to ask yourself:

- Are you examining a phenomenon, as opposed to a bounded case?

- Is determining the lived experience of people in relation to a specific phenomenon going to directly answer your question or fill a gap in research or practice?

- Does the basic premise of phenomenology—that perspective directly affects or is affected by the nature of the phenomenon—fit your study?

- Will you be able to collect information from the appropriate participants?

If the answer is "Yes" to all of the above, then phenomenology may be an appropriate research method for you.

CONCLUSION

Phenomenology is the collection and analysis of people's perceptions of their lived experiences related to a specific, definable phenomenon. Phenomenology originated as a philosophical movement founded by Edmund Husserl, and the main traditions commonly in practice today include descriptive (or transcendental) and interpretive phenomenology. Appropriate research topics for phenomenological research involve questions that consider how and why people do what they do or how they feel or interact with a phenomenon. You as researcher must be careful to avoid bias when collecting data and must follow general ethical considerations that apply to human subject research.

Phenomenological data must capture individuals' responses to a phenomenon in their own words. Appropriate ways to collect data include interviews, focus groups, journals, and open-ended questionnaires. Data analysis involves reviewing the data, identifying themes and patterns, and synthesizing the results through a process that includes open, axial, and selective coding. Techniques will vary based on the type of phenomenological study and its purpose.

Questions for Reflection

1. What is the main purpose for a phenomenology, and how does that differ from other methodologies?

2. Why do all phenomenology data sources require the collection of individuals' own words?

3. How appropriate is it to collect participants' opinions in a phenomenological study or to use phenomenology as an aspect of another methodology?

4. How do researchers accomplish epoché, and how does that fit with bracketing and reflexivity?

5. Why is an emic perspective essential to phenomenological data analysis, and what can happen if it is not used?

Key Sources

Giorgi, A. (2009). *The descriptive phenomenological method in psychology: A modified Husserlian approach*. Pittsburgh, PA: Duquesne University Press.

Moustakas, C. (1994). *Phenomenological research methods*. Thousand Oaks, CA: SAGE.

Sokolowski, R. (1999). *Introduction to phenomenology*. Cambridge, UK: Cambridge University Press.

Vagle, M. D. (2014). *Crafting phenomenological research*. Walnut Creek, CA: Left Coast Press.

van Manen, M. (1997). *Researching lived experience: Human science for an action sensitive pedagogy*. London, Ontario, Canada: Althouse Press.

References

Ahern, K. J. (1999). Ten tips for reflexive bracketing. *Qualitative Health Research, 9*(3), 407–411. doi:10.1177/104973239900900309

DeCanio, C. (2000). *A phenomenological study of perceived presence/spiritual encounters with SIDS parents: A definition based on philosophical perspective* (Doctoral dissertation). Retrieved from ProQuest dissertation database.

Flick, U. (2013). *The SAGE handbook of qualitative data analysis*. Thousand Oaks, CA: SAGE.

Friedman, M. L., Friedlander, M. L., & Blustein, D. L. (2005). Toward an understanding of Jewish identity: A phenomenological study. *Journal of Counseling Psychology, 52*(1), 77–83. doi:10.1037/0022-0167.52.1.77

Ghaffari-Nejad, A., Ziaadini, H., Saffari-Zadeha, S., Kheradmand, A., & Pouya, F. (2014). A study of the phenomenology of psychosis induced by methamphetamine: A preliminary research. *Addiction & Health, 6*(3–4), 105–111.

Giorgi, A. (1991). *Phenomenology and psychological research*. Pittsburgh, PA: Duquesne University Press.

Groenewald, T. (2004). A phenomenological research design illustrated. *International Journal of Qualitative Methods, 3*(1), 1–26. doi:10.1177/160940690400300104

Heidegger, M., & Krell, D. F. (Eds.). (2008). *Basic writings*. New York, NY: HarperCollins.

Huguelet, P. (2014). The contribution of existential phenomenology in the recovery-oriented care of patients with severe mental disorders. *Journal of Medicine & Philosophy, 39*(4), 346–367. doi:10.1093/jmp/jhu023

Husserl, E. (1962). *Ideas*. New York, NY: Macmillan.

Johnson, L., & Federman, E. J. (2013). Pathways and barriers to care for LGBT veterans in the U.S. Department of Veterans Affairs (VA). *Journal of LGBT Issues in Counseling, 7*(3), 218–235. doi: 10.1080/15538605.2013.812928

Katz, J., & Csordas, T. J. (2003). Phenomenological ethnography in sociology and anthropology. *Ethnography, 4*(3), 275–288. doi:10.1177/146613810343001

Khiat, H. (2010). A grounded theory approach: Conceptions of understanding in engineering mathematics learning. *Qualitative Report, 15*(6), 1459–1488.

Kozin, A., Landweer, H., & Rosenmueller, S. (2016). A phenomenological ethnography of shame in the context of German criminal law. *Empedocles: European Journal for the Philosophy of Communication, 6*(1), 57–75. doi:10.1386/ejpc.6.1.57_1

Maso, I. (2001). Phenomenology and ethnography. In P. Atkinson, A. Coffey, S. Delamont, J. Lofland, & L. Lofland (Eds.), *Handbook of ethnography* (pp. 136–144). Thousand Oaks, CA: SAGE.

McCormick, M. L. (2011). The lived body: The essential dimension in social work practice. *Qualitative Social Work: Research & Practice, 10*(1), 66–85. doi:10.1177/1473325009359452

Moustakas, C. (1994). *Phenomenological research methods*. Thousand Oaks, CA: SAGE.

Renshon, S. A. (1975). Political learning and support for political participation: An examination of some students and their parents. *Nonprofit & Voluntary Sector Quarterly, 4*(3–4), 200–218. doi:10.1177/089976407500400309

Rice, E. M. (2011). *Transitioning from practical to registered nurse: A phenomenological inquiry of graduates of a competency based nursing program* (Doctoral dissertation). Retrieved from ProQuest dissertation database.

Sallmann, J. (2010). Living with stigma: Women's experiences of prostitution and substance use. *Affilia, 25*(2), 146–159. doi:10.1177/0886109910364362

Schutt, R. K. (2014). *Investigating the social world: The process and practice of research*. Thousand Oaks, CA: SAGE.

Sorsa, M. A., Kiikkala, I., & Åstedt-Kurki, P. (2015). Bracketing as a skill in conducting unstructured qualitative interviews. *Nurse Researcher, 22*(4), 8–12. doi:10.7748/nr.22.4.8.e1317

Stein, K. (2012). Experiences of selected emerging adults with emotional or behavioral difficulties in higher education. *Career Development & Transition for Exceptional Individuals, 35*(3), 168–179. doi:10.1177/0885728812438940

Tsui, A. B. M., & Ng, M. M. Y. (2010). Cultural contexts and situated possibilities in the teaching of second language writing. *Journal of Teacher Education, 61*(4), 364–375. doi:10.1177/0022487110364855

Vagle, M. D. (2008). Locating and exploring teacher perception in the reflective thinking process. *Teachers and Teaching: Theory and Practice, 15*(5), 579–599. doi:10.1080/13540600903139597

Vagle, M. D. (2013). Grafting the intentional relation of hermeneutics and phenomenology in linguisticality. *Qualitative Inquiry, 19*(9), 725–735. doi:10.1177/1077800413500933

van Manen, M. (1997). *Researching lived experience: Human science for an action sensitive pedagogy.* London, Ontario, Canada: Althouse Press.

Welton, D. (Ed.). (1999). *The essential Husserl: Basic writings in transcendental phenomenology.* Bloomington, IN: Indiana University Press.

West, E. T. (2013). A phenomenological case study of the experiences of African American high school students. *SAGE Open, 3*(2). doi:10.1177/2158244013486788

Zhou, Y. R. (2010). The phenomenology of time: Lived experiences of people with HIV/AIDS in China. *Health (London), 14*(3), 310–325. doi:10.1177/1363459309358596

GROUNDED THEORY

Annie Pezalla

In this chapter, I provide an overview of the concepts associated with the grounded theory approach and grounded theory analysis. First, I introduce some of the origins and philosophical underpinnings of grounded theory, followed by examples of how grounded theory has been used in several disciplines, with information on appropriate sample size and matters related to data collection and analysis. I discuss *constant comparative analysis*, a technique that is shared by some other methodological approaches but that originated with grounded theory and results in interviews whose focus can change over the course of a study. I then clarify the role of the literature review in grounded theory research and its importance in crafting a proposal that has a defensible argument. Finally, I discuss the benefits of grounded theory research.

BACKGROUND

Grounded theory is a qualitative research design that researchers use to develop theory inductively from data. In grounded theory, you do not begin with a theory and then attempt to support or disprove it. Instead, you begin with an area of study and allow what is relevant within that area to emerge into a theory.

Origins of Grounded Theory

Grounded theory design emerged from two sociologists, Barney G. Glaser and Anselm L. Strauss, and their 1960s research on dying in hospitals, a topic that was rarely studied at that time. Glaser and Strauss (1967) observed dying patients and how awareness of their impending death influenced their interactions with relatives and hospital staff. As they constructed their analyses of dying, they developed systematic methodological strategies that social scientists could adopt for studying other topics. Their book, *The Discovery of Grounded Theory* (1967), first articulated these strategies and advocated for developing theories from research grounded in data rather than deducing testable hypotheses from existing theories.

Philosophical Underpinnings of Grounded Theory

Grounded theory marries two contrasting and competing traditions in sociology, influenced by differences in the backgrounds of Glaser and Strauss. Glaser came from Columbia

University, where quantitative methods were a strong influence. Glaser's positivist training resulted in his focus on codifying qualitative methods, generating "middle-range" theories (i.e., abstract renderings of specific social phenomena that were grounded in data), and maintaining a dispassionate and empirical process. Glaser saw the need for a well-thought-out, explicitly formulated, and systematic set of procedures for both coding and testing hypotheses generated during the research process. His background also emphasized empirical research in conjunction with the development of theory.

Strauss came from the University of Chicago, which has a long history in qualitative research. In contrast to Glaser, symbolic interactionist and pragmatist writings heavily influenced Strauss. Symbolic interactionism emphasizes understanding the world by interpreting human interaction, which occurs through the use of symbols, such as language. Strauss's background in symbolic interactionism contributed to the following aspects of grounded theory:

- The nature of experience and undergoing as continually evolving

- The active role of persons in shaping the worlds in which they live

- An emphasis on change and process, and the variability and complexity of life

- The interrelationships among conditions, meaning, and action (Strauss & Corbin, 1990)

DISCIPLINE-SPECIFIC APPLICATIONS OF GROUNDED THEORY

Any discipline can use grounded theory as an approach to a research question, as shown in the examples below. What matters in grounded theory are the procedures, and they are not discipline bound.

- In psychology, therapists have used grounded theory to understand the experiences of parents who have difficult-to-treat teenagers with attention deficit/hyperactivity disorder (Brinchmann & Sollie, 2014).

- Sociologists have used grounded theory to discover the meaning of spirituality among cancer patients and how spiritual beliefs inform patients' attitudes toward cancer treatments (Facchin, Saita, Barbara, Dridi, & Vercellini, 2018).

- Public health researchers have used grounded theory to examine black men's views of cancer risks (Mulugeta, Williamson, Monks, Hack, & Beaver, 2017).

- In business, managers have used grounded theory to explain the ways in which top-level corporate managers can be politically successful (Adjognon, 2014).

- Engineers have used grounded theory to explore the relationship between frugality and innovation in business models (Rosca, Arnold, & Bendul, 2017).

- Information technology researchers have used grounded theory to investigate older adults' use of computer technology in the first year after a stroke (Gustavsson, Ytterberg, Nabsen Marwaa, Tham, & Guidetti, 2018).

Pragmatism emphasizes practical consequences as the primary criteria in determining meaning or truth. Strauss's background brought a pragmatist influence, which stressed the need to get out into the field if one wants to understand what is going on and the importance of theory grounded in reality to the development of a discipline. Grounded theory's emphasis on humans as active, rather than passive, agents is a result of Strauss's influence. Strauss also emphasized the notions of emergent processes and social and subjective meanings.

A common question among new scholars with regard to this approach is whether grounded theory is qualitative or quantitative. Researchers traditionally view grounded theory as a qualitative design because it often uses qualitative data sets, such as interview transcripts or observational notes. Although there are certainly grounded theory studies that employ quantitative methods (e.g., Guetterman, Babchuk, Smith, & Stevens, 2017), because of the preponderance of qualitative-based grounded theory studies, this chapter focuses on qualitative grounded theory.

GROUNDED THEORY: ALIGNMENT AND DESIGN

In this section, I provide information on the types of research topics and questions explored with grounded theory, along with examples illustrating the use of grounded theory with other methodologies. In addition, I discuss the role of the researcher, as well as sample size and ethical considerations, in grounded theory research.

Research Topics for Grounded Theory

Grounded theory research topics should aim to discover emergent ideas or connections and increase understanding of meaning, context, process, how things happen, and the ways in which *X* affects *Y*, with an end goal of generating explanatory theory. For example, Ellingson's (2017) study increased understanding of how long-term cancer survivors construct alternative narratives of survivorship.

Other examples of research topics explored with grounded theory include the following:

- The meaning of chronic illness (Charmaz, 2006b)

- The context of successful leadership among senior executives (Ramazani & Jergeas, 2015)

- The meaning of "successful feeding" among mothers in a neonatal nursery (Reissland, Lewis, Lal, & Patterson, 2016)

- Insights on compassion and patient-centered nursing in intensive care (Jakimowicz, Perry, & Lewis, 2018)

- The influence of storytelling, sugar snacking, and toothbrushing rules on children's health and oral health literacy (Freeman, 2015)

- How middle-aged women find empowerment in menopause and with issues of hormone therapy (Yazdkhasti, Negarandeh, & Behboodi-Moghadam, 2016)

In exploring topics such as those listed above, research questions should always be open-ended (i.e., they cannot be answered with a simple yes/no response). For example, the research questions from the Yazdkhasti et al. (2016) study were "What is the nature of empowerment for menopausal women?" and "How can this process be explained from menopausal women's perspectives?" (p. 511). Note that both of these questions are open-ended questions and are nicely amenable to a qualitative grounded theory approach.

Can You Use Grounded Theory Techniques With Another Design?

You can use grounded theory or grounded theory techniques with other research designs. For example, such techniques can be used in a mixed methods study as a first step toward identifying testable constructs and hypothesizing about their relationship to one another. You could also employ a quantitative, cause–effect design after you have carried out a grounded theory design to further test the grounded theory. For example, Jakimowicz et al.'s (2018) action research study used grounded theory to help a group of nurses understand (a) why they experienced compassion fatigue and (b) the ways they could alleviate that weariness. As another example, Freeman (2015) employed a case study research project within a grounded theory design to examine, and then create a theory of, the processes by which adult health messages can be converted into child-friendly information for better oral health. Both examples illustrate that different designs can be used within the grounded theory approach. The important thing to remember is that, no matter the design, if a grounded theory approach is involved, the end product of the study must be a theory, one that is grounded in the data.

Determining Sample Size for Grounded Theory

Determining an appropriate sample size for grounded theories has been an elusive process. The main goal in any grounded theory study is to gather enough data until theoretical saturation has occurred, or the point at which no new properties emerge from the identified categories in one's theory. This goal focuses more on the amount of descriptive data than on the number of people to recruit.

Despite grounded theory's focus on saturation rather than sample size, qualitative researchers have continued to discuss the general parameters of when saturation *might* occur within particular sample sizes. Qualitative researchers have recommended sample sizes ranging from as few as 6 participants to as many as 30 for a grounded theory study (Creswell, 2013); however, no rationales exist for those recommendations. Only one study has currently investigated saturation in a quantifiable way, by examining the point in data collection at which codes were created and the point at which the distribution of code frequency stabilized (Guest, Bunce, & Johnson, 2006). In this study, no new codes emerged after 12 interviews; in fact, basic codes were present as early as after six interviews. Although Guest et al. (2006) did not intend to generalize their results to all grounded theory studies, their findings could be helpful for researchers who hope to establish an initial goal for the number of participants to recruit. Based on this information, a sample size ranging from 12 to 30 might be appropriate for a grounded theory study.

A smaller sample size of 10 to 12 is appropriate if your sample is relatively homogeneous; your participants possess "cultural competence" (Guest et al., 2006, p. 74), or a certain degree of expertise in the domain of inquiry; and your objectives in your research are fairly narrow. A larger sample size of 25 to 30 is appropriate if your sample is diverse, your participants possess varying levels of expertise in or familiarity with your domain of inquiry, your research objectives are fairly broad, or you are looking for disconfirming evidence or trying to discover "maximum variability" in your phenomenon of interest.

DATA COLLECTION AND ANALYSIS

"All is data" (Glaser, 1998, p. 8). This statement means that grounded theory can use any kind of data. As a grounded theory researcher, it is up to you to figure out what data to gather. All kinds of data can be the building blocks of a grounded theory, including field notes, interviews, audio recordings, observations, and information from records and reports. The kind of data you pursue depends on the topic and the access available.

You should also gather "rich, thick data" (Geertz, 1973, p. 10) for a grounded theory study. Obtaining these data means writing extensive field notes of observations, collecting respondents' written personal accounts, and/or compiling detailed narratives (e.g., transcribed tapes of interviews).

Data Collection

Interviews, audio recordings, observational research, memos, and open-ended questionnaires are common means of data collection in grounded theory studies, but almost any data collection procedure—within ethical limits, of course—is permissible in grounded theory. What is important to remember is that the data collection procedures may change throughout the course of the study as the grounded theory is refined and sharpened in focus. Charmaz (2006a) likened this process to that of a photographer honing in on a scene: "Like a camera with many lenses, first you view a broad sweep of the landscape. Subsequently, you change your lens several times to bring scenes closer and closer into view" (p. 14).

Grounded theory researchers often use semistructured, open-ended interviews in their studies, but these may change throughout the course of the study as the topic becomes more refined. With grounded theory, data collection procedures evolve as the theory becomes more refined. Uncertainty is common in grounded theory studies, and flexibility is an absolute must.

Data Analysis

Below I explain the general process of data analysis for grounded theory. These steps are not specific to grounded theory but, rather, are shared across other methodological approaches. More information on the analysis process is contained in Chapter 7.

The first step in any grounded theory is to become very familiar with your initial data. Establish this familiarity by reading and rereading your data and/or by listening to the audio recordings of your interviews (if you have collected them). Transcribing your own interviews is also an important way to become familiar with your data.

The second step is to start identifying *codes*, words or phrases that serve to indicate the meaning of a segment of data, and engage in a process of constant comparison, wherein you compare the codes you have created for other segments of data to determine if they are similar or different in meaning.

If you are conducting your first grounded theory study, it is wise to transcribe all of your materials. However, the actual transcribing may be selective. At first, you may decide to completely transcribe and analyze your very first interviews or field notes before going on to the next set of interviews or field observations. This early coding gives guidance for the next field observations and/or interviews. Later, as your theory develops, you may wish to listen to the tapes and transcribe only those sentences, passages, or paragraphs that relate to your evolving theory. Regardless of whether you transcribe all or part of your tapes, it is still important to listen to the tapes in their entirety. Listening as well as transcribing is essential for full and varied analysis.

The third step is open coding, which is the process of identifying, labeling, examining, and comparing your codes and categorizing them into larger, conceptual categories encompassing a variety of similarly themed codes.

The fourth step is the development of hypotheses, where you speculate about the relationship between the categories. In doing this step, you should also seek examples that contradict those hypotheses.

Throughout this process, *you should be collecting more data—as data collection and analysis are intertwined in grounded theory*—and you should continually refine your hypotheses until all examples are accounted for and explained. For example, as Ellingson (2017) collected her data, she used the constant comparative analysis process, where she constantly compared the survivorship stories of one patient with those of another, assessing their similarities and differences. Once she had developed some hypotheses about the patterns she observed, she collected and analyzed more data with which to test her hypotheses and develop more patterns, continually refining them in the process.

ROLE OF THE LITERATURE REVIEW

If a grounded theory study is about generating a theory, rather than testing a theory, is a literature review even necessary? Absolutely yes. No one, not even a grounded theory researcher, approaches a study "tabula rasa," or with a blank slate. Give earlier works their due. Completing a thorough literature review strengthens your justification of the importance of the research problem and, thus, the credibility of your project.

Glaser and Strauss (1967) proposed that data collection and analysis should occur before conducting a literature review because they did not want researchers to see their data through the lens of earlier ideas and become biased by any "pet theoretical ideas" or "received theories" (Strauss & Corbin, 1990). This perspective has been heavily disputed (see Charmaz, 2006a), particularly by funding agencies and those who work with doctoral students, who must, by the requirement of their programs, demonstrate a sophisticated knowledge of leading studies and theories in the field.

An important approach is to use your literature review without letting it stifle your creativity or "strangle your theory" (Charmaz, 2006a, p. 166). Equally important is the understanding that you may need to rewrite portions of your literature review after you have identified and developed your grounded theory in a way that adequately positions your grounded theory and clarifies its contribution.

For those of you working on a grounded theory thesis or dissertation, your results chapter may be significantly longer than your literature review chapter. This is because your contribution will be a substantial theory, one that is grounded in an abundance of rich, thick data. To even collect your data, though, you will need to demonstrate what is known based on existing research as well as what is not known. You cannot demonstrate that level of understanding without an adequate literature review. Just remember this practical point: The requirement for a thorough literature review for grounded theory studies is similar to that for any other major research project or any application for a grant. It will be difficult to gain approval for a thesis or dissertation proposal or funding for a study if a literature review is not part of the proposal.

Use of Memos in Data Analysis

Memos are an important aspect of data analysis in any qualitative study. Memos are particularly important in a grounded theory study because they stimulate thinking and provide you, the researcher, with opportunities to focus on emergent categories. There are different types of memos that you should write during the process of analysis. Memos common to all qualitative methods include textual, observational, and reflexive. Memos specific to grounded theory include conceptual/theoretical and operational.

Memos Common to Qualitative Methods

Textual Memos. These memos describe how you are thinking about a code you have assigned to a data segment or how you have assigned names and meanings to data. These are also known as *preliminary* and *orienting* memos. Their purpose is to stop you (briefly) from coding so that you can capture interpretive ideas and hunches. *Example:* "Participant A mentioned feeling overwhelmed with the idea of retiring when she felt so passionate about helping people in her career. I'm going to label that segment of our interview 'retirement as a moral conflict.'"

Observational Memos. These memos describe the context of interviews and observations. They focus on what your other senses are telling you in the research: what you have seen, felt, tasted, or experienced while doing the research. *Example:* "Participant B's home was filled with the smells of freshly baked bread and coffee. I also noticed that she had cleared off a space for me to rest my bag on her typically crowded dining room table. The baked goodies, the coffee, the clean house—all of it gave me the impression that she wanted me to stay awhile for today's interview."

Reflexive Memos. These memos could potentially cut across all the others. They are essentially observations of yourself—your voice, impact, and/or challenging roles throughout the process. These memos help you pay attention to your rising values, feelings, mistakes, embarrassments, and personal insights and to reflect on how those qualities might contribute to how you are making sense of the data. *Example:* "I can't help but wonder if my participants have been offering socially desirable responses to my questions about moral behavior in the workplace. Maybe I should complement my individual interviews with some open-ended and anonymous surveys? I'll talk with my committee members about that idea to get their feedback."

Memos Specific to Grounded Theory

Conceptual/Theoretical Memos. These memos ask the question "What is going on here?" They describe the development of a category and help develop ideas on the possible pathways for integrating the theory. *Example:* "Retirement as a Moral Conflict" seems connected to the code of "Isolated From Professional Acknowledgments." Those codes could be clustered together into a broader conceptual category of "Personal and Professional Identity Conflict."

Operational Memos. These memos are practical. They might have to do with reminding yourself to ask a new question that arose in a previous interview, with sampling strategies, or with whom to talk to next. They relate mostly to methodological procedures. *Example:* "Retirement as a Moral Conflict": Retirement is a profoundly moral conflict as well as a professional conflict. This code captures any narratives that reflect the clash of moral conflict (e.g., feeling conflicted at leaving a helping profession but wanting to spend more time with family) and professional conflict (e.g., feeling addicted to the accolades that come with professional accomplishments).

HOW TO PROMOTE QUALITY WHEN USING GROUNDED THEORY

You can ensure quality in your grounded theory studies by *complete transparency* in your data collection process. Through this transparency, a grounded theory researcher is able to demonstrate trustworthiness. Typically, terms like *validity* and *reliability* are not relevant in grounded theory research because those terms are quantitative in origin and are not directly applicable to grounded theory studies. Grounded theory studies, after all, do not necessarily hold that there is one unified Truth (with a capital *T*) in the world (a relativist position), so it is difficult to claim that one's approach is absolutely valid because truth (with a lowercase *t*) is assumed to be rather subjective and largely based on perceptions.

The same problem exists with claims of reliability in grounded theories. Reliability does not apply to grounded theories because reliability is not actually a goal. You should expect the research process to change throughout the study as the topic evolves and the grounded theory becomes more refined.

In lieu of the indicators of validity and reliability, then, grounded theories focus on trustworthiness, and there are four main indicators of trustworthiness that a grounded theory researcher should establish: credibility, transferability, dependability, and confirmability.

For example, Ellingson (2017) ensured quality by establishing confirmability and credibility in her work. Regarding confirmability, Ellingson kept extensive field notes during her observations (i.e., more than 300 pages). She also demonstrated credibility by staying extensively involved in the field. She conducted observations for years, visiting hospitals weekly for hours each time. She also amassed "thick" descriptions and triangulated her sources by using transcripts of interviews with patients along with her observations of them.

A well-constructed grounded theory will meet four central criteria for judging its quality (Strauss & Corbin, 1990):

1. *Understanding:* Because the grounded theory represents reality, it should be comprehensible and make sense to both the participants and those practicing in the area of study.

2. *Fit:* If a grounded theory is faithful to the everyday reality of a substantive area and carefully induced from diverse data, it should fit that substantive area. This means that the grounded theory should not be overly abstract or difficult to apply to real-life scenarios.

3. *Generality:* If the data are comprehensive and the interpretations conceptual and broad, then the grounded theory should be abstract enough and include sufficient variation to make it applicable to a variety of contexts related to that phenomenon; that is, you should be able to apply your theory.

4. *Control:* You should clearly spell out the conditions under which the phenomenon applies, and your hypotheses proposing relationships among concepts should relate to that (and only that) phenomenon.

Benefits of Grounded Theory

The benefits of using grounded theory include the following.

Ecological validity: Ecological validity is the extent to which research findings accurately represent real-world settings. Grounded theories are typically ecologically valid because they are close to the data from which they were generated. Although the constructs in a grounded theory are appropriately abstract (because their goal is to explain other similar phenomena), they are context specific, detailed, and tightly connected to the data.

Novelty: Grounded theories are often fresh and new and hold the potential for innovative discoveries in science.

Parsimony: Parsimony is about using the simplest possible description to explain a complex phenomenon. Grounded theories aim to provide parsimonious explanations about complex phenomena by rendering them into abstract constructs and hypothesizing their relationships. They offer helpful and relatively easy-to-remember schemata for us to understand our world a little better.

APPROPRIATENESS OF GROUNDED THEORY FOR YOUR RESEARCH PROJECT

To determine if grounded theory is a suitable approach for your research, keep in mind these questions:

- Is there no theory that adequately explains your phenomenon of interest? Often, there is a theory "out there," but you simply have not found it in the literature. You might need to seek out a librarian who will help you explore parallel fields with applicable theories.

- Is there a theory that partially explains your phenomenon of interest but it needs to be updated or changed in some way?

- Have other researchers identified various constructs in your field but not tested them in relationship to one another?

- If the answer to any of the above questions is "yes," the next question is "Are you ready to take on a grounded theory study?" Before taking on a grounded theory study, you must understand that it requires the following:

  o A substantial commitment of time and energy, without which you may have to decide against a grounded theory approach

  o A lot of flexibility and a level of comfort with uncertainty, because the focus of one's study is likely to change throughout the process

- ○ Intensive time in the abductive process—in practical terms, abduction is a continual process of collecting, transcribing, and analyzing data to create hypotheses, during which you will usually need to make changes to your protocol and then go back out into the field to test those hypotheses with more data
- ○ A thorough literature review and a standardized proposal process, in which you defend your research plans and provide a detailed plan of analysis
- ○ Institutional review board approval, with various contingency plans if your research interests evolve

Action Plan for Using Grounded Theory

It is important to work with a mentor who understands grounded theory and will provide structured guidance but who also gives you enough space to figure things out on your own. Glaser (2009) warned novice researchers of relying on mentors who do not understand grounded theory, holding that experienced researchers, in an effort to rescue the novice from confusion, "tend to block the novice researcher . . . by talking of his/her inexperience" and by "forcing their conclusions on the unformed, new novices" (p. 3).

Mentors should advise novice researchers that confusion and being overwhelmed are parts of the grounded theory process, "which are to be tolerated for a short while" (p. 4). It is essential to work with an advisor/chair who understands grounded theory and who will provide adequate support and flexibility. Conducting a grounded theory study is often overwhelming, but with a knowledgeable chair and an eager and open mind, you can employ this method with great success.

You might think that if you are going to do a grounded theory, you will not need to read the literature, because you do not want previous findings to bias you. Yet you will need to demonstrate to your readers (i.e., your research committee members) that you have sufficient justification to employ grounded theory. Otherwise, they will be less likely to approve of your work. Plus, you might be setting yourself up for failure because there could be an existing theory "out there" in the literature that sufficiently explains your phenomenon of interest (and if so, you may choose a quantitative approach that is deductive and proposes to test the validity of that theory).

There is a solution to guard against these pitfalls: Read, read, read. By reading, and critiquing what you read, you will ensure your own understanding of the existing literature and how it might justify a grounded theory. This kind of intensive reading will also provide you with ideas on how to write a proposal for a grounded theory.

Here is a second tip for novice researchers: Write, write, write. Writing a grounded theory is an ambiguous process because it involves more than mere reporting. Writing, like analysis, is emergent in grounded theory. Memo writing is important in grounded theories because it facilitates reflection, understanding, and analytical insight of emerging data and the evolving research study. Memo writing should be a frequent practice while conducting a grounded theory study. These memos should be spontaneous and not overly mechanical, with the purpose to "let your mind rove freely in, around, and from a category" (Charmaz, 2006a, p. 81).

A third tip is to join a network of grounded theory researchers. The Grounded Theory Institute (http://www.groundedtheory.com/) is one example of a network that offers access to an online forum with grounded theory researchers from all over the world. The site also offers a helpful publication and access to various seminars. The site is specifically geared toward novice grounded theory researchers, many of whom are working on theses or dissertations.

CONCLUSION

Researchers use grounded theory to develop theory inductively from data. Grounded theory differs from other designs in that its end goal is to generate theory rather than to test existing theories or generate only themes. Conceptual frameworks should guide—but not dictate—the focus of the grounded theory inquiry and observations. Grounded theory also uses an abductive process of data collection and analysis, in which you continually collect data, generate hypotheses from the data, and then test the hypotheses on more data. Grounded theory can be used to address research questions in any discipline; what is important is that the research topics should aim to increase understanding of meaning, context, or process with questions that are open-ended.

Questions for Reflection

1. How is grounded theory distinct from other research methods designs?

2. Describe abductive reasoning and its relationship with both inductive and deductive approaches.

3. Why are memos such an important component of a grounded theory study?

4. Why is it important to review the literature if the intent of a grounded theory study is not to test existing knowledge in the field but rather to create a new theory?

Key Sources

Charmaz, K. (2006). *Constructing grounded theory: A practical guide through qualitative analysis*. Thousand Oaks, CA: SAGE.

Gasson, S. (2004). Rigor in grounded theory research: An interpretive perspective on generating theory from qualitative studies. In M. E. Whitman & A. B. Woszcynski (Eds.), *The handbook of information systems research* (pp. 79–102). Hershey, PA: IGI Global.

Glaser, B. (1978). *Theoretical sensitivity: Advances in the methodology of grounded theory.* Mill Valley, CA: Sociology Press.

Glaser, B. (1998). *Doing grounded theory: Issues and discussions.* Mill Valley, CA: Sociology Press.

Glaser, B. (2009). The novice GT researcher. *Grounded Theory Review, 8*(2), 1–21.

Glaser, B., & Strauss, A. (1965). *Awareness of dying.* Hawthorne, NY: Aldine.

Glaser, B., & Strauss, A. (1967). *The discovery of grounded theory: Strategies for qualitative research.* Hawthorne, NY: Aldine.

Goetz, J. P., & LeCompte, M. D. (1981). Ethnographic research and the problem of data reduction. *Anthropology and Education Quarterly, 12,* 51–70. doi:10.1525/aeq.1981.12.1.05x1283i

Guest, G., Bunce, A., & Johnson, L. (2006). How many interviews are enough? An experiment with data saturation and variability. *Field Methods, 18*(1), 59–82. doi:10.1177/1525822X05279903

Smaling, A. (2002). The argumentative quality of the qualitative research report. *International Journal of Qualitative Methods, 1*(3), 62–69. doi:10.1177/160940690200100304. Retrieved from http://ejournals.library.ualberta.ca/index.php/IJQM/article/viewFile/4600/3753

Strauss, A., & Corbin, J. (1990). *Basics of qualitative research: Grounded theory procedures and techniques.* Thousand Oaks, CA: SAGE.

Website on Grounded Theory

Grounded Theory Institute: http://www.groundedtheory.com/

References

Adjognon, A. (2014). A grounded theory of political intelligentizing in business administration. *Grounded Theory Review, 2*(13), 20–29.

Brinchmann, B. S., & Sollie, H. (2014). Struggling with and for: A grounded theory of parents managing life with hard-to-treat ADHD teenagers. *Grounded Theory Review, 1*(13), 3–15.

Charmaz, K. (2006a). *Constructing grounded theory: A practical guide through qualitative analysis.* Thousand Oaks, CA: SAGE.

Charmaz, K. (2006b). Measuring pursuits, making self: Meaning construction in chronic illness. *International Journal of Qualitative Studies on Health and Well-Being, 1*(1), 27–37. doi:10.1080/17482620500534488

Creswell, J. (2013). *Qualitative inquiry and research design: Choosing among five traditions* (3rd ed.). Thousand Oaks, CA: SAGE.

Ellingson, L. L. (2017). Realistically ever after: Disrupting dominant narratives of long-term cancer survivorship. *Management Communication Quarterly, 31*(2), 321–327. doi:10.1177/0893318917689894

Facchin, F., Saita, E., Barbara, G., Dridi, D., & Vercellini, P. (2018). "Free butterflies will come out of these deep wounds": A grounded theory of how endometriosis affects women's psychological health. *Journal of Health Psychology, 23*(4), 538–549. doi:10.1177/1359105316688952

Freeman, R. (2015). Storytelling, sugar snacking, and toothbrushing rules: A proposed theoretical and developmental perspective on children's health and oral health literacy. *International Journal of Paediatric Dentistry, 25*(5), 339–348. doi:10.1111/ipd.12188

Geertz, C. (1973). *The interpretation of cultures: Selected essays.* New York, NY: Basic Books.

Glaser, B. (1998). *Doing grounded theory: Issues and discussions.* Mill Valley, CA: Sociology Press.

Glaser, B. (2009). The novice GT researcher. *Grounded Theory Review, 8*(2), 1–21.

Glaser, B., & Strauss, A. (1967). *The discovery of grounded theory: Strategies for qualitative research.* Hawthorne, NY: Aldine.

Guest, G., Bunce, A., & Johnson, L. (2006). How many interviews are enough? An experiment with data saturation and variability. *Field Methods, 18*(1), 59–82. doi:10.1177/1525822X05279903

Guetterman, T. C., Babchuk, W. A., Howell Smith, M. C., & Stevens, J. (2017). Contemporary approaches to mixed methods–grounded theory research: A field-based analysis. *Journal of Mixed Methods Research, 13*(2), 179–195. doi:10.1177/1558689817710877

Gustavsson, M., Ytterberg, C., Nabsen Marwaa, M., Tham, K., & Guidetti, S. (2018). Experiences of using information and communication technology within the first year after stroke: A grounded theory study. *Disability and Rehabilitation, 40*(5), 561–568. doi:10.1080/09638288.2016.1264012

Jakimowicz, S., Perry, L., & Lewis, J. (2018). Insights on compassion and patient-centered nursing in intensive care: A constructivist grounded theory. *Journal of Clinical Nursing, 27*(7–8), 1599–1611. doi:10.1111/jocn.14231

Mulugeta, B., Williamson, S., Monks, R., Hack, T., & Beaver, K. (2017). Cancer through black eyes—the views of UK based black men towards cancer: A constructivist grounded theory study. *European Journal of Oncology Nursing, 29*, 8–16. doi:10.1016/j.ejon.2017.04.005

Ramazani, J., & Jergeas, G. (2015). Project managers and the journey from good to great: The benefits of investment in project management training and education. *International Journal of Project Management, 33*(1), 41–52. doi:10.1016/j.ijproman.2014.03.012

Reissland, N., Lewis, S., Lal, M., & Patterson, L. (2016). What is successful feeding on the neonatal intensive care unit? A psychologist's perspective. *MIDRS Midwifery Digest, 26*(2), 231–235.

Rosca, E., Arnold, M., & Bendul, J. C. (2017). Business models for sustainable innovation: An empirical analysis of frugal products and services. *Journal of Cleaner Production, 162*, S133–S145. doi:10.1016/j.jclepro.2016.02.050

Strauss, A., & Corbin, J. (1990). *Basics of qualitative research: Grounded theory procedures and techniques.* Thousand Oaks, CA: SAGE.

Yazdkhasti, M., Negarandeh, R., & Behboodi-Moghadam, Z. (2016). Threat of the feminine identity: The emerging structure in exploring the process of women's empowerment for menopause management: A grounded theory study. *Health Sciences, 5*(11), 509–520.

CASE STUDY RESEARCH

Kurt Schoch

I n this chapter, I provide an introduction to case study design. The chapter begins with a definition of case study research and a description of its origins and philosophical underpinnings. I share discipline-specific applications of case study methods and describe the appropriate research questions addressed by case studies. I follow this description with methods considerations, including case study design, research questions, sample size, data collection, and data analysis. Note that there are many approaches and styles to case study research. This chapter focuses primarily on case studies that rely on qualitative methods; more advanced readings are listed at the end under Key Resources.

BACKGROUND

Case study research involves a detailed and intensive analysis of a particular event, situation, organization, or social unit. Typically, a case has a defined space and time frame: "a phenomenon of some sort in a bounded context" (Miles, Huberman, & Saldaña, 2014, p. 28). In terms of scope, a case study is an in-depth investigation of a contemporary phenomenon within its real-life context. The case study is appropriate especially if the context is relevant to the phenomenon—for example, investigating an achievement gap in a high school (the phenomenon) with a large second-generation immigrant population (the context). Because the boundaries between a phenomenon and its context are not always clear, case study design relies on multiple data sources for evidence (Yin, 2018, p. 15).

A *case* could be an individual, a role, a small group, an organization, a community, or even a nation (Miles et al., 2014, p. 28). Examples include the following:

- A remote town affected by a natural disaster, such as an earthquake (see Parrinello, 2013); the town or area constitutes the case.

- A refugee group resulting from a political conflict (Pedersen, 2012); the group is the case.

- A president or a high school principal. For example, Scribner and Crow (2012) reported on the case study of a high school principal in a reform setting.

Case studies are best conceptualized by the bounded phenomena of interest and not by specific methods; thus, different studies can be conducted under this broad umbrella. For example, two well-known case studies include Sigmund Freud's (1905) study of Dora and Graham Allison's (1971) case study of the Cuban missile crisis. Freud's case study of Dora used recollections, reconstruction, and dream analysis to depict a young woman suffering from hysterical symptoms, including difficulty breathing, nervous coughing, and headaches. Freud demonstrated that even an ordinary case can have an application in similar situations. The case study of the Cuban missile crisis is based on a broad range of data ranging from government documents to interviews with numerous officials. The results have served to instruct others about leadership styles and processes, in difficult situations. The Cuban missile crisis case study also clearly demonstrates how a case study is used for explanatory purposes and not just descriptive or exploratory purposes (Yin, 2018, p. 7).

Case study research typically fits in the postpositivist paradigm, which implies the existence of an ultimate reality that we can only approximately—not completely—understand. VanWynsberghe and Khan (2007) also suggest the possibility of critical theory and interpretivist paradigms for case study research, suggesting that "case study can make a substantial connection to each" (pp. 89–90).

Benefits of Using a Case Study Approach

Case study research offers benefits in terms of process and outcome. The case study design will help you focus your research within the confines of space and time on a specific case. A case study also gives you an opportunity to collect different kinds of data, such as interviews, documents, observations, surveys, and others, about the case and provides you with the chance to get an in-depth look at an organization or individual and the inner workings and interactions of that organization or individual.

In terms of the outcome, the case study provides a comprehensive understanding of a bounded unit and helps the reader examine that case so he or she can learn from it. It also allows others to apply the principles and lessons learned in a case to other cases or situations and leads to transferability (i.e., the ability to apply the case to another situation), which is different from the generalization that occurs in quantitative studies. For example, if someone wanted to learn more about being a high school principal, a case study could help that person learn about that experience and apply it to another situation or help that person decide whether being a principal is his or her best career path.

Focusing Case Study Research

Case study research focuses on a specific event, person, place, thing, organization, or unit (or if more than one, typically a small number). The key is to identify the case and the boundaries of that case; the question to ask is, "What is the *case*?" You can help yourself answer that by answering the question, "What is part of, and what is not part of, the case?" what Yin (2018) refers to as "bounding the case" (p. 31). Merriam (1998) writes, "I can 'fence in' what I am going to study" (p. 27). If the case is one school, then other schools are not part of the case; if the case is the principal,

DISCIPLINE-SPECIFIC APPLICATIONS OF CASE STUDY

Case study research is used widely across disciplines; this type of research is most common in education and other social sciences, as well as in law, political science, and health care. For example:

In this discipline . . .	a case study could investigate . . .
Health care	A hospital or specific type of patient
Education	A school or a principal
Business	A business, a chief executive officer (CEO), or a start-up organization
Public policy	A natural disaster and policy implications for responding to it

other teachers or administrators are not part of the case. Therefore, the specific unit of study, or unit of analysis, is a defining characteristic of a case study. Stake (2000) provides this perspective: "Case study is not a methodological choice but a choice of what is to be studied. . . . We concentrate, at least for the time being, on the case" (p. 435). Take care when defining the case because the research questions reflect the boundaries and definition of the case.

Examples of Case Study Research

These examples will be used throughout the rest of this chapter to provide examples of key elements of case study research. Note that each has clear boundaries of place and time, which is a defining characteristic of case studies.

- Militello, Schweid, and Sireci (2010) conducted a multiple-case study to explore the use of formative assessment systems (processes that students and teachers use to adjust their learning and teaching strategies). The authors wanted to better understand how educators seek and obtain assessment tools. The study lasted 18 months, used a sample of three school districts (representing a *multiple-case* study), and focused on the following overarching question: "To what extent does the fit between intended use and system characteristics foster or inhibit the ultimate utility of formative assessment systems for schools?" (p. 34). The results were focused on three key findings: (1) the reasons a school district might want an assessment system, (2) characteristics of the assessment systems, and (3) how formative assessment systems are used (p. 36).

- Joia (2002) conducted a single explanatory case study, analyzing the use of a web-based virtual learning environment for business students in Brazil. Although this is considered a single-case study (the case is the learning environment), three different cities (sites) were used for data collection. Five research questions were used, focusing on the collaborative nature of virtual learning environments, the influence of the physical location of students, use of a moderator, and the students' perceptions of a particular learning environment used in the school. Results were organized around each of the research questions, including the conclusion that there was collaborative learning in place, but the particular platform did not support the accomplishment of collaborative work.

- Scheib (2003) used a collective case study design to examine role of stress among four music teachers at a high school in the Midwestern United States. This study elaborated on previous literature that examined specific stressors in a music teacher's life to learn more about why those stressors exist. Scheib used observations, individual interviews, and document analysis to understand stressors related to areas such as role conflict, role overload, and resource inadequacy. Scheib noted the essential nature of triangulation in balancing all aspects of the data that were collected.

Conducting Case Study Research

The case study design includes components that connect initial research thoughts to the final research conclusions. Those first research thoughts begin with a research problem, which involves the identification of a lack of knowledge about some issue or phenomenon. Identification of the problem then leads to crafting the purpose statement and research question(s). Examining the research question(s) then allows you to determine whether a case study is the appropriate design.

Characteristics for selecting case study research versus other approaches focus on *how* or *why* kinds of research questions directed at exploring and understanding some phenomenon in depth (Yin, 2018). Once the decision is made to conduct a case study, a key decision involves selecting the case itself. Yin (2018) noted the two required elements as "defining the case and bounding the case" (p. 30). The former relates to clearly and concretely indicating the case, which can be a person, place, thing, organization, or phenomenon. The latter relates to scope—what is, and is not, included in the case, whether from time, structure, or other perspectives. Once the case has been identified, you can determine the types of data needed and how those data will be collected.

Case Study Sample Size

Typically, a case study has a sample of one (i.e., the bounded case, but note that sampling can also occur within the case), unless the research project is a multiple-case study. In a multiple-case study, having three to four distinct cases for comparison is probably the most cases that one can realistically handle. When using multiple cases or sampling within a case, it is effective to use a selection method known as *purposeful sampling*. By selecting the cases, and the individuals, documents, and artifacts within the case, purposeful sampling allows you to focus in depth on a phenomenon. It allows you to explore information-rich cases from which you can learn a great deal about issues of central importance to the research (Patton, 2002, p. 46).

One way to understand purposeful sampling used for case studies is to contrast it to sampling for quantitative research. Samples obtained for quantitative research studies are often probability samples that are presumed to be representative of the population being studied and are used to generalize to that population; it does not matter who the individuals in the sample are—only that they are statistically representative of the larger population. In purposeful sampling, however, the goal is to find individuals or cases that provide insights into the specific situation under study, regardless of the general population.

Case Study Sample Selection

Sample sizes in case studies are typically small, which is common in most qualitative research. Sometimes the selection of samples and cases to use is straightforward and clear, due to the uniqueness of the person or organization or because of special arrangements or access to the case. In some situations, however, there may be many qualified case study candidates, and you may have to use a screening procedure to select the proper ones. Yin (2018) suggests asking knowledgeable people about the case candidates or collecting limited documentation on them. What you clearly want to avoid is selecting a case that is representative of something other than what you want to study.

Joia's (2002) work is an example of a single-case study of a virtual learning community in Brazil. This particular case comprised 43 students enrolled in a graduate course on e-commerce. Scheib (2003), in his collective case study about the role of stress on high school music teachers, first selected the site based on the fact that he had access to it, that it had well-established music programs, and that the music department offered band, choir, and orchestra—a variety of musical programs. After selecting the site, the researcher focused on the four music teachers who taught there; the four teachers constituted the sample.

In other instances, screening for a sample can often be more involved. For example, Militello et al. (2010) used a sample of three schools from three different school districts in their research on formative assessment. They chose the schools by identifying prominent formative assessment companies and the districts that had contracts with these companies. After consulting with the state Department of Education to discover which districts were using assessment in a significant way (p. 34), the researchers narrowed their selection based on the use of formative assessments in middle school mathematics. The researchers then selected three school districts based on phone interviews with assessment personnel from the state Department of Education.

Case Study Research Questions

Research questions for a case study can be both quantitative and qualitative but frequently use terms similar to other qualitative research designs. For example, these kinds of questions focus on concepts such as *explain*, *explore*, *describe*, and *understand*. Typically, case study research questions use words such as *how* or *why*. Overall, the case study research questions need to address the substance of what (case) the study is about (Hatch, 2002, p. 10).

To formulate your case study research questions, think of conducting a case study like painting a picture. What does the case look like, whether it is an individual, organization, or situation? What image will the reader have in his or her mind after reading the case study? To paint that picture, what kinds of research questions would you need to ask?

Some case studies have one or two broad research questions. For example, Scheib's (2003) collective case study of school music teachers explored, through the lens of role theory, the open-ended question of why their work life is stressful. In another example, Campbell and Ahrens (1998) published a case study on rape victim services and set out to answer how and why coordinated service programs are effective. Other case studies state more specific questions. For example, Joia's (2002) case study on a virtual learning community had five specific questions, including "Why is a moderator needed, and how can his importance be measured?" (p. 309).

Some use an overarching question followed by subquestions, such as these from Militello et al.'s (2010) work. The main research question was, "To what extent does the fit between intended use and system characteristics foster or inhibit the ultimate utility of formative assessment systems for schools?" The subquestions were as follows:

1. Intended Use: What data and action did each district want from the assessment system?

2. System Characteristics: What were each of the formative assessment systems designed to do?

3. Actual Use: How are school district educators using the assessment systems? (p. 34)

Note that there is an important difference between the research questions for the case study and the interview questions used to elicit information from participants. Research questions are broad and focused on what the researcher ultimately wants to learn and not directed at any one person, document, situation, or occurrence within the case. Rather, the questions are directed at the case as a whole, and answers to the research questions will be derived from all the sources of data. Ask participants interview questions that will help you answer your research questions. Interview questions are directed at individuals or groups within the case and often contain the word *you*. For example, the questions might start with, "How do you . . . ?" or "Why do you . . . ?" As a hint, if the word *you* appears in a research question, it is probably an interview question, and not broad enough to be a research question.

DATA COLLECTION PROCEDURES

Types of Data Collection

In case studies, the research questions drive the data to be collected. From the research questions, the researcher determines the kinds of questions to be asked in interviews, what to observe, what documents to review, and what artifacts to examine. Therefore, multiple sources of data are used in a case study. Sources of evidence may include one or more of the following: (a) documentation, (b) archival records, (c) interviews, (d) direct observation, (e) participant observation, and (f) physical artifacts (Yin, 2018, p. 114). Stake (1995) supports the guidance provided by the research questions, noting, "What one does in the field, from gaining access to triangulating data, needs to be guided by the research questions" (p. 50).

If you use survey instruments for data collection, they need to be valid and reliable. For interviews, you will need interview protocols, or a list of questions and prompts used to interview participants. Protocols are useful to ensure the consistency of the interviews across the individuals being interviewed. You may also use different interview protocols for different groups within the case. For example, you might use different interview protocols for teachers and for students. Observations also require protocols; they ensure that interviewers understand what they are looking for and how the observations will help answer your research question(s). Similarly, be sure you know how documents and physical artifacts will help answer the research questions; know, in advance, what you are looking for. Yin (2018, pp. 126–137) also advocates the following general principles of data collection in case study research.

Table 16.1 provides important elements associated with data collection in case study research.

TABLE 16.1 ● KEY ELEMENTS OF DATA COLLECTION IN CASE STUDY	
Principle	**Explanation**
1. Use multiple sources and over several time periods.	Use different types of data and obtain different perspectives by using a variety of people and other sources. Scheib (2003) used direct observations of, and interviews with, the music teachers, school policy publications; documents sent to students and parents and music concert programs. Campbell and Ahrens (1998) included interviews with rape victim advocates, crisis center directors, police, prosecutors, and medical staff, as well as the rape survivors themselves; pamphlets and training manuals were made for each community program. Militello et al. (2010) collected data in three stages during one school year.
2. Build a case study database.	Keep your notes, documents, narratives, and other materials organized by maintaining a physical or electronic file system. This can include field notes, documents, surveys or other quantitative data, and other narratives. Consider using software to help you stay organized.
3. Establish a chain of evidence.	Be sure you are able to track the final conclusions backward through your notes or database to your approach, protocols, and research questions. Ask yourself, "Can I do a backward line of sight from my report all the way through to the research questions?" "Is there alignment between the conclusions, the evidence, and the research questions?"
4. Exercise care when using electronic sources.	The sheer volume of information available electronically can be overwhelming, so it is important to set limits on the amount of time you will spend collecting these kinds of data. Ensure you can make a strong case for relevance of this information to your research purpose. Also, the ease of posting and accessing data electronically requires caution regarding the credibility and accuracy of such data. Cross-check and double-check references and sources. Always seek permission to use electronic sources; just because information is on the internet does not mean it is in the public domain.

Stake (1995) also notes that data gathering almost always involves someone else's "home grounds," and thus "a small invasion of personal privacy" (p. 57). Be sure to obtain the required permissions, typically done as part of informed consent and institutional review board approval, including how the final report will be used or distributed.

Data Analysis Techniques

There is wide variation in case study research, but most scholar-practitioners tend to focus on qualitative data, which is where the focus of this section will be. Advice from Patton (2002) is well worth heeding: "The best advice I ever received about coding was to read the data I collected over and over and over. The more I interacted with the data, the more patterns and categories began to 'jump out' at me" (p. 446). Data, or content, analysis involves several phases: describing, interpreting, drawing conclusions, and determining significance. Specific techniques will vary based on the type of study and its purpose, and individual researchers will often develop their own approach and style. Typically, case study data analysis will involve the following steps.

Describing. This involves understanding the "who, what, when, where" of the situation under study. The descriptive phase of the data analysis involves several readings and reviews of all data collected. Field notes—those taken while at the research site or while studying parts of the case—are reviewed extensively to discover patterns or themes. Patterns tend to be descriptive, such as "most students are excited about the first day of class," whereas themes are often more topical, such as "excitement about school."

Emergence of Findings. Through the researcher's interaction with and immersion in the raw data, findings in the form of patterns, themes, or categories emerge, which is the essence of the inductive form of qualitative data analysis. The initial stages of this analysis involve open coding, which emphasizes recognizing any patterns that emerge from the data rather than analyzing data based on an existing framework as one might do in deductive analysis with quantitative data. These codes summarize and put labels on patterns, themes, or categories observed in the data.

Codes become brief shorthand labels to passages of data for easier organization and recognition. Coding is essential when multiple researchers are working on the same project to ensure common understanding and consistency. Codes can be identified in advance of the data analysis, which is known as *a priori coding*, based on what the researcher anticipates seeing in the data, or codes can be allowed to emerge from the data, either from the information itself or from the individuals interviewed. The latter is often called *in vivo coding*. Codes may also arise from a theoretical framework (hence the need for your research to be grounded in the literature). An accompanying step to open coding is axial coding, where relationships or connections are identified among the initial categories and themes identified during open coding.

Although researchers often think of open and axial coding as separate and sequential steps, Corbin and Strauss (2008) noted that "open coding and axial coding go hand in hand" (p. 198). Combining open and axial coding becomes a process of concurrently dissecting the raw data and reassembling it at the same time. While involved in this dissection/reassembly, you may find yourself comparing each piece of data with the ones that came before it; this *constant comparative analysis* is a common approach in many types of qualitative research. Selective coding is a final step in the coding process that allows you to create larger categories that connect the previously identified categories. Creswell (2007) referred to this as creating a "story line" (p. 67). One final thought on coding: It is helpful to maintain a description or definition of your codes, often in visual form, to allow for easy identification and revision later.

Cox (2011), in his doctoral dissertation, described some of his coding process:

> During initial coding, digital transcripts were hand-coded to establish patterns in the data and to identify the initial codes. . . . After the first five participant interviews and transcriptions, data were hand coded on the transcripts, analyzed, and preliminarily organized in the structure of an NVivo tree and case nodes. (p. 124)

Cox (2011) further explained that primary codes appear in bold and that "secondary codes, unbolded, appear to fit within the scope of primary codes" (p. 254, see Table 16.2).

Comparing. Final steps in case study data analysis can include making comparisons across the various themes that have emerged from the data, as well as making comparisons across different cases, if the study was a multiple-case study design. It is important to understand that these steps may not necessarily happen linearly, but in an iterative way. You may be comparing themes as you identify them. You may even need to go back and collect more data after completing these steps. Collecting new data to better conceptualize themes is common in qualitative research.

Examples of Data Analysis

- Joia (2002) used tables and charts to describe behavior and usage in the virtual community and the geographic distribution of its students in terms of participation. In addition, Joia analyzed the typology of the web-based community according to a taxonomy established by previous research.

- Lotzkar and Bottorff (2001) analyzed videotaped data in four steps. First, they reviewed the videotaped data to identify and describe behaviors of interest. Second, they reviewed the tapes to identify clusters of behaviors indicating the development of the relationship. Third, they described patterns of behavior within each cluster and compared the clusters, and finally, they constructed a detailed behavioral description, including conditions, cause or function, and consequences of the observed behaviors.

- Scheib (2003) used coding techniques to analyze interview transcripts, field notes, and documents. The researcher used codes identified by previous researchers to identify specific role stressors (e.g., role conflict, role ambiguity, role overload) in the artifacts.

- Militello et al. (2010) analyzed data using coding and comparative analysis (p. 36). The research team created memos from field notes and artifacts. They exported the memos, along with their interview transcriptions, into a computer database, and they described them using an open coding system. They applied codes to represent themes identified in existing literature and also to represent unreported findings. Using a similar coding system, they also analyzed the technical data. Then, they compared the data to analyze

TABLE 16.2 ● AN EXAMPLE OF THE INITIAL STAGES OF THE CODING PROCESS

Participant	1	2	3	4	5
Initial Codes	Values	Motivations	Tradition	Challenge	Goals
	Service	Teamsmanship	Expectation	Growth	Standards
	Socialization	Adventure	Symbolism of uniform	Adventure	Ethics
	Leadership as shaping	Direction	Value	Overcoming limits	Motivations
	Responsibility as shaping	Resilience	Integrity	Defining moments	Culture shock
	Culture shock	Agility	Proving self	Continuous learning	Growth
	Power of opportunity	Self-reliance	Growth	Ethics, values	Transformation
	Overcoming limits	Learning from leaders	Drive	Transformation	Risk taking
	Self-confidence	Integrity	Family	Politics vs. values	Learning
	Changed world view	Respect	**Responsibility**	Symbolism of rank	Self-worth
			Discipline	Definition of self	Values
			Identity	Calling	**Leadership**
			Change	Tradition	Civic duty
			Learning	Right thing	Role models
			Civic behavior		Selflessness
			Transformation		**Belonging**
			Sacrifice		Appreciation for country
					Tolerance
					Tested by experience
					Self confidence
					Judgment
					Mission

Source: Table reprinted with permission from Cox, R. (2011). The effects of military experience on civic consciousness (Doctoral dissertation).

Note: The primary codes appear in bold.

gaps between the intended and actualized use of formative assessments in the case study.

Case Study Reporting

The final step is case study reporting. Regardless of the purpose of your case study report—whether you are a student writing a thesis or dissertation or a researcher preparing an executive summary—be sure to do the following:

- Provide a thorough description of the case.

- Separate reporting from interpreting (reporting means presenting the facts: what happened, what did you see, etc.; interpreting involves finding meaning in the data).

- Include sections outlining your methods and your literature review, including how that literature led to your research questions.

- Ensure that the reader can easily follow the progression from your original problem, purpose, and methods to your analysis conclusions (there should be a clear sense of alignment among these items). Remember Yin's (2018) admonition to establish a chain of evidence.

- Make it clear what the case study informs and how it lays the groundwork for future studies.

- Write the report such that a person not involved in the case can understand it (limit the use of technical language so that a broader audience can learn from your experience).

Appropriateness of Case Study for Your Research Project

Embark on a case study as your research methodology when you want to better explore, understand, or explain "how" or "why" a phenomenon, within a particular context, is what it is. Case study research happens in the present, not the past; therefore, it explores a contemporary phenomenon. As a case study researcher, you will have little, if any, control over what happens in the phenomenon (as contrasted with controlled environments such as quantitative experiments); you will observe, review documents, conduct interviews, and collect other appropriate data in a manner that does not change behavior and minimally affects the phenomenon. You may collect quantitative data to help understand the "how" and "why," but your purpose is not to understand effectiveness or cause but rather provide a description of the phenomenon to enhance overall understanding. As with all research, begin with a problem statement and research purpose, followed by research questions that focus on "how" and/or "why" to provide "an extensive and 'in-depth' description of some social phenomenon" (Yin, 2018, p. 4).

The Role of the Researcher in a Case Study

Typically, the researcher conducts interviews, administers surveys, reviews and analyzes documents, and observes whatever is being studied. In a case study, the researcher is situated in the activity or organization being studied. In contrast, in quantitative research, the research may be done in a location other than where the object of study is located. For example, the researcher may not need to be present to conduct surveys. In qualitative research, the researcher is less separated from the object of study than in quantitative research.

As a researcher, be careful to avoid bias, or the tendency to prejudice or unduly influence the process or results of a research project. Be constantly aware of your own feelings, opinions, and prejudices, and make sure you are open to data and evidence that might not fit your notion or idea of what you might find. Do not enter into case study research, or any research, to demonstrate a previously held position or advocate a particular point of view. You can mitigate potential bias by using techniques shared by all qualitative research, such as journaling, triangulation of data, and member checking.

CONCLUSION

Case study research is an in-depth investigation of a contemporary phenomenon within its real-life context. A case study typically relies on multiple data sources and is bound by both space and time. Any discipline can use case study research, and case studies can be used with other research approaches; the key is to understand the "case" and ensure that the research questions support the case study design. Consistent with other qualitative designs, researchers need to attend to issues of researcher bias as well as quality in terms of trustworthiness (as discussed in Chapter 12).

Questions for Reflection

1. How does a clear definition of the "case"—that is, "bounding the case"—help with the management of the scope of the research?

2. Would you say that bias is more or less of a concern in case study research than in other types of research? How would you work to mitigate bias in case study research?

3. How does sample size affect the ability to effectively conduct case study research? How would a sample size of five or more make a case study much more difficult to do?

4. In speaking about data analysis techniques, Patton (2002) wrote, "I never even bothered to use the software program I installed on the computer because I found it much easier to code it by hand" (p. 446). Granted, that was written in 2002, and software has improved much since then. But even with that, what value do you see in simply reading the qualitative data several times rather than quickly entering it into a software program for analysis?

5. What limits our ability to generalize in case study research, which may include quantitative and qualitative approaches, in the same way that we generalize from designs that take a strictly quantitative research?

Key Sources

Baxter, P., & Jack, S. (2008, December). Qualitative case study methodology: Study design and implementation for novice researchers. *Qualitative Report, 13*(4), 544–559. Retrieved from http://www.nova.edu/ssss/QR/QR13-4/baxter.pdf

Merriam, S. (1998). *Qualitative research and case study applications in education.* San Francisco, CA: Jossey-Bass.

Miles, M. B., Huberman, A. M., & Saldaña, J. (2014). *Qualitative data analysis: A methods sourcebook* (3rd ed.). Thousand Oaks, CA: SAGE.

Patton, M. Q. (2002). *Qualitative research and evaluation methods* (3rd ed.). Thousand Oaks, CA: SAGE.

Stake, R. E. (1995). *The art of case study research.* Thousand Oaks, CA: SAGE.

Stake, R. E. (2000). Case studies. In N. K. Denzin & Y. S. Lincoln (Eds.), *Handbook of qualitative research* (2nd ed.). Thousand Oaks, CA: SAGE.

Tellis, W. (1997, July). Introduction to case study. *Qualitative Report, 3*(2). Retrieved from http://www.nova.edu/ssss/QR/QR3-2/tellis1.html

Yin, R. K. (2018). *Case study research: Design and methods* (6th ed.). Thousand Oaks, CA: SAGE.

References

Allison, G. (1971). *Essence of decision: Explaining the Cuban Missile Crisis.* New York, NY: Little, Brown.

Campbell, R., & Ahrens, C. E. (1998). Innovative community services for rape victims: An application of multiple case study methodology. *American Journal of Community Psychology, 26*(4), 537–571. doi:10.1023/A:1022140921921

Corbin, J., & Strauss, A. (2008). *Basics of qualitative research: Techniques and procedures for developing grounded theory* (3rd ed.). Thousand Oaks, CA: SAGE.

Cox, R. (2011). *The effects of military experience on civic consciousness* (Doctoral dissertation). Retrieved from ProQuest Dissertations & These Full Text Database. (UMI No. 3457222)

Creswell, J. W. (2007). *Qualitative inquiry and research design: Choosing among five approaches* (2nd ed.). Thousand Oaks, CA: SAGE.

Freud, S. (1905). Fragment of an analysis of a case of hysteria. In J. Strachey (Ed. & Trans.), *The standard edition of the complete psychological works of Sigmund Freud* (Vol. 7, pp. 1–122). London, UK: Hogarth Press. (Original work published 1901)

Hatch, J. A. (2002). *Doing qualitative research in education settings.* Albany, NY: State University of New York Press.

Joia, L. A. (2002). Analysing a web-based e-commerce learning community: A case study in Brazil. *Internet Research: Electronic Networking Applications and Policy, 12*(4), 305–317. doi:10.1108/10662240210438434

Lotzkar, M., & Bottorff, J. (2001). An observational study of the development of a nurse–patient relationship. *Clinical Nursing Research, 10*(3), 275–294. doi:10.1177/10547730122158932

Merriam, S. B. (1998). *Qualitative research and case study applications in education.* San Francisco, CA: Jossey-Bass.

Miles, M. B., Huberman, A. M., & Saldaña, J. (2014). *Qualitative data analysis: A methods sourcebook* (3rd ed.). Thousand Oaks, CA: SAGE.

Militello, M., Schweid, J., & Sireci, S. G. (2010). Formative assessment systems: Evaluating the fit between school districts' needs and assessment systems' characteristics. *Educational Assessment, Evaluation and Accountability, 22*(1), 29–52. doi:10.1007/s11092-010-9090-2

Parrinello, G. (2013). The city-territory: Large-scale planning and development policies in the aftermath of the Belice valley earthquake (Sicily, 1968). *Planning Perspectives, 28*(4), 571–593. doi:10.1080/02665433.2013.774538

Patton, M. Q. (2002). *Qualitative research and evaluation methods* (3rd ed.). Thousand Oaks, CA: SAGE.

Pedersen, M. H. (2012). Going on a class journey: The inclusion and exclusion of Iraqi refugees in Denmark. *Journal of Ethnic and Migration Studies, 38*(7), 1101–1117. doi:10.1080/1369183X.2012.681453

Scheib, J. W. (2003). Role stress in the professional life of the school music teacher: A collective case study. *Journal of Research in Music Education, 51*(2), 124–136. doi:10.2307/3345846

Scribner, S. P., & Crow, G. M. (2012). Employing professional identities: Case study of a high school principal in a reform setting. *Leadership and Policy in Schools, 11*(3), 243–274. doi:10.1080/15700763.2012.654885

Stake, R. E. (1995). *The art of case study research.* Thousand Oaks, CA: SAGE.

Stake, R. E. (2000). Case studies. In N. K. Denzin & Y. S. Lincoln (Eds.), *Handbook of qualitative research* (2nd ed., pp. 435–453). Thousand Oaks, CA: SAGE.

VanWynsberghe, R., & Khan, S. (2007). Redefining case study. *International Journal of Qualitative Methods, 6*(2), 80–94. doi:10.1177/160940690700600208

Yin, R. K. (2018). *Case study research: Design and methods* (6th ed.). Thousand Oaks, CA: SAGE.

PROGRAM EVALUATION

Louis Milanesi

In this chapter, I present a brief overview of program evaluation, emphasizing the central role of stakeholders, and explore the role of logic models in organizing evaluation studies. Key differences between process and formative evaluation, as well as outcome and summative evaluation, are described. I discuss sample size, data collection and analysis, and issues of quality and provide resources for conducting program evaluations. The presentation is oriented toward the practitioner who is trying to decide if program evaluation is the correct approach given the research question.

BACKGROUND

Evaluation is the systematic assessment of the operation and/or outcome of a program. Much like a scientific research study, program evaluation seeks to answer a question or set of questions. The scope and complexity of programs vary widely—from large-scale, national or international projects to smaller scale efforts of local governments or individual organizations. Thus, the scope and complexity of program evaluations also vary widely. Additionally, program evaluations are sometimes encountered as elements nested within broader studies related to policy development or policy evaluation. While, historically, program evaluation has focused on outcomes, the trend now is toward formative evaluation (Marshall, Crowe, Oades, Deane, & Kavanaugh, 2007).

Brief Overview of Program Evaluation

Program evaluation practice began as an application of scientific methods to address day-to-day problems faced by individuals and organizations. In the United States, evaluation models in education and organizational management can be traced to the 19th and early 20th centuries. Major investments in government-sponsored programs brought increased attention to the practice of program evaluation after World War II, and general theoretical orientations of evaluation practice began to emerge toward the end of that century. For a detailed understanding of the historical development of program evaluation, see Hogan (2007).

Program evaluators tend to embrace general theoretical orientations in their approach to evaluation (Alkin, 2004). These orientations can be understood as higher level theories regarding the different purposes and rationales of program evaluation. Examples would include utilization focus, methods, social valuing, accountability and control, and social inquiry. These varied theoretical orientations serve to define the specializations of professional practice among professional evaluators. Some evaluators opt to identify with one or more higher level theoretical perspectives, whereas others remain more eclectic in their approach to defining the field and practice.

Distinctions between these orientations toward program evaluation often reflect the individual practitioner's own orientation on the purpose of program evaluation, or the *why* of evaluation practice. However, how an individual evaluation is conducted links more specifically to the framework defined by its logic model, which guides the evaluation to results. For practical purposes, a logic model is critical for defining the nature and purpose of the evaluation, the questions it needs to investigate, and the best methods to employ.

The Role of the Researcher

Evaluators may have varying influence on the setting depending on whether they are internal or external to the program under review. External evaluators are independent of the setting that houses or sponsors the program being evaluated. Thus, they are viewed as more likely to be objective in their analysis and reporting. For example, major grants often specify that an external evaluator conduct the evaluation. External evaluators typically engage at specific milestones of the project.

Internal evaluators are members of the settings hosting or sponsoring the programs being evaluated. Since the internal evaluator is familiar with the program, the evaluator can be more agile in supporting the required adjustments to program delivery. For example, an internal evaluator can help in quickly identifying any impact of unintended events or gaps in initial planning that are undermining the program's progress or effectiveness. Early interventions based on this information can help conserve valuable resources and increase the program's likelihood for success.

External and internal evaluators need to guard against potential bias in the design, data collection, analyses, and reporting of evaluations. The accuracy and accountability dimensions of the Joint Committee on Standards for Educational Evaluation's (2011) *Program Evaluation Standards* speak to specific considerations in avoiding bias, and agencies that sponsor or require evaluations may provide additional guidance. For example, external evaluators often are required to file affidavits documenting their independence from the project under review. Internal evaluators must question whether their role creates a conflict of interest, their investment in the project will contribute to bias, or their friendships with program directors will make it difficult to provide objective feedback. Thus, it is best that all evaluators decline assignments where significant doubts exist regarding their ability to render an accurate, objective, and unbiased appraisal of a program. Additionally, the American Evaluation Association (2018) provides guidance for evaluators in its *Guiding Principles for Evaluators*.

IMPORTANT CONSIDERATIONS IN PROGRAM EVALUATION

The Role of Stakeholders

Collaboration among stakeholders is essential for the success of any program, and the program evaluator should be considered a key contributor in that collaboration. Understanding how other stakeholders view the evaluator's role is an important step in engaging with a project. The optimal situation occurs when the evaluator is recruited in the early planning stages and is seen as a long-term member of the program team. This allows opportunities for the evaluator to contribute to the program's successful deployment as well as to collect data that would contribute to a robust evaluation.

The terms *stakeholder* and *partner* are often used synonymously; in this chapter, however, a useful distinction is made between stakeholders who have key roles and investments in a program and partnerships between individuals and settings that exist outside the scope of the program. Stakeholders include individuals, organizations, and other settings that are involved in shaping and delivering a program as well as individuals who are involved in sustaining a program and those affected by the program. Some or all of these stakeholders may be connected with one another through cooperative partnerships that link their organizations.

Cooperative partnerships can serve to bind stakeholders in the execution of program activities; however, they may also bring background to the program project that can interfere with its execution. Cases where the connections between stakeholders involve only their work on the program being evaluated should prompt specific concerns for an evaluator because stakeholder commitment to the project's activities and timeline may become inconsistent.

Identifying and Engaging Stakeholders. The evaluator's initial contact with key stakeholders will usually occur during a collaborative meeting to define the role of the evaluator as well as the nature, scope of effort, and reporting of the evaluation. The evaluator should ask questions regarding who to contact and how best to engage with the groups and organizations within the project. As you identify the processes and outcomes that the evaluation may include, simultaneously ask about the key contacts with whom you need to interact. Some evaluators develop their own worksheets, following best practices, which flow much like a standardized interview, to help in documenting important stakeholders and contacts, including key informants, key collaborators, and gatekeepers. Best practices for engaging with stakeholders include the following:

- Strive to be regarded as a resource rather than a judge. Collaborate with stakeholders to define what successful outcomes would look like, and present the evaluation as a central means to achieving the objectives those outcomes represent.

- Avoid communicating weaknesses, which tend to imply judgment or static conditions, in favor of focusing on opportunities for improvement that lead to greater success.

- Be approachable as an empathetic listener; avoid both antipathy, which hinders engagement and information, and sympathy, which hinders objectivity.

- Consider how best to enter each group. Reflect on who introduces you and how this shapes the initial impressions stakeholders form regarding your purpose and trustworthiness.

- Learn the formal organization structure via organizational charts, and strive to be aware of informal social structures and opinion leaders.

- Explore how communication about the program is conducted within and across stakeholder groups.

- Be cautious of oversharing information across stakeholder groups.

- Avoid the perception of favoring individuals or groups within the community of stakeholders.

- Remain objective and consistent.

Developing the Program Logic Model

Evaluators can make significant contributions to the success of a program when they are engaged in the formative stages of its development. One such early contribution involves helping stakeholders formulate a detailed logic model describing how the program operates (Conrad, Randolf, Kirby, & Bebout, 1999; McDavid, Huse, & Ingleson, 2018; McLaughlin & Jordan, 1999; W. K. Kellogg Foundation Logic Model Development Guide, 2004). Program logic models are sometimes developed at the inception of a program and then used later as part of the evaluation. Logic models provide a causal map of how a program, policy, or initiative should work. In many ways, the logic model can be thought of as a program schematic that identifies the program/project priorities, inputs and outputs, and outcomes. It provides a visual aid of a program that can be shown to a potential funder, auditor, or organizational executive or that can be used by a program evaluator or team. Additionally, stakeholders may come to the project with different goals or agendas; therefore, this process can facilitate communication of the assumptions held by the various stakeholders and partners.

Moreover, well-constructed logic models will assist the evaluator in constructing the assessment model for the program by pointing to the *what*, *where*, and *when* dimensions of data collection and analysis. A robust logic model will help facilitate these pointed questions. The logic model approach is sometimes called the program theory of change (presented later in the chapter).

Logic models can take many forms, including flowcharts and tables (McLaughlin & Jordan, 2015). Regardless of how they are presented, logic models tend to contain the same four kinds of essential information: inputs, activities, outputs, and impacts. Inputs include the resources required for the evaluation, such as staffing, technology, and physical space. Activities include the events evaluators and participants conduct to achieve program goals. Outputs include the products that result from program activities that allow for evaluation. Finally, impacts ascertain progress toward goals as well as the expected influence of the program.

In some cases, a program evaluator may be recruited to assist a program that is already under way without the benefit of a detailed logic model. In that case, the evaluator will need to work quickly to get a clear sense of the needs of different stakeholder groups and the ways in which they relate to one another. The evaluator then engages stakeholders in a collaborative process in defining goals, objectives, and outcomes. The evaluator should assist stakeholders in defining immediate, intermediate, and long-term objectives as well as the outcomes that would represent successful achievement of each stage of the program's development.

The evaluator can draw on the commonly accepted standards in program evaluation related to the potential for the utility, feasibility, propriety, and accuracy of program evaluation designs. Then, the evaluation can determine what resources are or can be dedicated to the evaluation effort. Resources related to funding, as well as access to data, information, and people, directly affect the feasibility of the proposed evaluation.

There are many reasons why a program evaluator might decide not to engage with a program.

Why an Evaluator May Not Decide to Engage With a Program

- The evaluator may not feel adequately qualified within the program field of endeavor (utility standard).

- The evaluator is concerned that there is a high risk for misuse or misinterpretation of the results (utility standard).

- The evaluator believes that the opportunities for evaluation will not equitably represent the cultural or political interests of key stakeholders (feasibility standard).

- The evaluator perceives a threat to the rights or dignity of program participants or other stakeholders by performing the requested activities (propriety standard).

- The evaluator perceives limited opportunities to acquire dependable and consistent information to answer the key questions posed within the proposed evaluation model (accuracy standard).

Completing a Needs Assessment

Needs assessments (e.g., see Linfield & Posavac, 2018) can initially be used to determine the need for new programs in a community or an organization. Needs assessments direct attention to key opportunities for service and practice improvements. Examples include a community college seeking to identify current gaps in its program offerings, a nonprofit desiring to refine its focus and allocation of resources, or a human resources department surveying its employees to identify needs for new training programs. Methodologies for conducting needs assessments can include focus groups, personal interviews, review of administrative data, archival data analysis, or surveys. McKillip (1998) provides an easily accessible and concise guide to conducting needs assessments.

Type of Evaluation: Process/Formative and/ or Outcome/Summative

Process and Formative Evaluations. The terms *formative evaluation* and *process evaluation* are often used synonymously to classify evaluation activity. Although there is a distinction between the two approaches, it is important to note that they are complementary rather than contradictory (Dehar, Casswell, & Duignan, 1993). Process evaluation focuses on documenting and analyzing the way a program works to isolate and understand the influences that affect its operation. A process evaluation aims to understand how a program achieves the results it does. Formative evaluation differs in that it is ongoing and seeks to assist decision makers in refining and improving a program. Collection, synthesis, and feedback of information are continuous. Thus, formative evaluations would be employed to achieve continuous improvement of newly developed programs, especially those that have not yet achieved a desired level of efficiency or consistency (see Stetler et al., 2006, for an example of formative evaluation in a clinical setting).

Outcome and Summative Evaluations. *Outcome evaluation* and *summative evaluation* are often used interchangeably in discussing program evaluation, and this interchangeability may contribute to some confusion. A convenient way to draw distinctions between the two is to examine the differences in the scope and sophistication of the research involved. Outcome evaluations tend to be focused, whereas summative evaluations tend to be more comprehensive.

Outcome evaluations tend to focus on the specific objectives defined for a program. Program objectives are likely to be short-term compared with the long-term goals of the program. Thus, the achievement of program objectives can be more immediately measured and evaluated at specific points as the program elements are deployed. On the other hand, overall program goals may not be realized until years into the future and are more the focus of a summative evaluation. Trochim (2006) views summative evaluation broadly and subdivides it into several subtypologies of activities. Summative evaluations can have a significant impact on the future of the program and the

THE CENTERS FOR DISEASE CONTROL'S FRAMEWORK FOR EVALUATING INJURY AND VIOLENCE PREVENTION PROGRAMS

The Centers for Disease Control's framework for evaluating injury and violence prevention programs was developed for mixed methods evaluation. Nesbit et al. (2018) reported on how the program evaluation was designed and how the approach evolved to meet emerging challenges. The framework was used to build state health department capacity that was shown to affect short- and longer term outcomes. The basic framework was as follows:

- Development of SMART (specific, measurable, achievable, relevant, and time bound) objectives to assess health impact

- Analysis of evidence for the strategies being developed

- State health department organizational capacity indicators

- Performance measures (completing state-mandated annual activities)

- Qualitative success stories

Examples of Program Evaluation in the Literature

- Need for service programs: needs assessments (Altschuld & Kumar, 2009; Barnett, 2012; Soriano, 2013; World Health Organization, 2000)

- Efficiency of service program processes: formative/process evaluations and cost–benefit analyses (Coulon et al., 2012; Mohamadi & Malekshahi, 2018; Saunders, Evans, & Joshi, 2005; Steckler & Linnan, 2002; Wholey, Hatry, & Newcomer, 2004)

- Effectiveness of service program outcomes: outcome evaluations and impact analyses (Mohr, 1995; Rossi, Lipsey, & Freeman, 2003; Schalock, 2001; Williams-Reade, Gordon, & Wray, 2014)

- Efficiency of educational intervention processes: formative/process evaluations and cost–benefit analyses (Davis, Orpinas, & Horne, 2012; Jimison, Adler, Coye, Mulley, & Eng, 1999; Oakley et al., 2006)

- Effectiveness of educational interventions: outcome evaluations and impact analyses (Durlak, Weissberg, Dymnicki, Taylor, & Schellinger, 2011; Paul, Yeats, Clarke, Matthews, & Skrabala, 2015)

- Evaluation of instructional curriculum: formative/process evaluations, outcome evaluations, impact analyses, and cost–benefit analyses (Volkwein, 2010)

- The role of program evaluation in organizational transformation (Schalock, Verdugo, & van Loon, 2018)

stakeholders involved. Therefore, cost–benefit analyses, impact analyses, and other politically sensitive evaluations are major endeavors and are usually best performed by experienced evaluators.

Cost–benefit analysis attempts to determine the resources required to achieve a specific amount of change, whereas impact evaluations assess the intended or unintended effects of a program. Cost–benefit analysis often employs a more microlevel focus on the costs associated with achieving specific objectives within the program, which are then used to explore where more cost-effective alternatives may be needed. Such analyses can result in leaner programs that are more resilient to changes. Impact analysis tends to employ a macrolevel focus to measure the broad, holistic benefit of a program. For example, an impact evaluation could assess the degree of change, in relation to an overall problem, that would not have been realized in the absence of the program. Therefore, impact analyses are commonly associated with policy development and especially with policy evaluation.

PROGRAM EVALUATION ALIGNMENT AND DESIGN

Questions for the Evaluator

The most basic program evaluation question is "Does the program work?" There are, however, many other questions evaluators might choose to ask given the context of the program they are asked to address. Each of these alternative questions can be further specified. For example, the question "Can an existing program be improved?" could be approached as increasing efficiency, reducing costs, improving deliverables, expanding the scope of impact, or any combination of these possibilities. Examples of questions for evaluators to ask include the following:

- Is there a need for a new program?

- What would a new program require to yield success?

- Are there difficulties with program implementation?

- Can an existing program be improved?

- Is the operation of the program worthwhile?

- Does the current program still meet the needs of its participants?

- What is the impact of the program?

- Does the program produce any unintended consequences?

Methodological Approaches Used in Program Evaluation

Qualitative, quantitative, and mixed methods are commonly involved in program evaluation. Qualitative methods are especially valuable in the early stages of a program's development. Interviews, open-ended surveys, and/or focus groups are effective tools in starting the program. These approaches afford the opportunity to fill critical gaps in knowledge or understanding that may exist related to planning or guiding the program during the early stages of deployment.

Quantitative approaches are useful to answer how much and to what extent. They can provide powerful and convincing documentation of the problem a program seeks to address. Segmentation of such data can also guide program planning to target specific populations at greater risk.

Mixed methods research is commonly used in program evaluation. These designs leverage the advantages of both quantitative and qualitative approaches to address complex and often evolving research questions the evaluator must answer over the longitudinal cycles encountered in program evaluation. The quantitative and qualitative components of mixed methods designs can be applied either sequentially or concurrently to align with the research questions.

Data for Program Evaluation Studies

Data for program evaluations may be aligned to resolve a single research question or several different questions. Single research questions can be simple and straightforward (e.g., specific-outcome analyses) or complex and multifaceted (e.g., cost–benefit analyses, impact analyses). Alternatively, an internal evaluator is usually engaged with a project over an extended period and will face a series of questions that are aligned to a program's need for information. Thus, evaluation commonly requires collecting different types of data to triangulate in addressing more complex questions or to inform and guide a program over time.

Data Sources. Data analyses in program evaluation are often used for decision-making, planning, and deployment of the program. Because any delays in data collection and analysis can jeopardize the entire program, effective evaluators develop data collection plans, procedures, and permissions well in advance to ensure that the evaluation (and the program) is not compromised. Each of the data sources described in Table 17.1 is commonly employed in program evaluation, and all have benefits that must be weighed against the logistic requirements they present.

Because the specific elements of an evaluation design include a wide application of data analysis methods, sampling approaches need to be aligned to each research question and analytic strategy employed within each component of the overall design. Some factors to consider would include the size of the target population the program is intended to serve, the scope of the program's application within that population, adequate statistical power to support the quantitative analyses proposed, and a means of ensuring adequate saturation in the qualitative components.

Sampling strategies and techniques are critical in acquiring valid and meaningful data. These include aligning appropriate sampling methods for each component of the evaluation model. For example, a random sampling approach is often desired in controlling for alternative explanations of inferential quantitative analyses; however, purposeful-selection techniques may be better suited to answer research questions or in situations where subpopulations would be statistically underpowered. Purposeful selection of a smaller number of participants is common practice in qualitative components of an evaluation. Often, purposeful selection for interviews, narrative methods, or focus groups entails identifying and recruiting

TABLE 17.1 ● DATA SOURCES, ADVANTAGES AND DISADVANTAGES		
Data Source	**Advantages**	**Potential Disadvantages**
Archival data	Often a source of rich data; already exists and does not require collection; low logistical demand	Difficult to gain access/permission to use; limitations due to method of collection or coding; may be of poor quality or nonrepresentational; may be too old
Surveys	Easy and common method for collecting information from large numbers of people; average participant is familiar with surveys; moderate logistical demand relative to data collected; can be cost efficient	Logistic considerations related to identifying/accessing a sample relative to survey method used (internet, mail, phone, hand distributed hardcopy); language barriers; low return rates
Interviews	Allows more in-depth questioning/probing; can verify that participants understand questions; allows interviewer to verify that respondent fits the sampling criteria; potential to gain greater insight into nuances of research question	Logistic considerations related to identifying/accessing a sample relative to interview method used (phone, face-to-face); potential for interviewer bias; physical presence of interviewer may influence response
Field observations (including participant observation)	Direct observation of activity versus self-report; ability to recognize unanticipated influences stemming from social–ecological context surrounding observed activity; helps in understanding interrelationships between program stakeholders	Logistic considerations related to identifying/accessing appropriate observation site; potential for observer bias in coding data; physical presence of observer may influence behavior of those observed; safety of observer; requires significant time commitment for data collection
Document review	Qualitative alternative to quantitative archival data; good source of retrospective information; already exists and does not require collection; low logistical demand	Difficult to gain access/permission to use; may be biased; may be of poor quality or nonrepresentational; may be too old
Focus groups	Participant interaction can generate rich information; potential to gain greater insight into nuances of research question; can help in understanding interrelationships between stakeholders	Logistic considerations related to identifying/recruiting appropriate group; potential for group members to be overly dominant; potential for biased information; presence of group leader may influence responses of group

key informants who possess valid knowledge, information, and/or the expertise required to answer a research question.

Different sources of data can present unique challenges to devising an effective sampling strategy. For example, sampling protocols for observational data collection can require significant planning and previewing. Even the simple step of defining the sampling window needs to consider how the target activity varies across time and within social and physical environments to ensure that observers are in the right place at the right time of day and over an appropriate period of time to provide a valid accounting of the activity. Similarly, document analysis will require substantial advanced planning to map a sampling plan regarding how archived documents are located, how they are categorized for relevance to the research question, and how many are selected for coding and analysis.

For program evaluators who know how to use existing data effectively, archival data—information already stored by organizations (or data that *will be* collected and stored)—is often a valuable resource. Existing data can provide an efficient means of answering time-sensitive questions quickly or, alternatively, can provide comprehensive data to address other questions. Four simple questions to consider regarding archival data are the following:

1. Do the data exist?

2. Are the data good? The quality of the data is very important. What types of quantitative or qualitative data are available? What is the level of measurement for quantitative data? Are the data of adequate quality (free of obvious bias in the content or significant gaps in the data collected)?

3. Are the data relevant? What types of statistical analysis can be used with the data? What types of questions can one ask of these data? Do the existing data fairly and equitably represent all stakeholders' needs?

4. May I use the data? Which stakeholders need to grant permission to use the data? Will these stakeholders allow unbiased reporting of results?

Data Analysis Techniques

A wide variety of analytic techniques are employed in program evaluation. Combinations of the following techniques would be applied depending on whether a program is applying simple exploratory techniques in early needs assessments and formative evaluations or more sophisticated, multivariate analyses to perform summative, impact, or cost–benefit evaluations:

- Systematic coding and analysis of qualitative data for either emergent or a priori themes

- Descriptive statistics usually segmented by subpopulations or conditions

- A wide variety of inferential quantitative analyses

Analysis strategies should be considered within the logistic context of the availability of data or the ability to collect new data in a timely manner. An optimal technique looks good on paper; however, only the optimal *feasible* technique will produce a successful evaluation. Evaluation planning with stakeholders should also address new data collection in advance and tie data collection into the normal flow of routine activities whenever possible.

How to Ensure Quality: Evaluation Standards

Program evaluators must provide evidence of the trustworthiness, validity, and/or reliability of their measures and establish that the research designs answer the questions posed by the evaluation (see Chapter 12 for more detailed information on quality considerations in research). Since 1975, the Joint Committee on Standards for Educational Evaluation (http://www.jcsee.org/) has provided a coalition of professional associations dedicated to the quality of evaluation practice. Yarbrough, Shulha, Hopson, and Caruthers (2011) present detailed definitions that provide excellent references from which to benchmark the quality of the evaluation process and products. Evaluation processes should meet standards for utility, feasibility, propriety, and accountability, whereas the products produced in the evaluation should be held to standards of utility, propriety, accuracy, and accountability. Although initially focused on program evaluation within educational settings, the standards are largely generalizable to a variety of evaluation contexts.

Common standards that evaluations processes should meet include the following:

- Utility standards are intended to increase the extent to which program stakeholders find evaluation processes and products valuable in meeting their needs.

- Feasibility standards are intended to increase evaluation effectiveness and efficiency.

- Propriety standards support what is proper, fair, legal, right, and just in evaluations.

- Accuracy standards are intended to increase the dependability and truthfulness of evaluation representations, propositions, and findings, especially those that support interpretations and judgments about quality.

- Accountability standards encourage adequate documentation of evaluations and a meta-evaluative perspective focused on improvement and accountability of evaluation processes and products.

Finally, professional (and some private) organizations provide stewardship and guidance related to expectations for evaluation research ethics and quality within specific fields, including the following:

- The American Evaluation Association is the membership organization for professional program evaluators and offers professional development training.

- The Association of Institutional Research is a long-standing organization that specializes in institutional research specifically as it applies to research and assessment in higher education.

- The American Educational Research Association is generally regarded as the premier organization serving the practice of educational research.

- The W. K. Kellogg Foundation is a major philanthropic organization that hosts an excellent knowledge center that contains useful guides for logic model development and an evaluation handbook that is useful in program development and grant writing.

Questions for Reflection

1. You have been contacted by the new superintendent of a local K–12 school district, who questions the effectiveness of a vendor-produced reading intervention program. The claim is that the program leads to increased participation and success in advanced placement courses. The district has used the program for 6 years and has a database of state-mandated student reading scores and advanced placement course participation and performance that extends back at least 10 years. You are considering becoming the program evaluator. How might you proceed?

2. Zent Behavioral Counseling Services asks you to perform the final outcomes assessment for a two-year project that faced several delays in getting started. Moreover, confusion among the stakeholders delivering services led to some clients not receiving all the elements of the program, and only a few individuals have completed the full program due to these issues. What would you advise?

3. How would you have approached the Zent Behavioral Counseling Services case above had you been recruited at the planning stage for the grant application?

4. What program evaluation practices generally align to your current training and experience? What specific professional development activities would most enhance your evaluation skills?

Key Sources

Linfield, K. J., & Posovac, E. J. (2018). *Program evaluation: Methods and case studies*. New York, NY: Routledge.

Nesbit, B., Hertz, M., Thigpen, S., Castellanos, T., Brown, M., Porter, J., & Williams, A. (2018). Innovative methods for designing actionable program evaluation. *Journal of Public Health Management and Practice, 24*(Suppl 1), S12–S22. doi:10.1097/PHH.0000000000000682

Patton, M. Q. (2008). *Utilization focused evaluation* (4th ed.). Thousand Oaks, CA: SAGE.

Soriano, F. I. (2013). *Conducting needs assessment: A multidisciplinary approach* (2nd ed.). Thousand Oaks, CA: SAGE.

Steckler, A. B., & Linnan, L. (Eds.). (2002). *Process evaluation for public health interventions and research*. San Francisco, CA: Jossey-Bass.

Stufflebeam, D. L. (2014). *Evaluation theory, models, and applications*. San Francisco, CA: Jossey-Bass.

Wholey, J. S., Hatry, H. P., & Newcomer, K. E. (2004). *Handbook of practical program evaluation* (2nd ed.). San Francisco, CA: Jossey-Bass.

Yarbrough, D. B., Shulha, L. M., Hopson, R. K., & Caruthers, F. A. (2011). *The program evaluation standards: A guide for evaluators and evaluation users* (3rd ed.). Thousand Oaks, CA: SAGE.

References

Alkin, M. C. (2004). *Evaluation roots*. Thousand Oaks, CA: SAGE.

Altschuld, J., & Kumar, D. (2009). *Needs assessment: An overview*. Thousand Oaks, CA: SAGE. Retrieved from http://www.sage-ereference.com/view/needs-assessment-an-overview/SAGE.xml? rskey=5Br3kd&row=10

American Evaluation Association. (2018). *Guiding principles for evaluators*. Retrieved from https://www.eval.org/p/cm/ld/fid=51

Barnett, K. (2012). *Best practices for community health needs assessment and implementation strategy development: A review of scientific methods, current practices, and future potential report*. Report of proceedings from a public forum and interviews of experts, Atlanta, GA. Retrieved from http://www.phi.org/uploads/application/files/dz9vh55o3bb2x56lcrzyel83fwfu3mvu24oqqvn5z6qaeiw2u4.pdf

Conrad, K. J., Randolph, F. L., Kirby, M. W., Jr., & Bebout, R. R. (1999). Creating and using logic models: Four perspectives. *Alcoholism Treatment Quarterly, 17*(1–2), 17–31. doi:10.1300/J020v17n01pass:[_]02

Coulon, S. M., Wilson, D. K., Griffin, S., St. George, S. M., Alia, K. A., Trumpeter, N. N., . . . Gadson, B. (2012). Formative process evaluation for implementing a social marketing intervention to increase walking among African Americans in the Positive Action for Today's Health trial. *American Journal of Public Health, 102*(12), 2315–2321. doi:10.2105/AJPH.2012.300758

Davis, M., Orpinas, P., & Horne, A. M. (2012). Design and evaluation of prevention programs. In E. Vera (Ed.), *The Oxford handbook of prevention in counseling psychology* (pp. 91–108). Oxford, UK: Oxford University Press. doi:10.1093/oxfordhb/9780195396423.013.0007

Dehar, M. A., Casswell, S., & Duignan, P. (1993). Formative and process evaluation of health promotion and disease prevention programs. *Evaluation Review, 17*(2), 204–220. doi:10.1177/0193841X9301700205

Durlak, J. A., Weissberg, R. P., Dymnicki, A. B., Taylor, R. D., & Schellinger, K. B. (2011). The impact of enhancing students' social and emotional learning: A meta-analysis of school-based universal interventions. *Child Development, 82*(1), 405–432. doi:10.1111/j.1467-8624.2010.01564.x

Hogan, R. L. (2007). The historical development of program evaluation: Exploring the past and present. *Online Journal of Workforce Education and Development, 2*(4), 1–14.

Jimison, H., Adler, L., Coye, M., Mulley, A., Jr., & Eng, T. R. (1999). Health care providers and purchasers and evaluation of interactive health communication applications. *American Journal of Preventive Medicine, 16*(1), 16–22. doi:10.1016/S0749-3797(98)00105-6

Joint Committee on Standards for Educational Evaluation. (2011). *Program evaluation standards*. Retrieved from http://www.jcsee.org/program-evaluation-standards

Linfield, K. J., & Posovac, E. J. (2018). *Program evaluation: Methods and case studies*. New York, NY: Routledge.

Marshall, S. L., Crowe, T. P., Oades, L. G., Deane, F. F., & Kavanaugh, D. J. (2007). A review of consumer involvement in evaluations of case management: Consistency with a recovery paradigm. *Psychiatric Services, 58*(3), 396–401. doi:10.1176/ps.2007.58.3.413

McDavid, J. C., Huse, I., & Ingleson, L. R. L. (2018). *Program evaluation and performance measurement: An introduction to practice*. Thousand Oaks, CA: SAGE.

McKillip, J. (1998). Needs analysis: Process and techniques. In L. Bickman & D. J. Rog (Eds.), *Handbook of applied social research methods* (pp. 261–284). Thousand Oaks, CA: SAGE.

McLaughlin, J. A., & Jordan, G. B. (1999). Logic models: A tool for telling your program's performance story. *Evaluation and Program Planning, 22*(1), 65–72. doi:10.1016/S0149-7189(98)00042-1

McLaughlin, J. A., & Jordan, G. B. (2015). Using logic models. In K. E. Newcomer, H. P. Hatry, & J. S. Wholey (Eds.), *Handbook of practical program evaluation* (pp. 62–87). Hoboken, NJ: Wiley. doi:10.1002/9781119171386.ch3

Mohamadi, Z., & Malekshahi, N. (2018). Designing and validating a potential formative evaluation inventory for teacher competences. *Language Testing in Asia, 8*(1), 1–21. doi:10.1186/s40468-018-0059-2

Mohr, L. B. (1995). *Impact analysis for program evaluation.* Thousand Oaks, CA: SAGE.

Nesbit, B., Hertz, M., Thigpen, S., Castellanos, T., Brown, M., Porter, J., & Williams, A. (2018). Innovative methods for designing actionable program evaluation. *Journal of Public Health Management and Practice, 24*(Suppl 1), S12–S22. doi:10.1097/PHH.0000000000000682

Oakley, A., Strange, V., Bonell, C., Allen, E., Stephenson, J., & RIPPLE Study Team. (2006). Health services research: Process evaluation in randomised controlled trials of complex interventions. *British Medical Journal, 332*(7538), 413. doi:10.1136/bmj.332.7538.413

Paul, C., Yeats, J., Clarke, C. P., Matthews, M., & Skrabala, L. (2015). *Assessing and evaluating Department of Defense efforts to inform, influence, and persuade*. Santa Monica, CA: RAND Corporation.

Rossi, P. H., Lipsey, M. W., & Freeman, H. E. (2003). *Evaluation: A systematic approach*. Thousand Oaks, CA: SAGE.

Saunders, R. P., Evans, M. H., & Joshi, P. (2005). Developing a process-evaluation plan for assessing health promotion program implementation: A how-to guide. *Health Promotion Practice, 6*(2), 134–147. doi:10.1177/1524839904273387

Schalock, R. L. (2001). *Outcome-based evaluation* (2nd ed.). New York, NY: Kluwer Academic/Plenum.

Schalock, R. L., Verdugo, M. A., & van Loon, J. (2018). Understanding organization transformation in evaluation and program planning. *Evaluation and Program Planning, 67*, 53–60. doi:10.1016/j.evalprogplan.2017.11.003

Soriano, F. I. (2013). *Conducting needs assessment: A multidisciplinary approach* (2nd ed.). Thousand Oaks, CA: SAGE.

Steckler, A. B., & Linnan, L. (Eds.). (2002). *Process evaluation for public health interventions and research*. San Francisco, CA: Jossey-Bass.

Stetler, C. B., Legro, M. W., Wallace, C. M., Bownam, C., Guihan, M., Hegedorn, H., . . . Smith, J. L. (2006). The role of formative evaluation in implementation research and the QUERI experience. *Journal of General Internal Medicine, 21*(Suppl. 2), S1–S8. doi:10.1111/j.1525-1497.2006.00355.x

Trochim, W. M. (2006). *The research methods knowledge base* (2nd ed.). Retrieved from http://www.socialresearchmethods.net/kb/

Volkwein, J. F. (Ed.). (2010). *Assessing student outcomes: Why, who, what, how?* (New Directions for Institutional Research, Assessment Supplement 2009). Chichester, UK: Wiley.

Wholey, J. S., Hatry, H. P., & Newcomer, K. E. (2004). *Handbook of practical program evaluation* (2nd ed.). San Francisco, CA: Jossey-Bass.

Williams-Reade, J., Gordon, B. A., & Wray, W. (2014). A primer in program evaluation for MedFTs. In J. Hodgson, A. Lamson, T. Mendenhall, & D. R. Crane (Eds.), *Medical family therapy* (pp. 283–299). New York, NY: Springer. doi:10.1007/978-3-319-03482-9

W. K. Kellogg Foundation logic model development guide. (2004). Retrieved from http://www.smartgivers.org/uploads/logicmodelguidepdf.pdf

World Health Organization. (2000). *Workbook 3: Needs assessment*. Retrieved from http://www.unodc.org/docs/treatment//needs_assessment.pdf

Yarbrough, D. B., Shulha, L. M., Hopson, R. K., & Caruthers, F. A. (2011). *The program evaluation standards: A guide for evaluators and evaluation users* (3rd ed.). Thousand Oaks, CA: SAGE.

ACTION RESEARCH

Craig A. Mertler

INTRODUCTION

Action research is research conducted by practitioners to directly and immediately inform their own practice. It involves a process of studying real organizational settings to address problems or answer questions that are important at the local level of the organization. Action research is a systematic and cyclical process, where the outcomes of one cycle serve to inform subsequent cycles.

In this chapter, I describe action research as an effective and practical approach to solving contextualized organizational problems and answering related questions. I begin with an explanation of what action research is and is not—including comparisons with more traditional research conducted in social, behavioral, management, or educational settings, which is then followed by a brief history of the beginnings of action research. I then introduce and describe the action research process, including appropriate methods and procedures that can be used for data collection and analysis, and ways in which action researchers can establish rigor in action research studies. Finally, practical applications of action research in various contexts are discussed.

CHARACTERISTICS OF ACTION RESEARCH

Over the past couple of decades, action research has seen increased attention from professionals in a wide range of disciplines around the country (Mills, 2014). As an obvious indicator, one need only look at the typical research methods course as a required element in many graduate-level programs offered in colleges and universities. This required course in professional practice programs has begun to change from a traditional overview course on research methods to one focused on practically applied action research. This change has occurred largely due to the fact that professionals—at all levels—have increasingly begun to seek out research that is able to directly inform practice.

Action research has been defined as any systematic inquiry conducted by professionals or other practitioners with vested interests in learning more about how their particular organizations or other collaborative communities operate, how they lead or collaborate within the organization, and the extent to which their desired outcomes are met (Mertler, 2017; Mills, 2014). It is research done *by* practitioners *for* themselves; it is conceptualized by practitioners and is not imposed on them by someone else. Stated differently, action research is a process of studying actual social, behavioral, or educational settings or situations in an effort to better understand and to improve the quality and outcomes of actions or broader level work (Johnson, 2012). It is imperative to note that it is a systematic process and not a haphazard trial-and-error exercise. Action research represents a scientific and systematic set of procedures designed to help professionals and other practitioners—or groups of practitioners—identify a problem, design and implement an intervention or other alternative approach to the problem, assess the effectiveness of the proposed solution, and then develop a plan for where to proceed next.

Even though action research has been practiced for decades, there still tend to be some misconceptions about it as a means of conducting research. It is important to clearly understand what action research *is* and what it *is not*. The following two lists, compiled from several sources (Johnson, 2012; Mertler, 2017; Mills, 2014; Schmuck, 1997), is an overview of what action research is and is not. Action research is

- a process involving practitioners working together to improve their own practices.

- a process that improves organizations (or other collaborative communities) by incorporating change.

- a planned, systematic approach to understanding the processes.

- authoritative and persuasive, since it is done by practitioners for themselves.

- collaborative, in that it comprises practitioners talking and working with others in empowering relationships.

- practical and relevant to practitioners, since it allows them direct and immediate access to research findings.

- focused on developing critical reflection about one's own, specific practice.

- an open-minded process that allows us to "test" our ideas.

- a justification of one's professional practices.

Equally important is understanding what action research is *not*. Action research is

- not the usual thing that educators do when thinking about teaching; it is much more systematic and collaborative.

- not simple, haphazard, trial-and-error problem solving; it involves the specification of a problem, the development of something new (in most cases), and critical reflection on its effectiveness.

- not done "to" or "by" other people; it is research done by specific practitioners on their own practices.

- not the implementation of predetermined answers to problems or questions; it is more about exploration and discovery to find creative solutions to those problems.

- not a fad; it is a systematic process that should always be part of good professional practices.

Action research offers a process by which *current* practice can be changed to *better* practice. The overarching goal of action research is to improve practice *immediately* within a small, local setting or organizational community (McMillan, 2012). Because action research is so focused on examining and improving one's own practice, reflection is an integral component of the overall process (Mertler, 2019). Reflection is the act of critically exploring what you are doing, why you decided to do it, and what its effects have been. Professionals must become active participants in their various settings, as well as active observers of the processes that occur there. They must develop skills that enable them to observe, analyze, and interpret information—collected in a systematic manner—and then use that information as a basis for future decision-making (Mertler, 2019). This process of systematic collection of information, followed by active and engaged reflection—all with the goal of improving local practice—is the core of action research (Mertler, 2017).

Arguably, there are two general approaches to conducting action research—*participatory action research* and *practical action research*. The purpose of participatory action research is to improve the quality of the lives of individuals who make up organizations, communities, and families. Its focus is on empowering individuals and groups to improve their lives and to bring about social change on some level (Fraenkel, Wallen, & Hyun, 2012). Within the literature, this type of action research may also be referred to as community-based inquiry, collaborative action research, emancipatory action research, or critical action research (Creswell, 2005; Fraenkel et al., 2012; Gay, Mills, & Airasian, 2009).

In contrast, practical action research is focused on addressing a specific problem or need in a social, behavioral, or educational community (Fraenkel et al., 2012). Compared with participatory action research, the focus of practical action research is much more about the "how-to" approach to the process of actually conducting action research, as opposed to a more philosophical approach (Gay et al., 2009). Gay et al. (2009) list three guiding assumptions for the implementation of practical action research:

1. Individual practitioners or teams of practitioners are able to determine the nature of an action research investigation to be undertaken.

2. Action researchers are committed to continuous professional development and organizational improvement through a process of critical reflection.

3. Action researchers are capable of choosing their own areas of focus, determining plans for conducting the research, and developing action plans based on their findings.

For purposes of this chapter, in this book, our coverage of the methodological approach of action research will focus on practical action research.

Comparisons to Traditional Research in Organizational Settings

An additional approach to better understanding the nature of action research is to consider it alongside more traditional forms of research conducted in organizational settings. Traditional research is typically conducted by researchers who are, to varying degrees, removed from the environment or setting they are studying (Mertler, 2017). This does not mean that they are not committed to the research study and truly interested in the ultimate findings but rather that they are studying people, settings, or programs with which they are seldom personally involved (Schmuck, 1997). In fact, in many instances, they may be removed from the actual research site. Traditional researchers often seek to find explanations for existing phenomena and try to do so in an objective manner. The primary goal of traditional research is to describe, explain, predict, or control phenomena (Gay et al., 2009).

In traditional research, different research methods—that is, the specific techniques used to collect and analyze data—provide researchers with different ways to view a given reality. Qualitative methods involve the collection and analysis of visual and verbal data (e.g., observation notes, interview transcriptions, journal entries, sociograms, pictures, videotapes), whereas quantitative methods involve collection and analysis of numerical data (e.g., scores, ratings, attitude scales). Mixed methods research combines qualitative and quantitative in an attempt to reveal a more accurate picture of the phenomenon being studied.

While both traditional and action approaches to research rely on the use of systematic inquiry, there are several fundamental differences between action research and formal, traditional research, three of which are most salient here. First, the goal of all action research is to solve local-level problems and, ultimately, to make decisions, such as choosing which therapeutic model to adopt or which reading program to purchase. The goal of more traditional research is to develop and test theories and to produce knowledge that is applicable to broader populations of individuals. Second, action research is conducted by professionals and other practitioners, whereas traditional research is conducted by researchers who have been specifically trained to do so, and who are not usually involved in the local setting. Third, and perhaps most important, generalizability—while an important and necessary feature of traditional research—is not a goal of action research. The attention and priority in action research is only on the local setting and/or problem; being able to extend the findings to other similar settings beyond that which was studied firsthand is not an emphasis of action research.

Origins of Action Research

The origins of action research can be traced back to Kurt Lewin, who is credited with coining the term *action research* around 1934. His early research focused on workplace studies that compared the effectiveness of various methods of training factory workers (Hendricks, 2013). Lewin believed strongly that research conducted specifically *within* the context in which a problem existed was the key to arriving at a solution to that problem, or to institute some degree of change, and that more traditional forms of research could not accomplish this:

> The research needed for social practice can best be characterized as research for social management or social engineering. It is a type of *action-research* [italics added], a comparative research on the conditions and effects of various forms of social action, and research leading to social action. Research that produces nothing but books will not suffice. (Lewin, 1946, p. 35)

Lewin viewed action research as a process of spiraling reflection, inquiry, and action taken by stakeholders for the ultimate purposes of improving work environments and addressing social problems (Hendricks, 2013): "Rational social management, therefore, proceeds in a spiral of steps each of which is composed of a circle of planning, action, and fact-finding about the result of the action" (Lewin, 1946, p. 38).

Lewin's inclusion of the concept that democratic workplaces increase both worker motivation and productivity became a hallmark of his eventual theory of action research (Hendricks, 2013).

THE ACTION RESEARCH PROCESS

A critical feature of action research is that it is considered a *cyclical*—as opposed to linear—process. In other words, the process begins by examining current practices to identify a key problem or question or, perhaps more important, the cause of an identified problem. Analysis and considerations of that key problem or question then lead to the development or identification of an alternative approach or solution that is proposed and implemented. The implementation is accompanied by observations, monitoring, and/or other forms of data collection and analysis. Along with professional reflection, the result is some sort of action planned and taken for future implementation. This action plan and reflection serves as the impetus for the next cycle of action research. Many researchers have developed their own models of the cyclical nature of the action research process. My general model of the process, showing the four main elements of the cycle, is shown in Figure 18.1

The four stages of the model are as follows:

1. The *planning* stage
2. The *acting* stage
3. The *developing* stage
4. The *reflecting* stage

FIGURE 18.1   ⬡   THE CYCLICAL PROCESS OF ACTION RESEARCH

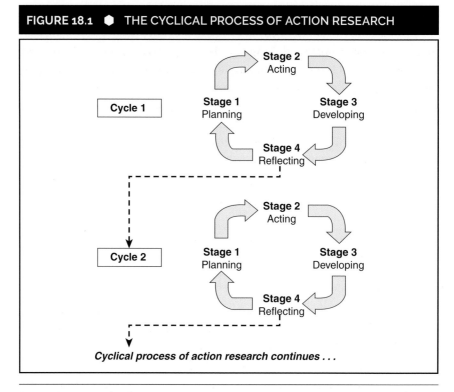

Cyclical process of action research continues . . .

Source: Mertler, C. A. (2017). *Action research: Improving schools and empowering educators* (5th ed.). Thousand Oaks, CA: SAGE. Figure 2.2

It is important to notice that the result of Stage 4—the reflecting stage—provides input and serves as the basis of Stage 1—the planning stage—of the subsequent cycle of action research.

Stage 1: The Planning Stage

Step 1: Identifying and limiting the topic. The first step of any research study is to identify what is going to be studied. In action research studies, the topic will typically stem from the personal and professional experiences of the practitioner(s) conducting the action research. It usually focuses on some issue or problem that the educators want to solve or resolve, which means they have a vested interest in the outcome of the study. The topic should also be limited, in that the practitioners must ensure that it is manageable; if it is too broad or general, it won't be possible to investigate it in a timely or practical manner. Some common topic areas for action research studies include trying a new teaching or assessment method (in education), identifying and testing an alternative counseling strategy (in behavioral sciences), and examining the effectiveness of a different communication style (in management) (Johnson, 2012).

Step 2: Gathering information. Once the topic has been identified and limited in scope, the next step is to gather preliminary information in a process known as *reconnaissance.* This gathering of information may be as simple as talking with colleagues or other coworkers to gauge their perceptions and perspectives on the proposed action research study and, perhaps, even to question them for their ideas. This process might also include reviewing professional materials to search for suggestions or ideas for new approaches to try. More formally, reconnaissance involves taking time to reflect on one's own beliefs as an educator and to get a better understanding of the nature and context of the proposed problem for investigation.

Step 3: Reviewing related literature. As with any educational research study, reviewing research that has previously been conducted is an essential step in the process. Doing so can provide a great deal of guidance in the development of an action research study. Note, however, that this is different from gathering preliminary information, as discussed in the previous step. That information is considered relatively "informal," whereas a literature review focuses on formally conducted (and published) research studies.

Step 4: Developing a research plan. The research plan is the specification of how the study will be conducted, how the intervention strategy or other alternative approach will be implemented, what data will be collected, from whom it will be collected, and how it will be analyzed. Since action research is not directly aligned with either qualitative or quantitative methods, either approach—or a mixed methods approach—may be most appropriate, depending on the nature of the action research problem. As a side note, it is largely for this reason that many researchers (e.g., Creswell, 2005; Ivankova, 2015, 2017; Mertler, 2017) see such a close alignment between action research and mixed methods research.

During this step of conducting action research, it is also important to consider various ethical issues and to pay attention to the appropriateness of the size of a desired sample. Many practitioners who are conducting action research are doing so with colleagues or other partners (some of whom may be subordinates, while others may be superiors). In action research, the researcher is also a participant, so establishing objectivity and guarding against bias will be different from other research approaches. It is important to recognize that in action research, especially when working with groups, there are often people with different knowledge levels about confidentiality and other ethical issues. It is a fundamental responsibility of the action researcher to ensure that all participants are aware of their ethical obligations and rights.

Sample size depends on the context of the project. Designs selected for inclusion in the action research process or cycles have their own sample size requirements. An action research teacher working without a team may consider focusing on improvement with an individual child ($n = 1$) or with the entire classroom ($n \approx 30$). When using a traditional quantitative or qualitative method within action research, the guidelines for choosing an appropriate sample size should be followed for that methodology. Keep in mind that sample size is different from the number of stakeholders. In action research, all stakeholders in the action research project are not necessarily members (i.e., participants) of a sample.

Stage 2: The Acting Stage

Step 5: Collecting data. In action research, virtually every type of data is a legitimate possibility to help address problems or answer questions. Action researchers are justified in using qualitative data, quantitative data, or a combination of both (i.e., mixed methods). The lone caveat is that one must be sure that the data are appropriate for the problem at hand and that their analysis and interpretation can logically follow from the nature of the problem.

Step 6: Analyzing data. Analysis of qualitative and quantitative data use different techniques and procedures, as do the analyses of data resulting from the conduct of mixed methods studies. Similar to the caveat offered in Step 5 above, the action researcher must be sure that the results of the analyses are appropriate to answer the question or problem central to the action research study.

Stage 3: The Developing Stage

Step 7: Developing an action plan. The action plan is the ultimate goal of any action research study—it is the *action* part of action research (Mertler, 2017). The action plan is the proposed strategy for implementing the results of the action research project. The plan typically consists of two parts: (1) a strategy for practical implementation of the findings within the specific context and (2) recommendations for the next cycle of action research, as the examination of the essential problem is likely to continue to be refined. Action plans can be developed and implemented at the level of an individual practitioner, a collaborative team of practitioners, or at the organizational level.

Stage 4: The Reflecting Stage

Step 8: Sharing and communicating results. Sharing the results of action research is somewhat different from traditional research. Since action research is typically done to provide benefit at the most local level, many outlets for dissemination of the results are predominantly found at the local level. Other practitioners can also benefit by learning from the experiences of others who have engaged in action research. For example, dissemination of action research projects in education settings can take many forms, including presentations at a faculty meeting or perhaps even a school board meeting; written summaries that can be provided to administrators, school board members, parents, and community members; or even presentations at larger conferences.

Step 9: Reflecting on the process. Since, at its core, action research is about critical examination of one's own professional practice, reflection on the process of conducting action research is a critical step. Professional reflection must be done at the end of each cycle of action research and may often be included as part of the action plan. However, highly effective educators and action researchers, in general, reflect on and critically examine all aspects of the action research process—before, during, and after the project. For the most part, professional reflection is done for the benefit of the actual action researchers and is often not part of what is shared or disseminated to others.

FIGURE 18.2 ● THE ACTION RESEARCH PROCESS, SHOWING SPECIFIC RESEARCH ACTIVITIES IN EACH STAGE

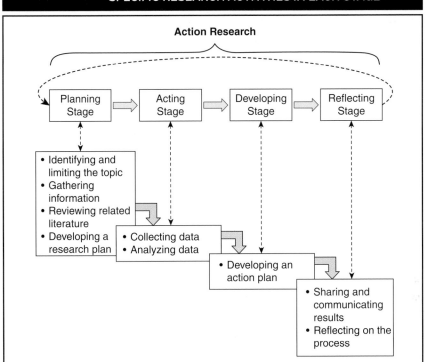

Source: Mertler, C. A. (2017). *Action research: Improving schools and empowering educators* (5th ed.). Thousand Oaks, CA: SAGE. Figure 2.1

Figure 18.2 integrates the four stages of the action research process with the specific activities or steps found at each stage. As depicted in Figure 18.2, the planning stage comprises the first four steps of the process—namely, identifying a topic for study, gathering any related background information, reviewing existing research literature, and developing a plan for the study. The acting stage consists of the actual conduct of the study, where data are collected and analyzed. The developing stage comprises a lone step—that of developing an action plan for future action and next steps. Finally, the reflecting stage includes sharing and communicating the results of the actual action research study and reflecting on the overall process. As shown in Figure 18.2, it is important to note that the reflection often leads directly into the next cycle of action research by providing the foundation for the nature of the next problem to be investigated.

RIGOR IN ACTION RESEARCH

Quality research must meet standards of sound practice (Mertler, 2019). The basis for establishing the quality of traditional research lies in the concepts of validity and reliability. Action research typically relies on a different set of standards for determining quality and credibility (Stringer, 2013). Because action research adheres to the standards of quality and credibility rather than validity and reliability, it has sometimes been criticized for being an inferior approach to research as well as for being of lesser quality. Rather than being considered lesser or inferior, action research should be viewed as being *different* from traditional research. Nevertheless, it is critical for action researchers to ensure that their research is sound (Mertler, 2019).

The extent to which action research reaches an acceptable standard of quality is directly related to the usefulness of the research findings for the intended audience (Mertler, 2019). This general level of quality is referred to as *rigor*. Rigor refers to the quality, validity, accuracy, and credibility of action research and its findings. Rigor is typically associated with the *validity* and *reliability* in quantitative studies—referring to the accuracy of instruments, data, and research findings—and with *accuracy, credibility,* and *dependability* in qualitative studies (Melrose, 2001). Melrose (2001) has suggested that the term *rigor* be used in a broader sense encompassing the entire research process and not just aspects of data collection, analysis, and findings.

Rigor in action research is typically based on procedures used to ensure that the procedures and analyses of the action research project are not biased, or reflective of only a very limited view from the researcher's perspective (Stringer, 2013). There are numerous techniques that can be used to help provide evidence of rigor within the parameters of practitioner-led action research studies (Melrose, 2001; Mills, 2014; Stringer, 2013). Among these techniques are the following:

- *Repeating the cycle:* Most action researchers tend to believe that one cycle of action research is simply not enough. Rigor can be enhanced by engaging in a number of cycles of action research into the same problem or question, where the earlier cycles help inform how to conduct later cycles, as well as specific sources of data that should be considered. In theory, with each subsequent cycle of action research, more is learned, and greater credibility is added to the findings.

- *Prolonged engagement and persistent observation:* For participants to fully understand the outcomes of an action research inquiry and process, the researcher should provide them with extended opportunities to explore and express their experiences within the study (Stringer, 2013) as it relates specifically to the problem under investigation. However, it is important to note that simply spending more time in the setting is not enough. Observations and interviews must be deliberately and carefully conducted and must be done in an ongoing manner (Mills, 2014; Stringer, 2013). It is not about the quantity of time spent in the setting, but rather, it is about the quality of the time spent.

- *Experience with the action research process:* As with virtually any type of research, experience with the process is invaluable. Rigor, itself, can be highly dependent on the experiences of the action researcher. If a professional educator had conducted previous action research studies—or even previous cycles within the same study—he or she can perform more confidently and have greater credibility with respective audiences (Melrose, 2001).

- *Triangulating the data:* Rigor can also be enhanced during the action research process by including multiple sources of data and other information. Using multiple sources of data allow the action researcher to verify the accuracy of the overall data (Mills, 2014) and clarify meanings or misconceptions held by those participating in the study (Stringer, 2013). Accuracy of data and credibility of findings go hand in hand (Mertler, 2019).

- *Member checking:* Depending on the purposes of the study, participants should be provided with the opportunity to review raw data, analyses, and final reports resulting from the action research process (Mills, 2014; Stringer, 2013). This process can be very influential in terms of validating the findings resulting from any action research study (although, it is important to note that this procedure may not be appropriate in all action research projects). Rigor is enhanced by allowing participants to verify that various aspects of the research process adequately and accurately represent their beliefs and perspectives. It also gives them the opportunity to further explain or expand on information previously provided.

- *Participant debriefing:* Similar to member checking, debriefing provides another opportunity to participants to provide insight into the conduct of the action research study. In contrast to member checking, the focus of debriefing is on their emotions and feelings, as opposed to factual information they may have provided.

APPLICATIONS OF ACTION RESEARCH

As a process for professional reflection, local-level problem solving, and data-informed decision-making, action research is an extremely versatile process. Its uses and applications are diverse, largely due to the flexible nature of the process. We have looked at action research as a process for critically examining one's professional practice, but this notion can also be extended to several important uses or applications of action research. These applications include (a) effectively connecting theory to practice, (b) improving practice, (c) fostering organizational improvement, (d) empowering participants (e.g., educators, clients, employees, and others), (e) promoting professional growth and learning, and (f) facilitating professional learning communities (PLCs; Mertler, 2017, 2019). These are described in detail below.

Connecting Theory to Practice. For many decades, the overwhelming approach for research to inform professional practice was for it to filter down from university-level, along with other researchers, to actual organizational settings. This sometimes results in a disconnect in the process, where a gap between theory and practice—in terms of what is learned by researchers and what is needed by practitioners—may be created. As we have seen in this chapter, action research conducted *by* practitioners *for* themselves can serve the needs of local-level problem solving and decision-making and may provide one possible mechanism for beginning to bridge the theory-to-practice gap.

Improving Professional Practice. The main focus of action research is the improvement of professional practices; however, leading and engaging in action research efforts require a shift in mind-set for practitioners, as well as for those who lead and supervise those practitioners. Practitioners must learn to be reflective and to critically examine their own practices. If they already do so, action research provides a systematic way to do what many already do. Once they are able to do this, they create opportunities to experience better-informed decision-making. Ultimately, this has the potential to influence and result in the direct improvement of practice at all levels.

Fostering Organizational Improvement. Generally speaking, organizational improvement is seen as large-scale, widespread, and systemic improvement. Its goals are very broad, which seems to be somewhat counterintuitive to the individualized focus of action research. However, action research is conducted in a *collaborative* manner—across classrooms in schools, departments in health facilities, and even units in business organizations. This broad, collaborative application of action research has the potential to lead to the widespread, cohesive and coordinated, and systemic improvement of virtually all aspects of the processes focused on measurable outcomes.

Empowering Participants. Action research can be used very effectively in promoting the notion of participant empowerment. When professionals take the initiative to investigate their own practices in critical and systematic fashions by identifying problems, developing interventions, collecting original data, and making informed decisions, they empower themselves to facilitate their own improvement efforts. In essence, these practitioners begin to take on roles of leadership, even if leadership is not part of their official roles or titles within the organization, department, or unit.

Promoting Professional Growth and Learning. The focus of action research is on improving practice, about discovering what works and what does not work. In most instances, it is about practicing professionals continuing to grow, develop, learn, and improve. This idea does not conform to the more traditional "one-size-fits-all" view of professional development, which typically takes the form of a training session where the focus and experience is the same for every attendee, regardless of level of experience or exposure to the topic of the training (Mertler, 2013). "More enlightened forms of professional learning operate on the assumption that educators already possess a great deal of professional knowledge and are highly capable of furthering their learning" (McNiff, 2002, p. 9). These types of professional learning capitalize on more appropriate forms of support to not only help educators celebrate what they already know, but also encourage them to develop new knowledge. Action research lends itself very nicely to this approach to professional learning. Practitioners see this type of professional development as considerably more meaningful and practical. In fact, action research is, perhaps, the epitome of *individualized* and *customizable* professional development for practitioners (Mertler, 2013).

Facilitating Professional Learning Communities. DuFour, DuFour, and Eaker (2008) have described PLCs as groups of practitioners who are committed to working collaboratively in ongoing processes of collective inquiry and *action research* to achieve better overall results for their organizations. PLCs are based on the notion that the key to improvements is continuous, job-embedded learning for practitioners. DuFour et al. (2008) go on to describe six key characteristics of PLCs:

1. A shared mission, vision, values, and goals—all focused on measurable outcomes

2. A collaborative culture

3. A collective inquiry into best practices and current reality

4. An action orientation, or learning by doing

5. A commitment to continuous improvement

6. An orientation focused on results and not on intentions.

Note that the fourth item in the list above—that is, an action orientation—essentially integrates the action research process into the culture of a collaborative group of professional practitioners. An additional key characteristic of PLCs is that innovation and experimentation are not viewed by its members as extra tasks to be completed, but rather as ways of conducting day-to-day business as a professional—directly in line with an action research mind-set.

Action Research Across the Disciplines. Action research has been used extensively and is represented in several disciplines, including business, education, sociology, psychology, organizational development, and leadership. It is deeply rooted in the politics of the oppressed, feminism, antiracism, and community transformation. Individuals and organizations in the fields of medicine, education, business, marketing, government programs, and international development are actively practicing action research today. Examples of research topics in various fields of study include the following:

- An inquiry into whether a pragmatic-oriented action research methodology may enhance the value of human capital of a business in France (Cappelletti & Baker, 2010)

- An exploration of how a high school teacher used a new way to engage his students in the required reading of classical texts in Greece (Tsafos, 2009)

- An investigation of the relationships between action research and general systems theory using the case study of environmental education activities in a rural community in Brazil (Berlinck & Saito, 2010)

- An analysis of the factors contributing to the longevity and achievements of an action group formed to improve dignity and respect toward patients and other service users at a hospital in the United Kingdom (Crow, Smith, & Keenan, 2010)

- A collaborative study exploring how teachers implemented a Spanish for Heritage Speakers course in Utah, an English-only state (Coles-Ritchie & Lugo, 2010)

- An investigation of aboriginal women, overrepresented in prisons in Australia, requiring "an Indigenous informed conceptual framework utilizing a decolonizing research methodology inclusive of enduring community and stakeholder dialogue and consultation" (Sherwood & Kendall, 2013, p. 83)

- An application of participatory action research to establish safe drinking water supplies in Bangladesh (Rammelt, 2014)

ACTION RESEARCH COMMUNITIES

Action research communities (ARCs) are defined as PLCs made up of practicing professionals, who are driven by a common goal of reflective practice as a means to guide improvement efforts (Mertler, 2016, 2018). PLCs integrate the notion of action research, but ARCs take that integration to the next level. Action research is not just an element of the learning community but is the core of it—it is the common means for all members of the ARC to achieve their individual learning and growth goals. An ARC is a PLC; however,

> the driving force behind an ARC is that action research serves as the overarching focus—the mechanism that drives a group of practitioners to its common mission and vision, and the common thread that provides the foundation for collaborative teamwork and professional growth. (Mertler, 2018, p. 68)

The only real difference between any PLC and an ARC is that the focus, mind-set, and *culture* are all based on and created around *collaborative action research in organizational settings*. In other words, the commonality shared by all the participants in the ARC is the fact that they engage in collaborative action research for the purposes of improving their practice and ultimately improving organizational outcomes. When a PLC is structured around collaborative action research at its core—thus, making it an ARC—not only is there a common vision for organizational improvement, but practitioners are also permitted to pursue school organizational improvement that is geared toward *their own identified areas* for professional growth and advancement. There is no existing structure—even for PLCs, in general—that provides practitioners these sorts of customizable professional growth opportunities (Mertler, 2018).

CONCLUSION

Action research is any systematic inquiry conducted by practitioners with vested interests in learning more about how their particular organizations or other collaborative communities operate, how they lead or collaborate within the organization, and the extent to which their desired outcomes are met. It is research done by practitioners for themselves and involves critical examination and professional reflection. Action research is distinguished by the fact that it focuses on solving local-level problems and that the results are not intended to be generalized to other settings. Many applications of action research focus on professional growth and learning for practitioners, as well as improvement of practice, general organizational improvement, and participant empowerment. ARCs are one way to implement widespread, collaborative action research in a wide variety of organizational contexts.

Questions for Reflection

1. As you think about action research, in what ways is it similar to and different from traditional qualitative and quantitative research methods?

2. What do you see as the value of professional reflection in the action research process? Why is it a critical component of action research?

3. In what ways can action research foster the improvement of individual practice, as well as the improvement of larger organizational effectiveness?

4. What might you see as potential benefits of engaging in action research as part of collaborative teams within your organization or field of study?

Key Sources

Creswell, J. W. (2005). *Educational research: Planning, conducting, and evaluating quantitative and qualitative research* (2nd ed.). Upper Saddle River, NJ: Merrill/Prentice Hall.

Hendricks, C. (2013). *Improving schools through action research: A reflective practice approach* (3rd ed.). Boston, MA: Pearson.

Johnson, A. P. (2012). *A short guide to action research* (4th ed.). Boston, MA: Pearson.

Mertler, C. A. (2017). *Action research: Improving schools and empowering educators* (5th ed.). Thousand Oaks, CA: SAGE.

Mills, G. E. (2014). *Action research: A guide for the teacher researcher* (5th ed.). Boston, MA: Pearson.

References

Berlinck, C. N., & Saito, C. H. (2010). Action research for emancipation informed by Habermas and Hierarchy of Systems: Case study on environmental education and management of water resources in Brazil. *Systemic Practice & Action Research, 23,* 143–156. doi:10.1007/s11213-009-9150-z

Cappelletti, L. G., & Baker, C. R. (2010). Developing human capital through a pragmatic oriented action research project: A French case study. *Action Research, 8,* 211–232. doi:10.1177/1476750309349976

Coles-Ritchie, M., & Lugo, J. (2010). Implementing a Spanish for heritage speaker's course in an English-only state: A collaborative critical teacher action research study. *Educational Action Research, 18*(2), 197–212. doi:10.1080/09650791003741061

Creswell, J. W. (2005). *Educational research: Planning, conducting, and evaluating quantitative and qualitative research* (2nd ed.). Upper Saddle River, NJ: Merrill/Prentice Hall.

Crow, J., Smith, L., & Keenan, I. (2010). Sustainability in an action research project: 5 Years of a Dignity and Respect action group in a hospital setting. *Journal of Research in Nursing, 15,* 55–68. doi:10.1177/1744987109352929

DuFour, R., DuFour, R., & Eaker, R. (2008). *Revisiting professional learning communities at work: New insights for improving schools.* Bloomington, IN: Solution Tree.

Fraenkel, J. R., Wallen, N. E., & Hyun, H. (2012). *How to design and evaluate research in education* (8th ed.). Boston, MA: McGraw-Hill.

Gay, L. R., Mills, G. E., & Airasian, P. W. (2009). *Educational research: Competencies for analysis and applications* (9th ed.). Upper Saddle River, NJ: Merrill.

Hendricks, C. (2013). *Improving schools through action research: A reflective practice approach* (3rd ed.). Boston, MA: Pearson.

Ivankova, N. V. (2015). *Mixed methods applications in action research: From methods to community action.* Thousand Oaks, CA: SAGE.

Ivankova, N. V. (2017). Applying mixed methods in community-based action research: A framework for engaging stakeholders with research as means for promoting patient-centeredness. *Journal of Research in Nursing, 22,* 282–294. doi:10.1177/1744987117699655

Johnson, A. P. (2012). *A short guide to action research* (4th ed.). Boston, MA: Pearson.

Lewin, K. (1946). Action research and minority problems. *Journal of Social Issues, 2*(4), 34–46. doi:10.1111/j.1540-4560.1946.tb02295.x

McMillan, J. H. (2012). *Educational research: Fundamentals for the consumer* (6th ed.). Boston, MA: Allyn & Bacon.

McNiff, J. (2002). *Action research for professional development: Concise advice for new action researchers* (3rd ed.). Dorset, UK: Author. Retrieved from http://www.jeanmcniff.com/userfiles/file/Publications/AR Booklet.doc

Melrose, M. J. (2001). Maximizing the rigor of action research: Why would you want to? How could you? *Field Methods, 13*(2), 160–180. doi:10.1177/1525822X0101300203

Mertler, C. A. (2013). Classroom-based action research: Revisiting the process as customizable and meaningful professional development for educators. *Journal of Pedagogic Development, 3*(3), 39–43.

Mertler, C. A. (2016). Leading and facilitating educational change through action research learning communities. *Journal of Ethical Educational Leadership, 3*(3), 1–11. Retrieved from http://www.cojeel.org

Mertler, C. A. (2017). *Action research: Improving schools and empowering educators* (5th ed.). Thousand Oaks, CA: SAGE.

Mertler, C. A. (2018). *Action research communities: Professional learning, empowerment, and improvement through collaborative action research.* London, UK: Routledge.

Mertler, C. A. (2019). *Introduction to educational research* (2nd ed.). Thousand Oaks, CA: SAGE.

Mills, G. E. (2014). *Action research: A guide for the teacher researcher* (5th ed.). Boston, MA: Pearson.

Rammelt, C. F. (2014). Participatory action research in marginalized communities: Safe drinking water in rural Bangladesh. *Systemic Practice and Action Research, 27,* 195–210. doi:10.1007/s11213-013-9280-1

Schmuck, R. A. (1997). *Practical action research for change.* Arlington Heights, IL: SkyLight Professional Development.

Sherwood, J., & Kendall, S. (2013). Reframing spaces by building relationships: Community collaborative participatory action research with Aboriginal mothers in prison. *Contemporary Nurse, 46*(1), 83–94. doi:10.5172/conu.2013.46.1.83

Stringer, E. (2013). *Action research* (4th ed.). Thousand Oaks, CA: SAGE.

Tsafos, V. (2009). Teacher–student negotiation in an action research project. *Educational Action Research, 17*(2), 197–211. doi:10.1080/09650790902914175

WRITING AND DISSEMINATING RESEARCH

PART VI

CRITIQUING AND SYNTHESIZING THE LITERATURE

Annie Pezalla

You might have assumed that the lessons you have learned thus far about research methods are only applicable to a methods chapter in a master's thesis or doctoral study, but this is not true. Understanding the lessons that have come before this chapter—the terminology of research, the philosophical underpinnings of research, the roles of theory, the various designs of research (qualitative, quantitative, and mixed methods), and the considerations of quality and ethics—will help you become a more critical consumer of information and, in turn, a better writer and thinker overall.

This chapter is organized into two major sections that reflect two important and parallel tasks in writing literature reviews: Critiquing the Literature and Synthesizing the Literature. Within both sections are four subsections: Definitions, where the basic meaning of each skill is clarified and elaborated; Important Considerations, where tips and guidelines are provided to facilitate the development of these skills; Common Mistakes, where examples are given of typical challenges and oversights from novice readers and writers; and Ways to Stay Organized, where strategies are offered to keep you organized.

Being able to synthesize the literature requires that you have the ability to critique it in the first place. Similarly, being able to critique the literature requires that you understand how the author(s) synthesized the work to present a coherent narrative. These skills are acquired through an abundance of *reading* not just the information provided in this chapter but also in the world of published literature. Many blossoming researchers assume that they will become proficient writers by practicing their writing. Although writing is certainly an important skill, the more pressing skill is that of reading the literature and analyzing it for all its various parts. I start this chapter on doing just that.

CRITIQUING THE LITERATURE

Definitions

Critiquing the literature means becoming an active rather than a passive reader and learning how to *interrogate* the literature. Acquiring these skills does not mean using harsh or personal criticism; rather, it requires an impersonal scrutiny of a piece of work using a balanced and objective approach. The purpose of critiquing the literature is to highlight a source's strengths as well as weaknesses in order to identify whether a piece of research is trustworthy and unbiased. As a scholar-practitioner, it is important to critically appraise the research in your field in order to identify and apply the best practices in your work.

Important Considerations

As a scholar-practitioner, you will be expected to read widely, but it is rarely possible to read *everything* that applies to your interests. To focus your attention on the most credible sources, you will need some kind of reading process, one that "progresses from the general to the particular" (Hart, 2011, p. 53). One recommended stage is the *pre-evaluation stage*, which allows you to quickly assess the utility of a source. A good place to start is to read the source's abstract, which can help determine if the study is relevant to your interests. It might also reveal the methods used in the study, the basic findings, and the recommendations for future research. If the abstract looks relevant, you can proceed with reading the article.

After reading the abstract, note the author(s) who wrote the study. Some authors carry a great deal of credibility in their work, so seeing a familiar author name can validate the quality of a source. This does not suggest that an article should be dismissed because it was written by an unknown author, but it would behoove you to become well-read on the giants of your field, those who are heavily published and well respected. If the source is written by a well-known author or even if you recognize some of the names in the source's references section, the source is likely credible.

Another consideration in this pre-evaluation stage is to note the publication date. Unless the source is considered a *seminal* source, serving as a pivotal piece in your field through a major breakthrough or insight or a new synthesis of ideas, if it was published more than 5 years ago, it may be less valuable to you and your research. Our understanding of trends, methods, and theoretical applications is continually changing, so reading the most recently published work will generally benefit you the most.

The type of publication is also important to note in this stage. You will likely be required to read and report on primarily peer-reviewed literature. This requirement ensures that the materials you are reading have been vetted by an established panel of professionals who abide by a common set of standards in accepting submissions. Journal editors are charged to look for manuscripts that "(a) contribute significantly to the content area covered by the journal, (b) communicate with clarity and conciseness, and (c) follow style guidelines" (American Psychological Association, 2010, p. 226). The reviewers of any peer-reviewed journal typically perform a masked review of the manuscript submissions to their journal; this means that they remain unaware of the author(s) who contributed the submission. This masked review process protects against any potential favoritism toward or unfairness against authors who are familiar to the reviewers; it also helps mitigate any potential gender bias. The important thing to remember is that if you are reading a peer-reviewed article, the odds are in your favor that you are reading a high-quality piece of literature that has withstood a lot of scrutiny and is, subsequently, viewed as credible.

You may be tempted to read other types of resources for your research, such as popular journals or magazines like *Business Week*, *Time*, or *People*. Those resources may be a good starting place to spark an interest in a topic. Indeed, they can be enjoyable to read because they tend to use more casual language than what you would find in a scholarly source. Walsh, Pezalla, and Marshall (2014) illustrated the language differences between popular- and peer-reviewed sources, contrasting a popular-source claim, "Grammar is dead! A new poll shows that text language is becoming more acceptable in the workplace, and we couldn't be happier! LOL!" with a scholarly-source claim, "The correct use of grammar in early college assignments has shown downward trends among young adults" (p. 61). Despite the focus on the same broad topic, however, the content of a popular source is unlikely to have withstood the same scrutiny as a peer-reviewed source. It is important, then, to rely most heavily on peer-reviewed sources.

After you have pre-evaluated a source, it is time to dig deeper, to review the value of that source in terms of its integrity. How robust is the research method? How appropriately did the researcher follow the steps in the research process? The answers to those questions will help you decipher the veracity of the source.

Determining the robustness of the research method requires, first and foremost, confirming that a method has been presented. Sometimes this information is omitted altogether, especially in sources that are not peer-reviewed. Perhaps the author provided no information about the sample that was recruited, the instruments that were used, or the inferential statistics employed to achieve the results. If that information has been omitted, the source lacks integrity, and you should use caution in including such a source in your research.

Most often, your assessment of a source's methods will be a little more ambiguous. An author may provide *some* information about his or her method but may never specify, for example, the instrument that was used to collect the data; alternatively, the author might list the questions in an instrument but never specify whether the instrument was tested for reliability or validity. Note these bits of detail that are provided and ask yourself whether the information is sufficient to justify the claims made in the results section. Also, note whether the approach is a logical one to address a problem and whether the information is clearly presented.

As you read a source, you will also need to decipher how appropriately and accurately the author follows the steps of the research process. All claims should be substantiated in the study, either with information from well-respected sources or from the author's own careful data collection or analysis. If you see any grandiose claims in a source (e.g., "All women desire to stay at home with their children"), with no substantiating evidence or a citation for support, you should question the credibility and integrity of that source. Noting all these limitations does not mean personally attacking a source; rather, it means critiquing it in a scholarly way.

Common Mistakes

There are a variety of common mistakes in critiquing the literature. One of the most common mistakes is using emotion instead of evidence to support the critique. You might attack a researcher because you dislike his or her results, not because of the way the research was conducted. Perhaps you are conducting a study on the utility of a particular educational intervention for struggling readers, and you find a study that shows no impact of this intervention. Maybe the source even shows that it has a harmful effect. If you personally believe that this intervention is effective and are hoping to generate support for such an intervention through your study, you may be tempted to dismiss this article as "bad" and may choose not to include it in your work. Use caution before you entertain such a response. Reflect on what the article really says, and focus on the methods of that study. Who was involved in the sample? How was the intervention tested? If you examine that study's methods, you will likely understand the study's reported results and why the findings of your proposed study—*in conjunction with the findings of that contradicting study*—would provide a more robust understanding of your phenomenon of interest. For example, the contradictory findings on that intervention might stem from the fact that the researchers tested the intervention on a very different sample. Perhaps they used a much smaller sample. Perhaps they only used a portion of the intervention. Those findings are powerful. The key takeaway: Do not dismiss an article simply because it tells a different story from the one you are hoping to tell in your own research.

Another mistake involves dismissing complex studies as "no good" simply because they are complex. Sometimes the findings in research studies are indeed overly complex (e.g., "Central aspects of Bronfenbrenner's theory are structurally represented in the schematic representation of the study's findings, wherein an explicit set of relations between variables in the interest domain is specified"), and the findings could benefit from a better presentation (e.g., "Bronfenbrenner's theory is supported by the findings of this research"). However, dismissing a long or complex article as unusable simply because it contains vocabulary that you are unaccustomed to or statistics that you have not yet learned is not appropriate. Trust yourself. Spend time with those articles, and do your best to interpret them. You will likely be able to interpret more than you would originally have expected at first glance of the study.

Ways to Stay Organized

It should be clear now that there are many factors to consider with any source you read. Below are some elements to help you organize your thoughts as you critique a source, regardless of its method.

Research Problem. What is it that the author(s) actually studied? The research problem is often presented after a short introduction, in which the general topic is introduced and the social problem is presented. The research problem should be distinguished from the social problem. A social problem should be seen as an undesirable situation in one's community or some other specified context (e.g., adolescents who affiliate with deviant peer groups tend to engage in risky, self-harming behavior). A research problem, on the other hand, is a topic that needs to be studied (e.g., little is known about how adolescents identify with those groups). Although the social problem might be the reason why you are interested in a particular study, take note of the research problem, and consider whether it has been clearly presented.

Literature Review. Is the review logically organized? Does it offer a balanced critical analysis of the literature? Does it explain the philosophical underpinnings of the study? These questions indicate the robustness and credibility of a literature review. A sparse literature review that is poorly organized and has little cohesion and flow should alert you that the foundation of the study might be questionable. You should look for a variety of authors and sources being used as well as the use of current sources. If dated sources (i.e., those older than 5 years) are being used, investigate their merit. Make sure they are from seminal research studies and ones that are highly respected within the field. This consideration is important because research is continually evolving. Any source that has an abundance of excessively old citations is likely not an accurate reflection of the current state of knowledge on a topic.

Theoretical or Conceptual Framework. Has a conceptual or theoretical framework been identified? Is the framework adequately described? A theoretical or conceptual framework provides an overall orienting lens that shapes the types of questions asked, informs how data are collected and analyzed, and/or provides a call for action or change. Take note of the framework, if there is one, and note its major tenets.

Research Question. Has a research question been identified? If so, is that research question clearly stated? Sometimes a research question is explicit: It is given its own space in an article and is clearly presented as a question, sometimes prefaced with the overt "Research Question" heading (e.g., "What is the relationship between adolescent peer group affiliation and the proclivity toward risk behavior?"). Other times, the research question is not a question at all but instead a declarative statement of intent (e.g., "The purpose of this study was to address the relationship between adolescent peer group affiliation and the proclivity toward risk behavior"). Research questions will also differ depending on the design of a study. Quantitative studies examine the relationship between two or more quantifiable variables, whereas qualitative studies examine the experience of a phenomenon with the intent to develop a complex picture of the problem or issue under study (Creswell, 2014). For example, a quantitative study might address the relationship between peer group affiliation, defined by an adolescent's self-identified peer group among a finite number of group options, and his or her self-reported risk behavior. A qualitative study, in comparison, might study the lived experiences of adolescents who identify with a particular peer group. Whatever the study design of the resource you are reading, make note of where the research questions are presented and how they are presented. Ideally, the constructs that are being studied have been clearly defined so that you know exactly what is being examined.

Methodology. Has the research design been clearly identified? Has the instrument used to gather data been described? Is the instrument appropriate? The answers to these questions might look different depending on the method used in the study. A quantitative study should describe the instruments that were used, including evidence of their reliability and validity. Ideally, the authors will provide a few example items from the instrument too, to give you a glimpse of how the items corresponded to the constructs that were studied. The same level of detail should be provided in a qualitative study, but the language will likely be different. Instead of using terms like *reliability* and *validity*, qualitative researchers are more likely to describe the rigor of their methods in terms of a variety of *trustworthiness* indicators. The important thing to look for, simply, is the level of detail the authors provide. The more transparent and clear the authors are in presenting their methods, the more rigor you can assume their study to have.

Results. Relatedly, look for information on the findings or results. Ask yourself the following questions. Are the results connected to the hypotheses and/or research questions and methods of analysis? Are all the major research questions answered in the results? There should be a clear sense of parallelism in the source: Each research question or hypothesis should correspond with its own findings report, and those findings should make sense in relation to the method of analysis that was used to achieve them. Each result should be presented in the same order in which its corresponding question was presented, with no superfluous details: Nothing tangential to the original research questions and no interpretive commentary should be included—for example, whether the findings were interesting or surprising. Such commentary should be reserved for the very end of the study, where the authors provide some of their own reflections about the study.

Cohesion. There are other factors to consider in evaluating the credibility and integrity of a source, and they are loosely bundled here under the overarching category of *cohesion*. The cohesion of a study speaks to how all the elements hang together. Once you have read through an entire study, take a moment to pause and reflect on its cohesion. Does the research report follow the steps of the research process in a logical manner? Do these steps flow naturally, and are the links clear? The introduction should lead into the problem statement and research purpose, which should lead into the methods, results, conclusions, and interpretations. These elements should flow together, much like a good story. The writing should be clear and accessible and should abide by the guidelines provided in the writing style manual adopted by your discipline or program.

In critiquing the aspects of a research study, these questions should foster more than just a simple *yes* or *no* response. They should stimulate you to consider the implications of what the researcher has done and how you might build on the research and/or improve it. Sociologist and scholarly writer Becker and Richards (2007) wrote about this consideration through the analogy of building a table, with some parts prefabricated and other parts hand crafted. It is likely that, as you read the literature, you will come across findings or techniques that spark a moment of inspiration, an idea to use a similar approach in your own work. Those bits represent the prefabricated parts of the table. There will be other ideas that are entirely yours, entirely new. Those bits represent the handcrafted parts of the table, which you will create yourself.

If critiquing the literature sounds like an active process, it should. It involves continually asking yourself about the utility of a source and its "fit" to your own interests. This active process pays off, though, as you move from critiquing the literature to synthesizing it. I turn to synthesis next.

SYNTHESIZING THE LITERATURE

As you develop your skills in critiquing the literature—essentially in analyzing or breaking down each source into its constituent parts—you will become better equipped to synthesize what you have read into a coherent whole. The second half of this chapter provides some guidance on engaging in that process.

Definitions

The term *synthesis* is often misused to describe an annotated bibliography, one that includes various sources presented alongside one another. Although an annotated bibliography is certainly a helpful start, it is not, in itself, a synthesized account of a particular topic. Instead, synthesis is defined as "an integrated analysis of different subtopics that help the writer and reader to come to a greater understanding of the state of knowledge on a larger issue" (Hart, 2011, p. 110). The unified, singular entity is the important feature in a synthesized narrative, because the source provides *a level of analysis* to relate the ideas of different sources together.

Important Considerations

A synthesized paper is an integrated, critical essay on the most relevant and current published knowledge on the topic. Hence, not everything needs to be included in a synthesized paper. It may not be necessary to report in your synthesis, for example, the type of instrument used in every study you have read, but a general overview of methods for your topic would be. Similarly, an individual account of sample sizes for each study you have read is probably not a helpful detail, but a summary of the sample sizes (e.g., large or small, homogeneous or diverse) would be informative. It will be up to you to decide on which details to include or omit, but the key thing to remember is that the information that is shared should be relevant to the larger story you are telling.

Beyond considering the level of detail in a synthesized paper, you must consider the ways in which those details are organized. Typically, the ideas of a synthesized paper are organized around major ideas or themes, including a discussion of theories, models, background, and trends. Once you identify those major ideas or themes, put them into an outline. Your outline can (and likely will) change as you continue to gather more sources, but the simple act of outlining major ideas will help you stay focused on the bigger, overarching story of your study, rather than on individual studies. Your initial synthesized draft might look very simple, something like this:

I.   Main Idea A
   1.   Supportive evidence (Author name, year)
   2.   Supportive evidence (Author name, year)
   3.   Supportive evidence (Author name, year)
      a.   Analysis that compares and contrasts the above evidence and relates it all to Main Idea A
      b.   Transitional sentence to guide the reader into Main Idea B

II.   Main Idea B
   1.   Supportive evidence (Author name, year)
   2.   Supportive evidence (Author name, year)
   3.   Supportive evidence (Author name, year)
      a.   Analysis that compares and contrasts the above evidence and relates it all to Main Idea B
      b.   Transitional sentence to guide the reader into Main Idea C

III.   . . . and so on

Some writers who have not done a lot of synthesis struggle to identify what synthesis looks like and wonder what sort of language typifies a synthesized paper. To help you get started, there are some phrases that alert the reader to a synthesized paper, such as "In line with these findings . . . ," "The results of X are consistent with Y . . . ," and "Although X suggests . . . , Y reaches a different conclusion." All illustrate synthesis, where two or more ideas are being analyzed alongside each other. In addition, the American Psychological Association's *Publication Manual* (2010) provides excellent guidance on the use of transitional phrases to demonstrate a synthesized analysis of two or more sources. For example, some phrases are helpful to demonstrate time links (*then, next, after, while, since*), some are used to demonstrate cause–effect links (*therefore, consequently, as a result*), some are used to demonstrate additions (*in addition, moreover, furthermore, similarly*), and others are used to illustrate contrasts (*but, conversely, nevertheless, however, although*). Consider these phrases as you begin to consider how your sources are related, and feel free to use them if they frame the relationship between your sources appropriately.

Of course, a synthesized paper is more than one that includes these synthesizing phrases. A synthesized paper should leave a reader with a holistic sense that the writer has conveyed his or her own new ideas and has drawn on a chorus of support. Synthesis gives you the opportunity to make your voice heard.

Common Mistakes

A common mistake in the attempt to synthesize is to include two or more sources in a paragraph. Here are some lighthearted examples:

Dark chocolate has been found to affect mood (Hershey, 2017); namely, the more dark chocolate one eats, the more cheerful one tends to be. White chocolate has little effect on mood. (Ghirardelli, 2018)

Synthesis does not mean simply having two or more sources. Having more than one source is an excellent first step, but real synthesis does not occur unless a relationship between the sources is apparent. In the examples above, the two sentences are broadly related (i.e., they both discuss chocolate), but there is no analysis given about how exactly they are connected. Something like this would be necessary to truly analyze the two sources together: "The *type of chocolate* may be an important consideration in the study of the chocolate–mood connection."

Another common mistake is to "throw in" random synthesis words for good measure but to stop there, without providing any level of description or analysis about how the various ideas are related. Here is an example:

One reason why chocolate should be on every elementary school lunch menu is that it makes students feel good. Rita Dove, president of Dove Chocolate, agrees, stating, "Chocolate is the perfect end to a satisfying luncheon." (Hershey, 2017, p. 18)

Did Rita Dove actually *agree* to the assertion that chocolate should be on every elementary school menu? Probably not. Use words deliberately. A word like *agrees* should be reserved for occasions when a real relationship has been explored. A more appropriate synthesis of those sources would be the following:

One reason why chocolate should be on every elementary school lunch menu is that it makes students feel good. Rita Dove, president of Dove Chocolate, provided a statement about the pleasant aftereffects of chocolate, saying that "chocolate is the perfect end to a satisfying luncheon." Such a statement would likely support the argument of chocolate's inclusion in the lunch menu.

Yet another common mistake in synthesized drafts is the overuse of quotes. Below is an example:

"Dark chocolate contains antioxidants" (Ghirardelli, 2018, p. 3); "antioxidants protect cells from free radical damage" (Oz, 2015, p. 27). "Dark chocolate can be incorporated into many snacks or meals." (Crocker, 2014, p. 22)

Always ask yourself whether you are interpreting quotes and furthering your own ideas or just piling quotes one on top of another. A more appropriate synthesis of those quotes would be something that takes the *ideas* of those quotes and translates them into a coherent whole:

> Dark chocolate is seen as a wise accompaniment to one's diet. This perspective is shared by those who have touted the antioxidants in dark chocolate (Ghirardelli, 2018), the ability of dark chocolate to protect cells from free radical damage (Oz, 2015, p. 27), and the ease with which one can incorporate dark chocolate into regular snacks or meals.

Using one source too often is an additional mistake that writers often make. Below is an example:

> Hershey (2017) has found that chocolate can boost one's mood. . . .
>
> Hershey (2017) has discovered a relationship between happiness and consumption of chocolate. . . .
>
> Hershey's (2017) study revealed that women eat significantly more chocolate than men. . . .

Make sure that one source is not driving the study. If every paragraph contains material from one particular source on the reference page or if whole paragraphs are not synthesized but, rather, offer this single, particular source alone, a reader could become suspicious that you have copied another author's structure and are relying too heavily on that source's argumentative structure rather than coming up with your own. Be on the alert for this problem.

Ways to Organize the Literature Review

One tool that may be helpful in organizing literature reviews is the literature review matrix (see Table 19.1), an organizational tool that was also recommended in the section Critiquing the Literature. The literature review matrix allows you to sort and categorize the different arguments presented on an issue. Across the top of the chart are the spaces to record different aspects of each study, and along the side of the chart are the spaces to record each separate article. As you examine your first source, you will work horizontally across the first row, recording as much information as possible about each significant aspect of the study. Follow a similar pattern for your following sources. As you find information that relates to an article you have already recorded, group those articles together in your matrix. If you are adept at Microsoft Excel, you can even sort your articles on keywords that allow you to group similar ideas. As you gather more sources, you will start to identify different subheadings or thoughts in the literature. You may organize your paper by these subheadings. Table 19.1 illustrates a literature review matrix that has been populated with a variety of related articles about adolescent drug abuse and cognitive–behavioral therapy (CBT), followed by an example of synthesis based on the information within the matrix.

Below is a synthesis of articles on adolescent drug abuse and CBT, using the articles from the literature review matrix in Table 19.1 to pull together a synthesized narrative.

TABLE 19.1 ◆ EXAMPLE OF A LITERATURE REVIEW MATRIX ON ADOLESCENT DRUG ABUSE AND COGNITIVE–BEHAVIORAL THERAPY (CBT)

Author/Date	Overview	Research Question/ Hypothesis	Methodology	Analysis	Results
Tangney, Baumeister, and Boone (2004)	Investigated restrained drinking and self-control in relation to alcohol consumption and problem drinking in a sample of adolescents	Lack of cognitive control will be associated with high levels of alcohol consumption in adolescents.	$N = 351$ undergraduates Completed questionnaires on levels of alcohol consumption, problem drinking, restrained drinking, and cognitive self-control	Correlations examined the association between self-control and alcohol consumption.	Low levels of cognitive self-control predicted high levels of problem drinking.
Studer et al. (2016)	Examined the relationship between the gambling behaviors and coping strategies of 4,989 Swiss males	Gamblers would report fewer coping strategies than nongamblers.	$N = 4,989$ Swiss adolescents Completed questionnaires on gambling behaviors, personality, and coping strategies	Latent class analysis was employed to determine gambling types. Analysis of variance determined gambling type × coping skills relationships.	Low problem-solving coping strategies were associated with the most extensive gambling behaviors.
Aebi, Giger, Plattner, Metzke, and Steinhausen (2014)	Examined stress coping and temptation coping as potential contributors to substance abuse	Stress coping and temptation coping will contribute to the most variance in adolescent substance abuse.	$N = 1,086$ Swiss adolescents Completed questionnaires over a 2-day period	Regressions examined the degree to which stress and temptation coping predict adolescent substance abuse.	Low coping skills in childhood predicted criminal outcomes in young adulthood.
Trudeau, Black, Kamon, and Sussman, (2017)	Examined the effectiveness of a cognitive–behavioral skills training program on adolescents in New York	Adolescents who receive cognitive–behavioral skills training will report lower cigarette, alcohol, and marijuana use than those who do not receive the training.	$N = 129$ adolescents in a Navigating My Journey program, split into an experimental and a control group. Data were collected at four time points	Linear mixed modeling examined differences by group in substance use and cognitive skills.	Those who received CBT reported greater motivation at all four time points to quit cigarette smoking, marijuana use, and alcohol use.
Fonagy et al. (2014)	Examined the current status of CBT for substance abuse treatment	What determines the effectiveness of CBT? Are certain CBT approaches superior to others?	Hundreds of studies were identified that examined the hypothesized mechanisms of action of CBT	Qualitative content analysis	CBT has been associated with a decrease in drug abuse, but *few conclusions have been made for the underlying mechanisms of CBT.*

Synthesis Example

Drug abuse may be a function of one's cognitive style. This idea has been supported in a variety of studies on cognition and drug abuse in adolescence. In comparison with adolescents who do not abuse drugs, past research has found drug-abusing adolescents to report lower levels of cognitive self-control (Tangney et al., 2004), fewer problem-solving coping strategies (Studer et al., 2016), and higher levels of stress (Aebi et al., 2014).

Because of these empirical findings, CBT has grown in popularity as an effective approach to reduce or prevent adolescent drug use. The effectiveness of CBT in reducing drug use, such as cigarette smoking, marijuana use, and alcohol use, has been demonstrated in a variety of clinical trials (e.g., Trudeau et al., 2017). Despite the promising findings from these studies, a recent content analysis of CBT studies found no explanation of the underlying mechanisms linking CBT to behavioral change (Fonagy et al., 2014).

If a literature review matrix is not an effective approach for you, an alternative tip is to use some sort of data management software program or electronic reference program in which you are able to create various folders, each containing summaries and hard copies of the articles you are reading. Alternatively, you can code by hand the sources you are collecting via highlighters, Post-it notes, note cards, or any other hard copy method to lay out your articles in front of you. Create piles, sort by theme, take notes, and highlight what seems important. Do what works for you.

CONCLUSION

This chapter brings together considerations on critiquing and synthesizing the literature, underscoring the importance of these skills and the need to practice them regularly. As you work on developing the ability to critique and synthesize, be patient with yourself. Being able to write an elegant, synthesized paper is not something that novice scholars can do at their first attempt. It takes practice, and just like any other practiced skill in life—such as playing the piano, throwing a curve ball, or cooking a soufflé—the skills to critique and synthesize require regular practice. Set aside some time every day for this practice, and you will reap the rewards.

Questions for Reflection

1. What personal practices will you adopt to become a more efficient and effective critical reader?

2. How is synthesis distinct from creating an annotated bibliography? Why is it so important to demonstrate your knowledge of the field?

3. What tools might you consider using to become a more organized reader?

4. What tools might you consider using to become a more effective synthesizer?

Key Sources

American Psychological Association. (2010). *Publication manual of the American Psychological Association* (6th ed.). Washington, DC: Author.

Walsh, M. L., Pezalla, A. E., & Marshall, H. (2014). *Essential guide to critical reading and writing.* Baltimore, MD: Laureate International Universities.

References

Aebi, M., Giger, J., Plattner, B., Metzke, C. W., & Steinhausen, H. C. (2014). Problem coping skills, psychosocial adversities and mental health problems in children and adolescents as predictors of criminal outcomes in young adulthood. *European Child & Adolescent Psychiatry, 23*(5), 283–293. doi:10.1007/s00787-013-0458-y

American Psychological Association. (2010). *Publication manual of the American Psychological Association* (6th ed.). Washington, DC: Author.

Becker, H. S., & Richards, P. (2007). *Writing for social scientists: How to start and finish your thesis, book, or article.* Chicago, IL: University of Chicago Press.

Creswell, J. W. (2014). *Research design: Qualitative, quantitative, and mixed methods approaches* (4th ed.). Thousand Oaks, CA: SAGE.

Fonagy, P., Cottrell, D., Phillips, J., Bevington, D., Glaser, D., & Allison, E. (2014). *What works for whom? A critical review of treatments for children and adolescents.* New York, NY: Guilford Press.

Hart, C. (2011). *Doing a literature review: Releasing the social science research imagination.* London, UK: SAGE.

Studer, J., Baggio, S., Mohler-Kuo, M., Simon, O., Daeppen, J. B., & Gmel, G. (2016). Latent class analysis of gambling activities in a sample of young Swiss men: Association with gambling problems, substance use outcomes, personality traits and coping strategies. *Journal of Gambling Studies, 32*(2), 421–440. doi:10.1007/s10899-015-9547-9

Tangney, J. P., Baumeister, R. F., & Boone, A. L. (2004). High self-control predicts good adjustment, less pathology, better grades, and interpersonal success. *Journal of Personality, 72*(2), 271–324. doi:10.1111/j.0022-3506.2004.00263.x

Trudeau, K. J., Black, R. A., Kamon, J. L., & Sussman, S. (2017). A randomized controlled trial of an online relapse prevention program for adolescents in substance abuse treatment. *Child and Youth Care Forum, 46*(3), 437–454. doi:10.1007/s10566-016-9387-5

Walsh, M. L., Pezalla, A., E., & Marshall, H. (2014). *Essential guide to critical reading and writing.* Baltimore, MD: Laureate International Universities.

WRITING THE RESEARCH PROPOSAL

Linda M. Crawford, Gary J. Burkholder, and Kimberley A. Cox

A research proposal is a thorough plan for conducting a study. Specifically, a dissertation or thesis proposal usually contains chapters, or some other organizational structure and presentation order, that include the rationale for the study and a description of how the study will be carried out. In this chapter, we discuss the elements of a research proposal, the development of a plan for conducting the study, and alignment among the research design, research questions, and methods. This chapter is oriented to those writing thesis or dissertation proposals; however, the principles easily apply to many kinds of research proposals. We saved this chapter for the end of this book because it draws on information presented in each of the preceding chapters. Our intent is that this chapter will serve as a practical organizing principle for the research proposal.

Constructing the proposal is an iterative process that does not proceed linearly. When writing the proposal, you will often go back and forth among the elements, filling in some parts and moving to other parts until you are assured that all the parts are fully aligned. In that light, although we discuss the elements of a research proposal in this chapter in what we believe to be a logical order, we do not expect that you will write a proposal sequentially, nor do we imply that every institution will require every element in the order discussed. Understanding each of these proposal elements, though, will help you conceptualize your proposal and prepare it in the manner required by your institution.

RESEARCH PROPOSAL ELEMENTS

A research proposal generally contains two main elements: (1) a study rationale and (2) a study implementation plan (Figure 20.1). The rationale for a study is rooted in an exhaustive literature review, often summarized in a background section that builds context for and establishes the need for the study, succinctly stated as a gap statement. The rationale is further specified in the problem, purpose, research questions, and conceptual framework. The implementation plan describes the overall design of the study and the methods to be used for selecting participants, identifying instrumentation, collecting data, and analyzing data. The implementation plan also delineates the study in terms of definitions, assumptions, scope and delimitations, limitations, and significance.

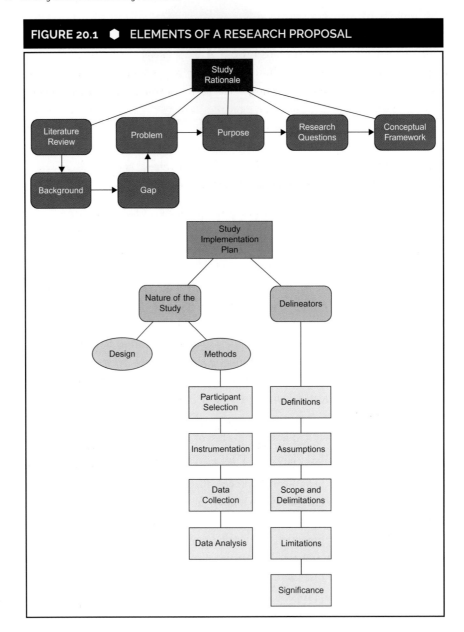

FIGURE 20.1 ● ELEMENTS OF A RESEARCH PROPOSAL

STUDY RATIONALE

The rationale begins with the literature review, which establishes context and the need for the study by presenting what is already known and what yet needs to be known or understood about a topic. The literature review may be summarized in a background and gap statement, which leads to a problem that the study is designed to solve. The rationale is further specified in a statement of purpose for the study, the research questions/hypotheses, and the conceptual framework of the study.

Literature Review

When approaching a study, you begin with some wondering in your mind concerning a question about some topic of interest. For example, you may be wondering how decisions are made in collegial groups, what motivates employee loyalty to organizations, or why some leaders generate more productivity among workers than other leaders. You then seek to determine if this interest is of concern not only to you but also to the profession at large, and you also seek to determine what is already known and not known about the topic, which formulates a need for the study. To ascertain that need for the study, you will delve into the related literature.

The literature review, fully discussed in Chapter 19, is a systematic synthesis of prior research and knowledge on your topic. There are a number of purposes that are served by the literature review, and it is good for you to be aware of these purposes as you begin the process of reading and synthesizing. These purposes include (a) providing evidence for what researchers know and do not know about the topic, (b) showing how addressing what researchers do not know will advance discipline-specific knowledge, (c) identifying the research designs that have been used to address the phenomenon of interest, (d) understanding the seminal thinking on the topic, and (e) gathering evidence to support your choice of methods. Thus, a literature review is much more than a summary of the research; it represents a critical understanding of the relevant scientific discourse in your discipline.

Note also that when we use the word *synthesis*, we mean something different from summarization. For example, a summary of an article reiterates the contents of the article in a briefer form. Synthesis requires you to find similarities and differences among articles that reveal understanding. For example, you might summarize the point of one article but find that three other articles reiterate that idea and one article contradicts the idea. A literature review combines, or synthesizes, these findings to create context for the study and to identify what is not yet known or understood about the topic that is of concern to the profession.

Discerning if the line of research you intend to pursue is of concern to the profession is important. For example, it may be that it is not known at what age toddlers typically learn to tie their shoes, but there is no indication in the literature of a need to know that. If you wish to pursue that line of research, you will need to convincingly establish that need beyond support in the literature.

Literature reviews may be organized in different ways, but typically, a literature review presents the seminal content and theoretical literature on the topic; the literature related to the independent variables, dependent variables, or phenomenon under study; studies conducted on the topic with various populations; and the research designs that have been used to study the topic. Based on the literature review, you determine what is lacking in knowledge or understanding of your topic that people in your profession are wondering about.

Although the literature review is usually quite extensive, the research proposal normally summarizes the literature review in a section sometimes labeled "Background." Such a summary orients the reader to the major understandings related to the topic and provides context for the study. The background ends in what is known as a gap statement. The gap statement clearly and succinctly states the nexus of the state of knowledge that calls for the study. For example, a gap statement might read like this: "Although we already know X, Y, and Z about A, only limited studies have explored W, resulting in a lack of the understanding needed to implement A." This gap statement leads to the problem statement.

Problem Statement

A problem statement is a description of what is not known or understood about your topic that is of interest to the profession (Booth, Colomb, Williams, Bizup, & Fitzgerald, 2016). The problem statement is one of the three most important elements of a research proposal, along with the purpose statement and research questions/hypotheses. In writing the problem statement, you should use precise, parsimonious language that clearly signals the problem to your reader. Although some institutions might require additional elements in a problem statement, there are three essential parts of a problem statement:

1. The research problem itself

2. For whom and why studying the problem is important

3. How the current study will address the problem

It is best to begin the problem statement with a clear declarative sentence, such as "The problem to be addressed by this study is that [something is not understood or not known]." If the sentence reads, "The problem to be addressed by this study is to . . . ," then the statement is probably a purpose rather than a problem statement, because it is indicating what your study will do rather than what problem it will address. Be sure to indicate what is not understood or not known rather than stating what your study will do.

Also, recognize the difference between a *situation*, which often comes from personal experience, and a *problem*, which is a literature-based concern across the profession—for example, "The problem to be addressed by this study is that principals do not use fair means of evaluating teachers." This is a statement of a situation and is likely rooted in the researcher's personal experience. The statement does not state what is not understood or not known based on the research literature. Compare that statement with the following: "The problem to be addressed by this study is that the means of establishing equity in teacher evaluations conducted by principals are not known." This second statement reflects that the literature has not yet provided sufficient research related to equity in teacher evaluation.

The problem statement indicates for whom and why studying the problem is important. This element is a precursor to stating the study's significance, described later in this chapter. In the problem statement, you need to indicate why the profession considers an investigation of the topic important and also how addressing the problem may affect the lives of stakeholders to the problem. For example, for a study on voting patterns in rural areas, this part of the problem statement might state, "Understanding voting patterns in rural areas might reveal issues of importance to politicians and the general public that affect accessibility to voting sites."

The problem statement also states in general terms how the current study will address the research problem. For example, for a study on minority parents' satisfaction with screening procedures for their children for acceptance into a talented and gifted program, this part of the problem statement might state, "This study will describe minority parents' perceptions of the procedures for admittance into talented and gifted programs."

The problem statement can be written in one concise paragraph. Below is a sample problem statement from a completed dissertation. The dissertation topic was the use of a social skills curriculum strategy, video self-modeling (VSM), with twice-exceptional students. *Twice exceptional* refers to those students recognized as intellectually gifted who also have a special needs diagnosis (Allard, 2014).

> The problem addressed by this study is the underuse of VSM as part of a comprehensive social skills curriculum for twice-exceptional students. Understanding the reasons for underuse of this potentially viable intervention for twice-exceptional students is important for school personnel invested in ensuring the social skills success for this population. This study addressed the problem of underuse of VSM by gaining an understanding of the experiences of school personnel in relation to the use of VSM as an intervention to improve social skills in twice-exceptional students, including the incentives and disincentives for its use in the school setting. Themes generated from interviews of the team members contribute to a more informed understanding of VSM as an intervention with this student population, as well as better informed practice by understanding the lived experiences of staff who are actually carrying out the VSM intervention. (pp. 6–7)

Notice that the problem statement begins with a clear identification of what is at issue—the underuse of a model for a certain population. Next, Allard (2014) explains why understanding the reasons for the underuse of this intervention is important and for whom it is important. Finally, the reader learns that the study will focus on gaining insight based on the experiences of school personnel who have used the intervention with the defined student population.

Purpose Statement

The final section of a problem statement, how the current study will address the problem, leads to the purpose statement. The purpose statement describes the

(a) study design; (b) the theory being tested (quantitative) or central phenomenon being investigated (qualitative), or both (mixed methods); (c) the study's intent; (d) the variables (quantitative) or definition of the phenomenon (qualitative), or both (mixed methods); (e) the participants; and (f) the site or context. That seems like a lot of information, but it can actually be presented in one or two concise sentences.

We provide below a format for writing a purpose statement that includes the items listed above; the format is an adaptation of purpose statement scripts provided by Creswell and Creswell (2018, pp. 119, 124). Although your purpose statement does not need to follow this somewhat formulaic presentation, your purpose statement does need to include all the items identified earlier. Formats of purpose statements for qualitative and quantitative studies are provided. Mixed methods studies would combine the two statements shown below.

> *Qualitative purpose statement:* The purpose of this _____ (design: case study, ethnography, etc.) is to _____ (understand, describe, explore, develop, etc.) the _____ (central phenomenon) for _____ (participants) at _____ (site). The central phenomenon is generally defined as _____ (general definition).

> *Quantitative purpose statement:* The purpose of this _____ (design: experimental, quasi-experimental, descriptive) study is to _____ (test or describe) the theory of _____, which _____ (describes, compares, or relates) the _____ (independent variable) with _____ (dependent variable), controlling for _____ (name the control variables if appropriate) for _____ (participants) at _____ (site). The independent variables are generally defined as _____ (general definition). The dependent variables are generally defined as _____ (general definition). The control and intervening variables, _____ (identify if appropriate), will be statistically controlled in the study.

As an example, following from the Allard (2014) problem statement cited earlier, her purpose statement was as follows:

> The purpose of this qualitative, phenomenological study was to explore the lived experiences of special education team members who have incorporated VSM as a social skills intervention for twice-exceptional elementary students. I examined the nature of these experiences in an attempt to understand the underuse of VSM and to explore incentives and disincentives for the use of VSM in the context of an elementary school setting with this population. (p. 7)

Notice how Allard (2014) identified the design as a qualitative, phenomenological study. The central phenomenon is incorporation of the VSM intervention, which is defined as a social skills intervention. She used an infinitive verb form, *to explore*, which signals study intent. The participants are specified as special education team members who have incorporated VSM for twice-exceptional students. The site is an elementary school setting.

In this example, all six elements of a strong purpose statement are clearly identifiable, and extraneous information is absent. We recommend that, when writing your purpose statement, you notate your content beside each of the six items listed earlier prior to formulating a purpose statement paragraph. Then, double-check to see if your paragraph incorporates all six items. Furthermore, we recommend that your purpose statement begin with a clear declarative sentence, such as "The purpose of this [design] is to [verb]. . . ." Writing your sentence in this way offers the reader a precise understanding of your study purpose.

In summary, you should begin proposal development by writing your literature review, which is a synthesis of prior research and knowledge on your topic. You summarize the literature review in the background section and end that section with a gap statement, which serves as a precursor to the problem. The problem statement contains three elements: (1) the problem itself, (2) for whom and why studying the problem is important, and (3) how the study will address the problem. The last part of the problem statement, how the study will address the problem, is a precursor to the purpose statement. The purpose statement specifies the study design, theoretical context, intent, variables or phenomenon, participants, and site. The next step is the development of research questions.

Research Questions and Hypotheses

Research questions and hypotheses should be a direct extension of the problem and purpose statements. The decisions you will subsequently make about your research design and methods largely rest on clearly stated research questions and/or hypotheses. Research questions appear in quantitative, qualitative, and mixed methods studies; hypotheses appear in quantitative and some mixed methods studies.

Research Questions. Research questions are interrogative statements that serve three functions. First, research questions frame the focus of the study. Second, research questions set the boundaries of the study to establish its scope. Third, research questions point you toward the data needed to answer them (Onwuegbuzie & Leech, 2004). In the process of developing research questions, your ideas about the concepts under study become clarified as you consider how to operationally define them and link your research questions with a particular approach to inquiry and research design (White, 2013).

There are several possible types of research questions, with the most apparent distinction being the approach to inquiry—qualitative, quantitative, or mixed methods. Within each approach, various types of research questions are possible, such as those that speak to the relationship between variables or those that compare groups. Your research question wording is important because the words you use to write research questions should be aligned with the selected approach to inquiry and research design. For example, a quantitative research question that uses the word *relate* or *relationship* typically signals the use of a correlational design; an example is the question "What is the relationship between affiliation and loyalty among employees in midlevel managerial positions in Northeastern nonprofit organizations?" This strategy, where the research question informs design decisions, is referred to as a *question-led* strategy (White, 2013), and it is the strategy we recommend for research projects such as theses or dissertations. A *methods-led* strategy, which we do not recommend, is characterized by initially selecting a design and then developing the research question to fit that design (White, 2013).

A common mistake in developing research questions is to write questions too broadly, without mention of the context (e.g., the population or setting) in which the study is situated (Agee, 2009)—for example, "What is the relationship between affiliation and loyalty among employees?" This research question fails to indicate the type of employees being studied or the setting. A better question might be "What is the relationship between affiliation and loyalty among contract (nonpermanent) employees working in a technology innovation company?"

Another common mistake is to confuse *interview* or *survey* questions with *research* questions. Research questions guide your overall study. Interview or survey questions are questions you ask the participants to obtain data to answer the research question. Following from the earlier example, the research question would be "What is the relationship between affiliation and loyalty among contract (nonpermanent) employees working in a technology innovation company?" An interview or survey question might be "How would you describe your employer's expression of loyalty to you as an employee?" As a way to check your questions, note whether you use the word *you* in the research question. If you use the word *you*, then you are likely writing an interview or survey question rather than a research question.

In addition to providing context, another characteristic of a good research question is its alignment with the problem and purpose of the study. As one example of alignment, let's return to the earlier hypothetical study and follow the development from research problem to purpose and finally to research question.

Problem statement: "The problem to be addressed by this study is that the relationship between affiliation and loyalty among contract (nonpermanent) workers is not fully understood. Understanding this relationship may influence the opportunities employers provide for contract employees to build a sense of affiliation in the workplace. This study will address the problem by correlating contract employees' sense of affiliation with their self-reported loyalty to the company."

Purpose statement: "The purpose of this correlational study is to describe the theory of X by determining the relationship between affiliation and loyalty among contract (nonpermanent) employees working in a technology innovation company. *Affiliation* is defined as Y, and *loyalty* is defined as Z."

Research question: "What is the relationship between affiliation and loyalty among contract (nonpermanent) employees working in a technology innovation company?"

In reviewing this example, note the similarity in wording, which helps provide internal coherence to each of the key components of the study—research problem, purpose, and question—and the consistency of ideas threading through each of them.

Qualitative Research Questions. Agee's (2009) analogy of a research question as a camera lens that brings focus to a study is a helpful way to think about writing questions in qualitative research:

> A question can be thought of as a tool that is much like a steady-cam lens used to document an event or a journey. In the initial stages of study design, the researcher uses the steady-cam to frame an ever-changing broad landscape and then narrows the focus to frame and follow a specific set of events or actions in the broader terrain. However, that terrain is not just any place; it is a specific place with a dense, rich history. (pp. 441–442)

Qualitative research questions are typically characterized by their intent to describe, discover, or explore an experience or process (Onwuegbuzie & Leech, 2004). For example, Creswell and Creswell (2018) recommended using the word *what* or *how* to start a qualitative research question and verbs that reflect the exploratory nature of qualitative research designs, such as *discover* and *explore*. We recommend using an approach that starts with a broad question, called a *central question*, followed by subquestions that further narrow the scope of the study (Creswell & Creswell, 2018). For example, returning to the example study involving the relationship between affiliation and loyalty in contract employees, a broad qualitative research question might be "What are the lived experiences of contract employees working in a technology innovation company with regard to affiliation and loyalty?" Some subquestions might include (a) "How do contract employees experience their affiliation to their company?"; (b) "How do contract employees experience their affiliation to other employees?"; and (c) "What does loyalty mean to a contract worker who may not have the company as his or her primary source of income?" We recommend three to five, and no more than seven, subquestions.

Qualitative research questions may evolve as data are analyzed during the conduct of the study. Analysis of transcripts of interviews or other artifacts may lead the researcher to generate new questions that allow for continued exploration of a particular phenomenon. Thus, qualitative research questions may change somewhat to reflect the new understandings that emerge during analysis. Revised research questions need to remain within the bounds of the study as stated in the problem and purpose statements and as approved by the Institutional Review Board. This tendency for qualitative research questions to evolve as the study is carried out is a characteristic that distinguishes qualitative research questions from quantitative research questions, which are typically developed before the study is conducted (Agee, 2009).

Quantitative Research Questions. Quantitative research questions are commonly characterized by their intent to make comparisons or examine the relationships between variables. Creswell and Creswell (2018) identified three common categories of quantitative research questions. First, groups may be compared on an independent variable to examine the effect on a dependent variable. Second, one or more predictor variables may be related to one or more criterion variables. Third, responses to variables may be described, such as frequency. For quantitative research questions, the use of words such as *relate*, *influence*, and *affect* is appropriate (Creswell & Creswell, 2018).

Onwuegbuzie and Leech (2004) provided a typology of quantitative research questions that is similar to Creswell and Creswell's (2018) categories. Their typology includes three categories of research questions: descriptive, comparative, and relationship. Descriptive questions are those that quantify a response on a variable, and they typically start with words such as *what is*. For example, a descriptive question might be "What is the retention rate among contract employees in a technology innovation company?" Comparative questions are those that compare groups, and they typically use words such as *compare* and *differ*. For example, a comparative question might be "What is the difference between contract and full-time technology innovation company employees with regard to affiliation with and loyalty to their company?" Relationship questions are those that speak to the relationship between or among variables, and they typically use words such as *association*, *relationship*, or *relate*. For example, a question of this type might be "What is the relationship between affiliation and loyalty among contract employees working in a technology innovation company?" We agree with Onwuegbuzie and Leech (2004) that researchers should not begin quantitative research questions with words that will yield only a yes/no answer, because these questions should provoke more complete understanding. This advice can also apply to writing qualitative and mixed methods research questions.

Mixed Methods Research Questions. There are different approaches to the development of mixed methods research questions. For example, you might write one or more quantitative research questions and one or more qualitative research questions (Onwuegbuzie & Leech, 2004). Creswell and Creswell (2018) advocated the use of three distinct types of questions in mixed methods research—qualitative, quantitative, and mixed methods—with the mixed methods question explicitly speaking to the mix of the qualitative and quantitative approaches of the study. Tashakkori and Creswell (2007) referred to this type of question as an integrated or hybrid research question. Based on a literature review of common practices that researchers used to write mixed methods research questions, Tashakkori and Creswell offered the following guidance on possible writing approaches:

(a) Write separate quantitative and qualitative questions, followed by an explicit mixed methods question (or, more specifically, questions about the nature of integration); (b) Write an overarching mixed (hybrid, integrated) research question, later broken down into separate quantitative and qualitative subquestions to answer in each strand or phase of the study; or (c) Write research questions for each phase of a study as the study evolves. If the first phase is a quantitative phase, the question would be framed as a quantitative question or hypothesis. If the second phase is qualitative, the question for that phase would be framed as a qualitative research question. (p. 208)

For example, a mixed methods research question to complement the qualitative and quantitative examples provided earlier might be "How do the findings of the qualitative phase of the study complement the quantitative understanding of the nature of the relationship between affiliation and loyalty among contract employees in a technology innovation company?" As shown in this example, mixed methods questions should provide a direction for the integration of approaches to understand the phenomenon.

Hypotheses. A hypothesis is written as a statement, as opposed to a question, to reflect the proposed relationship between variables and the study outcome before data are collected. Formal specification of a hypothesis to be tested is a key characteristic of most quantitative research in the social sciences. Two types of hypotheses are commonly used: (1) the null hypothesis and (2) the alternative (sometimes called *research*) hypothesis. The null hypothesis states that there is no difference (or relationship) between two or more variables, and it is typically designated H_0. For example, in a quantitative research study that intends to compare groups, the null hypothesis would speak to no difference or no relationship between the variable(s) under study between the groups. The alternative hypothesis would state that there is a difference or relationship between the variables, and it is typically designated H_1.

Hypotheses can be written as either nondirectional or directional. A nondirectional hypothesis states that a difference exists, but it does not indicate the nature of that difference. A nondirectional null hypothesis example might be as follows: "There is no relationship between employee affiliation, as measured by the X scale, and employee loyalty, as measured by the Y scale, among contract employees in Company Z." Another example, which reflects a test of group differences, could be "There is no difference between nonpermanent contract employees and permanent full-time employees in Company Z on loyalty, as measured by the Y scale."

In a directional hypothesis, the nature of the predicted difference or relationship is explicitly stated. Directional hypotheses are typically used when you have some knowledge of how the variables are related based on prior research. An example directional alternative hypothesis might be "There is a negative correlation between employee affiliation, as measured by the X scale, and employee loyalty, as measured by the Y scale, among contract employees in Company Z." In this example, the appropriate null hypothesis would be as follows: "There is no correlation or a positive correlation between employee affiliation, as measured by the X scale, and employee loyalty, as measured by the Y scale, among contract employees in Company Z." An example of a directional alternative hypothesis for a test of group differences might be "Full-time employees will report higher levels of employee loyalty than contract employees, as measured by the Y scale, in Company Z." The corresponding null hypothesis would be "Full-time employees will report lower levels of employee loyalty, or no difference in scores, as measured by the Y scale, compared with contract employees in Company Z."

A good hypothesis clearly states the variables under study based on their operational definitions, that is, how they are defined for the study. You should use similar phrasing when writing research questions and hypotheses, including the order in which the variables are presented, such that the independent variable is stated first, followed by the dependent variable (Creswell & Creswell, 2018). A good hypothesis permits empirical testing such that the statistical analysis performed will indicate whether or not the null hypothesis is supported. In hypothesis testing, if the null hypothesis is rejected, the alternative hypothesis is accepted. Also, note in the example in the previous paragraph that the hypothesis contains information indicating how the variables are operationalized in the research study; this is also a characteristic of a complete and clearly stated hypothesis.

To summarize, hypotheses are predictive statements, or educated guesses, of the outcomes of statistical tests designed to answer the research question in quantitative studies, wherein the research question is looking at differences between groups or relationships between variables. Hypotheses are written to cover all possible answers to the research question. The null hypothesis states that the data will not support the prediction. The alternative hypothesis states that the data will support the prediction. Hypotheses can be either nondirectional or directional. A nondirectional hypothesis predicts that any difference or relationship between groups or variables can be either more than or less than. A directional hypothesis assumes that any difference or relationship is only more than or only less than and tests only for the expected direction.

Conceptual Framework

The conceptual framework, elaborated on in Chapter 3, argues for the importance of studying a topic and why the chosen design and methods are appropriate and rigorous. A conceptual framework ordinarily contains a theoretical framework that explicates how the study either generates or tests theory and situates the study in the dialogue of the profession.

Summary of the Study Rationale

The rationale for a study is typically presented as part of the introduction section of the research proposal. The background section summarizes the more extensive literature review and ends with a gap statement of what is not yet known or understood about the topic. The gap statement is the basis for the statement of the problem, which incorporates at least three elements: (1) the problem (what is not known or understood), (2) for whom and why studying the problem is important, and (3) a general statement of how the study will address the problem. How the study will address the problem is further specified in the purpose statement, which describes the study design, theory or phenomenon of focus, intent, variables/phenomenon, participants, and site. The research questions turn the purpose statement into operable interrogatives, reflected in hypotheses for quantitative research questions, which will be answered through the study implementation. A conceptual framework presents both justification for and explanation of the study.

STUDY IMPLEMENTATION PLAN

As shown in Figure 20.1, one of the purposes of the research proposal introduction is to summarize the design, methods, and other delineators that specify how the study will be implemented. In this section, we will briefly define how the proposal presents those elements in the nature of the study and further delineations of the study.

Nature of the Study

The nature of the study section in the introduction of a proposal may be termed differently by different institutions, but, regardless of the heading, it contains a summary of the research design and methods, which are usually detailed in a major section, or chapter, of the proposal.

Design. The research design includes the selected approach to inquiry (quantitative, qualitative, or mixed methods); the design selected within the approach, with an appropriate rationale; and what other approaches and designs were considered but rejected and why.

For example, you might select a qualitative phenomenological design because the study purpose is to describe the lived experiences of participants about some phenomenon. You may have considered case study but rejected that design because you are not examining a bounded unit.

Methods. In the nature of the study section, you will state the methods for the study by describing participant selection, instrumentation, data collection procedures, and data analysis strategies. These methodological elements are examined in other chapters in this text. The point here is to emphasize clear presentation of each element in your research proposal.

Study Delineators

The implementation plan portion of the proposal specifies a number of delineators that clarify the study, including term definitions, assumptions, scope and delimitations, limitations, and significance.

Definition of Terms. Definition of terms is critical for positioning a study within the professional conversation on a topic. To converse, professionals need to know what terms mean, and the definitions should leave no ambiguity. Dictionary definitions are irrelevant for a research study. For example, it is easy to draw a definition for *depression* from the dictionary. However, a dictionary definition does not explain how depression is being operationally defined in your study. You need to provide definitions that explicate how you will use the term in the study (Leedy & Ormrod, 2015). You should provide definitions to specify the participants in the study, the variables (quantitative) or phenomena (qualitative), and any other terms that are particular to your study.

For example, in relation to defining participants, the dictionary definition of *teacher* is insufficient to inform a reader how the researcher identifies teachers in the study. Is the researcher including anyone with an educational license, such as a school counselor or librarian, or is the researcher including only those licensed individuals who instruct students in a classroom? Is the researcher including specialists, such as special education teachers? Are the teachers eligible for the study only those who work in public schools, or are teachers who work in private schools also eligible? For example, a definition of *teacher* for a study might read "an individual licensed as an elementary teacher by the state of X who currently holds a position teaching in K–3 regular education classrooms in a public school in the state of X."

For a concept that can have various definitions, operational definitions specify the bounds around the concept. An operational definition states what will be recorded as evidence of the concept contained in the term, that is, what can be seen or heard to evidence presence of the concept. Given the earlier example of employee motivation, you might define *employee motivation* as frequency of contribution to group goal attainment. Your definitions of variables and phenomena must be rooted in the professional literature. In other words, you cannot create your own definition of, say, motivation, but must cite one or more sources in the professional literature that support your definition of the concept.

Assumptions. In a proposal, you must state any assumptions on which your study is based. Leedy and Ormrod (2015) defined an assumption as "a condition that is taken for granted without which the research project would be pointless" (p. 23). For example, in a study of a new method of teaching arithmetic to second graders, it would be important that the teachers using the new method had been trained in the method. An assumption of the study, then, would be that the teachers had been trained in the method. If they had not been trained in the method, then the study integrity comes into question. There needs to be a basis for an assumption, a reason why it is valid to hold the assumption. For example, a basis for the assumption that the teachers had been trained in the new arithmetic teaching method may be that the districts have documentation for the training.

Crawford (2015) identified three critical attributes of an assumption:

1. The assumption must relate to a critical, not trivial, condition of the study.

2. There is a basis for making the assumption.

3. The assumption must relate to a procedure of the study that is not fully within the control of the researcher.

The first attribute of an assumption is that it must relate to a critical condition of the study. For example, to state an assumption that all participants in the study can read

English when all participants in the study are English teachers may be considered trivial because reading English would be a characteristic of the population. However, it may be important to state an assumption that the teachers in the study can read English if the study is being conducted with social studies teachers in a country where Spanish, not English, is the first language and the study is conducted in English.

The second critical attribute requires statement of a basis for the assumption. For example, following from above, if the study is being conducted in a country where Spanish is the first language and there is the assumption that the teacher participants can read English, the basis for assuming that the members of the population can read English must be stated. Perhaps all the teachers in the population must pass an English reading examination to obtain teaching credentials, or there is some other documentation of the English reading competency of the participants.

Finally, assumptions must relate to a procedure of the study that is not fully within your control. For example, implementation of a certain reading program with prior training is a study procedure. You do not control the training, but the school district requires all elementary teachers to receive professional development in that program. You can assume that the teachers you select for the study have received the required training based on the district requirement.

A well-written assumption statement will incorporate all three attributes: (a) a critical condition, (b) a basis for making the assumption, and (c) a study procedure that is not fully within your control.

Scope and Delimitations. The scope of a study frames the group to which the study might be applicable. For example, a study might examine friendship patterns among highly mobile (defined as having moved five or more times within the past 3 years) female military spouses within the European and Asian military sectors. This study, therefore, would be applicable to that population; that is the scope of the study, or the broad group for whom the study might be applicable.

Delimitations narrow the study in terms of participants, time, and/or location by stating what the study will not include. For example, the study of friendship patterns of highly mobile military spouses might be delimited by not studying male military spouses and by defining *highly mobile* to exclude those female military spouses who have moved fewer than five times within the past 3 years. The study might further be delimited by not studying female spouses who have moved beyond the European and Asian military sectors.

Beyond setting the boundaries of the study, stating the scope clearly helps in writing the study title, and stating the delimitations clearly helps in specifying the study population. Therefore, the study title and scope must be aligned, and the study delimitations and population definition must be aligned.

Limitations. Delimitations and limitations are often confused. Delimitations narrow the study by stating what the study does not include. Limitations identify weaknesses in the study design or methods. All studies have design and/or methods weaknesses; the point is to declare known weaknesses and describe what has been done to overcome them and/or what has prevented overcoming them. For example, a weakness (limitation) of a study may be that parents in the population typically work several jobs and availability for interviews is limited. To overcome that limitation, you might extend a broad range of hours and locations for your interviews. A study of adoption practices may be limited if the study is conducted in only one state or region, with unknown applicability to other states or regions. If you found yourself in that situation, you may declare that the limitation could not be overcome because of a feasibility issue in accessing participants beyond the stated geographic area.

Significance. As discussed earlier, the problem statement suggests for whom and why the study might be important. That part of the problem statement can evolve into the significance section of the proposal. Studies are significant for one or more of three reasons. They can (1) influence practice, (2) affect policy, and/or (3) generate future research. For example, a study might be of practical importance to therapists in that it identifies a population for whom a particular therapeutic strategy is effective. Another study might influence policymakers considering budget allocations for preschool education by identifying the long-term benefits of preschool education. In terms of generating future research, a study might provide new questions for understanding how parental behaviors influence the development of self-esteem in children.

Summary of Study Implementation

After providing a rationale for the study, in the study implementation plan you summarize how the study will be conducted, including design, methods, definitions, assumptions, scope and delimitations, limitations, and significance. The rationale and implementation plan sections of the study proposal must be consistent with each other and among their elements, which is an issue of internal alignment.

ALIGNING RESEARCH DESIGN, RESEARCH QUESTIONS, AND METHODS

The issue of internal alignment is an important aspect of the research proposal. In earlier parts of this chapter, we described the key proposal sections. In this section, our focus is on how to ensure consistency among the proposal sections. For example, you must take care to ensure that the research question(s) and the methods are consistent with the research design. As another example, the problem and purpose statements both must align with the research question, design, and methods. Alignment not only evidences a coherent research design but also demonstrates scientific rigor.

Research Design

Within qualitative, quantitative, and mixed research approaches to inquiry, you have several design options. The research design is the strategy chosen to answer the study questions. Alignment starts with the approach to inquiry. If you are primarily looking to generate theory or to explore a topic in more depth and through an interpretive lens, a qualitative research design is likely most appropriate. On the other hand, if you seek to test theory to ascertain cause and effect, you would likely be choosing a quantitative research design. The correct choice of research approach is the result of a thorough investigation and analysis of the literature that yields a clear understanding of the state of development of the topic within the discipline. For example, it is important to understand whether a phenomenon of interest has been the subject of extensive research or whether research on that topic is still underdeveloped. Such knowledge leads to the best choice of approach to inquiry based on whether the particular topic area requires more descriptive development to support theory generation (qualitative) or whether theory development is advanced to the point that strategies to ascertain cause and effect are needed (quantitative).

Research Questions

Research questions define the key objective of the study. The way research questions are worded usually suggests a particular approach to inquiry and, within that approach, a particular research design. For example, from the perspective of approaches, questions that include words such as *describe* and *explain* signify a qualitative approach, whereas words such as *compare*, *correlate*, and *difference* tend to be associated with a quantitative approach. A question such as "What are the lived experiences of female chief executive officers of Fortune 500 companies?" would best be addressed by a phenomenological research design because the focus on lived experience is consistent with a phenomenological epistemology. Such a question embedded in a grounded theory design would likely not make sense because the purpose of grounded theory is to generate theory rather than to describe lived experiences. In that case, the research questions and design would not be aligned as they should be.

Methods

As specified earlier in this chapter, methods include components of the study that describe how you plan to arrive at answers to the research questions, including participant selection, instrumentation, data collection, and data analysis. The methods must be aligned with the research design.

Each particular design has its own characteristic methods that are derived from its ontological and epistemological roots, as discussed in Chapter 2. For example, grounded theory, a qualitative design, comes from an ontologically relativist perspective with a subjectivist epistemology. Grounded theory designs require a relatively small (purposive) sample. The sample (as in all designs) is constrained by the delimitations and the setting of the study. The instrumentation used in a grounded theory design includes semistructured questions meant to address aspects of the phenomenon under consideration, and the research questions can change as the interviews progress; in grounded theory, analysis starts with the very first interview, and questions are shaped by that interview, which guides the next interview. This evolving of research questions as the study progresses is an aspect of the methods that is a unique but essential feature of grounded theory. This feature also reinforces the relativist and subjectivist orientations of this kind of design.

A randomized controlled trial, on the other hand, begins with a positivist philosophical perspective that is ontologically realist and epistemologically objectivist. There is a sampling method that is specified; for example, the sample may be obtained randomly or by convenience. The sample size is prescribed in advance of the study and is based on specific formulas that support achieving the statistical power necessary for generalizability of results. The method of data collection and analysis is always articulated. Data are then collected in their entirety, and analyses are specified in advance by the research questions and hypotheses. The analyses selected must be consistent with those that can provide answers to the research questions. Thus, quantitative designs tend to be much more prescribed in advance of data collection and analysis. It is important to note, however, that once data are collected and analysis begins, additional analyses may be conducted that complement the results from tests of the null hypotheses.

Each of the above examples describes key components of the specific approach to inquiry, design, and methods that require alignment. Ontological and epistemological choices drive interest in the approach to inquiry. The designs best suited for the research questions are selected, and tools and settings appropriate to those designs are selected and described. In the grounded theory example, semistructured interview protocols are developed that serve as the instrumentation. We noted that specific interview questions change as interviews progress, which is a defining feature of grounded theory. In the case of the randomized controlled trial, specific, structured questionnaires (or other data collection tools) are used to gather data for analysis of a priori hypotheses. This, also, is a defining characteristic of quantitative research in general and randomized controlled trials in particular. To summarize, you need to ensure that all aspects of the approach to inquiry, design, and methods are internally consistent and aligned with other aspects of the proposal.

Table 20.1 provides some questions that can be used to help guide the alignment process. In addition, members of your research committee or team can be invaluable in providing verification that the proposal makes logical sense.

Table 20.2 provides information that you may find helpful in aligning various aspects of quantitative, qualitative, and mixed methods proposals. Within a given paradigm, you can see aspects of the scientific approach, philosophical foundation, nature of the study, research design, instrumentation, data, analysis strategies, software, and reliability/validity considerations that would be consistent within that paradigm. During proposal writing, if one of these components you are describing falls into one of the other paradigms, it can be a sign that misalignment may be occurring.

TABLE 20.1 ● ALIGNING RESEARCH QUESTIONS, RESEARCH DESIGN, AND METHODS
Before Writing the Proposal
Have you conducted a thorough review of the literature in the field that provides evidence for the state of advancement of knowledge?
From the literature review, can you clearly identify what is known as well as what is not known?
Have you framed knowledge of what is known and not known into a research question that is of sufficient scope that it can be answered in the context of your study?
Have you thoroughly reviewed the literature related to the design, including the study of seminal resources in the field, which provides its theoretical and philosophical underpinnings?
Have you reviewed research studies that are similar to your own to generate evidence to support decisions on methods, including population, sample, context, instrumentation, and analysis?
Writing the Proposal
Does the research question make sense (i.e., can it be answered) in the context of the research design? Does it make sense in terms of the chosen approach to inquiry?
For quantitative studies, are the statistical hypotheses consistent with the research question(s) (i.e., will answering the hypotheses adequately address the research question)?
For qualitative studies, are the interview questions and subquestions consistent with the research question(s)? Will the interviews likely generate data that can answer appropriately the research question?
In qualitative and quantitative studies, is the required sample size consistent with the research question and design?
Are the analysis strategies consistent with the chosen research design?

Table 20.3 provides another useful tool. The Historical Alignment Tool can be used in the earliest stages of proposal writing to track the development of the proposal's key components. By reading across the columns, it is easy for you or those reviewing the research project to obtain a quick snapshot of the proposal elements described earlier and to check for alignment. In addition, you can track any changes based on conversations with other committee members or research team members and identify the changes made to ensure overall alignment once the adjustment is made. This tracking of changes results in a document that shows the evolution of your study.

CONCLUSION

A precisely written proposal will serve you well as you conduct your study. The proposal is a structured outline of the study that conveys to other scientists exactly how you plan to proceed. Writing the proposal is an iterative process; using the Historical Alignment Tool document (Table 20.3) will help you ensure that the key aspects of your proposal—the problem, purpose, research questions/hypotheses, conceptual/theoretical framework, and design—are aligned. We encourage you

TABLE 20.2 ● ALIGNING STUDY COMPONENTS WITHIN RESEARCH PARADIGMS

	Qualitative	Quantitative	Mixed Methodologies
Scientific approach	*Inductive* (generating meaning or understanding from data)	*Deductive* (test hypotheses are derived from theories)	Inductive and deductive approaches
Philosophical foundations	*Postmodernism/constructivism* (knowledge is shared or constructed; focus on individual meanings, points of view)	*Positivism* (there is an objective reality, or truth, that can be measured)	Includes aspects of both, but mixed methodologists likely would embrace more of a postmodern/constructivist perspective
Nature of studies	Descriptive	Correlational, quasi-experimental, experimental	Descriptive, correlational, quasi-experimental, experimental
Research designs	*Grounded theory* (developing theory in an area where theory is lacking or existing theory is inadequate)	*Surveys* (self-administered; interviewer administered; computer assisted [CASI and ACASI systems]; internet based)	Parallel qualitative and quantitative approaches
	Phenomenology (understanding the meaning a phenomenon has for participants; lived experience)	*Observations* (counting behaviors; counting and reporting behaviors in experiments)	*Sequential studies* (qualitative → quantitative or quantitative → qualitative)
	Case study (examining a particular event, occurrence, phenomenon in its natural context; understanding the factors influencing participants in the case)	*Experiments* (quasi experiments in which groups are predetermined; randomized controlled trials, in which participants are randomly assigned to groups, as in drug efficacy studies)	*Example of qualitative → quantitative:* Interviewing people in a community, and from this, developing instruments that are appropriate to that community
	Ethnography (in-depth analysis of a culture)		*Example of quantitative → qualitative:* Participants complete an instrument/ scale and then participate in in-depth interviews to understand more about why they answered the way they did
	Narrative (an approach that analyzes stories of life experiences and the meaning people make of those experiences)		
	Participatory action research (in which those being researched are coresearchers and work together with the researchers to solve socially relevant problems)		

	Qualitative	Quantitative	Mixed Methodologies
Instrumentation	*Interview protocols* (typically, unstructured or semistructured interviews that use more open-ended questions) *Observations* *Documents* (e.g., school records, meeting minutes, mission statements, organizational planning documents, annual reports, historical records, government documents, journals, diaries, etc.)	*Scales or instruments* (they require responses on some kind of forced scale of measurement, e.g., yes/no or Likert scales) *Observation and counting protocols* (e.g., counting specific behaviors on a playground that provide quantitative data for analysis)	Combination of interviews and scales/instruments, depending on the objectives/goals of the mixed method study
Data	Text (interview transcripts, observation notes, documents, etc.)	Numerical	Text and numerical
Analysis strategies	*Open coding* (initial coding of data into blocks) *Axial coding* (emerging concepts are dimensionalized in a grounded theory approach) *Constant-comparative analysis* (comparing emerging codes across participants) *Thematic analysis* (searching for themes) *Narrative analysis* (analyzing stories and narratives by structure, function, or oral performance)	*Correlation and regression* (Pearson's r, Spearman's rho, multiple and logistic regression, path analysis and structural equation modeling) *Group comparison tests* (analysis of variance, analysis of covariance, multivariate analysis of variance) *Instrument development* (factor analysis, item response analysis)	Qualitative and quantitative analysis methods chosen as appropriate to the mixed method study
Software examples	NVivo ATLAS.ti Ethnograph (Use of software is not required in qualitative research, but many use it to help manage data)	SPSS SAS R Stata	Uses both

(Continued)

TABLE 20.2 ● (Continued)

	Qualitative	Quantitative	Mixed Methodologies
Reliability and validity	Trustworthiness, including credibility, confirmability, and transferability (Lincoln & Guba, 1985) (strategies include prolonged engagement with data; persistent observation of the phenomenon under study; triangulation of findings; debriefing of findings and analyses with peers; member checks [checking results with those who provided the original data]; thick description) *Note:* This is just one set of criteria for evaluating the validity of qualitative research. There are other sets of criteria proposed by other authors.	*Test–retest reliability* (measures the same construct in the same person at two different times) *Internal consistency reliability (Cronbach's alpha)* (assesses how well items in a scale are correlated with each other) *Split-half reliability* (splits scale in half and correlates the items in each half) *Concurrent validity* (the measure correlates with an existing measure that assesses the same construct) *Discriminant validity* (the measure does not correlate with a measure to which it is not theoretically expected to be related) *Construct validity (face validity* [the instrument appears to measure what it is expected to measure] and *content validity* [experts review items]) *Predictive validity* (the construct predicts another construct to which it is theoretically expected to be related)	Approaches appropriate to the needs of the study (triangulation is popular in mixed methods research [multiple sources of evidence converge on the same findings])

Source: Table 20.2 used with permission of G. Burkholder and M. Spillett. ACASI, audio computer-assisted self-interview; CASI, computer-assisted self-interview.

Note: ACASI = audio computer-assisted self-interview; CASI = computer-assisted self-interview.

TABLE 20.3 ● HISTORICAL ALIGNMENT TOOL

Planned Research Focus	Enter Your Planned Research Focus Here							
	Dissertation Research Components							
	Research Framework				Research Design and Methodology			
Dissertation Planning and Revision History	Problem Statement	Purpose	Significance	Theoretical Framework	Research Question(s)	Nature of Study/ Approach to Inquiry	Possible Sources of Information or Data	Possible Analytical Strategies
Original plan								
Rationale for change								
Revised plan								
Rationale for change								
Revised plan								
Rationale for change								
Revised plan								
Rationale for change								
Revised plan								

to read dissertations from your own and other institutions to gain perspective on research proposal development. Following the process outlined in this chapter will maximize the probability that you will have a proposal that shows strong internal consistency and rigor.

Questions for Reflection

1. How does the literature review support a research study?

2. What does it mean for the problem, purpose, and research questions to be aligned?

3. What might interfere with the feasibility of participant selection, instrumentation, data collection, and data analysis, and how can those challenges be addressed?

4. How might the evolution and alignment of a proposal be tracked over time?

Key Sources

Krathwohl, D. R., & Smith, N. L. (2005). *How to prepare a dissertation proposal: Suggestions for students in education and the social and behavioral sciences.* Syracuse, NY: Syracuse University Press.

Leedy, P. D., & Ormrod, J. E. (2015). *Practical research: Planning and design* (11th ed.). Boston, MA: Pearson.

Simon, M. K., & Goes, J. (2013). *Dissertation and scholarly research: A practical guide to start and complete your dissertation, thesis, or formal research project.* Dubuque, IA: Kendall/Hunt.

References

Agee, J. (2009). Developing qualitative research questions: A reflective process. *International Journal of Qualitative Studies in Education, 22*(4), 431–447. doi:10.1080/09518390902736512

Allard, K. E. (2014). *Special education team member perceptions of video self-modeling with twice-exceptional students* (Doctoral dissertation). Retrieved from ProQuest Dissertations and Theses database. (UMI No. 3645160)

Booth, W. C., Colomb, G. G., Williams, J. M., Bizup, J., & Fitzgerald, W. T. (2016). *The craft of research* (4th ed.). Chicago, IL: University of Chicago Press.

Crawford, L. (2015). *Assumptions.* Unpublished manuscript.

Creswell, J. W., & Creswell, J. D. (2018). *Research design: Qualitative, quantitative, and mixed methods approaches* (5th ed.). Thousand Oaks, CA: SAGE.

Leedy, P. D., & Ormrod, J. E. (2015). *Practical research: Planning and design* (11th ed.). Boston, MA: Pearson.

Lincoln, Y. S., & Guba, E. G. (1985). *Naturalistic inquiry.* Beverly Hills, CA: SAGE.

Onwuegbuzie, A. J., & Leech, N. L. (2004). Linking research questions to mixed methods data analysis procedures. *Qualitative Report, 11*(3), 474–498. Retrieved from http://www.nova.edu/ssss/QR/QR11-3/onwuegbuzie.pdf

Tashakkori, A., & Creswell, J. W. (2007). Exploring the nature of research questions in mixed methods research [Editorial]. *Journal of Mixed Methods Research, 1*(3), 207–211. doi:10.1177/1558689807302814

White, P. (2013). Who's afraid of research questions? The neglect of research questions in the methods literature and a call for question-led methods teaching. *International Journal of Research & Method in Education, 3*, 213–227. doi:10.1080/1743727X.2013.809413

DISSEMINATING RESEARCH

Cultivating a Healthy Dissemination Attitude Among New Scholars

John H. Hitchcock

How will my research influence my field? To whom shall I send my work? How can I make sure that I am being heard? Is publishing worth the effort? In my early days as a scholar, in graduate school and shortly thereafter, I did not give much thought to these questions. I was largely concerned about finishing a degree and getting a job. I would have considered it presumptuous to send copies of my manuscripts and other writings to colleagues. Over and above that, I counted only my fellow classmates as my colleagues (certainly not people in the field) and figured they had their own work to worry about. Hence, as far as I was concerned, disseminating my research was not an important topic.

My thinking at the time is probably not so very different from that of most new scholars, who represent my intended readers (i.e., students who are close to completing a doctoral degree, or recent graduates). Hence, I wish to offer a more seasoned perspective. As of this writing, I am now a mid-career professional and have gone from having no opinion on dissemination to seeing it as an essential part of the research process and my own professional growth. Since I am a social research scientist, human beings have directly or indirectly given me information about themselves to answer a research question, and I owe it to them to honor their efforts by making sure that my findings have an audience.

The central purpose of this chapter is to help you cultivate a similar attitude and to share some views about publishing and, more broadly, dissemination. In the pages that follow, I offer some information about research dissemination, with the caveat that some details will quickly become dated given anticipated changes in information technology. To counterbalance this concern, I think it equally true that the notion of cultivating a *healthy dissemination attitude* will hold up over time.

Having described the purpose of the chapter, it might help to describe my own background. I have worked for consulting research firms that exist to get good research into the hands of policymakers and as a university professor with the responsibility of directing research centers. To date, I have coauthored more than 40 scholarly contributions, presented at conferences more than 100 times, and have about 8 years of editorial experience. Few of my manuscripts were published with no trouble; in fact, I have experienced manuscript rejection more than 100 times. Normally, such rejection came with an invitation to resubmit the work after revision (more on this below), but I have also experienced complete and total rejection. I have had to learn to deal with critique and the fear that my work might not be seen as good enough for some person or some journal. Assuming that you will feel some anxiety at the prospect of critique and rejection, which comes with dissemination, I offer some thoughts about cultivating a healthy dissemination attitude.

CULTIVATING A HEALTHY DISSEMINATION ATTITUDE

Experiencing rejection is not easy. However, cultivating a healthy attitude about the importance of dissemination can come in part from (a) understanding the peer-review process and (b) knowing that everyone, even the best scholars, experience rejection and other complexities with dissemination. It is likely that I will experience up to 150 more rejections before I wrap up my career. At the risk of seeming masochistic, I might be considered lucky if this is roughly accurate, because it means I'll be in a profession I enjoy for years to come and will be getting feedback needed to sharpen my work. So rather than seeing rejection as a thing to avoid, I find that it helps to see the event, when it happens, as part of the peer-review process.

Beyond understanding critique and rejection as just part of a process, it helps to see publishing as being well worth the effort. By far, the most important reason for publishing is that doing so informs the field. Indeed, publishing is a key form of dissemination, and without dissemination, there is hardly any point to conducting research. If that is not enough of a reason for getting one's work out into the hands of the public, widespread dissemination and publishing work provides a backbone for professional advancement and security. It is critical that you try to learn to take rejection in stride, be prepared to learn from critique, and understand that without dissemination your research will provide little if any benefit to others. Keep these ideas in mind and you will be on your way toward cultivating a healthy dissemination attitude. This attitude is so important that I will revisit it throughout this chapter. Now I turn to thoughts about one of the key paths for dissemination: publishing a manuscript in a peer-reviewed journal.

PUBLISHING YOUR MANUSCRIPT

Assume that you are in the process of authoring a manuscript and plan to publish it. The typical process will entail the following steps:

- *Develop your full ideas in written form:* Edit the work, edit it again, and see if you can get constructive critiques from a colleague before sending it out for review.

- *Select a journal outlet that should be a good fit:* Carefully review the journal's directions on scope, style (e.g., if the manuscript must be blinded,[1] follows a particular style guide such as the one developed by the American Psychological Association [APA]), page limits, and so on. Shape your manuscript accordingly. If you cannot make your work fit the journal (either because of topic or style), find another venue or your work might be desk-rejected, which means that your work will not go through the full review process because an action editor either does not see a topical fit or you did not follow key submission directions.

- *Submit the work and be prepared to wait:* Different journals have different review times, but most require several weeks to several months because reviews entail soliciting feedback from peers and collating feedback into an editorial decision. Consider working on another manuscript while you wait for an editorial decision.

- *Receipt of feedback:* The day will arrive when you will get notice of an editorial decision. The general decision categories are as follows: (a) reject, revision and resubmission are not encouraged; (b) reject, but resubmission of an updated manuscript is encouraged after revision (sometimes these are major revisions); (c) accept with minor revisions; and (d) the manuscript is accepted. In both my experience as an editor and as an author, the fourth option is rarely offered for a first-time submission. For some perspective, I am excited if I achieve a revise and resubmit decision on my first go around as long as the feedback is manageable (this excitement is part of my healthy dissemination attitude).

Yes, the work might be rejected in future review, but the editor wants to see it again after addressing peer-review feedback. Should it get rejected at that point, then I am free to send the manuscript elsewhere. Note that it is not unusual to go through two or three rounds of resubmission until the manuscript is accepted, and there is no guarantee that a revise and resubmit means the work will eventually be published. If your manuscript is rejected outright (resubmission is not invited), then maintain that healthy attitude and do not give up! Use the feedback to sharpen the work as best you can and then see if it fits another journal.

This overview raises an important concept with respect to cultivating a healthy dissemination attitude: *perseverance.* When thinking about perseverance, we can stand on the shoulders of some giants. There is an open-access special issue of *Research in the Schools* that offers ideas from what is affectionately called the *Century Club* (Onwuegbuzie & Slate, 2016a, 2016b). To be in this club, one needs to publish more than 100 times. This is an arbitrary cutoff, of course, and publishing more than 100 times does not mean that centurions get special treatment at restaurants, sporting events, or otherwise have spectacular lives. What they do have is knowledge

---

[1] "Blinded" means that any information that can identify the authors of the manuscript has been removed. This is done to promote the chances of receiving an unbiased review.

about this type of dissemination, and a few have stepped forward to offer some tips. The reference list below shows how to access the issue, and reading it is encouraged because in it you will find humor, humility (there is a lot of open discussion from these authors about rejected manuscripts), and concrete steps to follow during publication and dissemination.

To revisit a key point, the centurions are elite scholars, yet part of their hard-won experience is that their manuscripts have nevertheless been rejected. They have, in my view, cultivated healthy dissemination attitudes. Rejection can hurt, but it is also important to keep in mind that the typical peer-review process is imperfect and is carried out by volunteers who are busy. If one has to tolerate an imperfect process where even top scholars experience the sting of rejection as almost a routine by-product, then perseverance is the answer. Know also that even though peer-review is an imperfect process, it is meant to produce the best science. In short, take the feedback, improve and update the work accordingly, and try again knowing that everyone (even centurions) experience rejection from time to time.

Some additional wisdom from the journal issue, which I present as themes are (a) *know your audience*, (b) *work on your writing and presentation*, and (c) *be fastidious when revising a manuscript that might be accepted*.

Know your audience. Be a scholar of journals (Johnson & Johnson, 2016; one of the articles in the Centurion special issue). This means knowing about and reading the different journals in your field and what makes them different from one another. This expertise will guide you to the best outlet for your work. Once you identify an outlet that matches your work, your chances of publishing the manuscript will improve. Being a scholar of the journals in your field can also help should you need to shop your manuscript around. I publish in different arenas, including program evaluation, mixed methods, and special education. I have a good working understanding of about a half-dozen journals in each area, and this is useful when I try to be strategic about where to send my work.

Work on your writing and presentation. Few of us are capable of producing a polished manuscript in one sitting. If you take pride in your writing, try not to let your ego get in the way of seeking and accepting critical feedback. Think of your writing as being more of a triathlon with intermittent breaks than a sprint. A triathlon has distinct phases (swimming, biking, and running) and so too does manuscript development and refinement. There is initial development, editing, and dissemination, so be prepared to shape your work, revisit it, and shape it again until it is finally published.

Be fastidious when revising a manuscript that might be accepted. If an editor is interested in publishing your manuscript, you will almost always have to make changes. Be careful to delineate all changes requested in a cover letter to the editor and offer a point-by-point response to each request. There are many benefits to being careful here. First, you are showing that you are taking the feedback seriously.

Second, if you show exactly how you addressed a point in a response letter and also providing a page number where a change can be found in the new manuscript iteration, the editor might read it with a less critical eye.

There can be times when a reviewer or editor requests (or worse, requires) a change to the manuscript that you think you should not make. When this occurs, first do your best to ascertain if the change is in fact a required revision. You might, for example, be told that you should delete some text to meet some word count limitation, but in the process of review, you find that other revisions could make the manuscript short enough for the journal's needs. In this case you are not dealing with a strict requirement and should explain in a response letter why you are keeping the writing but otherwise are addressing the key feedback. In other cases, you might be asked to make a change that will render a factual error, muddle a key point, and so on. Should this happen, explain your reasoning in a respectful manner. If you are preventing an honest editorial error, then you should not have anything to worry about; if you are dealing with a difference of opinion, then you should have an opportunity for additional dialogue and you can take things from there. It is possible that you might have an insurmountable disagreement and then you will need to decide for yourself how to proceed, but for what it is worth, I have yet to see a case where some agreement could not be reached.

Finally, note that there can be times when you receive contradictory or confusing feedback. Again, the peer-review process is sometimes imperfect and is almost always complex. When this happens, it is acceptable to write to the editor and ask for additional direction. It would of course help to be as specific as possible when asking for more guidance.

With that overview of themes drawn from the special issue from *Research in the Schools*, I think it is important to emphasize that publishing is worth the reward. Publishing in journals is the coin of the realm for academics and can also help the careers of PhD-level researchers outside of academia, and the process will do a lot to sharpen and improve your work. A good peer-review process will yield a solid article (no longer a manuscript) that the journal will promote and stand behind once it is released to the public. Above all, this process will help you spread the word about your work and this in turn can be a benefit to society.

Know also that once your work is published, you can continue to promote and discuss it in venues like conferences, trade journals, internet sources, book chapters, and so on. In fact, your work might be more easily found should you present it in other settings, and it is certainly fine to recast your work so that it gets better exposure. By recast, I do mean you can use some variant of it again. Here it becomes critical to be aware of standard copyright agreements and one aspect of self-plagiarism. In fact, these ideas interlink. Self-plagiarism is defined in APA (2010) *Publication Manual* as follows:

> Just as researchers do not present the work of others as their own (plagiarism), they do not present their own previously published work as new scholarship (self-plagiarism). There are, however, limited circumstances (e.g., describing the

details of an instrument or analytic approach) under which authors may wish to duplicate without attribution (citation) their previously used words, feeling that extensive self-referencing is undesirable or awkward. When duplicated words are of limited scope, this approach is permissible. When duplication of one's own words is more extensive, citation of the duplicated words should be the norm. What constitutes the maximum acceptable length of material is difficult to define but must conform to legal notions of fair use. (p. 16)

This notion of legal fair use also connects to copyrighted material. As you develop your manuscript and get it to a fixed state, you and your coauthors own the copyright to it. Typically, when your work becomes published (and not before), this copyright is transferred to the entity that is publishing the work (see APA, 2010, p. 236). This means that, absent some other arrangement, you and your coauthors normally no longer own the work once the copyright transfer is complete; the publisher owns it. In fact, if you wish to reuse a part of your published work like a graph, you will need to seek permission from the new owner to do so. Hence, you will want to attend to these expectations when you disseminate your work in different venues. Furthermore, be aware that publishing the work in a trade journal or book chapter typically means you are handing over a copyright.

PRESENTING WORK IN CONFERENCES AND MEDIA

Can you discuss your work before you transfer copyright? Absolutely! The most common venue for doing so is to present a paper at a conference. This is so typical that it is understood that presenting your paper at a conference is part of the normal evolution of the manuscript. I like presenting a paper at a conference and then taking any critique I receive and then accounting for it when transforming the conference paper to an article. Note that it is inappropriate to present the same paper (or nearly the same paper) more than once at conferences because this inflates the sense of your productivity, and conferences are put on to showcase new scholarly contributions. I have however found it is okay to recycle some aspects of a prior paper when aggregating some of my ideas to offer a larger story about my research to professional audiences. I just properly cited my own work, which incidentally helped with dissemination. As an aside, consider reviewing paper submissions to conferences as a way to serve professional organizations. This will yield important experience with dissemination by seeing how others present their work; you will also learn about the review process, and for some conferences, this mirrors how journals conduct peer review.

Popular Press and Venues. A great dissemination skill is to learn how to explain research so that media representatives can appreciate and understand your work. Much has been written on this topic; one accessible source is an online article by McCurry-Schmidt and Ono (2014). To distill their brief guidance even further, *be prepared*. Prepare by figuring out how to get succinct messages across, prepare by thinking through how you might stumble so that this is more easily avoided, and prepare by thinking about the venue through which you will communicate. Will you answer a couple of brief questions in a phone call or email exchange? Will you get into a debate with another expert in front of a large crowd? Are you dealing with a topic that might engender controversy (e.g., what if your research about sex education for high school freshmen)? Will a reporter give you a chance to review and correct advanced copy? You can also prepare by learning about the media representative in advance (consider the reports this person has written, if you think these are fair), and it is fine to establish some ground rules on what you can and cannot speak to. There are many ways in which you could interact with media personnel relative to what you might be studying; thus, the only universal advice is to just be prepared.

Three pieces of advice that might make the *be prepared* missive a little more practical are as follows: (1) Talk in advance with your institution's media representative and/or a more senior colleague. Almost all institutions have a main point of contact who handles media requests. This person is usually experienced in these matters and sometimes is a former reporter himself or herself. Reach out to this person for help in crafting a message that does credit to you and your institution. This will be true even if you are a student. University administrators are often happy to extol the efforts of their students and should provide a lot of support. (2) Do not be afraid to say no and take some control of the correspondence with a reporter. (3) Be fast and responsive to a reporter, but do not agree to be interviewed or otherwise answer questions before you are ready.

Some elaborations are warranted. During an interview or other type of correspondence, you might find that you are asked questions that might make you uncomfortable, either because you see that you are unqualified to answer, or because you might now be on record for taking a position that you have not yet had a chance to consider (e.g., *That is a fascinating finding from your study about sex education in high school. Tell me, what does this say about the governor's state policies and funding priorities?*). If you're not sure that you are ready to answer, then say so. Sometimes reporters might not realize that they raised an issue that you should not speak to as an expert. If this happens, more often than not you will be thanked for knowing your limitations, since most reporters who write about research are into facts and not sensationalism. Finally, it is okay to demure if you are just not ready to talk; if you need time, ask for it. But remember, reporters are busy and are generally trying to produce articles or radio shows in tight timelines.

One other point worth raising is that you can proactively advertise your work to the media with a press release. If you think that there is something important to say that will have widespread interest, you can approach your institution's media team and they will help you craft a short set of paragraphs covering what your research questions were, how they were answered, and why anyone should care about your findings. I have been fortunate enough to work with savvy media representatives who helped craft press releases for a center I formerly directed. These releases received national attention and made my job easy because they said most of what a reporter wanted to know, if not everything, and the center's work was mentioned in newspapers and websites with routine interactions with the press.

You can also be creative with dissemination by utilizing your own website or your institution's website. I know professors who each has a website that describes their body of work and where to find books and articles; some even include blogging. This might seem like a vanity project, but the examples that come to mind strike me as a humble and ethical effort to ensure that their work matters. An excellent website example belongs to Daryl J. Bem's of Cornell University; do an internet search to find and explore his personal website. My former research center presented on its website a series of interactive data visualizations based on Tableau software, because we were tired of presenting education policy information in tables. I took real enjoyment in showing off the staff's data visualizations and found that these were great approaches for disseminating work. More generally, it is very likely that your institution would be open to your using their websites to showcase and disseminate your research. This is almost always a win–win for all involved.

SOME DISSEMINATION RESOURCES

The missive for this section of the chapter is to pay attention to whether your work is getting attention, and act accordingly. See Table 21.1 for a summary of different resources that can be used to help spread word of your work and ensure that it is properly cited and credited to you.

Three resources I have been interested in supporting and using are ORCID, Crossref, and Google Scholar. The motivation behind ORCID is to help connect research to the people who are authoring it so that credit is properly applied. Sometimes, researchers change names during the course of their career, and of course, many researchers share the same name. This identification service will affix a persistent, unique identification to each and every researcher who is registered with the system. Establishing an ORCID takes just a few seconds once you pull up the relevant website. Listing all details about you might however take a while, but this can be done at a leisurely pace. Many journals now require that you submit your ORCID as part of the publication process.

Crossref connects to ORCID, but rather than identifying the researcher, this service focuses on getting a unique digital object identifier (DOI) affixed to published articles that are electronically available. Not all articles list a DOI yet, but this will likely change over time. This will help with dissemination, because a DOI can simplify search efforts and delineating between articles with similar names.

I have personally found Google Scholar to be a useful service. It collates a number of statistics on scholarly productivity and likely helps researchers find one another's work. Google Scholar also automatically builds your profile as you publish more. As of this writing, it is imperfect (most services are), so you might need to add that hard to find article written in a small journal that is not yet online. In general, the service

TABLE 21.1 ● EXAMPLES OF CURRENT RESOURCES THAT CAN FACILITATE RESEARCH DISSEMINATION

Resource[a]	Description	Dissemination Tips
Crossref: https://www.crossref.org/	If you do not do so already, start thinking about publications as multidimensional objects that can be updated as new links across a body of work emerge, corrections are added, and findings are generated as work evolves. Publishers pay for Crossref so that processes like peer review, who funded what work, and so on, can be showcased. Crossref will link your work to something called an "ORCID" (see below) and it captures a persistent digital object identifier (DOI) that is now affixed to almost all articles that are made available electronically. A DOI is a unique alphanumeric code that begins with a "10" and is used to ensure one article is not confused with another. Crossref provides a metadata search at Crossref.org that allows you to find (and list) a DOI.	Be sure to share the DOI attached with your articles. In fact, when citing articles, it is now proper to add the DOI (see examples in the below reference list). When in Crossref.org Click on "Search MetaData" and do a search based on an article title.
Google Scholar: https://scholar.google.com/	Google Scholar is both a search tool and a way to keep track of/showcase your articles, book chapters, and so on. Google Scholar lists a number of indices that summarize your productivity (e.g., number of times you've been cited, how many times one of your works has been cited). This can be a great dissemination tool because people who become interested in one of your articles can find your profile and find other things you have written, as well as find your coauthors.	Once in the system, Google Scholar will automatically update your profile. Once in a while, you might need to manually update information. I provide a link to my Google Scholar profile on my resume.
ORCID: https://orcid.org/	ORCID is a nonprofit organization that allows data about your scholarly activity to be linked to a persistent digital identifier, an ORC "ID" (as in identification). This "ID" links sundry scholarly activity (articles, grants) and helps one address complexities like other scholars having the same name. The same ID can be used throughout one's career so can be handy should your name change. This relates to research dissemination because participating parties can use an ORCID for proper identification.	Keep your ID updated. We all change employers from time to time so consider using a persistent email account (e.g., gmail). Some journals now request an ORCID.
Research Gate	Research Gate is a social networking site and should be treated accordingly. It is a place where people can share articles, working manuscripts, and engage in dialogue around thorny research concerns. Note that, in the past, the site has sent unsolicited emails to users. Should you use the site, treat it as you would other social networking schemes.	Be careful about infringing copyright laws when uploading and sharing published papers. Be sure that you maintain control of your profile and content.
Other social media outlets	Other sites like LinkedIn, Facebook, and Twitter might also be of use when disseminating your work.	

a - Internet links might change. The links presented here are current as of this writing. All of these sources are easily found with a standard search engine.

has not only helped me to disseminate my work but also provided a simple way for me to summarize different productivity metrics that can be helpful when applying for jobs or a competitive grant.

Scholar Metrics. Although I am not enthusiastic about number-based metrics for assessing productivity because they do not tell the whole story about one's scholarship, these are now part of the landscape. Understanding the basics of these metrics will help you think about dissemination. One metric that most publishers can furnish is the number of times your article has been downloaded, just like how many times a book has been purchased. If download rates are low, then this suggests you might want to do some more advertising.

Another basic metric that is captured by Google Scholar is the number of times work has been cited. I can think of a couple of my own articles that are not yet being cited; since I believe they offer something interesting, I can account for this in my dissemination plans. There is also now a metric, the *h* index, which is a count of how many articles have been cited the corresponding number of times. For example, if one's *h* index is 16, this means the person has coauthored 16 articles (or other works like books, book chapters) that have been cited at least 16 times. In contrast, the i10 index is the number of publications with at least 10 citations (Hirsch, 2005).

Social Media. Sometimes the best dissemination technique is to send a message through Twitter to a specific audience. One of the best tips that I can offer is to rely on your professional organizations to navigate the social medial realm. If, for example, I do some work pertaining to mixed methods, I will send word to the leadership of the Mixed Methods International Research Association. They will then generally send notice via their Twitter accounts and a membership listserv. Even if I'm not a member of an organization, I still might send along word of a publication or other work so long as there is a clear reason to do so. This is because the purpose of professional organizations is to help keep members current with respect to changes in research and other matters. Since most research professionals carry memberships in multiple organizations, it is not long before messages of newly released work snowball and reverberate back and forth across social media. If I notice there is limited saturation of my publication, I would do a little nudging by sending along word to a new organization.

CONCLUSION

It is essential to think of research dissemination as a skill, and it is important to cultivate a healthy dissemination attitude. The most important ideas offered in this chapter are as follows:

- *Persevere:* I often say to students and colleagues that there is little meaningful variation in IQ (whatever that is exactly) among people with graduate degrees with respect to research dissemination, which includes publishing. What does vary is perseverance, which is likely a good predictor of publication rates and dissemination efforts. You will probably experience the pain of rejection. Nevertheless, you owe it to your field and to your research and practice agenda to persevere.

- *Be flexible:* Be flexible both in terms of the journals in which you wish to publish and also the venues you use to get the word out about your research.

- *Network:* One of the most effective ways to network is to serve as a reviewer for conferences, if you can, join editorial boards, and so on. This opens up natural communication lines with colleagues in your field and yields experience with publication and dissemination processes.

- *Be prepared:* This applies primarily when talking with media. But this is also true when presenting at conferences and so on. Prepare interesting summaries of your research and why the research matters.

- *Do some advertising for your research:* Pay attention to whether your work is getting attention, and act accordingly. Advertise via the professional associations in which you have membership. Determine if your institution can prepare a media release about your research.

- *Evaluate:* You can evaluate your dissemination efforts by obtaining metrics like download and citation rates. Understanding those metrics can help you focus your dissemination plan to improve those rates. Services such as ORCID and Google Scholar ensure you get proper credit. If you see there is limited attention being given to your work, identify ways to spread the word.

Reflection Questions

1. Review some of the resources you used to prepare the literature review for your own research. Pick one of the researchers from the list who appears to be well published, and do a search of the author.

   a. Where has the author disseminated his or her research? Has the research been disseminated in different forms and in different venues?

   b. If the author has a personal or institutional website, what information is contained there? Does the author use the website as a venue for dissemination? Does it seem to be effective? Why or why not? What things might you suggest in a dissemination plan?

2. If you have not done so, set up an ORCID and Google Scholar account.

3. Where are your strengths and areas of opportunity related to dissemination of your research?

4. Identify five to six journals that might be a good fit for publishing your work. What qualities or characteristics of these journals factored into your selection?

Key Resources

McCurry-Schmidt, M., & Ono, M. (2014). 10 Tips for scientists on talking to the media. *News and Views. Online Weekly of the Scripps Research Institute, 14*(9). Retrieved from https://www .scripps.edu/newsandviews/e_20141013/mediatips.html

Onwuegbuzie, A. J., & Slate, J. R. (Eds.). (2016a). How to publish: Tips from centurions [Special Issue]. *Research in the Schools, 23*(1). Retrieved from http://msera.org/docs/rits-2016-spring-v23n1.pdf

References

American Psychological Association. (2010). *Publication manual of the American Psychological Association* (6th ed.). Washington, DC: Author.

Hirsch, J. E. (2005, November 15). An index to quantify an individual's scientific research output. *Proceedings of the National Academy of Sciences, 102*(46), 16569–16572. doi:10.1073/pnas.0507655102

Johnson, D. W., & Johnson, R. T. (2016). How to publish: Tips from two centurions. *Research in the Schools, 23*(1), 29–30.

McCurry-Schmidt, M., & Ono, M. (2014). 10 Tips for scientists on talking to the media. *News and Views. Online Weekly of the Scripps Research Institute, 14*(9). Retrieved from https://www .scripps.edu/newsandviews/e_20141013/mediatips.html

Onwuegbuzie, A. J., & Slate, J. R. (2016a). Editorial: To publish or not to publish? An introduction to tips from centurion authors. *Research in the Schools, 23*(1), i–ii.

Onwuegbuzie, A. J., & Slate, J. R. (Eds.). (2016b). How to publish: Tips from centurions [Special Issue]. *Research in the Schools, 23*(1). Retrieved from http://msera.org/docs/rits-2016-spring-v23n1.pdf

INDEX